Theatre of the Rule of Law

Theatre of the Rule of Law presents the first sustained critique of rule of law promotion – the drive to shape laws and institutions that pervades international development and post-conflict reconstruction policy today. While successful in disseminating a comparable set of ideas about law and policy, this expansive global enterprise has largely failed in its stated goals of alleviating poverty and fixing 'fragile states'. Moreover, in its execution, the field deviates sharply from 'rule of law' principles as commonly conceived. To explain this, Stephen Humphreys examines the history of the rule of law as a term of art and considers a spectrum of contemporary interventions as well as earlier examples of legal export to other ends. Rule of law promotion, he suggests, is best understood as a kind of theatre, a staged morality tale about the good life, intended for edification and emulation but blind to its own internal contradictions.

STEPHEN HUMPHREYS is Lecturer in Law at the London School of Economics and Political Science. He previously worked at the International Council on Human Rights Policy in Geneva, as Research Director, and before that at the Open Society Institute in New York and Budapest. He writes regularly on international law, in both academic and policy contexts, and is the editor of *Human Rights and Climate Change* (Cambridge University Press, 2009).

CAMBRIDGE STUDIES IN INTERNATIONAL AND COMPARATIVE LAW

Established in 1946, this series produces high-quality scholarship in the fields of public and private international law and comparative law. Although these are distinct legal sub-disciplines, developments since 1946 confirm their interrelation.

Comparative law is increasingly used as a tool in the making of law at national, regional and international levels. Private international law is now often affected by international conventions, and the issues faced by classical conflicts rules are frequently dealt with by substantive harmonisation of law under international auspices. Mixed international arbitrations, especially those involving state economic activity, raise mixed questions of public and private international law, while in many fields (such as the protection of human rights and democratic standards, investment guarantees and international criminal law) international and national systems interact. National constitutional arrangements relating to 'foreign affairs', and to the implementation of international norms, are a focus of attention.

The Board welcomes works of a theoretical or interdisciplinary character, and those focusing on the new approaches to international or comparative law or conflicts of law. Studies of particular institutions or problems are equally welcome, as are translations of the best work published in other languages.

General Editors James Crawford SC FBA *Whewell Professor of International Law, Faculty of Law, and Director, Lauterpacht Research Centre for International Law, University of Cambridge*
John S. Bell FBA*Professor of Law, Faculty of Law, University of Cambridge*

Editorial Board Professor Hilary Charlesworth *Australian National University*
Professor Lori Damrosch *Columbia University Law School*
Professor John Dugard *University of Leiden*
Professor Mary-Ann Glendon *Harvard Law School*
Professor Christopher Greenwood *London School of Economics*
Professor David Johnston *University of Edinburgh*
Professor Hein Kötz *Max-Planck-Institute, Hamburg*
Professor Donald McRae *University of Ottawa*
Professor Onuma Yasuaki *University of Tokyo*
Professor Reinhard Zimmermann *University of Regensburg*

Advisory Committee Professor D. W. Bowett QC
Judge Rosalyn Higgins QC
Professor J. A. Jolowicz QC
Professor Sir Elihu Lauterpacht CBE QC
Judge Stephen Schwebel

A list of books in the series can be found at the end of this volume.

Theatre of the Rule of Law

Transnational Legal Intervention in Theory and Practice

Stephen Humphreys

CAMBRIDGE UNIVERSITY PRESS
Cambridge, New York, Melbourne, Madrid, Cape Town,
Singapore, São Paulo, Delhi, Mexico City

Cambridge University Press
The Edinburgh Building, Cambridge CB2 8RU, UK

Published in the United States of America by Cambridge University Press, New York

www.cambridge.org
Information on this title: www.cambridge.org/9781107411647

© Stephen Humphreys 2010

This publication is in copyright. Subject to statutory exception
and to the provisions of relevant collective licensing agreements,
no reproduction of any part may take place without the written
permission of Cambridge University Press.

First published 2010
First paperback edition 2012

A catalogue record for this publication is available from the British Library

Library of Congress Cataloguing in Publication Data
Humphreys, Stephen, 1971–
  Theatre of the rule of law : transnational legal intervention in theory and practice /
  Stephen Humphreys.
    p. cm. – (Cambridge studies in international and comparative law ; 73)
  ISBN 978-1-107-00078-0 (hardback)
  1. Rule of law.   2. Rule of law–Political aspects.   3. Rule of law–Economic
  aspects.   4. International economic relations.   I. Title.
  K3171.H86 2010
  340′.11–dc22
                                                              2010038760

ISBN 978-1-107-00078-0 Hardback
ISBN 978-1-107-41164-7 Paperback

Cambridge University Press has no responsibility for the persistence or
accuracy of URLs for external or third-party internet websites referred to in
this publication, and does not guarantee that any content on such websites is,
or will remain, accurate or appropriate.

For My Parents

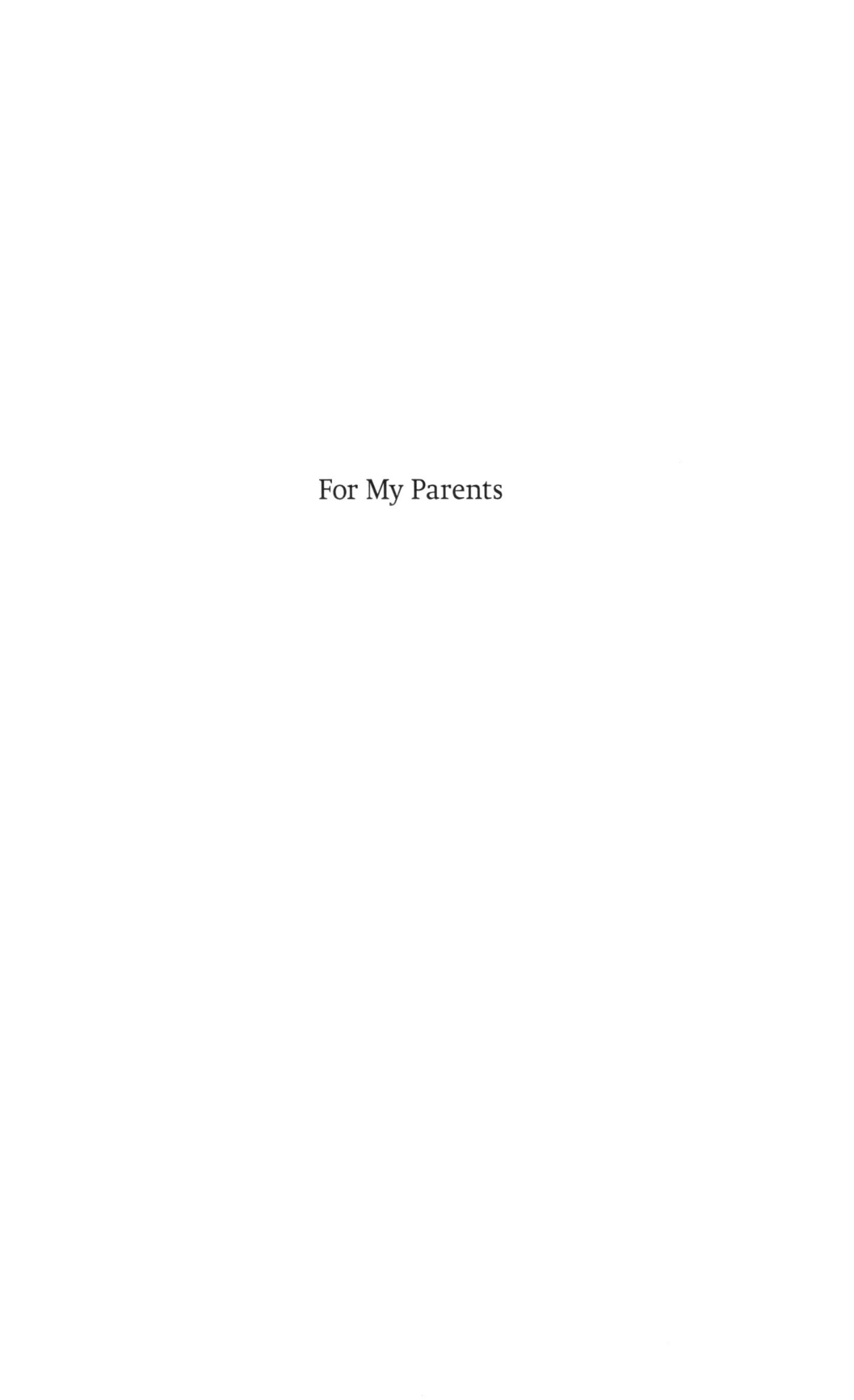

Short table of contents

Prologue	*page* xii
Acknowledgements	xxvii
Introduction	1
Part I Parameters: 'rule of law' as a term of art	27
Chapter 1 Society	29
Chapter 2 Economy	57
Chapter 3 Sovereignty	89
Interlude Precursors: colonial legal intervention	109
Part II Theatre of the rule of law	123
Chapter 4 Market	125
Chapter 5 State	149
Chapter 6 Public	175
Conclusion	219
Bibliography	233
Index	287

Contents

Prologue	page xii
Acknowledgements	xxvii
Introduction	1
What we talk about when we talk about the rule of law	3
Rule of law promotion as a field	6
The rule of law at home and abroad	9
The theory and the practice of rule of law promotion	12
Part I: the rule of law as term of art	14
Interlude: colonial precursors	17
Part II: theatre of the rule of law	18
Part I Parameters: 'rule of law' as a term of art	**27**
1 Society	29
The immanent rule of law	29
Dicey: 'the habit of self-government'	30
Oakeshott: a 'moral association' (the *jus* of *lex*)	35
Habermas: mutual respect among strangers	38
Summary: the 'modern' rule of law	41
Between state and society	45
The public sphere	45
A tripartite distinction	53
Conclusion	55
2 Economy	57
Two perspectives on law and the state	59
Dicey on *droit administratif*	59
Weber on 'compulsory political association'	62

The realist critique: four charges of judicial bias	66
Bias one: the choice of rights	69
Bias two: the choice of policy	70
Bias three: the choice of evidence	72
Bias four: the blindness to bias	73
After the realists	75
The rule of law and welfare as mutually incompatible	77
Social rights within a rule of law framework	83
Conclusion	84
3 Sovereignty	**89**
Aristotle: Nomarchy (the sovereignty of law)	89
Law's umpire	93
The Aristotelian tradition	96
Agamben: the law of sovereignty	98
Sovereign exception	99
Sovereign extension	101
Sovereign expansion	104
Conclusion	106
Interlude Precursors: colonial legal intervention	109
Part II Theatre of the rule of law	**123**
4 Market	**125**
US foreign assistance	125
The world according to USAID	128
The World Bank	131
After 1989: governance and PSD	132
The economy of law	138
Conclusion	147
5 State	**149**
The United States	149
The United Nations	155
The rule of law and order?	162
The lure of law	166
Conclusion	173
6 Public	**175**
The theme: modernisation	176
The reform constituency	183

Lead roles: public and private	187
Governance	190
Corruption	191
Privatisation	193
A public sphere of private ... investors?	194
Supporting roles	195
The judiciary: autonomy and prestige	196
Civil society: public education	204
'The poor': investors in waiting	207
Denouement: global integration	213
Conclusion	217
Conclusion	219
Bibliography	233
Index	287

Prologue

With the fall of the Berlin Wall still fresh in 1991, I drove to Prague, just to see what it looked like. Beautiful and drab at once, it was a city that preserved a copious history, both ancient and recent, and a sensibility quite unlike any I had come across before: erudite, yearning and humble all at once. A few years later I moved to Budapest, a very different city, but one that shared a similar sense of wounded magnificence and of informed, tentative hope. Remaining there over much of the decade, I developed some sense of what it means to live through history. For these countries were, in those years, at the centre of a tremendous transformation, one that spiralled quickly outwards and came to engulf much of the rest of the world – extending, as I learned during a two-year stint in Senegal some time later, to Africa and beyond. As the Cold War thawed, it seemed to unleash all sorts of flows across the world's previously unyielding borders: of money, of people and, perhaps most of all, of ideas.

This book began life in my desire to understand and articulate my personal and professional experiences from those years, much of which I spent working in a field that has come to be known as 'rule of law promotion'. That is the name given to an immense and still expanding body of practice aiming to reform and improve the laws and institutions of countries across the world. I wanted to make sense of the contrast I perceived between, on one hand, the exuberant rhetoric that was then (and is still today) habitually deployed to describe and explain the extensive interventions into the economic and legal structures of the countries I spent time in, and, on the other, the difficult and often deteriorating conditions of life I witnessed in my time living in and visiting the same 'beneficiary' countries. Was there a connection?

To begin *in medias res*, I agreed in 2000 to oversee a project that was part of a wider programme to monitor compliance with the Copenhagen criteria, as they are called, for accession to the European Union, in ten countries that were then 'candidates' for EU membership. The criteria are remarkably concise. They state:

> Membership requires that the candidate country has achieved stability of institutions guaranteeing democracy, the rule of law, human rights and respect for and protection of minorities, the existence of a functioning market economy as well as the capacity to cope with competitive pressure and market forces within the Union.[1]

In retrospect, the criteria – proclaimed in 1993 – are a product of their era. In the midst of familiar perennials from the lexicon of liberal constitutionalism – democracy, human rights, minority protection – another keyword appears that, despite comparably deep roots, was only then, in the early 1990s, acquiring at last a mien of impartiality: the market economy. It is now difficult to recall, but in previous decades, particularly in Europe, the invocation of 'market forces' had retained a controversial, even combative, colouring. After 1989, however, the Copenhagen criteria signalled not only the budding confidence of this language in mainstream political discourse, but also the abandonment, in the same gesture, of another key aspirational vocabulary of the postwar settlement: social welfare and a whole accompanying register of solidarity, economic equality, social justice, and so on. Absent from the criteria, these aspirations were apparently not sought – or were disavowed – for the candidate countries. In this, the criteria endorsed and ratified a change in the prevailing political wind that had been gaining throughout the 1980s. They proclaimed a triumph of a kind, even if it was, at the time, essentially rhetorical.

And there, in the middle, sits this curiously bland term: 'the rule of law'.

It took me some time to admit that, if I was honest, I wasn't fully sure what 'the rule of law' meant. It took me a little longer to realise that, in fact, few others were either, and more time still to begin to be able to articulate my sense of the significance of a term that was, at the time, something of a newcomer in the arena of 'international assistance'.

---

[1] SN 180/1/93 REV 1, European Council in Copenhagen, June 21–22, 1993, Conclusions of the Presidency, 13. The criteria also state: 'Membership presupposes the candidate's ability to take on the obligations of membership including adherence to the aims of political, economic and monetary union.'

But it was a fast mover. For I soon discovered that the rule of law was not simply a 'condition of membership' for aspiring EU countries. In the very recent past, it had become a key new term in the vocabulary of international affairs, increasingly cited as both a goal and a condition of assistance of all kinds in countries all over the world. But what did it mean? And what was it doing in the field of international development?

I put these questions at the heart of my doctoral research, begun in 2003, of which the present book is the outcome. I looked in detail at the principal texts comprising the history and theory of the concept of the rule of law and at the extensive literature in which the promoters of rule of law programmes explain their objectives and rationale. Recourse to a vocabulary of the rule of law had become, I quickly discovered, extraordinarily widespread in international activity. Moreover, its usage escalated throughout the period of my writing, to the extent that what was already an elusive and fungible term seemed to become, over time, ever more abstracted from real world referents. So widely is the term 'rule of law' used today, so many desirable political, economic and legal attributes are incorporated within it at a stretch – and it is repeatedly stretched – and so few common elements are required across the visions channelled through it, that it has become something of a challenge simply to capture what is specific about 'the rule of law' today.

And yet, from the perspective of my starting point – the turn to the rule of law in international development assistance – it was clearly not adequate to say merely 'the rule of law is a site of contestation'. After all, a striking aspect of contemporary international usage is how little scope for argument or contestation it leaves – how quickly and thoroughly it seems to dominate the space of political debate. One thing everyone can agree on, it seems, whatever the context, is that the rule of law is a good thing, and more of it must be good too. Even though its specific content is often murky, to invoke the rule of law is nevertheless to posit that we already know a lot about how things work and (more to the point) how they *should* work, that 'the challenge' is 'to implement' this knowledge, and that to open up discussion on 'the basics' 'again' would be fruitless, counterproductive or wrong-headed. Transnational funders may argue over how best to improve the rule of law: no-one argues against the thing itself.

Mindful of the ubiquity and plasticity of this notion, I chose to pursue it through its associations, locations and effects. If its deployment could have a chilling effect on political possibility, I conjectured, perhaps that was in part *because* of its rich associative history – it can encompass *so much*. It can reveal itself (to revisit the Copenhagen criteria) as an indispensable condition of both 'human rights' and the 'market economy', while leaving the content or effects of these and other desiderata essentially empty. To speak of 'the rule of law' could, it seemed, substitute for all sorts of questions about what society should look like – how to organise the political and economic. And yet, the inhibiting effect of rule of law language on political debate might also be because it is *itself* so comparatively empty of determinative content. When the rule of law is raised, talk turns easily to processes and procedures: monitoring, arbitrating, adjudicating, and so on, with reference to a set of procedural principles: transparency, efficiency, accountability, generality, and so on. To invoke the rule of law is to prioritise procedure over substance and to defer discussion of the latter; a focus on 'building the rule of law' suspends, for the time being, questions about the direction and effects of public action.

But there is also, I gradually realised, another reason the rule of law register can apparently void the policy space. A certain hostility to the policy function itself runs through many influential accounts of the rule of law. Key exponents of the term – Albert Dicey, Michael Oakeshott and Friedrich Hayek – explicitly invoke the rule of law to warn against or ward off government intervention of any but the most minimal kind. Today, still, the concrete procedures associated with rule of law act as brakes on the policy apparatus and provide limits on public action, preferring private over public ordering and prioritising courts as decision-makers. The problem of policy, when framed in rule of law terms, can quickly reduce to an assumption that there is *already too much* of it; the immediate task is to fend off, guard against, or roll it back – to liberate the private by constraining the public. This association, it turns out, is embedded in its conceptual history.

If the turn to 'rule of law promotion', then, as a guiding motif in the work undertaken by the principal development bodies – the international financial institutions, bilateral aid agencies, private foundations and main organs of the UN – tends to forestall political possibilities, this was, it seemed to me, not only because it is consistently presented as *apolitical*, as above or prior to politics, and not only because the measures it announces are not *policy* steps in the ordinary sense – they are rather structural or procedural – but also because the expression is habitually deployed to query the policy-making apparatus itself, on *moral* as well as practical grounds. If to talk about the rule of law is, as I began to realise, always to take a position on the proper ordering of society, it is also always to signal a studied neutrality on that same question.

And yet, it did not seem correct to describe the role of the rule of law in contemporary development as 'apolitical' or anti-policy, I realised, if only because the *actual* policy orientation of this immense body of work is, in fact, stark and unmistakable. From the outset, the World Bank, the prime sponsors of this vocabulary from 1989, placed it at the centre of a new vision of wealth-creation: 'private sector development', supposed not only to generate growth but ultimately to eliminate poverty (the Bank's motto is 'working for a world free of poverty'). And over time, as other development actors acquired the language, the rule of law label began to appear in proliferating contexts, notably, from about 2000, in relation to security and crime in post-conflict and 'fragile' states. New goals and subgoals were continually added: 'encouraging investment', 'achieving governance', 'strengthening civil society', 'protecting human rights', 'fighting impunity', 'combating corruption', even 'ending the cycle of hatred'.

Despite an insistent suspicion about 'central planning' and indeed planning of any kind in economic affairs, the programmes to make all this happen are themselves centrally planned by a small group of large organisations based in a handful of world capitals, and, notwithstanding some inter-agency jockeying, working in close coordination. Rule of law programmes are implemented uniformly (if not always successfully) wherever development assistance is delivered: that is, in much of the world. It struck me that recourse to a rule of law register in this context can mute or disguise the extent to which strong policy preferences do, in fact, accompany and structure its promotion country by country. So my questions began to change. What becomes of this thing called 'the rule of law', if it is invoked specifically to produce broader policy goals? What do we learn about the immense body of contemporary work under the rule of law rubric by acknowledging and articulating its policy function?

The more I looked at the history of this idea, the more paradoxes like the above I uncovered. Sure, the ambitious policy to construct and reform many of the world's states in fulfilment of a given set of economic goals essentially reverses a classic vision of the rule of law as a bulwark against, in Michael Oakeshott's words, 'teleocracy' or a 'technological conception of the state'. But this is not the only way in which the field of rule of law promotion deviates from the tradition it lays claim to. Three other examples quickly became apparent. First, rule of law is classically conceived as describing the normative base or *legitimacy* of the law in force, a legitimacy derived, in turn, from the community itself that is subject to that law. That is, the rule of law is intended to express a minimal societal consensus or 'deal' about 'the rules of the game'. In development work, however, local laws and procedures are consistently perceived as problematic – as, for example, informal (customary), discriminatory, outdated, or corrupt – with a notional 'rule of law' imported from outside as solution. Persistent attempts to promote 'local ownership' of rule of law projects, as I had witnessed, merely underline this structural reality.

Second, the existence and pursuit of a procedurally rigorous legislative process grounded in a representative and legitimate legislature are generally regarded as fundamental to most conceptions of the rule of law. However, funders are typically impatient with these processes, preferring to push through legislative templates developed elsewhere with the help of 'reform-minded' executives and elites, bypassing legislative process where possible. In this, the programmes reproduce their own political origins, for they too arrive into the toolbox of development actors not through agreement with 'beneficiary states' but through decisions of the Security Council (in the case of much UN rule of law work, notably in peacebuilding operations), or of the executive boards of the international financial institutions, or of the executive arms of donor states themselves, operating through bilateral aid agencies. Ironically, since the rule of law is deemed to be 'apolitical', it is also essentially non-negotiable.

Third, despite the insistent assumption of a non-intrusive state in rule of law literature, the work itself has increasingly focused, in its state-building mode, on the construction of a state apparatus that is both pervasive and coercive: whose coercion is, indeed, pervasive. Increasingly, as the rule of law became the moniker of choice for state-building, particularly in 'fragile states' perceived as prone to becoming 'havens' or 'breeding grounds' for terrorists, its meaning is practically indistinguishable from 'law and order' – the consolidation of a trained and equipped police force and of a functioning criminal law system, including through increasing prison capacity and setting targets for arrests, prosecutions and convictions. As policy measures pursued through development agendas, these are somewhat novel. But what is really surprising is how they too have been housed under the rule of law umbrella, which, for all its polysemy, has never before stood behind the policing state quite so unequivocally. Here, as elsewhere, the term is apparently stretching towards novelty.

At this juncture, there is a danger of drawing a too sharp contrast between the contemporary practice of rule of law promotion and some earlier 'purer' or more 'authentic' notion which has, if this account were to run, been sidelined, undermined or overturned in a contemporary practice that might therefore seem hypocritical or conspiratorial. So I should note that the intended contrast is with an ideal or concept, not a historical fact. There is every reason to believe that the classic vision of the rule of law is itself largely mythical or idealised. Certainly, when he advanced the expression in his 1885 *Introduction to the Study of the Law of the Constitution*, Albert Dicey embarked on deliberate mythmaking. Harking back to a fabulous land of rights and freedoms acquired in habit and legal practice, he grounded the rule of law in a combination of chauvinist accounts of the English legal system, on one hand, and assimilated elements of modern European statehood, on the other. As many have noted since, this picture, constructed explicitly to counter the rise of a modern bureaucracy in England, was neither theoretically coherent nor empirically accurate on the actual functioning of law in contemporary England. Another view, most coherently articulated by Max Weber in 1921, saw the rise of extensive administration as *inhering* in a modern rule of law state, a view shared by later commentators on Dicey (including in apologetic prefaces to later editions of his work).

The broader European tradition encompassing these related visions was laid out in some detail in an early text by Jürgen Habermas. In this tradition, as Habermas recounts it, the emergence of constitutional government was conceived as the triumph of an autonomous (modern) private civil society over an authoritarian (medieval) public sovereign. This new 'public' – that is, the aggregate of private persons – comes into being through rational discussion in a notional 'public sphere' by means of which the 'public interest' is determined. The public becomes the source of legitimacy for government, which is set the task of assuring both the public interest and the private freedoms that underpin it, but its powers are bounded within sharp limits.

According to this story, then, the state (that is, the public *sector*) is both the product of the public sphere and its guarantor. The rule of law comes to describe the system of legislative and judicial balances and mechanisms that underpin this construction. As Habermas points out, however, this picture of the European state has always constituted an idealised archetype rather than a historical reality, a package of eighteenth-century political ideals recast retrospectively, in the late nineteenth century, as historical directives. As such – a 'regulative idea' (to use Immanuel Kant's term) towards which the modern state should ideally strive – it constituted a powerful tool in contests over the ordering of European society through the late nineteenth and twentieth centuries. More worryingly, Habermas suggests that the relative hegemony of this ideal leaves the 'public sphere' (i.e. the media and other channels of public discourse) open to manipulation by powerful private or public interests with the capacity to do so. Given the assumptions of formal equality and private freedom that the 'rule of law' instantiates, manipulation of this sort may be difficult to perceive.

Habermas's account is enormously helpful in explaining much of the *latent* theory that appears to underpin rule of law work today. A similar set of assumptions about the respective roles of public and private actors, the existence and purpose of a public sphere, and the role of the rule of law in maintaining this set of conditions, runs through the field as a whole without apparently needing to be demonstrated or queried. Obvious questions arise here about the appropriateness of basing contemporary actions on a model of state and society derived from a particular moment in European history, and one that was largely mythical even then. But setting these doubts aside momentarily, I found myself wondering how to square the central notion of an *autonomous public* in this picture – of the public sphere as a meeting place for a society in congress with itself to determine the public interest – with the equally central fact, in rule of law promotion, that the relevant principles and procedures, and even expressions of the public interest, amount essentially to ready-made imports from elsewhere. Are there precedents that explain what seems an obvious contradiction?

In search of an answer, I looked at the *practical* precursors of this body of work: earlier attempts to transplant laws and procedures across borders in the service of social, political and economic goals. The obvious antecedent is, of course, European colonialism. Focusing on colonial interventions in Africa, I found numerous parallels with contemporary rule of law promotion, both substantive and performative. These included a clear consonance of motivating themes, on one hand – economic development, humanitarianism, and progress, or modernisation; and, on the other, of modes of intervention – a concentration on policing (and peacekeeping), constructing criminal systems, building market structures, establishing judiciaries, training administrators, all with a view to allocating and safeguarding economic and political capacities. Like colonial authorities, rule of law promotion prefers expedient legislative processes, working with small groups of 'reform-minded' locals to achieve lasting effects. There are clear differences of course, dictated at least in part by the quite different conditions of operating in post-independence states. But the similarities are nevertheless striking.

And yet, while the continuities between contemporary rule of law promotion and the colonial legal intervention that preceded and indeed laid the foundations for it are stark, if often obscured from view (including by terminological shifts, such as the turn to rule of law language itself), there is at least one innovation in contemporary work that has no obvious parallel in the colonial era. That is its concentration on the *public* itself, a notion generally neglected or treated ambiguously in colonial times. The rule of law literature orients itself towards a notional public as its relevant audience and justifies itself in terms of the specific benefits that will accrue to 'the public'. Moreover, it often speaks as though *representative* of a wider public. But beyond all this, and perhaps most strikingly, considerable resources are expended on bringing a public into being. This is done through projects to fund and 'strengthen' civil society, to expand and 'diversify' the media (in the name of 'freedom of expression'), to train lobby groups, including chambers of commerce and NGOs, and so on. In keeping with the public/private divide that runs through rule of law programming generally, these latter projects are generally (though not exclusively) the domain of private rather than public funders.

Rule of law work, I began to perceive, doesn't simply presuppose a certain vision of society that is reliant in particular on the distinction between public and private actors, the latter a locus of freedom and entrepreneurship, the former a space of discipline and security. It proactively sets about creating such a vision, by funding, 'nurturing' and training whole sections of society – judiciaries, police, soldiers and civil servants, of course, but also private lobbying groups, the media, and 'civil society' itself. Underlying rule of law promotion, it turns out, is a fairly complete vision of what society is and how it should look. The goal of 'rule of law programmes' is not simply to construct or reform 'institutions', it is actively to reform the way people, *in general*, in host countries behave, public and private persons alike. The aim is, apparently, to normalise and universalise very specific ideas about state and society and their inter-relation.

Ambitious though the programme literature – to which I turned for detailed accounts of the field – is, it rarely expresses the full implications of its own presuppositions. These larger claims, hopes and intentions are rarely openly acknowledged or proclaimed, indeed, they are perhaps not always fully appreciated, as I could myself attest. And yet they are pervasive. They are indicated by, and necessary to, a consistent narrative which is thoroughly embedded in the body of programmes wherever performed. They are *staged* rather than stated. (I will come back to this idea of 'staging' in a moment.) Furthermore, the extraordinary scale of ambition behind this work is, unsurprisingly, not generally met in practice; indeed it is difficult to see how it could be. Yet, perhaps because the larger premise is so rarely articulated, the literature evinces recurrent surprise and disappointment at the failure to achieve its stated aims, as though these more modest objectives could somehow be uncoupled from the wider transformation that rule of law programmes mutely expect.

Certainly this work is not easy. Practitioners struggle hard in difficult circumstances to produce modest change, and then struggle again to demonstrate to their sponsors that the change is real. A number of ironies or tensions run through all this that may contribute to the pervasive perception of failure. For one, there is an evident tension between the purported emphasis on diversity of opinions and interests in the public sphere, on the one hand, and the thorough consistency of the message transmitted through the programmes in support of rule of law, on the other. In the same way, second, there is a remarkable tension between the constant talk of transparency and accountability in the literature and the relative absence of these qualities when it comes to the key institutions themselves, certainly in relation to their 'beneficiaries'. A third source of tension arises between the insistent emphasis on the importance of lobbying in the public interest, on one hand, and the relative inaccessibility of the key funders to actual expressions of the public interest from those in host countries, on the other. That is to say, the particular set of principles and modes of intervention found in rule of law promotion are not supplied from within target countries and adapt only marginally in response to pressure from the recipients – channels to 'lobby' the key funders are, ironically, not readily available. Fourth, there is a niggling tension between the formal equality and diversity presumed to be constitutive of the public sphere in principle and the importance in practice of access to funding, generally from these same (foreign) funders, in determining which voices actually get heard.

Taking account of all this – the repeated narrative tropes, the moral overtones, the ambiguous or contradictory motives and reflexes, the recurring set of principal actors and motifs – it gradually struck me as most appropriate to characterise rule of law promotion as a kind of theatre or performance. As the *staging*, in the way I suggested earlier, of a certain story or morality tale about the good life – about state and society, law and economy, about the appropriate way to set priorities and the appropriate priorities to set. As pedagogical: rule of law promotion is theatrical in its mode of persuasion: it does not attempt to *demonstrate* the rightness of its propositions through empirical evidence (there is little), nor through the discipline of reasoned competitive discourse in the public sphere (it is not itself open for debate), nor through the clarity of historical analogy (no analogy seems appropriate). Rather, the field bases its appeal on the force of repeated narrative itself, and on the consistent reproduction of a cast of strangely inscrutable terms that follow a similar choreography regardless of context. These comprise, on one hand, a set of immutable themes (governance, corruption, privatisation, transparency, accountability, impunity, judicial independence) and, on the other, a group of recurrent morally-tagged actors (civil society, the judiciary, 'the poor', 'the elite', the media, public officials, 'reform-minded constituencies').

The plotlines too are simple, bold, familiar and repeated. Governments tend to tyranny. Independent courts protect the rights of ordinary people. Corruption obstructs 'governance' and constitutes a tax on the poor. Privatised services are more efficient than public. An 'enabling environment' for investment is a prerequisite of 'development'. 'Integration' in the global economy is good for everyone, local and global alike. 'The poor' are essentially entrepreneurial, waiting for the right environment to step forward and contribute to (and benefit from) wealth generation. The 'right environment' is a matter of incentives.

I will end this prologue soon, but first I want to flag two further points that emerged from my investigation. First, there is a striking contrast between the state-bounded nature of 'the public' as ordinarily (and historically) conceived, and of the government tasked with responsiveness to it, on one hand, and the *essentially* transnational nature of the public as it consistently appears in rule of law programme literature, on the other. Who is this transnational public? Presumably it is the aggregate of private interests with an identifiable stake in how a given government organises policy, which would seem to mean, as rule of law literature indeed clarifies, private firms and investors large enough to operate in multiple states. Can the interest of these relatively powerful actors really be understood as equivalent, or indispensible, to the 'public interest' of host countries? Does the mismatch of boundaries between state and public not distort the principles supposedly underpinning rule of law work? Or does it point to the emergence of something quite novel: a nascent public body at the global level to match the public sphere to which it is to respond? If the latter, such a global public sector might be thought to reside in the very institutions themselves promoting rule of law globally. And of course, this body *does* appear responsive to precisely the same transnational public so often cited as 'beneficiary': a transnational private sector and a global 'civil society'. And yet, if this is right, even roughly, it receives no acknowledgement in rule of law literature, which remains relentlessly state-centric. Why so? These intriguing questions deserve more scrutiny than I can give them here.

Second, there seems to be at least one way in which rule of law promotion has been a clear if qualified success – and that is precisely in its performative or pedagogical dimension, in the dissemination of rule of law language itself, and of the morality tale it transmits, at least at the rhetorical level. There seems little doubt that the turn to rule of law language has consolidated its hold in international relations, in international development assistance, and in the shared discourse of public authorities and civil society organisations everywhere. Adopted now by all the major international actors, extending to bilateral and UN-based agencies as well as private funders, the language has also, unsurprisingly, become increasingly common among government bodies that must perforce deal with and respond to these agencies. Governments are evaluated on their adherence to this notional rule of law, investment flows towards it, funding is made conditional upon it. And NGOs too find themselves having to invoke this register to expedite funding applications. To have near-universalised a particular vocabulary in regard to fundamental concerns of state and society is no mean feat. Perhaps the question is not so much whether all this rhetoric is leading to 'improved rule of law' 'on the ground', as the literature often wonders, but rather, what sort of international and transnational transactions are facilitated by this widely shared language, and who benefits from them?

This set of themes, broadly, comprise my focus in the book that follows. I look first at a range of arguments that have played out on the ground of the rule of law in the century-odd since the term was first introduced. I then provide a brief account of earlier efforts to mobilise law abroad to achieve development, focusing in particular on colonial Africa. Finally I turn to a thorough analysis of a large body of project and explanatory literature from a number of key rule of law funders and implementers – in particular, the US Agency for International Development (USAID), the World Bank and various organs of the United Nations.

It should be clear, I hope, that I am not attempting in what follows to fix a final definition of 'the rule of law': to the contrary, I am querying whether such a fixed definition is attainable at all for a term which appears to owe its prominence to its plasticity. Likewise it should be clear that the grander values and desires that implicitly or explicitly underpin articulations of the rule of law are not themselves the object of my critique here: such a study would require another book-length investigation. Here, it is rather the radically uneven application of these principles in this particular field of practice that I wish to interrogate.

It might be worth clarifying a number of other things I am *not* doing in this book. As indicated above, I am not attempting to assess whether 'rule of law promotion' as a technique 'works' or not – that is, whether it successfully 'improves' certain attributes of state or society articulated beneath a rule of law rubric. There is a considerable literature already evaluating rule of law export, much of which concludes that it is *not* successful on its own terms. I am content to allow those studies to tell their own story: poor self-assessment within the field provides a backdrop to my own research, but not its impetus. I do not presume to offer any such assessment, neither as to the *existence* of the rule of law (however defined) in a given context, nor the extent to which funded programmes can 'improve' it (if at all), nor the degree to which it would be possible to measure such improvement, should it take place.

Neither am I making any claims about whether something called the rule of law really *is* good for development or not. There has been an extraordinary surge in global economic growth over the last thirty years, coincident with the promotion of the rule of law and in particular the 'integration' of 'emerging markets' and 'transitional economies' into the global economy, with which it is frequently associated. There has been, at the same time, an unprecedented rise in economic inequality both within and between countries – hence the deterioration I have seen at first hand in countries I visit often. It seems reasonable to assume that these trends are inter-related and that they may all have something to do with the injection of a uniform vision of economic relations channelled through the replication of legal forms and institutions. If so, this would appear to indicate another kind of 'success' for rule of law promotion, but it is not part of my goal in the present work to establish such a connection.

Furthermore, I have made no attempt in the following to represent the views of those in recipient countries who are subject to, or beneficiaries of, rule of law assistance. It is common in this field to pursue case studies aiming to show what the impact of these programmes is 'on the ground'. My focus, however, is quite different: it is to look at the field in terms not of its targets, nor of its substantive impact, but of its rationale. What are rule of law funders promoting exactly? How do they explain this work? What are the underlying assumptions? What is the worldview that sustains the field of rule of law promotion? If the field has developed to a degree in response to its reception in its countries of operation, and to obstacles met in implementation, the reflexive response has generally been to translate these hurdles back into the familiar language of the overarching rule of law narrative, rather than to introduce new themes or undertake fresh inquiry. My focus on implementers – on the agents of the rule of law, so to speak, rather than on those at the receiving end – has entailed a choice not to attempt to speak for the latter. The degree to which these programmes are embraced, resisted or simply ignored in their countries of implementation – and the politics of embrace, resistance or indifference, important though these clearly are – remain beyond my scope in this book.

Lastly, I do not wish to question the intentions, motivations, or achievements of the many individuals involved in rule of law promotion. Having had the privilege to work within the field myself, and with some truly remarkable individuals, I am aware of the extraordinary commitment common in this field to bettering the conditions of life for persons who have been victims of political and economic upheavals beyond their control. By corollary, I am not suggesting that some particular public goods frequently ushered under the rule of law moniker are not themselves valuable objects of study and pursuit. The present study would suggest that as a blanket term intending to cover multiple public goods, 'the rule of law' is overused, of limited analytic or descriptive value, and potentially distorting. But that is not, of course, to say that identifiable injustices swept into the broad embrace of rule of law rhetoric are not deserving of engagement. I am conscious that specific interventions frequently result in outcomes that are genuinely beneficial to specific individuals and communities and that, where they are not, the causes are often complex. I know that those working from the best motives operate in a strategic environment requiring careful framing of aims, methods and objectives. My goal is not to question their integrity. Rather, it is to take a few steps back from the self-evident decency of the acts and intentions in this field, to scrutinise the language that frames and sometimes (therefore) channels or redirects them, and to place them within their systemic context, with a view to the 'big picture'.

Some things are easy to miss when working at the coalface, so to speak. It is my hope that the investigation that follows will be read by people working in the field not as an indictment, but as an invitation to a conversation, as an opportunity, or perhaps a provocation, to think a little further into the causes and consequences of a hugely significant enterprise which leaves few in the world untouched today.

Acknowledgements

There are many people I must thank. My deepest gratitude goes to my parents, Niall and Eileen Humphreys, who taught me the value and elusiveness of autonomy, and consistently showed by example that justice runs deeper than law can express. My brothers Ciarán and Macartan Humphreys were, and are, always among my first and most stimulating discussants of these and many other subjects besides. My wider family created a wonderfully nurturing environment for critically and ethically informed inquiry: I must mention Eithne Cullen, Deirdre Curran, Dympna Moore, Kevin Curran, Mary Humphreys and, especially, Michael Humphreys. Very special mention is due to Jacobia, to Valerie, to my niece Aoife and nephew Odhran.

My warmest thanks to Susan Marks, my supervisor at Cambridge. I was extremely fortunate to have such a conscientious and perceptive interlocutor, whose close readings, spare but targeted comments, and generous availability for discursive inquiry well beyond the parameters of the text, were indispensable in nurturing my conviction to pursue the shape of work that seemed most appropriate to this topic. Professor Marks is an exceptionally bright light in international law today.

Many others will recognise their imprint throughout the text. Great thanks are owed my colleagues in Cambridge, who provided the ideal intellectual environment for discussing these and related topics over the years. First, the members of the self-styled Cambridge Forum on International Law Theory, where scintillating conversation was always accompanied by cosy hospitality and good food: Alex Mills, Alison Kesby, Daniel Joyce, Douglas Guilfoyle, Isabelle Van Damme and Margaret Young. Also in Cambridge, Freya Baetans, Conway Blake, Anton Burkov, Geert De Baere, Ana Gerdau de Borja, Jessie Hohmann, Kathryn Hollingsworth, Kirsty Hughes, Mecky Kaapanda, Laura

Kirkley, Andrew Lang, Zachary Lomo, Yseult Marique (warm thanks), Conor McCarthy, Jacqueline Mowbray, Sarah Nouwen, Kate Parlett, Zoe Rose and (belatedly) Kimberley Trapp. It was my exceedingly good fortune to have been a participant in such an extraordinary community.

I am especially grateful to James Crawford, a truly exceptional presence at Cambridge, for his insightful comments on much of the text that became this book, his encouragement in pursuing it into publication, and his habitual demonstration of the compatibility of meticulous professionalism with far-reaching intellectual curiosity. I also had the privilege of discussing these themes with the consistently remarkable Philip Allott. The intellectual stimulus at Cambridge generally, and at Sidney Sussex College in particular – the privilege of peace and security there and the consistently high standards of faculty and students alike in the Law Faculty and elsewhere – provided a superb location within which to pursue this work. Special thanks too to the ever-resourceful Alison Hirst.

Peter Fitzpatrick at Birkbeck has been immensely inspirational, not only in his fearless approach to critical inquiry, but also in his unfailing demonstration that intellectual integrity and warm-hearted gentility make excellent companions. He is, in addition, an unstinting and incisive commentator. A reading group in Birkbeck under his tutelage was always a source of astonishing intellectual excitement from a range of disciplinary and political perspectives. Thanks are also due to Bill Bowring, Oscar Guardiola-Rivera, Elena Louizidou, Anthony Anghie, Sundhya Pahuja, Costas Douzinas, Richard Joyce and Ruth Buchanan for conversations in and around Birkbeck, to David Kennedy for occasional jousts in various venues, and to the members of the London reading groups led by Susan Marks and Matthew Craven.

I must also reserve particular thanks for the faculty and fellows at the Hauser Global Law School in New York University where, in 2005–06, I came under Joseph Weiler and Philip Alston's impressive guidance, with Fiona Kennedy's always professional help. A fertile intellectual experiment has been cultivated there, and it is one from which I benefited tremendously in a year of pivotal importance in translating my experience into the analysis that informs the present book. I am grateful for immensely stimulating discussions that year in New York with, among others, Christine Bateup, Nehal Bhuta, Olivia Coldrey, Cathryn Costello, Jean d'Aspremont, Frank Haldemann, Xin He, Satoko Kitamura, Nanda Kumar Krishnachar, Shahar Lifshitz, Shamiso Mbizvo, Rufus Pichler, Julie Ringelheim, Tracy Robinson,

Benjamin Straumann, Michal Tamir, Sophie Truslow, Kate Young and Tuula Mouhu-Young. Thanks too to the members of the NYU *JILP* editorial board, especially Elizabeth Rasmussen and Cindy Lin. Special thanks to Simon Chesterman, who went out of his way to make my experience at NYU comfortable, memorable and fruitful, and to Kevin Davis, for helpful discussion of these topics.

I have been remarkably lucky with teachers and mentors who have contributed to the shape of this work over time: Tom Docherty, Bill McCormack and Brendan Kennelly at Trinity College Dublin, István Géher and Ferenc Takács at ELTE University in Budapest, and Youba Sokona at ENDA Tiers Monde in Dakar, Senegal, have all been deeply influential on my thinking and orientation. At SOAS, Matthew Craven's ease with unpretentious critical encouragement has been a regular source of envy and aspiration to me over many years. Jim Goldston at OSI in Budapest and then New York has consistently been a formidable interlocutor and a rousing combination of transformative energy and strategic acumen – I cannot properly assess my debt to him. Thanks too to Peter Doherty, whom I will always remember warmly.

Most of all my thanks go to the many individuals I have had the privilege to meet, work and associate with personally and professionally over the years, and who have shaped my understanding of the topics discussed in this book and much more besides. I cannot possibly name them all, but must mention at least the following, conscious of how inadequate such a list inevitably is: Robert Archer, Pál Békés, Bruce Broomhall and Barbara Bedont, Bríd Cannon, Claude Cahn and dear Cosmina Novacovici (and Kali and Johanna), Kate Carlisle, Brian Conway, Tyson Cosby, Jacobia Dahm, Csilla Dér, Axelle Devun, Esther Doorly and Kelly McErlean, Fairouz El Tom, Agnes Enyedi, Rita Erdős, Lilla Farkas, Sophie Frezza, Valerie Gammell, Thea Gelbspan, Ailbhe Gerard (and Cathy and the family), András Gerevich, Joe Gerhardt and Ruth Jarman, Howard Goldkrand and Beth Coleman, Mariette Grange, Stefanie Grant, Rachel Guglielmo and Timothy Waters, Selina Guinness, Tracey Gurd, Julia Harrington, David Hecht, Richard Herriott and Christina Fiig, Hadil Hijazi and Hannes Schloemann, Scott Jerbi, Hina Jilani, Geoff Johnson, Eva Karadi, Sabrina Lambat, Karen Laxton, Matilda Leyser, Katy Mainelli, Susan Mathews, Karin Maugé, John and Margaret May, Yvonne McDevitt, Desmond McGrath and Monika Kovács, Henrikas Mickevicius, Sonya Mooney, Ger Murphy, Gnilane Ndiaye and Jean Charles Mamadou Tall, Scott Newton, Chidi Odinkalu, Andrea Pavoni, Joss Peto, Dimitrina Petrova, Anna Piekarzewski, Priya

Pillai, Markian Prokopovych and Agnes Kelemen, Judit and László Rajk, Mary Robinson, Dalindyebo Shabalala and Karin Dijkstra, Sue Simon, Gábor Soós, Krithika Srinivasan, Veronika Leila Szente, Wilder Tayler, Zsuzsanna Vidra, Valerie Wattenberg, Emma Webb and Chris Michael, Allen White, Emma Young, and Péter Zilahy. Peter Shaw was a pioneering presence in my life and a constant friend. I will miss him profoundly.

Warmest thanks to Rita Kéri (and Gergely, Sára, Guszti and Bandi) for the joy of cross-border commensuration from Synge through Szentkuthy. Priscilla Hayner for multiple insights in the final months of writing. Vijay Nagaraj, for his extraordinary patience and dependable support as I entered the last phase of this work. Barbora Bukovska for unstinting and intelligent criticism and advice, often scathing, always warranted, and for much more besides over many years. Anne Barron, for helpful last-minute commentary – and to the rest at LSE Law Dept for their warm collegiality. Nida Gelazis for tactful comments on this text and profound generosity of spirit generally. Most especially, heartfelt thanks to Kinga Dornacher for quietly showing me how life might be lived well (if only I would learn) and for that consistency of wisdom and sensibility to which I continue to aspire and within which my godson Mihàly (Misu) Heincz and his siblings Emma, Miklós Balambér and Zsóka have the good fortune to dwell.

Finally, Cambridge University Press have been professional, efficient and encouraging throughout. For that, and for patiently bearing with me through this process, my great thanks to Finola O'Sullivan, Nienke Van Schaverbeke and Richard Woodham, and also to Laurence Marsh, who copy-edited with admirable precision, restraint and gentility.

Introduction

In June 2008, a 'blue ribbon' Commission issued a report claiming that 'four billion people around the world are robbed of the chance to better their lives and climb out of poverty, because they are excluded from the rule of law'.[1] According to a report in *The Economist*, the Commission had difficulty, over its three years of work, reaching consensus on how precisely 'the rule of law' would 'empower' the poor. Nevertheless, the *articulation* of the problem in this form commanded unanimous support.[2] A month later, the press release of an equally high-level 'World Justice Forum' in Vienna announced its participants' 'collaborative programs to strengthen the rule of law and thereby solve problems of corruption, violence, sickness, ignorance and poverty in their communities'.[3]

Whatever else we might think about these two proclamations, they feel firmly anchored in a certain *zeitgeist*. The claims appear both breathlessly novel and yet somehow already on the cusp of anachronism. They seem tense and stretched: extraordinarily broad in the scope of the challenges they address (poverty, ignorance, violence, corruption) and yet strangely narrow in their proposed remedy (something called 'the rule of law'). They assume a kind of immanent agency: they are

---

[1] See Empowerment Commission (2008a), 1, discussed further in Chapter 6. The Commission was chaired by Madeleine Albright and Hernando de Soto, and included Lawrence Summers, Arjun Sengupta, Ernesto Zedillo, and Justice Anthony Kennedy. Robert Zoellick, President of the World Bank, was a member of the Advisory Board.

[2] 'The Law Poor', *The Economist*, June 5, 2008.

[3] American Bar Association (ABA), 'Proposals to Strengthen the Rule of Law Incubated at World Justice Forum; Funding for Projects Announced' (July 7, 2008). The World Justice Forum is the successor to the ABA's Rule of Law Symposia of 2005 and 2006. Participants included Presidents Jimmy Carter, Petar Stoyanov and Ferenc Mádl, Justices Richard Goldstone and Ruth Bader Ginsburg, and leading scholars.

both oddly passive (who has 'robbed' and 'excluded' these people?) and exuberantly active ('strengthen ... and thereby solve'). Their evident hubris appears to derive from faith: the term 'rule of law' seems to play a magical, or at least talismanic, role in both pronouncements. Such faith is possible, presumably, when its object has reached a position of such normative pre-eminence, political authority and discursive ubiquity that its key tenets are largely assumed to be broadly shared, understood and unquestioned.

Pronouncements of the kind cited above rely upon or embed some shorthand grasp of their motivating terms, a grasp that is presumably shared, at a minimum, by a relevant target audience. In this case, the audience is relatively clear: 'policy-makers' or 'opinion-shapers' in international organisations, private foundations and bilateral and multilateral development agencies; a coterie of academics (political science, economics and law), think tanks and research institutions and international organisations; and the governments of, as well as the general public in, those countries known as 'developing'. If the above statements function as shorthand for this audience, it is a result of almost thirty years of circulation and augmentation of a particular register about their object, something called 'the rule of law'. In that time, ambitious programmes have been undertaken and vast sums spent to 'promote the rule of law' throughout the world. An enormous body of work – writings, projects, convened conferences, public education programmes – had served, by 2008, to buttress and disseminate the notion that this thing called 'the rule of law' is necessary to most policy ends.

This wider contemporary phenomenon – 'rule of law promotion' – is my subject in what follows. I will look at the phenomenon both in terms of the activities undertaken under this broad rubric and of the ideas about law that are promulgated through and in support of those activities. I will do so in two main parts, the first investigating the parameters of the concept of the rule of law itself, the second undertaking an extensive exploration of the documents and literature produced by the various development agencies who conduct rule of law promotion. I will also, in an intermediary section, look briefly at historical precursors to this current work.

Throughout I will adopt a vocabulary that borrows from and embellishes that used in the field itself. So I will be talking interchangeably about 'donors' and 'funders', both of which refer to development and aid agencies – whether bilateral, multilateral or private – who fund and implement rule of law work. I will frequently use 'rule of law' as a modifier, to denote aspects relevant to the worldview or objectives of these actors – thus, for example, 'rule of law work' to fulfil a 'rule of law vision' of a 'rule of law society', 'rule of law economy' or indeed 'rule of law state'. I will likewise be referring to rule of law 'activities', 'projects' and 'programmes' – referring to concrete operations that range from the training of police officers or judges or other legal professionals in the application of certain bodies of law (or on 'the rule of law' itself) to the building and equipping of 'rule of law institutions' such as court houses and administrations, prisons and police forces, to 'technical assistance' in drafting laws, to providing financial support for bar associations, law schools and law students. These activities are in turn frequently referred to as rule of law 'reform', 'assistance', 'promotion' or even 'export'. I will speak of 'project literature' and 'strategic literature' in reference to the extensive documentation produced by donor agencies in the course of their work, and which provide the raw material for much of Part II.

It seems appropriate to begin this introduction – which will lay out the argument as a whole in synopsis – with a brief discussion of what we mean when we talk about 'the rule of law'.

What we talk about when we talk about the rule of law

'The rule of law': four clipped syllables, two iambs, two hard nouns. What could be more concise? And yet, perhaps because the nouns are near synonyms, yet neither is semantically unambiguous, its meaning is not really self-evident at all. 'Rule of law' sounds like tautology. What is law if it doesn't rule? Or: isn't it precisely the fact that it 'rules' that distinguishes a 'law' from a 'rule'? What, in short, does the phrase 'rule of law' capture or add that mere 'law', the positive law itself, lacks?

In both the above illustrations, something called the rule of law is posited as the answer – or an essential element of the answer – to a profound malaise, indeed to the somewhat epic problems afflicting a global society. Such claims cannot be made on behalf of 'law' per se. In a given context, law may condone or underpin poverty, violence, or ignorance. Here, however, reference to the 'rule' of law is apparently thought to supply some extra ingredient, injecting some *quality* into law, or denoting a particular configuration of law, that insures against these outcomes.

But what? Let me step back a little. The above examples are characteristic of the particular story of the rule of law that is the focus of the present book. But it is worth noting at the outset that there are other stories available and that this particular framing does not command universal assent among those who would claim 'the rule of law' as part of their professional vocabulary. Few constitutional or administrative lawyers, for example, and few philosophers of law, would accept that the rule of law can or should 'cure' poverty or ignorance. Many would offer a modest definition of the 'quality' of law denoted by the expression 'rule of law'. Some would, like Joseph Raz, consider it to signify the 'specific excellence of the law'.[4] The rule of law is to law, Raz said, as sharpness is to a knife: it is that which permits law to function effectively. But if that is all it is, the rule of law has little to say directly about social or economic goods. Extreme poverty, for example, is quite compatible with the rule of law according to Raz.[5] This point, that the rule of law is primarily about the *procedures* of law rather than its substance (and so that procedure and substance can be strictly separated), runs through numerous accounts of the rule of law.[6]

And yet, in most rule of law narratives, the formal-substantive distinction constantly threatens to collapse. Tom Bingham, who provides a recent exemplary account of a procedural rule of law, finds he must add that '[t]he rule of law must, surely, require legal protection of such human rights as, within that society, are seen as fundamental.'[7] Raz himself includes 'the principles of natural justice' as inherent within the rule of law, without really explaining what these are or where they come from.[8] Both accounts nod to Lon Fuller's famous suggestion that law contains an implicit morality: that if it is to function at all (if 'law' is to 'rule'), the procedural apparatus for the task will necessarily embed certain substantive qualities: equality before the

---

[4] Raz (2001), 303.
[5] Raz (2001), 291: 'a non-democratic legal system, based on denial of human rights [and] on extensive poverty ... may, in principle, conform to the requirements of the rule of law better than any of the ... Western democracies.'
[6] See for a good account, Craig (1997). Or for a recent example, Tom Bingham: 'the core of the existing principle is ... that all persons and authorities within the state, whether public or private, should be bound by and entitled to the benefit of laws publicly and prospectively promulgated and publicly administered in the courts.' Bingham (2007), 69.
[7] Bingham (2007), 77.   [8] Raz (2001), 296.

law, publication of laws, transparency of legislation, procedural predictability, non-retroactivity of criminal law, access to courts, equality of arms, and so on.[9] At what point do these 'fundamentals' and 'principles' slip into the 'promiscuity' or 'perversion' that Raz identified in the New Delhi Declaration of the International Commission of Jurists? That document claimed, fifty years before the above examples, that the rule of law requires 'not only the recognition of [each individual's] civil and political rights' but also 'the establishment of the social, economic, educational and cultural conditions which are essential to the full development of his personality'.[10] While this formula would seem to foreshadow those of the blue ribbon commissions cited above, there is clearly a very different tone here.

What are we to make of all this? Clearly we are on contested rhetorical terrain: the expression 'rule of law' is a locus of numerous, varied, and sometimes apparently incompatible claims. But what if it were the very existence of this contest that is the most salient feature of the rule of law? What if its significance lies in the fact that *something is at stake* whenever the rule of law is invoked? If so, the stakes are evidently high – they concern the very structuring of the political, the social, and the economic. What is at stake, presumably, is the values or objectives that may attach to the fact of law: what kind of 'quality' does the invocation of a 'rule of law' add to the (mere, positive) law? Is it, perhaps, that the expression 'rule of law' tends to unsettle the very idea that there is such a thing as 'mere positive law'? Might it be, perhaps, that to speak of the rule of law is to suggest that law is *always* freighted with values? If so, reference to the rule of law in any given context might tell us *how* to interpret the law, how to read the law such that our reading remains truly *lawful*, that is, faithful to the law. The set of values assumed in the phrase 'rule of law', then, would allow us to determine the *legitimacy* of both law and of legal interpretation in any given instance. They would provide the master key to law: the 'rule of law' would be a kind of meta-law, the law of law.

---

[9] Fuller (1969).   [10] Cited in Raz (2001), 290.

Rule of law promotion as a field

The notion that 'the rule of law' captures a particular *quality* of law or of a legal system, a quality that may be more or less present or absent in a given legal system and that thus provides a basis for evaluating such a system, imbues most accounts of the rule of law. The present book explores one such account among many, one that today, however, is sufficiently prevalent as to be potentially transformative of the term's normative terrain. This is the particular register adopted in international development work and applied liberally to a range of activities undertaken by hundreds of agencies around the world as a means of framing, explaining and justifying their activities.

In this book, then, I will not be attempting to determine what the rule of law 'actually is'. I treat the systematic overburdening of this necessarily fungible expression as a symptom of a more generalised tendency which comprises my main concern: the intensive exportation of laws and institutional models around the world, under the rubric of 'rule of law' promotion. For the deliberate sponsorship and financing of 'rule of law reform' by leading private, bilateral and multilateral agencies in most of the world's countries has, it seems, been successful on at least one count: rule of law language is ubiquitous and increasingly associated with a broad span of public goods. In what follows, I am going to ask about the 'quality' or qualities that attach to the expression 'rule of law' in this register. I am going to look into the origins, both theoretical and practical, of this way of thinking and speaking about law. I will investigate the implicit, and often, explicit, assumptions about the relationship between law and 'society' and 'politics' and 'economy' that are found within it. And I will ask how this register is mobilised – what it is supposed to do, and what it actually does in practice.

The book thus aims to lay out for inspection the extravagant claims made on behalf of a field of practice that, despite having grown exponentially in size and reach in recent years, nevertheless remains barely explored *as a field*. Beginning in the mid-1980s, initially financed primarily by the US government's Agency for International Development (USAID) and the World Bank, rule of law promotion soon becomes a staple of every major donor.[11] It has undergone two phases of

---

[11] These include: bilateral donors particularly the United Kingdom (Department for International Development; DfID) and Swiss (Swiss Development Agency for Development and Cooperation; SDC) governments; multilateral donors, including

significantly accelerated expansion: first with the end of Communism, where it became the rallying call for the 'transition' to 'free market democracies' in Eastern Europe and beyond. Then again after 2001, with the surge in counter-terrorism and wars in Afghanistan and Iraq, both reinforcing and escalating calls for the creation and nurturing of robust rule of law institutions in 'fragile states'. A steadily increasing amount of time, money and effort has thus been devoted, over the last quarter century, to helping most of the world's countries 'improve the rule of law' through 'technical assistance' in drafting laws, direct support for courts and judiciaries to strengthen 'independence', training for security services, including police, army and prisons, and support for 'civil society' and private associations to advocate in favour of human rights and against corruption. Rule of law reform is now at the forefront of the UN's 'peacebuilding' mandate and has become the rallying banner around which a broad variety of old-style law-and-order activities are conducted in countries characterised as 'developing', 'post-conflict' or 'transitional'. At the same time a long-standing policy of economic restructuring continues to drive international development policy under the rule of law rubric.

Rule of law promotion is, in short, explicitly bound up with the primary currents of international political and economic development, and today provides a leading language for the articulation and justification of overarching public policy orientations. The work undertaken beneath this sprawling heading has now begun to spawn a significant literature of its own.[12] That commentary, like the work it refers to, deals

---

the EU (the Commission and Council), the Council of Europe, the Organisation for Economic Cooperation and Development (OECD – whose Development Assistance Committee (DAC) provides a forum for coordinating donor policies) and Organisation for Security and Cooperation in Europe (OSCE, notably its Office for Democratic Institutions and Human Rights (ODIHR)); and multilateral banks – the European Bank for Reconstruction and Development (EBRD) and the Asian, African and Inter-American Development Banks. There are also many privately funded institutions promoting the rule of law, including operational programmes and funders (notably the American Bar Association (ABA), the Ford Foundation and the Open Society Institute (OSI)) and some research institutions/think-tanks (such as the International Peace Academy and the Carnegie Endowment for International Peace).

[12] See, for examples, Allen et al. (2005), Belton (2005), Carothers (2006) (and contributions therein), Caruso (2006), Channell (2005), Chong and Calderon (2000), Clarke (2003), Dam (2006a), Dam (2006b), Davis (2004), Davis and Kruse (2006), Djankov et al. (2002), Faundez (2000), Golub (2007), Hurwitz and Huang (2008), Jansen and Heller (2003), Jayasuriya (1999), Kossick (2004), Li (2006), Magen (2004), Mattei and Nader (2008), Mednicoff (2005), Michaels and Jansen (2006), Nader (2007), Neumayer

with serious stuff: the deliberate re-engineering, at a legal-structural level, of the economic, political and social basics of countries throughout the world. And yet the burgeoning literature remains essentially unreflective with regard to the field's overarching self-justification and rationale. With few exceptions,[13] it is fundamentally technocratic in its overall thrust, broadly credulous of practitioners' claims to be mere functionaries, and sanguine about the prospects for eventual 'success' of this work, despite few examples. It is as though the association between something called 'the rule of law' and contemporary ideas of the good life has grown so strong as to inoculate efforts undertaken in its name against serious scrutiny. Although critical views exist, they tend to be limited to specific projects, methodologies and orientations; the most ambitious concern is with, as one collection has it, 'the problem of knowledge' – how is the rule of law to be measured; how can it be improved; what examples are there of successes and how can they be emulated; what can be learned from the many failures?[14]

My concerns in the present book extend beyond these essentially (and self-consciously) technocratic considerations. I aim rather to describe the *inner logic* of rule of law promotion: what kind of world is imagined in these programmes; what theoretical and historical drivers orient and legitimate it; and how do donors go about making that world a reality? Given how heavily the field has come to rely on the expression 'rule of law' itself as its guiding rhetoric, the book is also concerned with the changing parameters of this term of art: what does 'the rule of law' now encompass, how does current usage differ from its past referential scope, and what factors have contributed to its evolution? The present book couches its critique of this field in the field's own world, through immersion in the repeated self-sustaining narratives that permeate the programmatic and strategic literature, set against the broader history and conceptual evolution of the rule of law 'itself', as it has come down to us.

What that examination finds is that rule of law promotion relies for its normative force on the consistent reproduction of a particular narrative embedding a certain set of assumptions about the optimal role

---

(2003), Ohnesorge (2003), Peerenboom (2002), Purvis (2006), Sachs and Pistor (1997) (and contributions therein), Spence (2005), Stephenson (2006), Stromseth *et al.* (2006), Thomas (2007), Trubek and Santos (2006) (and contributions therein).

[13] Among the few exceptions, contributions to Trubek and Santos (2006), Mattei and Nader (2008), Purvis (2006).

[14] Among many examples, contributions to Carothers (2006).

of law in society – rather than relying on, say, theoretical or critical inquiry, historical analogy, reasoned deduction, or empirical demonstration. For this reason – its reliance on the techniques of story-telling and intuitive appeal rather than on the tools of analysis and demonstration – rule of law promotion is perhaps best viewed as a sort of theatre, a morality tale staged as a spectacle, drawing on the techniques of rhetoric and the power of performance.

The rule of law at home and abroad

The tremendous drive among development agencies and other donors to 'promote' the rule of law cannot be entirely dissociated from a larger preoccupation with the rule of law in contemporary life. On the one hand, the rise of rule of law language in international development is concomitant with, and indissociable from, deregulation and the gradual pruning of the welfare state back home: in each case something called the rule of law is pitted against the overpowering and stifling discretion of an intrusive, 'bloated', ineffective and/or corrupt bureaucracy, that is to be made leaner, more efficient and more accountable. On the other, rule of law language has contrasting associations with counter-terrorism measures at home and abroad. At home, the accumulation of executive powers in the war against terrorism is regularly challenged as violative of something called 'the rule of law'. Abroad, by contrast, the training and arming of security forces to counter terrorism is *itself* carried out under the rule of law banner. In both cases, the parameters of state capacity to project coercive violence are at issue, but rule of law language is deployed to dramatically different, even opposite, ends in each.

There is thus both a relation and a distinction between the rule of law 'at home' and the rule of law 'abroad'. For whereas the language has a comparable sphere of reference in each domain, it has different specific significations. In the field of development assistance, rule of law language is deployed to eclipse or minimise entire areas of government activity (social welfare and public spending) that are considered quite compatible with the rule of law 'at home'. Rule of law state-building, moreover, is more strictly concerned with reinforcing and channelling than merely constraining or interrogating the state's coercive capacity. Furthermore, whereas – at least at the rhetorical level – the rule of law at home is a good in itself, an *end*, the rule of law abroad is rather a *means*, motivated by other goods, notably prosperity (a market economy) and stability ('peace and security'). Indeed, rule of law promotion rhetorically links and buttresses these two objectives: global security to underpin global prosperity. These distinctions in the applications of a rule of law register at home and abroad are not quite contradictory; it is the weight, or centre of gravity, of the expression that has shifted, not its entire associative canvas.

Rule of law promotion is premised on a further core distinction: the *presence* of the rule of law at home is contrasted with, and privileged over, its *absence* abroad. Whereas donor countries are thought to 'have' the rule of law, recipient countries do not, or not yet, or not sufficiently: the rule of law is the basis for prosperity/stability at home; its relative absence is a contributory cause or explanation of comparative poverty/insecurity abroad. This distinction again mobilises a relation – *we* can (and should) help *them* attain the rule of law. To assist in establishing the rule of law abroad is thus a moral duty; but it is also enlightened self-interest: in an increasingly integrated world everyone everywhere stands to benefit from an improvement in the rule of law (and so prosperity and stability) anywhere. This relation is not formal – it is not a product of international obligation. Rather it is voluntary, a matter of charitable 'assistance'.

Rule of law promotion is thus an activity undertaken by agents in (and of) one set of countries but conducted in another set of countries. It is a *transnational* activity. The term 'transnational' is appropriate here, rather than 'international', because the relationship is both non-obligatory (it is moral rather than legal) and unidirectional (it flows from one set of parties to another but not vice versa), in contrast to the binding and reciprocal relations that characterise international law. But I also use the term 'transnational' for three other reasons.[15] First, the relationship between donors and hosts is neither a relation of equals (it is premised on inequality) nor truly a free association (it is a riddled with conditions and incentives), two conditions generally thought necessary to an association under international law. Second, rule of law promotion is not fundamentally concerned with relations *between states*; it does not result from or express the interaction of formally equal sovereigns. Rather it is concerned with

---

[15] See on this subject the special 2004 issue of the *Penn State International Law Review* compiling papers from the American Society of International Law symposium on 'Transnational Law: What is it? How Does it Differ from International Law and Comparative Law', 23 *Penn State International Law Review* 795 (2004), especially Reimann (2004).

the *intra*-statal, the *content* of sovereignty. It involves the reproduction of statehood, and of the functions appropriate to the state, in recipient countries. Third, as a matter of rhetoric, rule of law promotion privileges private agents over the state actors that people public international law – non-statal transnational actors that pass through and between states, and whose passage is fostered and signposted by rule of law promotion.

For these reasons, while I will frequently refer to the subject of my inquiry, in what follows, as 'transnational rule of law promotion', 'reform' or 'assistance', the modifier 'transnational' refers to the agents and beneficiaries of this work, not to some notional ideal of the 'rule of law' that might be thought 'transnational' rather than international or national.

These various concerns of contemporary rule of law promotion place a significant burden on the term; tension is generated when new and motivated deployments of the register rub up against other settled site- or discipline-specific uses. In the following pages, I will trace some of the many threads that have led to the tangled and often confused notion that is the contemporary rule of law. To do so requires stepping back from the seductive appeal of rule of law language and focusing on its actual deployments. It becomes quickly apparent that there are several kinds of 'rule of law'. And that the particular deployments that dominate in transnational rule of law promotion, despite many superficial resemblances to those conceptions well-known from legal and constitutional scholarship, are in many other respects almost unrecognisable.

The thrust of the book, then, is to uncover the objectives, techniques and internalised lessons that propel the field from within, as it were – what might be called the *latent theory* of the rule of law field, a field that ordinarily eschews theory altogether in favour of a robustly pragmatic orientation. Once articulated, however, this background theoretical structure will, I believe, appear very familiar to rule of law practitioners and observers alike. And, since internal consistency is not the same as contextual aptness, it may also help explain why rule of law reform so rarely succeeds, even on its own account. Beyond this, the book provides a guide to one of the key dynamics of contemporary international and transnational development, an area of practice that has considerable substantive implications for the evolution of legal systems throughout the world and that, by nudging jurisdictions everywhere towards a convergent set of norms, principles and institutional mechanisms, drives and underpins the legal architecture of economic and cultural globalisation.

Having laid out the broad parameters of the field, I will now turn to the structure and argument of the book itself.

The theory and the practice of rule of law promotion

The book that follows is in two parts, separated by an 'interlude'. A first part provides a broad conceptual account of the rule of law, investigating the historical and theoretical influences that have, over time, imbued the term with the immense rhetorical force it enjoys today; it does so with reference to three paradigmatic fields of its ordinary application – that is, with regard to the optimal ordering of society (how should we relate to one another?), of the political (what is a state and how should it function?) and of the economic (how do we organise and manage wealth creation and distribution?). The second part looks in detail at the projects and programmes today undertaken in the name of the rule of law, organised according to the same three broad areas, rearticulated as state (polity), market (economy) and the 'public' (society). Between Parts I and II, I step away from the rule of law register for a moment to examine a relevant precursor to contemporary efforts to establish political and economic goals through legal intervention abroad, in the transposition of law and legal systems in colonial Africa.

The juxtaposition of these bodies of thought and practice clarifies something often missed in the literature (justificatory, evaluative and critical alike). That is: in its ordinary mode of production and application, rule of law promotion looks *almost nothing like* the ideal habitually represented in the language of the rule of law, either in its conceptual framing since the late nineteenth century or in its contemporary talismanic deployment. Certainly, powerful themes gleaned from the rule of law's broad conceptual terrain foreshadow the work undertaken in its name. But even so, the specific weighting these themes are given in rule of law reform and, in particular, the means by which this global practice is produced and effected tends to displace, disfigure, and even deny, some of the core precepts associated with the term.

The very operation of the field of rule of law promotion opens up rich and non-trivial conceptual conundrums. As we shall see in more detail, a number of the basic mechanisms of today's rule of law promotion appear, at first glance, to contradict outright some core principles regularly asserted under the rule of law rubric: the fact, for instance, that the field explicitly treats law as instrumental rather than autonomous; that it generally avoids standard legislative processes in favour of decrees or other expedient shortcuts; that it systematically supplies a source for law external to the specific social, historical or cultural conditions of those subject to it; that it privileges the state as central subject while nevertheless transcending, surpassing or simply ignoring sovereignty as a conceptual or political matter; and that, perhaps most strikingly, a language consistently deployed as a bulwark against public policy and centralisation is today a key trope of what is in practice a centralised and guided public policy applied globally. In consequence, if it was ever possible to assign a concrete and identifiable signification to the term rule of law – itself a doubtful proposition – such an assignation is increasingly impossible today.

This paradox cannot be explained by reference to the genealogy of the rule of law as term of art alone, which, as we shall see in Part I, consistently dissociates the rule of law from political and economic motives of any kind. But contemporary rule of law promotion does not derive from that tradition alone; indeed it is partly a new name for an old phenomenon. There is nothing new about the export of legal forms to economic ends – and the focused and directed manner in which it is now taking place has especially clear precedents in late colonial activity, as we shall see in the interlude below.

In practice, contemporary rule of law literature is unfussily amnesiac about its own history: the experience of the past century is either forgotten altogether or repressed. For example, the fraught battles over the welfare state undertaken in the name of the rule of law throughout much of the mid-twentieth century, as we shall see in Part I, are treated as over and won; they are not acknowledged, much less revisited, in contemporary rule of law promotion. At the same time, the language of the rule of law itself is wielded specifically to draw a line under the colonial period. Whatever rule of law promoters do, the necessary assumption is of a rupture with the colonial era; there is little space for remarking, much less assessing, continuities.

As a result of this generalised repression, it is at least as necessary, in the inquiry that follows, to attend to what contemporary rule of law language does *not* include as to examine its own stated parameters. A constellation of terms associated with the rule of law in everyday language – constitutionalism, legalism, formalism, proceduralism, fundamental rights – must be defamiliarised and reset in their historical and ideational context. I do this not by revisiting the standard historical narrative of the rule of law (which runs along familiar symbolic milestones: Magna Carta, Edward Coke, the Glorious Revolution, *Marbury* v. *Madison* and so on), but by revisiting other relevant histories and seeking to identify what has been neglected or excised in the various advances that have given the term its particular character and dominance today. A synopsis of the argument follows.

Part I: the rule of law as term of art

Chapter 1 examines a number of influential accounts of the rule of law, in order to identify some core attributes of the term. It aims to reach beyond the usual litany of attributes of a legal system habitually produced when the rule of law is reviewed (accountability, transparency, generality, predictability, non-retroactivity, and so on), in order to identify whether a deeper set of grounding presumptions underpin these notions. I turn to three influential commentators for guidance: Albert Dicey, Michael Oakeshott and Jürgen Habermas. Despite their different backgrounds, each of these three emphasises the *societal* dimension of the rule of law, approaching it first and foremost as an attribute of a modern European society: something that *binds* the members of a given polity to one another, indeed in the presumed absence of any other necessary bond (of community or faith, for example).

Having gleaned a series of elements common to all three accounts of the rule of law – nine 'family resemblances', so to speak – I then take a step back, guided in particular by the writing of Jürgen Habermas, to examine a prior moment in European history that is assumed, implicitly or explicitly, in all three accounts. That is the emergence, prior to and during the late eighteenth century, of certain core ideas about the relationship between state and society, positing a *civil society* as a fundamental basis for a modern state. In this configuration, private persons come to regard themselves as the proper agents of society, with the public machinery of the state subordinated to them and constrained to act on their behalf, in the 'public interest'. While Habermas focuses on the rise of a 'public sphere' during this period, the point for present purposes is the emergence at the same time of a set of principles and procedural mechanisms to constrain the public and safeguard the private that we would today recognise as constituting the 'rule of law' (these are, again, the familiar principles of accountability, transparency, generality, predictability, non-retroactivity, and so on).

Turning to the *economy*, Chapter 2 picks up a later formative moment in the history of the term, its relationship with the policy apparatus of the state. In its earliest formulation, Albert Dicey introduced the term to describe a specifically English guarantee that 'there can be with us nothing really corresponding to the "administrative law" ... of France'.[16] However, this absolute opposition between 'rule of law' and the 'administrative state' is difficult to sustain on other accounts of the role of law in the economy, notably that of Dicey's near contemporary Max Weber, for whom fidelity to law and legal process (i.e. the *Rechtsstaat*), is the guarantor both of an efficient bureaucracy and of the smooth functioning of a market economy. The chapter engages more closely with this set of arguments by way of the American legal realist critique of 'formalism' in judicial interpretation. The realists observed that techniques of legal interpretation then common in US courts were flawed in a number of respects, serving to abstract law from the realities with which it necessarily must deal. Pointing to a series of recurrent biases and errors they perceived in the judicial processes, writers such as Oliver Wendell Holmes and Robert Lee Hale called for a fuller appreciation of the policy function inherent in law and in judicial decisions. Initially, however, these realist insights were strenuously resisted in the US courts.

By the late 1930s, with the New Deal and the establishment of a far-reaching administrative apparatus in the United States, the realists appeared to have won this argument, but in the process Dicey's foundational opposition between 'the rule of law' and the 'administrative state' became if anything more deeply entrenched: scepticism towards state 'policy' or 'planning' of any kind was an often unstated assumption of a rule of law perspective. This view was most clearly articulated and theorised by Friedrich Hayek in the 1940s. Hayek's definition of the rule of law, a principle he viewed as a bulwark against 'planning' in general – and redistributive welfare in particular – moved to the political centre in the 1980s, infecting not only domestic Anglo-American politics, but also the policies of the international financial institutions and, eventually, development organisations in general.

Chapter 3 turns to *sovereignty*, a perennial locus of contestation in the name of the rule of law. The chapter examines the claim commonly made that Aristotle was the 'founding father of the rule of law'. Aristotle asked how the law – the *nomos*, as opposed to the statutes

---

[16] Dicey (1962), 202–203.

promulgated through a democratic legislature – might be made to 'rule'. This breaks down into two related questions: how the *nomos* itself is to be *known* and how a public authority can be construed so as to faithfully apply that law, rather than usurp it in their own interests. Finding no final answer to these questions, other than the mirage of a 'godlike man' who might know the law intuitively and rule selflessly – but whose existence he admitted to be unlikely – Aristotle bequeathed a political conundrum that reappears throughout the medieval and early modern period in controversies over the figure of the political sovereign, through the writings of Bracton, Aquinas, Montesquieu, Bodin and others.

The chapter then examines a contemporary perspective on sovereignty, in the work of philosopher Giorgio Agamben. For Agamben, sovereignty seeks constant self-expansion, and does so through the invocation of 'states of exception' (wars, public emergencies, and so on), which allow the reach of the law to extend. Implicitly, Agamben's account challenges the very idea that something called 'the rule of law' might restrain the sovereign. Rather, since legal measures initially framed as exceptional become progressively normalised, the procedural values associated with the rule of law might themselves tend to facilitate the consolidation of sovereign reach. With a nod to Michel Foucault's work on disciplinary power, the chapter suggests that even as it apparently constrains sovereign power, the procedural rigour assumed by a rule of law may equally serve to refine, focus and augment that same power.

With that, Part I comes to a close. The combination of rereadings, reminders and critiques of the rule of law in Part I is not intended to debunk the rule of law as ideal but rather, in the main, to destabilise the highly attenuated usage that appears in the enormous volume of project literature that I will turn to in Part II. The point is not to show that the rule of law, although it may appear simple, is 'actually' complex, or to 'uncover' its true complexity. The complexity of the rule of law as term of art is familiar and largely uncontroversial. The point here is rather to revive some of the nuances, ambiguities and conundrums traditionally associated with the term, to increase the space for discursive inquiry surrounding its usage, and so to recognise that its complexity may in fact be a virtue. For what is new today is not so much the apotheosis of a venerable term as the relatively simplistic, rigid, unambiguous and largely ahistorical tenor bestowed upon it within the field of transnational rule of law reform, and, oddly, that this deployment has been adopted so widely, rapidly and uncritically.

First, however, I look quickly at the historical precedents for contemporary practice.

Interlude: colonial precursors

Antecedents for the contemporary field of rule of law reform are not, of course, to be found only in legal history and political philosophy. The field also has roots in a solid body of past *practice*; there is, indeed, no shortage of experience in the export of legal norms and institutions abroad to further economic and political goals. An obvious precursor is the colonial period, during which a wholesale transfer of legal institutions and norms took place, that still provide the basis for state administrations in much of the world today.

The relationship between these colonial and contemporary practices bears scrutiny for a number of reasons. For one, the legal systems built, or at a minimum reconstituted, by colonial authorities, are often those that are today the subject of fresh interventions. For another, the explicit objectives of colonial legal intervention are remarkably consonant with those currently put forward to explain and motivate rule of law reforms. Three shared themes stand out in particular: free trade, humanitarianism and development.[17] A third reason to look back at the colonial export of law is that it seems reasonable to expect that the techniques adopted in the present to facilitate the transfer of legal systems and institutions might owe something to methods developed during that era.

Legal export was central to the colonial endeavour in at least three ways. The first was the role of international law in framing the colonial encounter. The General Acts of Berlin (1885) and Brussels (1890) agreed between the Powers regulated their entry into, and authority in, future colonial acquisitions in Africa, in order to establish free trade and abolish the slave trade. Concomitant with the negotiation of these Acts, in allocating African territories, sovereignty was finally fixed to statehood (accelerating the elimination of the residual category of sovereign *person*hood), which in turn was defined in terms of effective territorial control and the existence of government. It then fell to the Powers to supply this control and government, and to raise the money locally to do so, which in turn opened the way for extensive construction of administrative apparatuses in the territories.

---

[17] See generally Anghie (1999), Anghie (2005).

Second, widespread transplantation of laws and institutions was central to the successful management of these tasks. For all the Powers, African colonisation was speedy and deliberate. The physical landscape and the behaviour of the populations were swiftly subjected to new overarching normative orders which drew on and reshaped existing customs, but superimposed a level of statehood overhead that served, on one hand, to make all subject to a single overarching authority and, on the other, to found that authority in law, represented as both the product and vehicle of 'modern civilisation'. So successful was this endeavour that these structures – legislative bodies, prisons, criminal and civil courts and appeals processes, local administrations – as well, of course, as the overarching authority of the state itself, were retained through decolonisation and beyond.

Finally, a third area in which law was central to African colonisation was the injection of *legalism* itself: everywhere the authorities insisted on the primacy of law, instilled through reliance on court mechanisms and (generally) the promulgation of laws prior to the initiation of policy. Colonialism largely justified itself in legal terms and its battles were frequently fought in the name of upholding the law. To function, it sought acquiescence not just in the factual authority of the colonial order, but also in the principles of legalism that underpinned it. Indeed, the latter was achieved even where the former was not. While contemporary rule of law export clearly does not simply continue or repeat the colonial endeavour, many of the themes and techniques from that period do reappear in today's work, as we shall see in Part II.

Part II: theatre of the rule of law

Where Part I was concerned with the kinds of ideas and background norms that provide the normative penumbra of the 'rule of law', Part II turns to a body of practice undertaken by concrete actors in specific places, through projects and programmes that claim as their motive and justification to be furthering and promoting this same 'rule of law'. Part II thus looks to the mechanics of a global daily activity, an *industry* of a certain kind.[18] As such, the three chapters of this Part involve a change of tone and tempo from the first three: they are

---

[18] That is, 'systematic labour especially for some useful purpose or the creation of something of value'. Merriam-Webster's Online Dictionary, http://www.merriam-webster.com/dictionary/industry, at 2(a).

steeped in project literature and programmatic rhetoric rather than the canon of political or legal philosophy; in the minutiae of technical applications and project goals rather than the narrative of broad historical intervention or conceptual evolution; in the logic and self-justification of institutional actors with limited budgets in competitive environments rather than the disinterested inquiry of the impartial observer. The chapters ask what is *specific* to rule of law promotion as a field or industry. To grasp that specificity requires submersion in the field's own self-representations, a now extensive body of incantation of ideals, goals and techniques.

Throughout, therefore, I attempt to reach below the surface of an immense and somewhat repetitive body of project literature, which is at least as important a part of the rule of law landscape today as the projects themselves, in order to grasp the vision of the social, political and economic, the relation between the national and the international, and the unifying themes and concepts that lie beneath the rhetoric. Although the language is technical and often stultifying, the themes raised in this literature are remarkably broad. But they are at the same time bounded, consistent and exclusive in terms of what figures and what does not, what is emphasised and what is brushed over or obscured.

The questions these chapters ask, then, are not 'how can the rule of law be promoted?' much less 'how can progress be measured?' or 'where has rule of law promotion been successful and why?' These have been the standard inquiries undertaken in the field to date, and asking them serves to propel it further. Here I am asking different kinds of question: 'what sort of world does rule of law promotion imagine?', 'what are the gaps it intends to fill?', 'what sectors of society does it target and privilege?', 'who does it neglect and why?', 'what governmental powers does it activate and what suppress?', 'what sort of activity is a rule of law activity, and which activities are ruled out?' As in Part I, then, inquiry in this Part too does not aim to define or describe the rule of law 'itself' in countries of application, as though it were simply available for observation and description. Rather the focus is on the specific associations the term produces in the particular circumstances of project work; the rule of law as banner, umbrella, activity, technical specification, package, condition, censure, threat. What, in these circumstances, does the rule of law signal among its promoters and what does it signify in their relationship with its 'beneficiaries'?

Despite the proliferation of topic-areas and actors in this field over the last two decades, it is possible to pick out a number of core themes and actors – the principal waterways, as it were – along which rule of law promotion runs, as distinct from the myriad tributaries it picks up along the way. The chapters in Part II focus on three main actors: the World Bank, United States foreign assistance agencies (especially, but not only, the Agency for International Development (USAID)) and the United Nations. These three are chosen as the largest and most influential rule of law actors, and also because they mobilise their extensive convening capacity to disseminate rule of law language and themes far beyond their immediate contexts. They further represent different strands of the contemporary rule of law: the Bank focuses mainly on market mechanisms, the UN on state-building, and the US foreign assistance sector on both (albeit through different agencies). Additionally, USAID and the Bank are chronologically the earliest agents of contemporary rule of law promotion, having begun in the mid to late 1980s (the UN joined considerably later). Their work has provided the yardstick against which later initiatives are measured, the paradigm on which they are modelled or against which they chafe.

Given the vast scope of the rule of law promotion field today, the chapters are inevitably selective. My approach has been to concentrate on the principal lines of activity – the discourse-setting and norm-generating bodies of work – against which background other bodies of work appear largely derivative, both chronologically and thematically. As a result, numerous rule of law actors – bilateral, multilateral and private – are not dealt with directly in Part II.[19] I also touch only obliquely upon the growing subindustry of rule of law 'indicators'.[20]

---

[19] For a fuller list of rule of law donors, see note 11 above. Police and military rule of law training is undertaken by DFID, OSCE ODIHR, the Council of the European Union and the Council of Europe. Market-centred rule of law work is undertaken by the multilateral development banks and the OECD; the private funders focus on human rights, judicial strengthening and civil society building.

[20] A recent count undertaken by the American Bar Association (ABA) lists 60 relevant indices produced by 42 different agencies. See ABA, 'Rule of Law Index – Exhibit B' (2008). Seven of these are produced by the World Bank, foremost among them the Bank's Governance Matters and (through the IFC) Doing Business surveys, published annually. Other leaders are ABA CEELI's Judicial Reform, Legal Profession and Prosecutorial Reform Indices; the Business Environment and Enterprise Performance Surveys (BEEPS), produced by the World Bank and the EBRD; the International Country Risk Guide (ICRG) of the Political Risk Services Group; the Business Environmental Risk Intelligence (BERI) surveys on 'Business Risk Service' and 'Country Risks Forecast for International Lenders'. BERI also produces

These appear to have three main functions: first, to provide guidance to investors on the security of investing in certain countries; second to attach conditionality to grants, loans and debt cancellations made by the major donors (higher rule of law scores bring eligibility for larger grants or debt relief); third to allow governments to compare their rankings, thereby generating competition to attract investment and donor funding/debt relief.[21] The role of these indicators in disseminating rule of law language and creating pressure for the adoption and achievement of rule of law objectives is worthy of a study in its own right.

The three chapters of Part II break down as follows. The first two sketch rule of law assistance aimed respectively at market-promotion and state-building. Having drawn the relevant parameters of the field, each chapter than queries the rationale for deployment of rule of law language in these different contexts, in the light of a number of glaring deviations from the rule of law parameters outlined in the first Part. Following these, the final chapter picks up the main theme of Chapter 1 – the articulation of 'the public' per se in the language of the rule of law.

Chapter 4 describes the turn, in the late 1980s, away from post-colonial 'developmentalism' and towards market promotion, with rule of law as a central premise and objective. Post-colonial states are charged with having mismanaged their economies and allowed state bureaucracies to become bloated and corrupt. Following on the sovereign debt crisis and introduction of structural adjustment programmes, the World Bank (and other international agencies) established new priorities for development assistance aimed at encouraging growth – 'private sector development' and 'governance'. The language of 'the rule of law' was introduced at this time in support of these aims: promotion

---

a cross-country 'Quality of Workforce Index' and 'Financial Ethics Index'. The US Millennium Challenge Corporation, which determines allocations from the President's Millennium Challenge Account, produces its own ratings for that purpose. Standard and Poor's sovereign credit ratings frequently include rule of law indicators. Academics too have sought to produce rule of law indicators, notably Knack and Keefer (1995) (their results provide the basis for numerous later studies correlating the 'rule of law' with a variety of other public goods) and the Harvard group initially led by Andrei Shleifer, later by Simeon Djankov (at time of writing, Bulgarian Minister of Finance). For critique, Davis (2004) and Davis and Kruse (2006).

[21] See, for example, Presentation of Ambassador Fritz Poku, Ghana's envoy to the United States, on the occasion of the International Rule of Law Symposium in Washington, DC, hosted by the American Bar Association, November 2005.

of the rule of law was explained by the Bank as 'structural' rather than 'political', a mere technical exercise in support of other economic reforms: supporting courts and other legal institutions, nurturing judicial 'independence' and so on.

The deployment of rule of law language, with its long-standing associations with the autonomy of law, to these explicitly motivated ends is, perhaps, surprising. Chapter 4 therefore probes a little further, to query the Bank's counterintuitive usage and suggest some possible effects this may be expected to achieve for the Bank and others doing development work. I identify three such effects. First, the Bank might expect to gain in *legitimacy* by associating its often controversial work with a universally recognised public good such as the rule of law. Second, the particular economic configuration preferred by the Bank, de-emphasising government action, taxation and regulation, and prioritising private freedom of action, may be *naturalised* by association with the rule of law. Third, reference to the rule of law in this context, with its presumption against *policy* interventions, may tend to obscure the extent to which Bank projects themselves embed policy preferences in their own right.

Chapter 5 turns to the immense expansion of state-building 'rule of law' work, generally under a 'peace and security' rubric. Initially undertaken by the US in Latin America, this work received a boost after September 11, 2001. From that time, and especially after the invasion of Iraq in 2003, it was also increasingly deployed by agencies of the United Nations. By 2004, the UN Secretary-General was speaking of the UN's unique role in addressing the 'rule of law vacuums' in post-conflict countries, where law and order had broken down. The rule of law became a centrepiece of the UN's new peacebuilding mandate, and peppered the language of the Department of Peacekeeping Operations (DPKO) and other agencies, such as UNODC, OHCHR, and UNDP who produced rule of law 'handbooks' and 'toolkits' for 'rule of law officers' and NGOs working in post-conflict environments.

Again, this deployment of rule of law language is somewhat incongruous, given the term's history, in that it refers in the main to the expansion of the state's coercive capacities – police forces and armies, prisons and criminal courts. Although reliable, prisons and policing are obviously compatible with most visions of the rule of law, the traditional emphasis had nevertheless been on the restraint of these arms of the state. To put effective policing front and centre of the term's referential scope is certainly an innovation and, like Chapter 4, Chapter 5 goes on to suggest a number of expectable effects of this novel recourse to rule of law language in lieu of 'law and order' (or 'rule *by* law', as it is sometimes called).

These are: first, this focus on the institutions of law tends to saturate the terms of post-conflict settlement, prioritising *retributive* modes of justice over others that might otherwise be available. Second, to refer to police, military and criminal structures as the institutions of the 'rule of law' tends to reinforce their *disciplinary* function both internally, as themselves disciplined institutions, and externally, as institutions requiring discipline and obedience from the public. Third, as with the use of rule of law to promote markets, here too it may be expected to bestow *legitimacy* on international actors, distance them from previous (colonial) enterprises that otherwise look similar, and obscure the extent to which countries are subject to an overarching *policy* objective set elsewhere.

Perhaps the newest innovation in the work reviewed in Chapters 4 and 5 is the attachment of rule of law language to a series of international efforts that are not, in and of themselves, especially new in international affairs. However, in the final chapter, Chapter 6, I turn to a genuine innovation of this body of work, one that stems directly from the turn to rule of law language and that draws upon the history of the term. That is the concerted effort to mobilise a 'public', along the lines of the 'public sphere' recounted in Chapter 1, in rule of law target states: a public imagined as the proper guardians of the public interest, and to which the state owes obedience. It will be quickly apparent that such a framing is not properly descriptive of the relations of allegiance constructed through rule of law reform. But it nevertheless provides the principal narrative to explain much of this work, one that is echoed through a broad variety of sources, both international and national, public, 'private sector' and 'civil society' alike. This notional public plays a central role in rule of law reform, not only as the *addressee* of projects and programmes, but also as their supposed *source*.

Chapter 6 takes up the narrative of the public in rule of law work, as source, target and indeed product of interventions throughout the political and economic spheres. For what is perhaps most striking about rule of law reform is the degree to which it presents itself not so much as a reasoned response to a specific set of problems, but rather as a broadly applicable fix for society as a whole. Its ubiquity of application derives not from analysis of local problems, nor from analytic reasoning more generally, nor from historical contextualisation or proven demonstration in analogical contexts. Rather its appeal derives from the narrative itself, its moral force from its capacity to persuade, itself premised on the existence of a public, imagined as both audience and key participant.

The theatre of the rule of law comprises a remarkably consistent set of themes and characters, playing out in multiple locations around the world along very similar lines. The setting is an overarching backdrop of modernisation in a post-ideological and globalising world. Narrative tension is supplied by the conflict between *public* and *private*. Weakened or confused, these two realms and sectors must be disentangled and reoriented towards the roles and duties proper to a modern society and prospering economy. The lead characters are: the judiciary, civil society, a 'reform constituency' (the natural allies of rule of law funders), and finally, 'the poor', posited as the ultimate beneficiaries of reform (but who in practice appear to suffer from its application).[22]

Together, and with the help of the 'international community', the protagonists undertake a series of set ordeals, which provides the plot. Foremost among these are the achievement of governance, elimination of corruption and submission to privatisation. At the denouement, a higher purpose to the story is disclosed. Having accomplished their tasks and thus proved themselves responsible and competent, the lead actors may join in the larger project of 'global integration', in particular through adherence to the rules of international trade and investment (which, according to the literature, both rely upon and in turn encourage 'more' rule of law in host states) and can look forward to sharing in the fruits of (global) security and prosperity.

Chapter 6 draws the threads of the preceding arguments together in order to represent contemporary transnational rule of law promotion as a whole, an exercise premised upon a number of theoretical principles that it claims but does not demonstrate, and a number of practical principles that it demonstrates but does not claim.

The Conclusion makes explicit the connections between the previous sections, noting how in contemporary rule of law reform, a mix of colonial era priorities (the dominance of public policy; the encouragement of and support for private enterprise; the creation of an 'enabling environment' for development; the protection of foreigners' rights on a par with locals; the facilitation of expected justice) meets with the implicit logic of the rule of law ideal (the primacy of the judiciary; the

---

[22] See the three-volume World Bank Study *Voices of the Poor*, especially World Bank (2002b), 471–476.

sharp separation of public and private; the role of law as a bulwark between them). Rule of law reform looks like colonial law in precisely those attributes where it deviates most from the 'classical' concept of the rule of law.

There are many other conclusions that might be drawn from this inquiry, most of which can only be touched upon in my concluding chapter. Among them, this story raises questions regarding the future impetus and direction of the rule of law as a term of art, which appears to be in a process of becoming both narrower in its range and aspirations while simultaneously becoming attached to a greater number of public goods. More pressingly, perhaps, another question that is raised but not answered here concerns the kind of transnational *polity* or *society* involved in the production of a global network of rule of law states, and that may perhaps be coming into being, if not through the mechanisms of rule of law promotion alone, then through a broader set of global processes of convergence to which it belongs.

The conceit of a 'global civil society' that itself seeks rule of law reform is somewhat belied by the constant background presence of the immense public and private actors that fund and mobilise this 'civil society' (perhaps, if we believe the Habermas of *Structural Transformation*, it was always thus). The parallel conceit is of a newly burgeoning global *sovereign*, comprised presumably of the same public and private actors – an entity whose presence is just as difficult to pinpoint, if indeed it exists at all. These twin rising stars appear emblematic of that peculiar dialectic between state and society that a rule of law register instantiates and, as we have seen, actively transmits. But if it is the case, as the foregoing inquiry suggests, that this dialectic is in fact deliberately reproduced and disseminated, we might ask whether there is not another more fundamental contest also taking place, albeit largely concealed behind the comfortable spectacle of the more familiar rule of law struggle, now apparently underway everywhere. And if so, who does it involve and how is it taking place?

PART I

PARAMETERS: 'RULE OF LAW' AS A
TERM OF ART

1 Society

Part I of this book tracks the parameters of the rule of law as a term of art, with a view to determining the scope of its referential field. I aim in these chapters to capture not only the broad set of conceptions and suppositions – political, social, and economic – assumed within the term's ordinary penumbra, but also its historical weight: its role as a battleground for competing conceptions of the good life and as signalling an assumed outcome to those battles.

THE IMMANENT RULE OF LAW

In perhaps its most influential early articulation, drawing on a long tradition of political philosophy and in turn frequently reiterated today, the rule of law appears as a sort of social glue, a connective tissue holding society together. In this picture, a generalised obedience to the law combines with a pervasive legalism in both public and private spheres. The law itself functions in the background, largely internalised and functionally independent of the coercive and administrative power that guarantees its efficacy. Associated with the 'social fabric', this rule of law is *immanent*. It is already present in the everyday interaction of law-abiding citizens. Its reappearance in official and legal processes is the concrete expression of profoundly held principles and habits of thought – but not their source. Legal actors and public officials, in this view, do not arrive at law-sustaining conduct merely by following preassigned rules. In the first instance, they draw on an ingrained, even intuitive, understanding of the proper operation of the polity. This is the rule of law as *habitus* in the Aristotelian sense of a quality so thoroughly culturally embedded that it is difficult to alter.[1]

I take three authors as initial guides to this set of themes – Dicey, Oakeshott and Habermas – chosen in part for the clarity and richness of their accounts, but also because they are associated with politically diverse perspectives. Any themes common to all three might, in consequence, be considered representative of a core set of qualities. If the rule of law is something that essentially holds the 'social fabric' together, as each of these three suggests, it may be possible to identify through them some of the weave and pattern that go to make it up. In a second section I will turn to Habermas again for his account of the 'public', which is an elementary component of the kind of society thought to be modern and, by corollary, an indispensable, if generally implicit, element of most visions of the rule of law.

Dicey: 'the habit of self-government'

Albert Dicey did not conceive of the rule of law as a universal good. To the contrary, it is irremediably local: 'one of the most marked peculiarities of English life'.[2] Dicey placed the expression at the centre of his influential restatement of the English Constitution. Given the tangled mass of law possibly relevant to his subject, he introduced the term 'rule of law' as a structuring device to tease out the constitutional wheat from the sundry legal chaff, so to speak. To begin, he reminds us that the English Constitution had, before then, generally been thought of in a somewhat mystical vein:

> the fruit not of abstract theory but of that instinct which (it is supposed) has enabled Englishmen, and especially uncivilised Englishmen, to build up sound institutions, much as bees construct a honeycomb, without undergoing the degradation of understanding the principles on which they raise a fabric more subtly wrought than any work of conscious art.[3]

The obvious hyperbole in this passage – 'instinct', 'uncivilised', 'the degradation of understanding' – serves to consolidate the *organic* nature of England's 'sound institutions' which, Dicey indicates, are

---

[1] See generally Nederman (1997), 87–110. Pierre Bourdieu (1987) uses the term 'habitus' in a related sense to mean the *ésprit* and norms common to a given profession, such as lawyers.

[2] Dicey (1962), 187–188. The rule of law might also be found in 'countries which, like the United States of America, have inherited English traditions'.

[3] Dicey (1962), 3, 4.

neither the creation nor the prerogative of legal professionals alone. Indeed this is a vision that evinces scepticism of 'expertise' of any kind, a sort of Everyman simplicity that already had a long pedigree in English self-representation, supplying a bedrock theme of the laissez faire liberalism that was reaching a peak at the time Dicey wrote. Thus the reference to 'bees construct[ing] a honeycomb' would have struck Dicey's contemporary audience as an allusion to Bernard de Mandeville's Fable of the Bees, a short parable from his 1714 *Private Vices, Publick Virtues*. Mandeville's observation – that individual bees, in the ordinary pursuit of their own interests, subject to no higher intelligence or authority, manage to produce general welfare and excellence (honeycombs and honey) – was a conceptual forebear of Adam Smith's 'invisible hand' and a cornerstone of the now flourishing discipline of economics.

Dicey, however, makes clear that he will abstain from these 'attractive mysteries' (and I will do so too for now, picking them up again in the next chapter); his aim instead is to mature or graduate this long tradition of political (or analogical) English constitutionalism into hard positive law. From Blackstone and Edmund Burke he derives the notion that the rights of an Englishman are better protected than the constitutional rights of the French (and others), because they subsist not in written proclamation, but in the minds and habits of the people and in the common law principles of the ordinary courts. The rule of law, a term Dicey popularised and may even have coined,[4] will serve as the kiln within which he will recast these principles of right, these habits and legal practices, as hard law. Since, Dicey says, Englishmen often miss what is most distinctive about their own system and character, he introduces the rule of law by means of a long citation from Alexis de Tocqueville comparing England and Switzerland. The gist of it is summed up at the end: 'in England there seems to be more liberty in the customs than in the laws of the people. In Switzerland there seems to be more liberty in the laws than in the customs of the country.'[5] Dicey comments:

[De Tocqueville's words] direct attention to the extreme vagueness of a trait of national character which is as noticeable as it is hard to portray. De Tocqueville, we see, is clearly perplexed how to define a feature of English manners of which he at once recognizes the existence; he mingles or confuses together the habit of self-government, the love of order, the respect for justice and a

---

[4] See discussion in Chapter 3 below.   [5] Dicey (1962), 187.

legal turn of mind. ... [W]e ourselves, whenever we talk of Englishmen as loving the government of law, or of the supremacy of law as being a characteristic of the English constitution, are using words which, though they possess a real significance, are nevertheless to most persons who employ them full of vagueness and ambiguity.[6]

In its first appearance, then, the rule of law has an inherited intangible quality – at the outer limit, a 'trait of national character' or 'legal turn of mind'. The deliberate application of a vocabulary of imprecision – 'habit', 'love', 'respect', 'vagueness', 'ambiguity' – to the supposedly hard concepts of government, order, justice and law, gives Dicey's formulation a peculiar (and enduring) colour that continues to imbue (and cloud) the rule of law as term of art. The task of Dicey's *Introduction to the Study of the Law of the Constitution* is nevertheless to dissipate, as far as possible, ambiguity from this English 'habit', and sharpen it into a principle, the rule of law, that he will then demonstrate to be a thread running through the Constitution, holding it together, and distinguishing its true design.[7] Dicey's rule of law effectively rethreads the *fabric* of ancient English constitutionalism, subsuming its mystery without succumbing to its mysticism. As a result, the *Introduction* is part comparative constitutionalism, part English particularism.

In Dicey's subsequent analysis, the rule of law not only distinguishes English law from other bodies of law, it renders it superior.[8] It is 'a formula for expressing the fact that *with us* the law of the Constitution, the rules which in foreign countries naturally form part of the constitutional code, are not the source but the consequence of the rights of individuals, as defined and enforced by the courts'.[9] The rights of Englishmen, rooted in 'love' of law and order, and defended in the common law, are more concrete than their declaratory continental cousins because they are built on a broader consensual base than mere positive law alone. This rule of law is thicker than dogmatic or fearful obedience of the law but thinner than custom. A texture of pervasive legalism is its most distinctive trait. If it signifies, for the individual, a predilection for obedience to the precepts expressed in law, this is at least in part because the law itself reflects norms and habits that are

---

[6] Dicey (1962), 187.
[7] Dicey (1962), 407. Martin Loughlin calls the rule of law a 'golden thread'. Loughlin (2000), 68.
[8] Dicey (1962), 417. [9] Dicey (1962), 203 (emphasis added).

already deeply ingrained in each individual. The rule of law supplies a source of legitimacy for the English constitutional order by grounding the 'law of the land' in the ancient tradition of rights and liberties peculiar to English subjects.

I will return to Dicey in Chapters 2 and 3. For now, however, two quick observations. First, Dicey clearly regards the rule of law as an Englishman's 'entailed inheritance', in Burke's words; there is no implication that it can be consciously or deliberately produced. Indeed just the reverse – it is precisely deliberative meddling that has rendered continental constitutions weak in his eyes; if the United States escapes it is only because English habits and principles underlie its brash constitutionalism.[10] So although Dicey's narrative occasionally touches upon the talismanic beads of 'English liberty' related in Blackstone's *Commentaries* – the Magna Carta (1215), the jurist Edward Coke's challenge to James I (1610), the adoption of the first habeas corpus bill (1679), the Glorious Revolution (1689) – these serve rather as props than directives.[11] The superiority of the 'ordinary law of the land' and the 'ordinary courts' is not demonstrated but assumed.[12] Its primary characteristics, indeed, are non-replicable: the long diatribes against French 'administrative law' that animate the *Introduction* largely conflate the *ancientness* of English liberties with their *Englishness*.[13] Indeed, the rule of law is a guard *against* tinkering with the legal system. The sixteenth-century attempt to impose an administrative apparatus on England failed, Dicey wrote, because it 'was opposed to those habits of equality before the law which had long been essential characteristics of English institutions'.[14] English parochialism, in Dicey's *Introduction*, is thus inseparable from conservatism.[15] Nothing could be further from

---

[10] Dicey (1962), 200: 'in many foreign countries the rights of individuals, e.g. to personal freedom, depend upon the constitution, whilst in England the law of the constitution is little else than a generalisation of the rights which the courts secure to individuals.' Nevertheless, 'the rule of law is as marked a feature of the United States as of England', a result of their English common law heritage: 'the statesmen of America have shown unrivalled skill in providing means for giving legal security to the rights declared by the American constitutions.'

[11] Dicey has no time for what he calls 'the historical method': Dicey (1962), vii.

[12] See, for example, Dicey (1962), 194.

[13] Dicey has been charged with getting this wrong – misunderstanding both the French and English systems, and showing ignorance of contemporary Prussia. See, in this regard, Allan (2003), 125; Shklar (1987), 6; Hayek (2006), 203–204.

[14] Dicey (1962), 373.

[15] Judith Shklar referred to the book as an 'unfortunate outburst of Anglo-Saxon parochialism'. Shklar (1987), 5.

his understanding of the rule of law than innovation in or importation into the legal order.

Second, Dicey's rule of law assumes no surefire check on government discretion beyond 'convention'. His positivism is not purist; he regularly reaches outside law to explain its source and force. Neither of his two interlocking sources of constitutional legitimacy, the rule of law and parliamentary sovereignty, is itself 'law': rather, both impose shape on the legally possible. Parliamentary sovereignty expresses the immediacy of the democratic will (such at least is Dicey's assumption); the rule of law injects a profound historical and cultural esteem for individual liberty into the law. As Dicey notes, we might expect these two principles to act as 'counterbalancing forces', each acting as a restraint on the other.[16] But for Dicey, they are rather co-generative: 'The sovereignty of Parliament ... favours the supremacy of law, whilst the predominance of rigid legality throughout our institutions ... increases the authority of Parliamentary sovereignty.'[17] Parliament can, in principle, pass any law it deems fit. But since public obedience of the law is conceived of as habitual and autonomous rather than fearful or coercive, parliamentary restraint is best understood as a matter of rational or pragmatic 'convention', which Dicey defines as the 'customs, practices, maxims or precepts which are not enforced or recognised by the courts [and] make up a body not of laws, but of constitutional or political ethics'.

It is this relation between the law and *conventions* of the Constitution that is, for Dicey, the 'most striking instance of that supremacy of the law which gives to the English polity the whole of its peculiar colour'.[18] Such is the strength of the rule of law *habitus*, Dicey implies, that it casts a penumbra of limitation that everywhere checks the positive law. The rule of law implies *both* a generalised habit of 'rigid legality' *and* a generalised affirmation of long-established rights, a prelegal container that circumscribes the limits of legislation. Together, these elements preserve and sustain the 'conventions' that underlie legal

---

[16] 'The sovereignty of parliament and the supremacy of the law of the land – the two principles which pervade the whole of the English constitution – may appear to stand in opposition to each other or to be at best only counterbalancing forces. But this appearance is delusive...': Dicey (1962), 407.

[17] Dicey (1962), 407. See also 417, 422–423. See Allan (2003), 13: 'Dicey's influential discussion seemed to leave the tension between legislative supremacy and the rule of law unresolved.'

[18] Dicey (1962), 418.

conservatism. The rule of law, stitching convention to law to obedience, must therefore depend for its effect on 'respect', rather than 'enforcement'.

Oakeshott: a 'moral association' (the *jus* of *lex*)

Like Dicey, Michael Oakeshott describes the rule of law both as 'a work of art' and as a 'somewhat vague relationship' among individuals.[19] Unlike Dicey, he is uncertain that it has been achieved anywhere; it is rather something 'glimpsed, sketched in a practice, unreflectively and intermittently enjoyed, half understood, left indistinct'.[20] If it exists at all, it is to be found in 'the modern European state',[21] by which he broadly intends a certain kind of contemporary political structure only loosely bound to geographical location.[22] For Oakeshott, the rule of law is a 'moral association', one that imposes certain obligations on all agents – assumed to be 'related transactionally' in performing 'self-chosen' activities – to observe certain 'noninstrumental' conditions in their interaction.[23] Oakeshott describes the development of this association as a cumulative process, much like Dicey's English constitutional fabric, a product of human agency that is nevertheless beyond human intentionality:

> The political dwelling we inhabit never had an architect [but is rather] the net result of all the temporary and contingent enterprises of these centuries of European politics. The path and direction of modern European political activity is neither more nor less than the footprints of those who engaged in politics. Some footprints have been firmly placed and remain individually distinguishable; others are blurred and obscured, the trampling of many feet which have gone this way and that. But they are all the marks of men necessarily ignorant of any ultimate destiny, who took their direction from their immediate circumstances.[24]

According to Oakeshott, the agents in this (as in any) 'mode of association', are *personae* who are all equal, because all, in his idiosyncratic

---

[19] Oakeshott (1999), 163, 131. [20] Oakeshott (1999), 131.
[21] There is, says Oakeshott, enough evidence 'to intimate to some that a modern European state might be made to become, might need to become, and might even be on its way to becoming something like an association in terms of the rule of law'. Oakeshott (1999), 165.
[22] Oakeshott (2006), 359. Even so, 'the rule of law *cannot*, without qualification, characterize a modern European state.' Oakeshott (1999), 168 (emphasis in the original).
[23] Oakeshott (1999), 144. [24] Oakeshott (2006), 360–361.

vocabulary, are 'indistinguishably and exclusively related'.[25] To be practicable, such a relationship would appear to presuppose some form of ethics or morality, which thus emerges at the centre of Oakeshott's account. Morality in this context is 'not a list of licences and prohibitions, but an everyday practice ... a vernacular language of intercourse', with respect to which moral conduct is 'a kind of literacy'.[26] The obligation imposed by a moral association is 'not merely a disposition usually to comply with what a rule prescribes – what has been called a "habit of obedience". It is neither more nor less than the acknowledgement of the authenticity of the [relevant] rule.'[27] The 'sole terms' of the relationship described by the rule of law are, therefore, the 'recognition of the authority and the authenticity of the laws'.[28] This 'recognition' in turn relies on two qualities. First, the laws must issue from a 'sovereign legislative office'.[29] Second, they must contribute to the 'shape' of the overarching set of rules 'as the desirable conditions of an invented pattern of noninstrumental human relationships'. This convoluted formula for rule construction appears to be designed for consistency with one of Oakeshott's 'fundamental principles of moral obligation': 'that no man can become obligated save by a choice of his own'.[30]

Fulfilment of the first condition can be easily ascertained by means of procedural tests. The second, however, is harder to monitor – some form of evaluation is needed. Oakeshott frames this task as the 'deliberation of the *jus* of *lex*'. He rejects immediately the notion that the *jus* of the law can be known by comparison with a 'higher law' of some sort; nor, he says, is it exhausted by the formal characteristics of lawmaking.[31] It is rather a 'moral consideration':

---

[25] Oakeshott (1999), 174.
[26] Oakeshott (1999), 144. Compare Michel Foucault's definition of morality: 'a set of values and rules of action that are recommended to individuals through the intermediary of various prescriptive agencies': Foucault (1990), 25.
[27] Oakeshott (1999), 141. Oakeshott appears to be taking issue with both Austin and Dicey. Compare Hart's objections to Austin on this same point in Hart (1997), 51–61. Despite real differences, both Hart and Oakeshott are concerned with the source of authority that engenders an authentic habit of obedience – rather than mere unreflective customary practice – and both ultimately locate this source in sovereignty.
[28] Oakeshott (1999), 149. See also 150, 142, 171.   [29] Oakeshott (1999), 150.
[30] Oakeshott (1999), 163. For the state to ignore this maxim would also likely fall foul of Oakeshott's requirement that the rule of law state not be 'managerial'. See Oakeshott (1999), 165.
[31] Oakeshott (1999), 173, 174.

[T]he prescriptions of law should not conflict with a prevailing educated moral sensibility capable of distinguishing between the conditions of 'virtue', the conditions of moral association ('good conduct'), and those which are of such a kind they should be imposed by law ('justice').

The rule of law, for Oakeshott, is thus not merely a procedural attribute, it also says something about the content of law – law should be *restricted* to the task of ensuring that 'justice' prevails. It should not extend to the establishment of other public goods ('virtue', 'good conduct'). How are we to tell the difference? Whose is this 'prevailing educated moral sensibility', this capacity to 'deliberate' the *jus* of *lex*? Oakeshott does not, as Dicey did, attribute any special facility with this general sensibility to the English, nor to the 'ordinary courts'. The sole role of the judge, in Oakeshott's account, is to apply, as mechanically as possible, the positive law to individual cases; the judge has no legislative or review function whatsoever.[32] But neither does he appear to mean, by education, some form of indoctrination in the supremacy of law (as Plato suggested – see Chapter 3). The combination of adjectives – 'prevailing', 'moral', 'educated' – is nevertheless suggestive of an acculturated intelligence, representative yet refined, and of laws arrived at through reasoned debate.[33] The proper source of 'deliberation', which is the test of the 'authenticity' of law in a rule of law association, would appear to reside in the 'best men' in a given polity, an *aristocracy* in the sense recommended by Artistotle in the *Politics*.[34]

Oakeshott's rule of law therefore has no necessary connection with the institutions of democracy as usually articulated.[35] His 'sovereign legislative office' need not embody *popular* sovereignty: indeed, it is rather explicitly modelled on the somewhat authoritarian presumptions of Jean Bodin and Thomas Hobbes.[36] The critical point lies not, it

---

[32] Oakeshott (1999), 157–160. Cf. Dicey (1962), 63. Oakeshott here refers to Aristotle's famous statement that the judges are only needed at all because a general law cannot be mechanically applied to all particular cases: Aristotle, *Rhetoric*, 1345a–1345b in Roberts (2004).

[33] See, for example, Oakeshott (1999), 169, 174: the law's 'moral-legal acceptability [is] itself a reflection of the moral-legal self-understanding of the associates which ... cannot be expected to be without ambiguity or internal tension – a moral imagination more stable in its style of deliberation than in its conclusions.'

[34] See below Chapter 3, text at note 33.

[35] Oakeshott comments that the institution of political parties has 'hindered rather than advanced the emergence of states as associations in terms of the rule of law': Oakeshott (1999), 167.

[36] Oakeshott (1999), 163, 170–175.

seems, in discovering the right legislator, who need only be educated and disinterested to do the job well, but in the content of law – in particular, the preservation of the non-instrumentality of the law, that is, the requirement that the polity not become a vehicle for *projects*, that it not succumb to a 'technological conception of the state':[37]

> [L]aw is not concerned with the merits of different interests, with satisfying substantive wants, [or] with the promotion of prosperity. [It] cannot be identified with the successful provision of ... substantive benefits, measured by the efficiency or expedition with which they are provided or the 'fairness' with which they are distributed.[38]

Precisely this promotion of 'substantive interests' or a notional 'common good' is (again, as in Aristotle) the danger of democracy.[39] And (again, as in Dicey) constitutional declarations are necessarily inferior to the cumulation of law and legal principle over time: the idea that parliamentary supremacy might be constructed 'ex nihilo' is 'absurd'. More likely that a 'legislative office might emerge and *acquire* authority than ... that it might be endowed with it in a constitutive act'.[40] In a similar vein, '"freedom" does not follow as a consequence of this association: it is inherent in its character'.[41] Elsewhere Oakeshott calls this value-neutral rule of law state a *nomocracy*, which he contrasts to a *teleocracy*, a state that exists for a purpose.[42] The nomocracy has no purpose other than the preservation, by means of law, of a 'moral' association of free individuals. The rule of law in this view is the evidence of the existence such a non-purposive association, the condition of its continuation, and the outcome of its deliberation. Such a view carries easily from the construction of the 'social' into that of the 'economic', precisely the thrust of a similar vision elaborated by Friedrich Hayek, as we shall see in Chapter 2.

Habermas: mutual respect among strangers

Whereas Oakeshott constructs a schematic 'moral association' as a heuristic device to describe and explain a (rarely achieved) political and social ideal, Jürgen Habermas does the reverse: he imagines a

---

[37] Oakeshott (1999), 166.   [38] Oakeshott (1999), 153.
[39] See, in this regard, Aristotle *Politics* 1292a, 27–31 (translation of *Politics* is from Saunders (1992), unless otherwise noted); Weber (1978), 811, 889.
[40] Oakeshott (1999), 163.   [41] Oakeshott (1999), 175.   [42] Oakeshott (2003), 313.

political and social model in order to demonstrate that a particular approach to lawmaking and enforcement – rule of law – is vital to the maintenance of viable human association in a modern society. Law has the role of providing a platform for 'social integration' in complex societies, a means by which individuals can coexist in the absence of any necessary shared background of values. The need for such a function is especially acute in 'modern' pluralistic societies: societies from which comprehensive worldviews and collectively binding ethics have disappeared; and in which a surviving ('post-traditional') morality of conscientious tolerance must substitute for a natural law grounded in religion or metaphysics.[43]

'Modern law', as Habermas calls it, supplies the social glue in these fragmented 'post-traditional' contexts. It acts as a 'transmission belt', transferring 'structures of mutual recognition' from familiar situations into interactions between strangers, in an 'abstract but binding form'.[44] Habermas reconstructs a sociology of law from within the Weberian tradition, according to which contemporary society exists in a condition of secular 'disenchantment', having abandoned the ancient authority of a sacred bind between the world and human morality.[45] Habermas's restatement of this problem appears in a claim that in such post-traditional societies a gap is opened between facts and values (or 'norms'), that is, between experiential claims and belief claims.[46] In modern states, individuals no longer interact on the basis of common experiences (facts) filtered through a shared belief system (values): instead the events are perceived and interpreted differently due to differences of outlook/worldview. Law, in such a state, provides a *necessarily* common interface that overrides differing belief systems (without necessarily discounting them). A shared and binding law stabilises behaviour and therefore expectations, creating a basis for meaningful (and indeed meaningless) interaction. According to Habermas, law is 'the only

---

[43] Habermas (1998), 448.
[44] Habermas (1998), 448: '[T]ogether with the constitutionally organised political system, law provides a safety net for [the possibility of] failure to achieve social integration. It functions as a kind of "transmission belt" that picks up structures of mutual recognition that are familiar from face-to-face interactions and transmits these, in an abstract but binding form, to the anonymous systemically mediated interactions among strangers.'
[45] Habermas (1998), 23–25, 43–51.
[46] Habermas (1998), 13–17. The somewhat cumbersome English terms used throughout the translation are 'facticity' and 'validity', which themselves would also translate the title of the book ('Between Facticity and Validity').

medium in which it is possible reliably to establish morally obligated relationships of mutual respect, even among strangers.'[47]

Law can only perform this role, however, where it is seen as legitimate in the eyes of all, regardless of their differences. An 'expectation of legitimacy' can arise where two conditions are fulfilled. First, the law must preserve for each individual enough personal autonomy from others (in the form of rights and liberties) that they can freely pursue the life they wish. To this end, the state must ensure 'at least average compliance' with the law.[48] Second, the state must guarantee 'the institutional preconditions for the legitimate genesis of the norm itself'.[49] 'Legitimate genesis' means in effect that all addressees of the law must also be able to situate themselves as its potential authors. This does not necessitate that each individual participate directly (or even indirectly) in lawmaking. It merely requires, in Habermas's (explicitly Kantian) terms, that only those norms be considered valid 'to which all possibly affected persons could agree as participants in rational discourse'.[50]

These two spheres of legitimacy, general compliance with and general ownership of the laws, are inextricably bound together. From the perspective of the individual, the result is dual subjectivity: a private autonomy (a personal sphere of rights and liberties) and a public autonomy (participation in the *demos*). Private autonomy is guaranteed by 'human rights' – first and foremost the 'classic liberties', later extending to basic 'social and ecological' [sic] rights.[51] (In Habermas's reading, debates on social welfare mistakenly centre on questions of 'distribution' or 'well-being', when the appropriate lens should be that of individual autonomy.) Public autonomy is the capacity to be a subject of and participant in a constitutional democracy. All are free to exercise both or neither of these autonomies to the extent desired – but at a schematic level the two are necessarily codependent or, to use Habermas's term, 'co-original'. The argument of *Between Facts and Norms*, he writes, aims to show 'that there is a conceptual and internal relation, and not simply a historical contingent association, between the rule of law and democracy'. The participation (and ownership) of the various members

---

[47] Habermas (1998), 25–27; see also 33–34, 37, 132–193, 460.
[48] It is up to individuals to decide on their motives for compliance: these may be 'strategic' – that is, based on a calculation of the probability of coercion – or 'performative' – that is, 'out of respect for the law': Habermas (1998), 448.
[49] Habermas (1998), 448, 107–110.
[50] Habermas refers to this as the 'discourse principle'.
[51] Habermas (1998), 454, 123, 400–409, 418–419, 449.

of a society in the construction of its laws is the guarantee both of their individual autonomy *and* of the authenticity of the 'transmission belt' itself. This is so not in spite of, but because of, the different value and faith systems in a 'modern society'.

Nevertheless, like Oakeshott's, Habermas's modern rule of law state is not constructed to fulfil any particular 'purpose' beyond providing basic conditions for mutual association. It is founded rather to mediate between personal and public autonomy, to provide a common language and set of expectations in the absence of a common morality. (Habermas devotes considerable space to mediating between conceptions of the positive law and of 'moral law', concluding that the two 'have different reference groups and regulate different matters'.[52]) The rule of law results rather, he says, from a 'societal learning process' than from any necessary moral imperative.[53]

Summary: the 'modern' rule of law

Each of these three broad yet nuanced accounts of the rule of law open the notion up beyond a checklist of technical attributes. Each also draws upon and processes a significant relevant body of background knowledge – the English constitutional tradition in Dicey's case (Coke, Burke, Blackstone), the European political tradition in Oakeshott's (Aristotle, Bodin, Hobbes) and the German enlightenment tradition in Habermas's (Kant, Hegel, Weber) – that are discrete and often divergent. The three accounts are nevertheless cumulative and mutually supportive in certain key respects. Some notion of constrained individual autonomy runs through all three, constantly re-embedded in an immanent rule of law, a quality of 'moral' or mutual obligation to preserve the liberty of each by marking out an equally autonomous space for all. In all three visions, the rule of law supplies the fabric of a contemporary society, a means to join together and maintain the integrity of the whole, a honeycomb of freestanding yet mutually dependent cells. [54]

---

[52] Habermas (1998), 451, 104–117. Compare Oakeshott (1999), 173; Dicey (1962), 62–63.
[53] Habermas (1998), 460.
[54] A similar understanding informs the recent writings of Roberto Unger: 'The rule of law and the experience of trust among strangers, backed ultimately by regulated coercion and diffuse love, are two of the three essential instruments for the preservation of the social bond': Unger (2006), 248.

As a result, in each of these visions, the coercive power of the state appears as a necessary, but secondary, aspect of the rule of law – a backup mechanism, viewed not as intrinsic to the social fabric itself, but nevertheless indispensable to its preservation. Oakeshott describes the role of state coercion as follows:[55]

[T]he fear of having to suffer a penalty may of course deter a potential delinquent and the expectation of a penalty may be a reason for fulfilling an obligation, but this mode of association [i.e. the rule of law] is in terms of the recognition of obligations – and penalties are extrinsic to obligations.

Habermas makes a similar point:[56]

[T]he state's guarantee to enforce the law [allows] for the stabilization of behavioural expectations ...[Nevertheless] modern law ... leaves the motives for rule compliance open while enforcing observance.

There are two points of broad disagreement. The first is the relationship between rule of law and democracy. The rule of law can either be viewed as constitutive of democracy (Habermas), parasitic upon it (Dicey), or indifferent or possibly hostile to it (Oakeshott). The second area of disagreement concerns the bond that binds the members of a rule of law state. All agree that the source of law's legitimacy, in a rule of law polity, lies not in God, nature, or any 'higher' authority, but in the polity itself.[57] Their disagreement concerns the *nature* of the polity's authority. For Dicey it is ethno-cultural (distinctively and instinctively English); for Oakeshott 'moral'; for Habermas pragmatic. Although Oakeshott and Habermas effectively agree that the law, if it is 'legitimate' (Habermas) and 'authentic' (Oakeshott), itself provides an overarching 'morality', a 'language' of interaction, for a pluralist society of differing belief systems – they prioritise inversely. For Oakeshott, a defined and shared morality is the source of the rule of law. For Habermas it is the rule of law that is rather the source of a minimal shared morality. Dicey's notion of 'morality',

---

[55] Oakeshott (1999), 160. Dicey speaks about the criminal law purely in terms of its procedural guarantees of liberty. For a contrasting view, see my account of Weber below, Chapter 2.
[56] Habermas (1998), 37.
[57] See Oakeshott (1999), 173: Regarding 'a supposed universal inherently just Natural Law or set of fundamental Values [or] an enacted Basic Law or Bill of Rights said to reflect these fundamental values', he writes 'the rule of law has no need of any such beliefs or institutions; indeed more often than not they are the occasion of profitless dispute.'

by contrast, resorts to a natural law basis that remains frankly communitarian.[58]

For all three, however, the rule of law is learned rather than inherent: with a narrow focus on English acculturation in Dicey; a broader 'educated sensibility' in Oakeshott; and the 'learned' experience of interaction in a complex society for Habermas. For all three, the rule of law is necessarily specific to a particular time and place: England; the 'modern Europe state'; postwar 'modern' (that is Western) society.[59] And yet, although all three accounts uphold the rule of law as a desirable social good, none of them recommend an educative or promotional role for the state in engendering it. This is because, for all three writers, any form of public indoctrination would undermine the very essence of the rule of law: the guarantee of the autonomy of the individual, and the non-purposiveness of their mutual association. Fundamentally, the process is rather gradual, accumulative and discursive: Dicey's ordinary law of the land, Oakeshott's 'trampling' footprints of 'necessarily ignorant' men, Habermas's morally disenchanted agents in search of stability in a post-traditional society.

It is possible, then, to list some fundamental family resemblances among the various accounts of the rule of law as this notion was received and articulated in the twentieth century:

i. The rule of law is historically and culturally contingent (rather than natural).
ii. It is organic (it has 'never had an architect').
iii. It requires a state (the 'community' is not adequate).
iv. It is non-instrumental (it has no purpose beyond 'moral association').
v. It can only be freely acquired, never imposed.
vi. It associates liberty/autonomy with submission to law/discipline.
vii. It is an expression of tolerance and pluralism: a means to achieve moral, rational association 'among strangers'.

---

[58] Dicey (1962), 62–63: 'judges, when attempting to ascertain what is the meaning to be affixed to an Act of Parliament, will presume that Parliament did not intend to violate the *ordinary laws of morality*' (emphasis added). The idea that the rule of law is essentially an Anglo-American virtue garners some support in contemporary rule of law literature. See in this regard Djankov *et al.* (2002).

[59] In 1964, Judith Shklar viewed the rise of the rule of law as a response to 'the Cold War and to the political organisation of ex-colonial, non-European societies which now challenge the European world'. 'These events have made us all culturally self-conscious. The result is a search for an identity, for a positive and uniquely Western tradition. The core of that tradition, for those who have discovered it, is essentially legalism, the rule of law': Shklar (1986), 21.

viii. It requires that the law, to be legitimate, must be produced by a body that is affirmed by the members of the relevant society/association to be both authoritative and authentic.
ix. It is *legalist*: that is, it associates law with procedural rectitude and regards it as functionally autonomous.

BETWEEN STATE AND SOCIETY

In this section I provide background for a central assumption that underpins much rule of law thinking, albeit often implicitly: that the preservation and consolidation of distinct public and private realms is an important good of a modern legal regime. Discussions of the public sphere habitually begin with a much earlier text by Jürgen Habermas than that just discussed, his 1962 *Structural Transformation of the Public Sphere*. His account begins with a glance to fifth-century BCE Athens, where the public realm of politics (the *polis*) was articulated as a zone of freedom founded upon mastery of the private household (*oikos*), the sphere of economic necessity or unfreedom.[60] For Habermas, modernity (that is the enlightenment period in Europe dating from the late seventeenth century) involves a revival of this structural relation, albeit quite altered. But he is also concerned with a quintessential mid-twentieth century problem – Hannah Arendt famously referred to it as 'the rise of the social'[61] – which brought with it a reconfiguration of the relation between state and society. That problem too is of relevance to the rule of law ideal, as we shall see in the following chapter. In the present section, I shall rely on Habermas's productive and nuanced articulation of the mutually constitutive roles of public and private as a structural framework for the institutional shape of the modern state. I will end by sorting through some of the intertwined (and often confusing) applications of the terms 'public' and 'private' as we inherit them today, as these terms are constantly reiterated, and play a central role, in contemporary rule of law reform.

The public sphere

In the first section above, we saw that the rule of law constitutes a bond, holding together the 'fabric' of society. But not of just any society; it is of relevance only to 'modern' societies, that is, those that are constitutively represented by and channelled through a modern state,

---

[60] Habermas (1994), 3–4. Arendt (1958), 22–78. The terms public and private are, of course, Latin not Greek – as Habermas notes: 'we are dealing with categories of Greek origin transmitted to us bearing a Roman stamp': Habermas (1994), 3. Arendt observes that the 'privation' of the Roman private sphere was precisely the lack of freedom found in the public: Arendt (1958), 38. Raymond Geuss comments that there was no Greek for our contemporary sense of privacy as *intimacy*. He remarks that the Greek *agora* (open/market) is closer to 'public', a point that would fit with Habermas's term for public sphere *Öffentlichkeit* (literally 'openness'), and of course contemporary notions such as 'open society' or 'marketplace of ideas': Geuss (2001b), 31–32.

[61] Arendt (1958), 38–49.

where the 'state' is the quintessential locus of generation and enforcement of a law that belongs to 'society' (rather than to the state).

In *Structural Transformation*, Habermas concentrates on the evolution of this co-dependence of modern societies and modern states. According to Habermas, the public sphere 'evolved in the tension-charged field between state and society';[62] it is 'a sphere that mediates between society and state'.[63] Its situation *between* gives the public its special role simultaneously as channel, 'mediator' or translator, and at the same time as substantive bond, hitching an emergent state up to an equally emergent society. The existence and security of this channel or bond, a *public*, constitutes the cornerstone of democracy and so the source of legitimacy of the modern state, on Habermas's account. But it must be immediately clarified that he has in mind not something empirically 'there' but an 'ideal type', in the Weberian sense – that is, he describes the parameters and constitutive elements of the public sphere as *conceived* in its heyday in eighteenth- and nineteenth-century Europe (and reconceived since). Yet this phenomenon did not necessarily exist as such then or ever.[64] Indeed, the public sphere essentially was, and remains, a convenient fiction: it describes neither a physical space nor an actual group of like-minded individuals, nor a unitary source of 'opinion' or 'interest'.[65] It is rather an ideal screen that allows these notions to be projected onto it, notions which in turn provide political legitimacy, at least so long as the ideal itself has traction among the public's putative members. In other words, to provide legitimacy, it is not necessary that a 'public sphere' actually exists in the ideal form in which it is imagined, but it *is* necessary that the *ideal* itself is widely shared by the relevant group identifiable as, and self-identifying as, the 'public'.

In what follows, I will look at two aspects of the ideal public sphere, its organisation of 'public' and 'private' as key attributes of a modern polity and its conception of the appropriate rules to ensure its own existence and political effect.

A public of private persons

A first point is, following Habermas, that the public sphere that emerges from feudalism is a public of *private persons*:

---

[62] Habermas (1994), 141.   [63] Cited in Eley (1992).
[64] See Habermas (1994), xvii (Author's Preface) and Habermas (1992), 422.
[65] In Michael Warner's words, Habermas's public might best be understood as 'a special kind of virtual object enabling a special mode of address': Warner (2002), 55.

[The] public sphere may be conceived above all as the sphere of private people come together as a public; they ... claimed the public sphere ... against the public authorities themselves, to engage them in a debate over the general rules governing relations in the basically privatized but publicly relevant sphere of commodity exchange and social labour.[66]

The public, in other words, is the space within which the polity can be subjected to the control (criticism and recommendation) of its 'members', that is, 'private' persons rather than of the sovereign, state or government. The basis and rationale for this control is the application of 'private' reason to public affairs, rather than dutiful submission to a public authority.[67] The value of privacy in this formula is broad and novel to the period: Habermas traces the expansion of personal privacy at this time through a number of contemporary cultural innovations.[68] Foremost among them is the arrival of new literary technologies: the novel (the first 'self-administered' art form, by means of which the public is engaged in a private capacity), the diary (whereby the private self becomes its own audience or public), and others premised on the existence of a public sphere where autonomous private persons think 'out loud' – such as published correspondence (the earliest novels, indeed, adopted the form of extended correspondence or diaries) and, crucially, newspapers which, from carriers of raw data, quickly become vehicles of 'opinion'.[69] Thus the private is itself formed by being set off against a newly forming public: the public and private are cogenerative.

But as Habermas notes, this new public sphere, reversing the ancient Greek formula, prioritised the private over the public. A rising middle class thought of themselves first and foremost as private persons, viewing family and economic activity as 'humanity's genuine site'; it was in just this way that they distinguished themselves from a fading nobility.[70] The preservation and protection of an

---

[66] Habermas (1994), 27.
[67] In this, as in much else, Habermas follows Kant. See Kant (1983), 42: 'nothing is required for this enlightenment, however, except ... the freedom to use reason *publicly* in all matters' [emphasis in original]; Habermas (1994), 104–107. For Habermas, 'The medium of this political confrontation was peculiar and without historical precedent: people's public use of their reason' (26).
[68] Habermas (1994), 43–51. He calls this the 'institutionalisation of a privateness oriented towards an audience' (43).
[69] Habermas (1994), 57–73. Newspapers and journals played the central role in the construction of the public sphere: Habermas locates Britain's abolition of censorship in 1695 as a crucial milestone in the consolidation of the press's role as the 'voice of the public sphere' in criticising government (59).
[70] Habermas (1994), 52.

'intimate sphere'[71] of family and production became a priority for a growing section of society.[72] With this preservation of the intimate private sphere in view, open criticism and public debate of government became a matter of 'public interest' *for private persons*, a theme that arises repeatedly from Locke and Montesquieu through Mill and de Tocqueville:[73]

> With the rise of a sphere of the social, over whose regulation public opinion battled with public power, the theme of the modern (in contrast to the ancient) public sphere shifted from the properly political tasks of a citizenry acting in common (i.e. administration of [the] law ... and [the] military ...) to the more properly civic tasks of a society engaged in critical public debate (i.e. the protection of a commercial economy).

Privacy thus becomes a positive value (discarding its earlier connotations of 'privation'[74]), the condition of self-constitution that empowers individuals to enter the public sphere. According to the same narrative, the public sphere as a *locus* is perhaps initially best represented by those salons and coffee-shops where private citizens met as such, where ideas and opinions were (in a perhaps idealised retrospection) the chief currency, and where attendees gradually became the source of, and intended audience for, the first newspapers. It is thus the very privateness of its members that guarantees the publicness of the public sphere. Private persons must ideally be autonomous, which is to say they have their own means (they are, to begin, property owners[75]) and their own opinions, arrived at through education and independent reflection.[76] The public sphere is that space wherein these autonomous

---

[71] Hannah Arendt refers to the 'older realm' of the private and 'the more recently established sphere of intimacy': Arendt (1958), 45.

[72] The private, on this account, is eked out from a universal public space in a process that can be traced to the consolidation of freedom of conscience/religion. See Habermas (1994), 10–12, 74–77. Raymond Geuss traces the earliest development of privacy in this sense of inwardness or introspection as access to truth to St Augustine's *Confessions*. Geuss (2001b), 58–64.

[73] Habermas (1994), 24, 52. See: 52–53, 97–98, 132–138.

[74] Arendt (1958), 38.

[75] The requirement of property ownership for 'autonomy' – and thus franchise – was given theoretical ballast by Immanuel Kant; Hegel suggested in response that some amount of property should therefore be guaranteed to all citizens. See Habermas (1994), 109–117.

[76] Habermas (1994), 85–86: '[T]he restriction on franchise did not necessarily have to be viewed as a restriction of the public sphere itself, as long as it could be interpreted as the mere legal ratification of a status attained economically in

persons meet, debate and compete, with a view to arriving at consensus, or compromise.[77] It nevertheless remains within the 'private realm', which is conceived in strict separation from the realm of public authority. Here Habermas supplies a sharp distinction, upon which I shall draw, between public *sphere* and public *realm*, with the latter term reserved for the state or public officials as against the private persons who make up the former.[78]

The private persons who make up the public sphere are familiar. Habermas alternates between the term 'bourgeois' (translating the still-current German term *bürgerlich*) and one we would be more likely to use today (in English): 'civil society'. The latter term too owes its origins to this period, in a formula expressed most clearly by Hegel, whose *Philosophy of Right* provides its first sustained account.[79] Hegel's civil society is one of his three pillars of the polity (the other two being the family and the state), characterisable as the zone of economic activity, personal autonomy in the public sphere, corporate affiliation and voluntary association.[80] Civil society emerges when political and economic activity is removed from feudal relations, in the extended family or manor, to private persons.

Law: equality, generality, rationality, transparency

Given the public sphere's critical (in both senses) role in legitimating law and statehood, much clearly depends on how this political ideal translated into legal fact. Habermas refers to this role as the 'ideological' function of the public sphere, by which he means 'what

---

the private sphere ... the public sphere was safeguarded whenever the economic and social conditions gave everyone an equal chance to meet the criteria for admission.'

[77] Habermas (1994), 64 remarks that the replacement of civil war with 'permanent controversy' forms the bedrock of party parliamentarianism. Arendt (1958), 49, links this quality back to the Greek *polis*, the space of *agon* (contest) and *aretē* (excellence).

[78] Habermas (1994), 175-176: '[The] model ... presupposed strict separation of the public from the private realm in such a way that the public sphere made up of private people gathered together as a public and articulating the needs of society within the state, was itself considered part of the private realm.' In principle this places the legislature in the ambiguous position of both comprising and opposing public authority (233). On a similar conundrum regarding 'general interest' see Habermas (1994), 234.

[79] Hegel borrowed the notion of civil society from Adam Smith and especially Adam Ferguson. See Habermas (1994), 85-87, 109, 118. See also Warner (2002), 40.

[80] Hegel (2005), especially Part 3, section 2 and, within that, paras. 211-229.

the public itself believed [itself] to be and to be doing'.[81] Throughout, Habermas notes correspondences between the public sphere's self-understanding of its own role and the common legal structures that emerged throughout the western world during this period. This new public was the practical inverse of its immediate medieval predecessor. 'Publicness' in the pre-modern state was an attribute of monarchs, princes and other sovereigns who represented *in their persons* that which was 'public'. Habermas calls this 'representative publicity' and traces its disappearance between about 1630 and 1780 in Britain, France and Germany.[82]

The public sphere that took the place of 'representative publicity' was sharply different. First, it was a realm of formal equality, maintaining

> a kind of social intercourse that, far from presupposing equality of status, disregarded status altogether. [Participants] replaced the celebration of rank with a tact befitting equals. The parity on whose basis alone the authority of the better argument could assert itself against that of social hierarchy ... meant ... the parity of 'common humanity'.[83]

The assumption of equality was, of course, a structuring ideal rather than a reality of the public sphere's composition or access: in practice only individuals from certain bands of society made it into the salons, theatres, reading rooms and coffee-houses (Habermas identifies illiteracy as a more conclusive obstacle than poverty). But '[i]f not realized', the principle of equality was 'at least consequential'. It was not the status of an individual, but the truth or reasonableness of their argument, that was to count. This leads to the second crucial feature of the public sphere according to Habermas: the primacy of rational and critical argument as the basis of truth-seeking and thus policy.[84] As Craig Calhoun summarises, 'However often the norm was breached, the idea that the best rational argument and not the identity of the speaker was supposed to carry the day was institutionalized as an available claim.'[85]

---

[81] Habermas (1994), 88. Indeed, he claims that the public sphere is itself the first example of an ideology, properly so called: 'If there is an aspect to [ideology] that can lay a claim to truth inasmuch as it transcends the status quo in utopian fashion, even if only for purposes of justification, then ideology exists at all only from this period on.'

[82] Habermas (1994), 5–14. For an enlightening discussion of this aspect of the European pre-modern monarch, see Bataille (1991), 237–252.

[83] Habermas (1994), 36.   [84] Habermas (1994), 54, 94, 99–107.   [85] Calhoun (1992), 13.

Third, the public sphere 'presupposed the problematisation of areas that until then had not been questioned'.[86] That is to say, the public sphere thematised issues of 'common concern' that had previously been subject to a 'monopoly of interpretation' of the overarching authorities of church and state. In part, Habermas notes, the rise of capitalism itself in the eighteenth century, with its need for increasingly detailed information, undid those monopolies. Matters of general interest were removed from the 'representative publicity' of premodern authority, stripped of that authoritative mystique and *profaned* – in the sense that they entered the vulgar public domain and lost their aura of sacredness.

Related to this generality of subject matter was, fourth, a generality of participation, at least in principle. Wherever a circle of discussants met to discuss public issues, they 'did not equate [themselves] with *the* public but at most claimed to act as its mouthpiece, in its name, perhaps even as its educator'. This, together with the other principles, of rationality and of the common good, involves a shift away from the secrecy associated with the absolutist state (and the representative publicity of the monarch) to an increasingly positive valuation of information transmission and (to use a contemporary term) transparency: the public sphere is a sphere of transparency (or to use the term preferred at the time, and continued by Habermas, *publicity*).[87]

These principles of equality, rationality, generality and transparency (publicity) comprised the groundrules for the public sphere's idea of itself and its own functioning. They also framed the relevant principles of law, in a process that was, from the start, mutually constitutive.[88] Habermas writes that where the state 'was sanctioned (as on the continent) by a ... basic law or constitution, the functions of the public sphere were clearly spelled out in the law'. In Britain, the same process was assumed to have taken place implicitly; the existence of similar

---

[86] Habermas (1994), 36–37.
[87] This shift is also characterised as moving society from a basis in *voluntas* (will) to one in *ratio* (reason): Habermas (1994), 53.
[88] Habermas (1994), 52–56, 79–84: 'The only reliable criterion for distinguishing the more recent from the older polemic was the use of a rigorous concept of law. Law in this sense guaranteed not merely justice in the sense of a duly acquired right, but legality by means of the enactment of general and abstract norms' (at 53).

safeguards is made explicit in the writings of Locke, Burke, Mill and Dicey. Habermas's description of this 'spelling out' bears quoting at length:[89]

> A set of basic rights concerned the sphere of the public engaged in a rational-critical debate (freedom of opinion and speech, freedom of press, freedom of assembly and association, etc.) and the political function of private people in this public sphere (right of petition, equality of vote, etc.). A second set of basic rights concerned the individual's status as a free human being, grounded in the intimate sphere of the patriarchal conjugal family (personal freedom, inviolability of the home, etc.). The third set of basic rights concerned the transactions of the private owners of property in the sphere of civil society (equality before the law, protection of private property, etc.). The basic rights guaranteed: the spheres of the public realm and of the private (with the intimate sphere at its core); the institutions and instruments of the public sphere, on the one hand (press, parties) and the foundation of private autonomy (family and property), on the other; finally, the functions of the private people, both their political ones as citizens and their economic ones as owners of commodities.

The assumptions that underlie the ideal type of the public sphere were thus concretised in law – and this was in turn reflected in modern constitutional arrangements. And, as we shall see in Part II, these same principles – equality, rationality, generality and transparency – provide a practical blueprint for the contemporary transnational rule of law. Where absent, they are to be generated by recourse to a similar set of societal arrangements as those from the Enlightenment period set out above, constructed (rather than self-producing) through the deliberate fashioning *from without* of a public sphere, comprising private persons conscious of, and motivated by, their self-distinction from the state (public *realm*).

A final relevant point: Habermas's account explores in detail the extraordinary importance allocated to 'public opinion' in constitutional theory of this period (in both civil and common law systems):

> A political consciousness developed in the public sphere of civil society which, in opposition to absolute sovereignty, articulated the concept of and demand for general and abstract laws and which ultimately came to assert itself (i.e., public opinion) as the only legitimate source of this law.[90]

---

[89] Habermas (1994), 83.   [90] Habermas (1994), 54.

(This view is further ratified in Dicey's explanation that public opinion provided the last and only constraint on parliamentary supremacy.[91]) Parliament was the voice *par excellence* of this public of private persons, a space that institutionalised precisely the open, rational discussion prized above all by participants. The parliamentary legislative process could thus be imagined as one in which lawmaking is conceived of as truth-seeking and consensus building, that is: as the actualisation of public opinion. Hence too the enormous significance attached to the free press, 'which stimulates the citizens themselves to seek after truth and to tell it to power'.[92] Everything from parliamentary integrity to judicial independence was to be guaranteed by public opinion.[93] By the late nineteenth century, Mill and de Tocqueville had already expressed concern about the tyrannical potential of this all-powerful public opinion, predicting (in Habermas's view) its evolution into mass-oriented systems of representation and manipulation that would finally clog or occlude the public sphere's ideal capacity for rational criticism.[94] There was, these writers warned, a danger and tendency for powerful actors to manipulate or manage public opinion, which would in effect corrupt the ideal of the public sphere.[95]

A tripartite distinction

Habermas's account of a public sphere of private persons allows for clarification of the terms public and private, which are used today in a wide variety of tangled and interrelated ways that are not always consistent and do not lend themselves easily to understanding in every case.[96] In practice Habermas introduces a *tripartite* distinction, rather than a dichotomy, between private and public. This tripartite structure fits well with Hegel's trio of family–civil society–state. Both 'private' and 'public', however, as commonly used, slide uncomfortably back and forth over the middle ground of Hegel's 'civil society' – which coincides with Habermas's 'public sphere'.

---

[91] See generally Dicey (2008).   [92] Guizot cited in Habermas (1994), 101.
[93] Habermas (1994), 83.   [94] Habermas (1994), 132–138.
[95] See in this regard, part two of Habermas (1994).
[96] Hannah Arendt, for example, in *The Human Condition*, published just before *Structural Transformation*, uses different terms.

The tripartite structure might be illustrated as follows:

	Family/ individuals (intimate sphere)	The public sphere of private persons	Government/ state
Public/private realm	Private realm		Public realm
Public/private sphere	Private sphere	Public sphere	N/A
Public/private sector	N/A	Civil society (including, though not exhausted by, the private sector)	Public sector
Public/private interest	Private interest	Public interest (aggregate of private interests)	

In practice, as the table shows, we can distinguish four different deployments of the public/private split. First, are the public and private *realms* – distinguishing state activity from non-state activity, public officials from private persons. Second, there are the public and private *spheres* – *both* of which, following Habermas, exist within the private realm.[97] The private sphere is the sphere of intimacy, of communion with oneself, friends or family, or otherwise outside the public gaze; the public sphere is the space of 'publicity'. In principle, an individual can move freely between these two spheres,[98] but only under conditions where the private realm is clearly distinct from (that is, protected from) the public realm. Third, the public and private *sectors* break down along lines of the public and private realms, but with the important difference that the 'private sector' comprises only a small part of the 'private realm' and of the public sphere, the latter also comprising (at a minimum) 'civil society' and the media (including the spheres of art

---

[97] As this terminology is taken from Habermas, it is necessarily dependent upon translation. The term 'public sphere' translates Habermas's *Öffentlichkeit*, properly meaning 'openness' or 'publicity' without the physical-spatial metaphor of the English 'sphere'. The distinction between 'sphere' and 'realm' in the English translation captures Habermas's original German, but must rely somewhat awkwardly on two barely differentiable spatial metaphors generally used interchangeably in English.
[98] Michael Warner associates public with light, circulation, accessibility, openness; private with darkness, concealment, inaccessibility, close(d)ness. See Warner (2002), 29–30.

and representation). Public and private *interests* break down differently again, with the public sphere comprising the public interests as the aggregate of private interests to be channelled through the state. This vocabulary and the distinctions it promulgates provide the contextual and conceptual underpinnings of contemporary rule of law work: separation of public and private *realms*; preservation of the integrity of both the private and public *sectors*; and a regulatory construction of the interaction between the public *sphere* of private persons and the public *realm* of public authorities.

CONCLUSION

Viewed in historical context, *Structural Transformation* appeared at the height of a cycle that can be traced back at least 40 years before its publication, to Max Weber's *Economy and Society* and the American legal realists, each of whom were concerned (in different and sometimes contradictory ways), with what they perceived to be a shift in the function of law away from a *Rechtsstaat* (a 'formalist', or frequently termed 'rule of law') orientation and towards a *Sozialstaat* (broadly, welfarist or, in Weber's terms, substantivist) orientation.[99] It is in this context that we must read the repeated assertions in postwar writing – of which Habermas's (and Arendt's) interventions are indicative – that the public-private divide had collapsed, or that its collapse was imminent.[100] Soon thereafter, however – or so a common account has it – the pendulum swung in the opposite direction: back to formalism and the 'rule of law', including its export variety. In a recent account, Duncan Kennedy highlights how *each* of these shifts in emphasis (from rule of law/*Rechtsstaat* to welfare/*Sozialstaat* and back) was exported in turn, in various distinct waves of 'globalization'.[101] My next chapter examines a second family of ideas about the rule of law, that occur in the writings of Max Weber and of the legal realists, and in the critiques generated

---

[99] For a good discussion of Weber's influence on Habermas in this context, see McCormick (2007), especially Chapter 2. On the American legal realists, see below Chapter 2.
[100] As John McCormick notes, this view – of a refeudalisation of society – was as common on the right (among writers like Carl Schmitt, Friedrich Hayek, and Michael Oakeshott) as it was on the left (besides Arendt and Habermas, Otto Kirchheimer and Franz Neumann, as well as others in the Frankfurt school, and later Michel Foucault). See McCormick (2007), 44–45.
[101] Kennedy (2006c).

in response, all of which set the stage for a specific and attenuated configuration of the term 'rule of law' in the register of economics.

As we shall see in Part II, however, historical contextualisation of this kind is habitually absent from contemporary rule of law accounts, which work rather with archetypal and universal visions of state and society, released from specificities of time and place other than as locations of enactment. Indeed, these archetypes underlie Western legal and political institutions at such a profound level and exert such a powerful gravitational force over political and legal thought that they are generally unavailable for diagnosis and debate. Habermas's achievement in *Structural Transformation* was to hold this archetypal imagery up to the light, specifically by articulating the great burden of political responsibility and legitimacy channelled through the enlightenment ideal of a mediating 'public sphere'. My goal in returning to his work in this section has been to reopen some of the key themes at the interface of state and society, the operating space of both the public sphere and, as we shall see, of rule of law reform. In short, an inquiry into the roots of the motivating language and justificatory norms of contemporary rule of law as it applies globally leads into a very particular time and place: late eighteenth-/early nineteenth-century Europe – to an ideal, furthermore, which, at least on Habermas's account, never actually came to pass, even there.

2 Economy

In a common formulation, the rule of law posits a relation between the individual and the state in which the former is a bearer of rights held against the latter, enforced by an independent judiciary. This story – with the protected rights varyingly termed 'ancient', 'fundamental', 'inalienable' or 'human' – is well known and need not be reproduced here.[1] However, there is a flipside to the story: the rule of law's mantle has not generally extended to – and has frequently been represented as antithetical to – a sizeable subset of the 'fundamental rights' enumerated in international human rights instruments – the covenants on, respectively, 'civil and political' and 'economic, social and cultural' rights. Thus, whereas the rule of law is frequently articulated as a 'guarantor' of human rights as such, in practice these articulations do not easily extend beyond that subgroup of rights termed 'civil and political'.

Silence on 'social and economic rights' pervades contemporary project literature, even though, as we shall see in Part II, economic governance is a primary subject and target of this literature. As such, the silence may appear to be a mere oversight or, at worst reflective of an institutional (as opposed to a conceptual) bias. Yet far from being peripheral to the historical reception of the rule of law ideal, state efforts to protect and promote welfare have in fact played a central role in determining the normative reach of the term. According to an influential view, state administrative and welfare apparatuses necessarily bestow significant discretionary powers on government officials,

---

[1] The following accounts and collections are representative: Reid (2004), Walker (1988), Tamanaha (2004), Hutchinson and Monahan (1987); contributors to Sandoz (1993) and to Shapiro (1994). For a thorough exposition of this relationship, see Allan (2003).

thereby interfering with the rule of law prima facie. Dicey presents the rule of law in just these terms, in part to contest and discredit the 'administrative state' at the very moment it was emergent throughout Europe. In the United States, the rule of law emerged as term of art at the peak of longstanding disputes over the public role of the state during the construction of the New Deal welfare apparatus, and as a counterweight to the latter.[2] This history comprises the subject of the present chapter.

In what follows, I first revisit Dicey's structured opposition between the rule of law and administrative law, which I go on to contrast with Weber's influential account of the role of law in a modern economy. I then concentrate on the legal realist debates of the early twentieth century in the United States, for two reasons. First, those discussions helped set the parameters of contemporary rule of law understanding, in a skeletal fashion that tends to influence contemporary notions at a largely subcutaneous level. A second reason to revisit the realists is that the incisiveness of their critique remains largely unsurpassed almost a century on and carries a renewed relevance in the context of contemporary transnational rule of law activities. Following this, in a third section I trace how the subsequent reception of realist analyses in the United States resulted in two divergent tendencies – the embrace of administrative discretion through the New Deal, on one hand, and an association of the rule of law with judicial formalism, on the other (contributing in turn to the attempted formalisation of welfare as 'social rights'). Finally, I trace a contemporaneous genealogy of the rule of law that begins with Hayek and is today dominant in the transnational promotion of the rule of law.

My aim in this chapter is not to defend any particular view of the rule of law as compatible or not with welfare, but to demonstrate rather the rhetorical hostility to welfare that a rule of law framework unobtrusively instantiates. This hostility is not absolute. Many countries that today retain relatively robust welfare systems are generally considered also to 'have' the rule of law. Theoretically, there is nothing self-evident in the notion that the protection of welfare requires excessive government discretion, or that courts (or other tribunals) cannot monitor welfare operations as they do other state operations (should

---

[2] James Landis, a principal architect of the new administration, defended his proposals as requiring a 'more modest' definition of the rule of law than Dicey's. Landis (1938), 123–134.

such oversight be thought inherent to a 'modern' state, itself a contestable notion). Nevertheless, a powerfully entrenched set of dichotomies over the last century has naturalised this hostility, associating the rule of law with 'procedural' or 'formal' justice, private law, civil and political rights, 'negative' freedom and government constraint; contrastable with 'substantive justice', public law, social and economic rights, 'positive' freedom, and administrative discretion. As a result, in a rule of law register, welfare is either absent or repeatedly postponed. It is this set of shaping arguments that comprise my subject here.

TWO PERSPECTIVES ON LAW AND THE STATE

Dicey on *droit administratif*

To contextualise this inquiry, it is helpful briefly to recall the background to Dicey's original statement of the rule of law in the late nineteenth century. The theme arises at a moment when the European state, including Britain's, begins to acquire its extensive modern policy function – with the arrival of new nationwide energy and transport infrastructures, the initiation of social security schemes, the need to 'manage' the economy, to prepare for 'modern warfare' and so on. The *Introduction* was published just as the advance toward universal suffrage was beginning to look inexorable in England. Around the same time, Bismarck introduced the first social insurance scheme in Germany, an example followed in England by H. H. Asquith's government in the first decade of the twentieth century, which had the effect of shifting embryonic welfare structures from private voluntary groups to the state, and universalising them. State pensions were introduced from 1908, rent controls from 1915; peaking with the introduction of full modern welfare structures in 1948.

Viewed from this perspective, Dicey's opposition to the state as regulator and administrator appears quixotic as well as conservative. He chose not to recognise the likely irreversibility of demands for a regulatory state, given the power of its technological and industrial motors; rather, his *Introduction* is reflexively anti-historical. He characterises the legal problems of his day as though they had altered little from the era of Edward Coke – turning on the freedom of an Englishman's person and property in the face of arbitrary monarchical tyranny. Indeed, Dicey does not acknowledge the existence of a state per se, preferring to keep quite separate the ethos and competence of the Crown, Parliament and the judiciary.[3] In contrast, the existence of just such a unitary framework in France provides a principal motive for the *Introduction*.[4] Dicey produces his English rule of law specifically to counter the spread of this French ideology; his famous tripartite definition is entirely constructed around a distinction between (French) administrative and (English) judicial authority:

> [First, the rule of law] excludes the existence of arbitrariness, of prerogative, or even of wide discretionary authority on the part of the government. Englishmen are ruled by the law and by the law alone ... [Second, it] excludes the idea of any exemption of officials or others from the duty of obedience to the law which governs other citizens or from the jurisdiction of the ordinary tribunals; there can be with us nothing really corresponding to the 'administrative law' or the 'administrative tribunals' of France ... [third it means] that with us the law of the constitution, the rules which in foreign countries naturally form part of a constitutional code, are not the source but the consequence of the rights of individuals as defined and enforced by the courts ...[5]

At root, Dicey's account is antipathetic towards 'policy' per se.[6] Rights are conceived in opposition to policy; they are permanent where policy is contingent, they are known where policy is opaque, they are rule-bound where policy is discretionary. In effect, Dicey recast the perceived *absence* of a functioning administrative law framework in England as the *presence* of a romanticised common law trophy. The rule of law, in Dicey's account, is thus *fundamentally* – not incidentally – defined by its effective opposition to administrative law and courts, and the capacity for public policy they imply; it is a point he returns to repeatedly.

And yet, on most subsequent accounts, even sympathetic ones, Dicey got it wrong.[7] He exaggerated the faults of the French system (often

---

[3] In 1951 Wolfgang Friedmann could still write that English law 'has no theory of the state'. Cited in Pound (1954), 21.

[4] Of the *Tribunal de Conflits* – in his estimation the most 'judicial' of French administrative courts – he writes: 'An Englishman, indeed, can hardly fail to surmise that the Court must still remain a partly official body which may occasionally be swayed by the policy of a Ministry, and still more often be influenced by official or governmental ideas.' Dicey (1962), 366.

[5] Dicey (1962), 202–203.

[6] Dicey's *Introduction* uses the term in a manner that is no longer standard, speaking (synonymously) of 'high policy', 'foreign policy' and 'imperial policy' without reference to any domestic or national equivalent.

[7] See, for example, Jennings (1959); Wade (1957); Allan (2003), 125; Shklar (1987), 6; Hayek (2006), 203–204.

resorting to nationalist-inflected impressionism[8]) and misrepresented the extent of the existing English apparatus. A later introduction to his opus observes:

> Had Dicey examined the full range of administrative law in the sense of the organisation, method, powers and control of public authorities, he would have been forced, even in 1885, to enumerate a long list of statutes permitting the exercise of discretionary powers which could not be called in question by the courts.[9]

Dicey's principal thesis was mistaken not only empirically but also as a matter of subsequent historical development. The 'ordinary English courts' did not provide significant resistance to the rise of administrative government – in health and safety, pensions, social insurance, labour protections and elsewhere. By the time of the *Introduction*'s eighth edition in 1915, Dicey could no longer ignore the increasing prevalence of an English 'official' or 'administrative' body of law. In a new preface to that edition, he speaks of a 'decline in reverence' for the rule of law, despairing that, with the passage of the National Insurance Act of 1911, 'something very like judicial powers have been given to officials closely connected with the Government'.[10] Elsewhere he worries that 'laissez faire ... has more or less lost its hold on the English people', and that 'collectivism' is on the rise.[11]

It is worth insisting on the centrality of this (supposed) misapprehension to Dicey's articulation of the rule of law, because a subsequent legal textbook tradition has tended to discount Dicey's 'errors of judgement' about French (and English) administrative law, regarding them as marginal to his overall statement. But, errors aside, Dicey's preferred emphasis, although often viewed as idiosyncratic within the legal profession, found fertile ground among economists, where a separate tradition of the rule of law, crystallised by Friedrich Hayek in the 1940s hewed closely to Dicey's initial presumption that individual freedom resides precisely in the incapacitation of government, as we shall

---

[8] See, for example, Dicey (1962), 401: 'No Englishman can wonder that the jurisdiction of the [French] Council of State, as the greatest of administrative Courts, grows apace; the extension of its power removes ... real grievances, and meets the need of the ordinary citizen. Yet to an Englishman imbued with an unshakeable faith in the importance of maintaining the supremacy of the ordinary law of the land enforced by the ordinary Law Courts, the *droit administratif* of modern France is open to some grave criticism.'

[9] E. C. S. Wade's introduction to Dicey (1962), cxvi–cxvii.

[10] Dicey (1915), 'Introduction', xxxvii–xlviii.   [11] Dicey (2008), xxix–xliii.

see in a moment.¹² That tradition also draws on the writings of a near contemporary of Dicey's, Max Weber, whose very different description of the role of law I will now describe briefly.

Weber on 'compulsory political association'

The modern European *Rechtsstaat* described by Max Weber appears, at first glance, to represent precisely the kind of state apparatus that Dicey produced the rule of law to oppose. And yet, as we shall see in Part II, contemporary rule of law promotion takes as much, if not more, from Weber's account of the role of law in the state and economy, as from Dicey's. These two contrasting, even opposing, accounts of modern law each provide a different parental branch for the contemporary hybrid.

As intimated in the discussion of Habermas in Chapter 1, Max Weber regarded European law and legal systems as the outcome of a long process of 'disenchantment', that is, of a recent and general emergence from superstition and religion.¹³ In *Economy and Society*, published in 1921, Weber undertook a detailed comparative exercise to determine what is specific to 'modern' Western law: which he identified as its combination of formality (ritual or procedural rigour), rationality (consistency over time of the relationship between facts, norms, rules, and decisions), secularity (its refusal as a matter of fundamental principle to turn for interpretative solutions to religious or supernatural or other non-secular authorities), and reliance on an extensive functional bureaucracy for its execution.¹⁴

The forms, processes and contents of 'modern law' were, in Weber's view, indissociable from the rise of capitalism, which required, and thrived upon, legal certainty, predictability and consistency – a legal

---

[12] Recently, Dicey's mistrust of continental law is again fashionable, reproduced in, for example, Djankov *et al.* (2002), whose authors launched the influential World Bank *Doing Business* series, claiming inter alia that common law systems are more supportive of entrepreneurship than civil law systems.

[13] Weber (1978), 671, 687, 705, 758–759, 761, 766, 771, 830, 842, 882; on comparable processes in Roman law see 792–802.

[14] See Kennedy (2004); Trubek (1972a); Trubek (1972b); Thomas (2006); Weber (1978), 687, 695, 698, 707, 754, 757, 775, 785–788, 801; on the rationalisation required for and promoted by bureaucracy, see 809–812. (Weber uses the term 'rationality' in a variety of contexts, including also as the basis for agreement between contractual parties and the premising of agreements and actions on the expectations of courts.)

system whereby 'universal rules are uniformly applied'.[15] However, if these qualities of the legal system were not purpose-built for economic ends, nor can they be understood primarily in terms of conserving a space of individual freedom from the state. To the contrary, conditions of generalised formal equality and rational 'calculability' under law are only conceivable under conditions of 'compulsory political association', a term Weber uses for the modern state.[16] Private contract, the quintessential vehicle of modern law in Weber's view, attains to certainty only when firmly backed by state coercion – that is, when contract and other private relations are thoroughly ensconced within a coercive public apparatus that alone can guarantee their execution.[17] Hence Weber's famous definition of the state as that institution enjoying a 'monopoly on legitimate violence' and hence too the ambiguity with which he viewed individual 'freedom' in such a state.[18] *Economy and Society* provides numerous examples of 'freedoms' entrenched in law that turn out, on inspection, to rely on direct state coercion and/or on the delegation by the state of its coercive power to certain private actors to wield over others, such that the 'autonomy' Dicey celebrated – apparently guaranteed by law – is neither truly autonomous not truly guaranteed, since it is premised on denial to some.[19]

---

[15] The citation is from Trubek (1972a), 7. See also Trubek (1972b), 724. Weber (1978), 671–672: 'The present-day significance of contract is primarily the result of the high degree to which our economic system is market-oriented and of the role played by money. The increased importance of the private law contract is the legal reflex of the market orientation of our society.'

[16] Weber (1978), 705. See also Weber (1978), 698, 902.

[17] Weber (1978), 694–695: Modern 'private' law 'is a product of the unification and rationalization of the law; it is based on the official monopoly of law creation by, and the compulsion of membership in, the modern political organization.' Generally on contract see 669: '[T]he most essential feature of modern substantive law is the greatly increased significance of legal transactions, particularly contracts, as a source of claims guaranteed by legal coercion'. Weber (1978), 680, 684, 813, 869–870.

[18] Weber (1978), 901–905, 902: 'Since political power has become the monopoly of organized, today "institutional", action, the objects of coercion are to be found primarily among the compulsory members of the organization.'

[19] Weber (1978), 668: 'Freedom of contract, for example, exists exactly to the extent to which ... autonomy is recognized by the legal order ... in no legal order is freedom of contract unlimited in the sense that the law would place its guaranty of coercion at the disposal of all and every agreement regardless of its terms.'
  Weber (1978), 699: '[Personal] autonomy ... always denotes the beginning of the state's legal supremacy. It always entails the idea that the state either tolerates or directly guarantees the creation of law by organs other than its own ... If, by virtue of the principle of formal legal equality, everyone, "without respect of person"

If the formalisation and rationalisation of law is constantly on the increase, as Weber viewed it as being, this is not only due to the acceleration of market economies, it is also a result of the entrenchment and expansion of these qualities within bureaucratic structures, and of the increasingly complex and self-reproducing nature of bureaucratisation itself, a development Weber regarded as profoundly transformational (as well as intrinsically worrying):[20]

[F]rom a purely technical point of view, [a bureaucracy is] capable of attaining the highest degree of efficiency and is in this sense formally the most rational known means of exercising authority over human beings. It is superior to any other form in precision, in stability, in the stringency of its discipline, and in its reliability. It thus makes possible a particularly high degree of calculability of results for the heads of organization[s] ... It is finally superior both in intensive efficiency and in the scope of its operations, and is formally capable of application to all kinds of administrative tasks.[21]

Bureaucracy is both a revolutionary and a conservative force in Western legal structures: the source of its resilience and of its transformational capacity. The modern bureaucracy is the means of structuring both public and private organisations in order to ensure the most efficient and predictable outcomes. Weber's description of its extent and expansion shares much with Dicey's administrative state:

The development of modern forms of organization in all fields is nothing less than identical with the development and continual spread of bureaucratic administration. ... Its development is ... at the root of the modern Western state. ... [I]t would be sheer illusion to think for a moment that continuous administrative work can be carried out in any field except by means of officials working in offices. The whole pattern of everyday life is cut to fit this

---

may establish a business corporation or entail a landed estate, the *propertied* classes *as such* obtain a sort of factual "autonomy," since they alone are able to utilize or take advantage of these powers.'

Weber (1978), 729-731: 'The formal right of a worker to enter into any contract whatsoever with any employer whatsoever does not in practice represent for the employment seeker even the slightest freedom in the determination of his own conditions of work, and it does not guarantee him any influence on this process. It rather means, at least primarily, that the most powerful party in the market, i.e., normally the employer, has the possibility to set the terms, to offer the job, "take it or leave it," and, given the normally more pressing economic need of the worker, to impose his terms upon him. The result of contractual freedom, then, is in the first place the opening of the opportunity to use, by the clever utilization of property ownership in the market, these resources without legal restraints as a means for the achievement of power over others.'

[20] Weber (1978), 988-989. [21] Weber (1978), 223.

framework. If bureaucratic administration is ... always the most rational type from a technical point of view, the needs of mass administration make it today completely indispensable.²²

State bureaucracies entrench the rationality and the formality of modern law. By 'formal' Weber meant a system of identifiable procedural rules in the administration of law and justice; the existence of formal equality between individuals, with a minimum of discretion in the treatment of individual cases by bureaucrats or judges.²³ The legal profession played a particularly important role in this picture – and it is one that again marked the modern European state out from many others – as the guardians of the procedural rigour, consistency and autonomy of law.²⁴ However, it was the steadily increasing subjection to rigid formality and rational demands, in the workplace as in the public domain, that led Weber to describe the experience of modern life, famously, as an 'iron cage'.²⁵

Weber contrasted the formal justice of the modern bureaucracy and judiciary with substantive justice – 'kadi justice' was his term – whereby cases are decided on an individual or discretionary basis.²⁶ Kadi justice had not disappeared from Western legal orders: elements existed notably, but not only, in the English system, particularly equity, trial by jury, and the powers of justices of the peace.²⁷ Elements of kadi justice are not only tolerated, they are often valued, because a capacity for substantive justice itself supplies necessary relief from the perceived inhumanity of the pure formalism of a 'slot-machine' justice.²⁸ Furthermore, Weber observed contemporary pressures tending towards the deformalization of law and an increase in substantive justice, principal among them are two: powerful private interests seeking special treatment or guarantees from the state, on one hand, and the increasing claims for 'social justice', on the other.²⁹

Weber's account clearly has much in common with Dicey's.³⁰ Like Dicey, Weber worried that the rise of bureaucracy/administration undermines the freedom of the individual as does constant subjection to a purposive formal rationality (i.e., policy). He too insisted that the *Rechtsstaat* – a formal rational state bureaucracy operating strictly

---

²² Weber (1978), 223.   ²³ Weber (1978), 225, 876–882.
²⁴ Weber (1978), 785–788, 875–877.   ²⁵ On the 'iron cage', Kennedy (2004), 1056–1031.
²⁶ Weber (1978), 891–892.   ²⁷ Weber (1978), 724, 841, 891.
²⁸ Weber (1978), 882–887.   ²⁹ Weber (1978), 813, 844–848, 883–888.
³⁰ Weber regarded the English common law as less 'rational' than continental civil law: Weber (1978), 724, 762, 788, 801, 813; Trubek (1972b), 746–749.

according to law – is not itself purposive; it does not exist to promote any given economic order; rather it has evolved side-by-side with a particular economics, which it supports implicitly. Furthermore, Weber provides no means of stepping from the analysis of a given social constellation to its programmatic construction.[31]

On a few points, however, Weber's story deviates significantly from Dicey's. First, Weber does not regard the rise of administrative structures as itself inconsistent with the subjection of the state to law – to the contrary, the two are mutually constitutive and self-reinforcing. For the same reason, the spread of administration is not viewed as reversible; it is by contrast the very essence of modern life. Second, Weber does not regard the advance of purposive rationality and its concomitant pressures on the freedom of the individual as limited to state administration; private organisation too is subject to similar principles that are, if anything, more stringent, demanding and constrictive. (It is therefore far from obvious that barring the state from 'interference' would in fact advance individual freedom; if anything, by giving private bureaucracies freer rein, the opposite outcome might be expected.) Third, Weber regarded the rise of welfarism as a reaction against, as much as a symptom of, the advance of the 'iron cage' of bureaucracy (both public and private).

Weber's analysis therefore questions both the historical and the sociological premises of Dicey's 'rule of law'. The latent tension between these two views is made explicit, as we shall now see, in the American realist critique of judicial 'formalism', a cognate phenomenon with the 'formalism' described by Dicey.

THE REALIST CRITIQUE: FOUR CHARGES OF JUDICIAL BIAS

Today, the term 'administrative law' is generally defined as having two distinct applications: first, the laws and regulations promulgated by administrative agencies; second, the complex of laws, case law and procedures designed to minimise administrative discretion.[32]

---

[31] Kennedy (2004), 1036, citing three papers by Weber, 'The Meaning of "Ethical Neutrality" in Sociology and Economics'; '"Objectivity" in Social Science and Social Policy'; and 'Science as a Vocation'. See also Weber (1994).

[32] Somewhat ironically, Dicey also appears to have coined the English term 'administrative law' from the French, according to Wade in his introduction to Dicey (1959), cxlvi.

Textbooks focus on the second – on judicial, legislative and executive mechanisms of oversight of administrative agencies.[33] The standard account is simultaneously a celebration of the superiority of the rule of law over administrative discretion and a disquisition into the reasons for court deference, where it exists, to administrative 'expertise'. The story generally repeats in refined form Dicey's assumption that the 'ordinary courts of the land' are the individual's best defence against the possible tyranny of empowered public officials. In the United States, with which I am predominantly concerned in the present section, textbooks start with the progressive development of the principles of property and liberty in judicial interpretations of the US constitution, in particular through the doctrine of 'substantive due process' in readings of the fifth and fourteenth amendments.[34]

These foundational principles were challenged, in the textbook account, with the creation of the first administrative agencies in the late nineteenth century.[35] During the New Deal period, 'powerful' independent administrative agencies were created through 'vague' congressional acts, and entrusted with 'sweeping' legislative, adjudicative and executive authority, including the regulation of hours and wages. The 1946 Administrative Procedure Act reasserted the rule of law, so the story goes, by imposing procedural burdens on administrative activity and requiring judicial review in contested applications of the law. Thereafter, the courts have increasingly refined these 'rule of law safeguards'.

An alternative history, however, views administrative law as the focal point for a quite different set of struggles and demands – those of vulnerable workers against exploitative employers, social 'progressives' against expansive private interests, and democratic legislatures against the courts.[36] I will use here a notorious Supreme Court case, the 1905 *Lochner* v. *New York*, to illustrate these areas of

---

[33] The following accounts are characteristic: Pierce *et al.* (2004), 23–40; Gellhorn *et al.* (1997), 1–7; Shapiro (1988), 36–49; Warren (2004), 12–31, 37–80.

[34] More circumspect histories nevertheless note that until the mid-nineteenth century, US law did not conceive of a private individual space free from state interference. See Singer (1988), 477–489; Horwitz (1978), 85.

[35] The first, the Interstate Commerce Commission, was founded in 1887 to impose controls over the actions of railroad companies – but also to circumvent court resistance to the controls imposed by state legislatures.

[36] See generally Horwitz (1992), Mensch (1998).

struggle and the relevant 'realist' perspectives, in order to spotlight some of the themes and the confusion that has complicated subsequent appreciation of the contesting accounts of the rule of law and welfare.

In *Lochner*, a Supreme Court majority struck down a New York State law that limited, on health grounds, the number of hours bakers could work to 60 per week. The court explained that, since 'almost all occupations more or less affect the health', statutes that limit the hours 'in which grown and intelligent men may labor to earn their living are mere meddlesome interferences with the rights of the individual'.[37] Were it to intervene, the state 'would assume the position of a supervisor or *pater familias* over every act of the individual'. The law's limitation of hours is 'so wholly beside the matter of a proper, reasonable and fair provision as to run counter to that liberty of person and of free contract provided for in the Federal Constitution'. Moreover, since 'it is manifest to us that the limitation of the hours of labor as provided for ... has no such direct relation to and no such substantial effect upon the health of the employé as to justify us in regarding the section as really a health law', the law must instead have been 'in reality passed from other motives'. The majority did not clarify what these 'other motives' might have been, confining their opprobrium for the law's 'real object and purpose' which was 'simply to regulate the hours of labor'. A minority dissented on the grounds that evidence made available to the court had indicated substantial and demonstrable health risks to bakers from overwork.[38] Justice Oliver Wendell Holmes, in a separate dissent, famously asserted that the case had been 'decided upon an economic theory' – indicating a majority bias towards what he called '*laissez faire*' – and that the court should not overturn democratic legislation except where 'fundamental constitutional rights' were involved.[39]

The realist reaction against Supreme Court rulings of the period can be approached through the identification of four different kinds of bias in this case, each of which presents an ingrained obstacle to

---

[37] *Lochner v. New York*, 198 US 45 (1905), 61–64.
[38] *Lochner*, 65–74. For this reason, the minority asserted that the Court's own bar – that legislation must be 'a plain, palpable invasion of rights secured by the fundamental law' to be struck down – had not been reached, citing *Jacobson v. Massachusetts*, 197 US 11 (1904).
[39] *Lochner*, 75–76. 'A constitution', Holmes observed, 'is not intended to embody a particular economic theory, whether of paternalism and the organic relation of the citizen to the state or of *laissez faire*.' See Fisher et al. (1993), 25.

judicial recognition of 'progressive' goals, and each of which drew its own realist response.[40]

Bias one: the choice of rights

In *Lochner*, the Court reframed a question on welfare as one concerning instead freedom of contract: 'a question of which of two powers or rights shall prevail – the power of the state to legislate or the right of the individual to liberty of person and freedom of contract'.[41] In this framing, the court protects the freedom of *both* employers and employees from the overweening 'paternalist' intrusion of the state. The Constitution provided little textual basis to privilege either freedom of contract or worker health, but in *Lochner* the Supreme Court 'read' contract protections into the fourteenth amendment's due process clause.[42] The doctrine of 'substantive due process' assumed that the Constitution's procedural protections must necessarily extend to specific individual rights not explicitly listed in the Constitution. It thus protects certain areas of private activity from the state's 'police power' – that is, the state's legitimate zone of interference.[43]

The 'realists' took issue with the Supreme Court's approach in this and similar cases, arguing that the court's reasoning failed to account for the full and actual effects of the law – failing in fact to extend equal protections. Robert Hale, in a series of sharply critical papers, argued along Weberian lines that contracts can be equally read to embody mutual coercion rather than a simple alignment of freedoms.[44]

---

[40] I do not cover all the many realist representatives and positions here, but focus on certain writings of Robert Hale (in particular), Morris Cohen, Felix Cohen, Walter Wheeler Cook, Karl Llewellyn, Oliver Wendell Holmes and Roscoe Pound. See Hale (1923), (1935), (1943), (1946); Cohen (1928); Cohen (1935); Cook (1918); Pound (1910), (1931); Llewellyn (1931); Holmes (1897), (1894). For background on the realists, see Singer (1988); Horwitz (1992); Mensch (1992); Fisher *et al.* (1993); Fuller (1934); anon. (1982); Kennedy (1993) and (1982).

[41] *Lochner*, 57.

[42] The Fourteenth Amendment to the US Constitution reads (at Section 1): 'No State shall make or enforce any law which shall abridge the privileges or immunities of citizens of the United States; nor shall any State deprive any person of life, liberty, or property, without due process of law.'

[43] Relevant cases in the evolution of substantive law doctrine include *Dred Scott v. Sandford*, 60 US (19 How.) 393 (1857); *Allgeyer v. Louisiana*, 165 US 578 (1897) (freedom of contract); *United States v. Carolene Products Co.*, 304 US 144 (1938) (restricting the scope of the doctrine to rights of the accused, political rights and minority rights). Justice Oliver Wendell Holmes criticised the doctrine's 'ever increasing scope' in *Baldwin v. Missouri*, 281 US 586, 595 (1930).

[44] See in particular Hale (1923).

Since each party seeks, within the contract, to invoke the state's coercive force in defence of their own interests, contracts cannot be regarded as wholly private affairs unmoored from public 'policy'. And the (formal, rational) principles brought to bear in the enforcement of contracts, which result in turn in predictable distributional outcomes, reflect implicit or explicit policy choices, so it is disingenuous to claim that private law and the courts are somehow disinfected of policy considerations. Furthermore, Hale said, a judicial assumption of contractual voluntarism made it difficult or impossible to assess the full spectrum of rights claims at stake in any given case. Negotiations between parties are marked by uneven access to bargaining resources. Other realists noted that in an era of increasing standardisation of contractual terms, the assumption that employees 'negotiated' the terms at all was already mythical.[45] According to the realists, then, the *Lochner* court's reading of the constitution demonstrated an overdeveloped respect for freedom of contract at the expense of other relevant elements of liberty. This might therefore be seen as a 'choice of rights' bias.

In the realists' view, a greater recognition of the full range of legal stakes, protections, and effects would lead to better judicial renderings of the law as it applied 'in action'.[46] Hohfeld's well-known categorisation of 'jural correlatives' and 'jural opposites' demonstrated how attention to the 'law in action' might reveal a deeper set of relevant interventions and outcomes to judicial rulings, rarely recognised by the courts.[47] Holmes later developed a corrective approach – that courts should rather aim to 'balance' rights than to regard each case as a contest between absolutes, as the *Lochner* majority had done.[48] Balancing tests would reveal to courts how they might better take account of each of the relevant interests. In all of this, the realists were suggesting that constitutional protections might be scrupulously interpreted as more extensive than the *Lochner* court had recognised.

Bias two: the choice of policy

A second bias, according to the realists, was the *Lochner* court's apparent preference for one party's interests over the other's, and their attribution of sinister unstated 'other motives' to the New York law. While

---

[45] Horwitz (1992), 30–39.   [46] See, in particular, Pound (1910).
[47] See Hohfeld (1913).   [48] *Pennsylvania Coal Co. v. Mahon*, 260 US 393 (1922).

related to the first, there is clearly a difference in kind between a formalist adherence to precedential notions of 'substantive due process', on one hand, and a manifest preference, on the other, for the interests of certain economic interests – the 'economic theory' of Holmes's dissent. On this view, the majority opinion, far from embodying a persuasive outcome of reasoned perusal of the relevant legal precedents, was poorly constructed and poorly argued. The majority dismissed without serious consideration both the circumstances of actual employees and the stated intent of the New York state legislature. *Lochner* took place during a period where courts were repeatedly striking down legislation,[49] leading Roscoe Pound to observe that the justices 'have now definitely invaded the field of public policy and are quick to declare unconstitutional almost any laws of which they disapprove, particularly in the fields of social and industrial legislation'.[50] There was an increasing sense that the courts were in fact taking sides during a period of significant popular support for legislative protections from industrial power, and clothing their bias in the supposed neutrality of 'formalist' reasoning.

The realists undertook close analyses of a number of rulings of this kind, uncovering apparent flaws in the reasoning that in many cases served one party over another by default. An excellent example is Walter Wheeler Cook's 'Privileges of Labor Unions', which subjects a Supreme Court injunction on union activity to a sustained Hohfeldian analysis, finding the logic incoherent, the reasoning inattentive to the precedents referenced in the opinion, and the outcome needlessly far-reaching in favour of the plaintiff.[51] Personal bias of this sort is attributable less to the law itself, or the history of constitutional interpretation, more to the social and personal preferences of the members of the court themselves. Conceivably, such a bias resides in judges less as individuals than as representatives of their class.

In response to this second dilemma, many 'progressives' concluded that the best assurance of welfare protections was to take the issues out of the hands of the antipathetic courts, insofar as possible. The legislature was the appropriate locus of policy decisions. Such a view found support in Holmes's *Lochner* dissent, where he speaks of his 'strong belief' that the court had no business interfering with the

---

[49] Pound (1910), 16, mentions 377 similar decisions in a five-year period.
[50] Pound (1910), 15, quoting Walter Dodd.
[51] See Cook (1918). The case was *Hitchman Coal and Coke Co.* v. *Mitchell*, 245 US 229 (1917).

democratic legislative process, except where to do so 'would infringe fundamental principles as they have been understood by the traditions and laws of our people'.[52] The gist of the complaint targets the majority's *activism* – their application of the law bluntly to suit their own 'economic theories'. Holmes's doctrine of judicial restraint advocates respect for legislative intent as a counter to the activism of the *Lochner* majority. This is a proceduralism that is fully compatible, in principle, with any legislative allocation of rights.

Bias three: the choice of evidence

Third, with their cursory dismissal that any health benefits might result from the statute, the justices further exhibited an unwillingness or incapacity to give probative weight to evidence resulting from empirical social research. A common realist complaint was that the courts were out of step with the times, lost in the 'law in books', unschooled in contemporary methods of information gathering, and unaware of the considerable expertise then being generated on the effects of industrialisation and the social costs of economic expansion. For certain realists – Karl Llewellyn is perhaps best known – the law needed to be updated by means of the newer authority of social science expertise.[53]

A question often raised in this context, both then and now, asks whether the courts are the appropriate places to determine policy responses that inevitably involve specialised expertise. James Landis spoke, for example, of a general 'distrust of the ability of the judicial process to make the necessary adjustments in the development of both law and regulatory methods as they related to particular industrial problems'.[54] In the event, the New Deal apparatus drew explicitly on recommendations like Llewellyn's for increased reliance on the new social sciences. The notion that judges are out of touch with social realities lent itself easily to the conclusion that experts should be given increased discretion in discovering and implementing the best policy options.[55] In the empowering of administrative agencies, assigned to deliver, inter alia, minimum health care and unemployment benefits and monitor wages, hours and prices, welfare policy objectives are sought through explicit circumvention of court oversight.

---

[52] *Lochner*, 75–76.   [53] See Llewellyn (1930).
[54] Landis (1938), 30.   [55] Horwitz (1998), 215–237; Friedman (2000), 1016–1023.

The traditional rule of law complaint along standard Diceyan lines finds a secure foothold in this environment. According to a common view, the doctrine of separation of powers was said to have been violated by the creation of a 'fourth branch' of government, shielded from court accountability. Others worried that these agencies would be vulnerable to 'industry capture'.[56] While the backlash was largely successful in triggering the zeal for restrictions on discretion that later characterised US administrative law, there has also remained a reticence on the part of US courts to become too closely embroiled in questions of policy. The compromise result has been an institutional separation of competences, notably of the courts' review role on 'questions of law' from administrative authority over 'questions of fact'. In principle, such a solution entrenches a rule of law balance between court and legislature, imposing few obvious preconditions on policy orientation. In practice, of course, much then depends on the extent that a court's review role appears 'activist', as we shall see from the US experience in a moment.

Bias four: the blindness to bias

Each of the three biases related so far can be located within an overarching realist critique. *Lochner* is often read as typifying the blindspots of 'formalist' legal reasoning, which (in Holmes's formula) treats rights as absolute, relies on deductive and analogical reasoning from first principles and presumes that a single correct interpretation of law exists and can be uncovered by judges through abstract reasoning.[57] The premise of formalism is that court adjudication should be insulated from policy considerations. Formalist reasoning captures the very essence of the 'autonomy of law', the idea that law has an existence independent of political and other considerations, and takes its course only from internal considerations applied by trained acolytes with specialist understanding. A decade before *Lochner*, Holmes, in a paper titled 'Privilege, Malice, and Intent', had already queried whether reasoning of this kind was actually feasible:

Perhaps one of the reasons why judges do not like to discuss questions of policy, or to put a decision in those terms upon their views as law-makers,

---

[56] 'Industry capture' of public administration amounts to a blurring of the divide between public and private – examined below in Chapter 6.
[57] Holmes (1897).

is that the moment you leave the path of merely logical deduction you lose the illusion of certainty which makes legal reasoning seem like mathematics. But the certainty is only an illusion, nevertheless. Views of policy are taught by experience of the interests of life. Those interests are fields of battle ... The danger is that such considerations should have their weight ... as unconscious considerations or half conscious inclination ... It seems to me desirable that the work should be done with express recognition of its nature.[58]

Holmes's famous text, written only shortly after Dicey's *Introduction*, tends in a sharply different direction. Not only is policy not barred from the courtroom, rather it is ever present and may infect every ruling, possibly even 'unconsciously'. Judges do not provide a simple defence against government; they may unwittingly be its agents. And rather than calling for the elimination, or minimisation of this tendency, Holmes instead recommends its 'express recognition' as an aspect of the judicial work. The charge of bias here is immanent. It targets the judicial conceit of legal autonomy itself. We might call it the 'rule of law bias' – or the rule of law *as* bias, or as *obscuring* bias.[59] The neutrality of the judge, in this charge, is a screen, even where faithfully adhered to, obscuring a series of other factors relevant to extant cases: personal prejudices, beliefs or foibles; considered policy preference; or simple gut reactions.

Holmes's critique anticipates later 'structuralist' analyses that would decentre standard 'neutral' or 'natural' explanations of a given phenomenon by exposing structural biases. And just as structuralism led to a wider-ranging post-structuralist critique – one that could find no ultimate criterion for identifying an appropriate or final centre of evaluation – so Holmes's observation opens up the possibility of inherent legal indeterminacy. Followed through, it implied that the Supreme Court, as final arbiter of the law, does not simply state the appropriate interpretation of the law, but actively generates it, in a move best understood as performative. The content of law is only knowable at the moment when the court enunciates it – and, in the same gesture,

---

[58] Holmes (1894), 7, 9. See also Horwitz (1998), 123–143. See also Holmes (1897) on contract adjudication: 'You can give any conclusion a logical form. You always can imply a condition in a contract. But why do you imply it? It is because of some belief as to the practice of the community or of a class, or because of some opinion as to policy, or, in short, because of some attitude of yours upon a matter not capable of exact quantitative measurement, and therefore not capable of founding exact logical conclusions. Such matters really are battle grounds where the means do not exist for determinations that shall be good for all time.'

[59] But see for comparison Dicey (1962), 176–177.

the law becomes that which the court says it is. This gives a decisionist spin to constitutional interpretation that tends to undermine formalism as a doctrine; indeed, that sits extremely uncomfortably with any procedural ideal of legal certainty as embodied in the rule of law as described by Dicey (and since). The effect in practice of this (no longer controversial) insight was to blur the clarity of distinction between judicial restraint and judicial activism: in a context of non-consensus over the meaning of justice ('social' or otherwise), the content of constitutional rights itself becomes the 'field of battle' for the 'unconscious considerations' and 'views of policy' in the court.[60] Thus the 'activism' of the *Lochner* court (according to the policy preferences of some) is superseded by the reverse 'activism' of the Warren court (in the view of others), and so on in a process that has haunted the US Supreme Court ever since. A continuous anxiety about the politicisation of the Supreme Court is the deeper legacy of the realists here. If the rule of law signifies an autonomy of law that might minimise judicial discretion – and by extension, government discretion generally, which must ultimately be accorded a determinate legal status – its foundations are clearly unstable.

AFTER THE REALISTS

The *Lochner* era ended, according to most accounts, in a series of Supreme Court rulings in 1936–7, during which the court's rigid defence of free contract gave way to other competing interpretations of the constitutional protection of liberty. When in 1937 the Supreme Court finally accepted legislative 'interference with freedom of contract', in the form of a minimum wage, it did so precisely by requiring a balancing of rights:

> The Constitution does not speak of freedom of contract. It speaks of liberty and prohibits the deprivation of liberty without due process of law. In prohibiting that deprivation, the Constitution does not recognize an absolute and uncontrollable liberty. Liberty in each of its phases has its history and connotation. But the liberty safeguarded is liberty in a social organization which requires the protection of law against the evils which menace the health, safety, morals, and welfare of the people.[61]

---

[60] See Rosenfeld (2005), 165–200, especially 177.
[61] *West Coast Hotel Co.* v. *Parrish*, 300 US 379 (1937). The case upheld the constitutionality of minimum wage legislation enacted by the State of Washington; overturning the 1923 case of *Adkins* v. *Children's Hospital*, 261 US 525 (1923).

This case, *West Coast Hotel Co.* v. *Parrish*, can be read as a success for realism.[62] The 'revolution' heralded by this ruling was expressed as the recognition of a 'flexible' or 'living constitution'.[63] Yet, like *Lochner*, it too is controversial. A majority was only achieved due to a sudden change in the voting habits of one judge (a Justice Roberts) whose famous 'switch in time' obviated the need for President Roosevelt's stated plan to 'pack' the court (that is, effectively to impose a new profile upon it). The case can therefore *also* be read as illustrative of the deeper problem raised by the realists: the inherent impossibility of insulating law from policy.

During the 30-odd years of court conservatism and realist ascendancy, various different realist tenets became deeply absorbed into both legal and political spheres – but in a manner that tended to pull in contrary directions. On one hand, the courts from the late 1930s incorporated much of Holmes's and Hale's critiques in a series of moves that led eventually to *Brown* v. *Board of Education*'s thorough reinterpretation of the fourteenth amendment, in 1954.[64] On the other hand, the New Deal at the same time signalled a push away from court oversight through the empowerment of expert administrative agencies initially subject to scant judicial controls. These tendencies respond to different aspects of the realist critique – and inform current notions of the rule of law in quite different ways.

The first outcome demonstrates that the courts need not inevitably pose an obstacle to a 'progressive' democratic will but may be, to the contrary, a potential fast-track to 'social justice'. This outcome might be thought, therefore, to provide evidence that the rule of law is in fact perfectly compatible with 'progressive' goals, by which I here mean the resort to policy in the interests of redistributing wealth or otherwise intervening in the economic realm. I shall return to this notion in a moment. However, two other readings of the rule of law can be gleaned from the Supreme Court 'switch'. It can be read as demonstrating that courts can never be insulated from 'policy', thereby problematising the very idea of the 'rule of law', at least as an ideal of legal autonomy. Or the *West Coast* and *Brown* rulings can be read

---

[62] Hale was cited as an authority in a number of relevant Supreme Court rulings. See Samuels (1973), 264–266.
[63] See Friedman (2000), 1013.
[64] *Brown v. Board of Education of Topeka*, 347 US 483 (1954). See the discussion of *Brown* running through Horwitz (1992).

as instantiating the collapse of the rule of law in the face of political pressure.

As it happened in practice, the second outcome – the turn to administrative agencies – tended to reinforce the latter reading, by frankly associating progressive goals with administrative discretion, and the rule of law with social conservativism. As noted earlier, the rule of law gained its specific normative traction in the United States at this time in the field of administrative law, where it functioned largely to slow down and moderate government-led initiatives generally framed in terms of the public welfare. Specifically, the rule of law became the banner beneath which court review of administrative action was entrenched. Together – and in combination with other historical contingencies, some of which I review below – these developments tended to further subsume core civil rights within the rule of law's ordinary normative penumbra and to associate the term with the 'pure' justice of the courts as against the interestedness of 'policy' or 'administration', which remains the locus of welfare. In short, the rule of law became critical to the vocabulary through which competing social and policy goals were discussed, where it represented a particular restraining perspective.

It is important to note that 'rule of law' did not signify the resulting 'compromise' or 'balance' (if indeed such a thing was ever achieved): to the contrary, 'rule of law' signified the opposing term, the counterweight, to the 'progressivism' of administrative agencies; it signified conservatism in opposition to that progressivism, a presumption in favour of caution and of non-intervention.

In the following section, I examine two sets of responses to this important period, with the aim of clarifying the principal post-realist rhetorical positions that have further driven a wedge between 'rule of law' and welfare as these two terms have developed. A first, dominant, response views the rule of law as posing a *fundamental* bar to state intervention in economic matters, even for reasons of public welfare; a second, residual, view seeks an answer to the rule of law-welfare dilemma through the judicial or constitutional entrenchment of a discrete set of 'social rights'.

The rule of law and welfare as mutually incompatible

The notion that the rule of law and social welfare are incompatible appears in two schools of thought that have otherwise little in common. One school comprises the 'critical legal studies' (CLS) movement, a group of American lawyers and law school professors who, from the mid-1970s, revived the realist tradition of legal critique. The other is the 'Austrian school' of economists, particularly Friedrich Hayek, whose 1944 *Road to Serfdom* and 1960 *Constitution of Liberty* became influential among economists, policy-makers and politicians from the late 1970s.[65] I will look at Hayek first, then CLS.

The rule of law according to Hayek

Hayek's writing was not a response to the realists, per se; rather it was a reaction against the general shift towards welfare in the 1930s, a broad shift in which the American realists comprised a representative and articulate strand. His target in *Road to Serfdom* was broad – the still new European welfare state and the New Deal, on one hand, the Soviet and National Socialist regimes, on the other. Hayek linked these vastly divergent systems together by identifying a position all shared, in his view – that the 'greater complexity' of modern society rendered inevitable a larger government role in steering the economy.[66] By contrast, Hayek argued, the greater the complexity of society, the less likely that it could be managed effectively, the better would be a 'technique which does not depend on conscious control'.[67]

Central to Hayek's work was a restatement of Dicey's rule of law; where Dicey had opposed the rule of law to a formal element of government, 'administration', Hayek opposed it to an activity, 'planning'.[68] For

---

[65] At her first party conference as leader of the Conservative Party in 1978, Margaret Thatcher reportedly held up Hayek's *Constitution of Liberty*: ' "This", she said sternly, "is what we believe", and banged Hayek down on the table': Ranelagh (1991), ix. Thatcher later wrote, 'For Dicey, writing in 1885, and for me reading him some seventy years later, the rule of law still had a very English, or at least Anglo-Saxon, feel to it. It was later, through Hayek's masterpieces *The Constitution of Liberty* and *Law, Legislation and Liberty* that I really came to think of this principle as having wider application': Thatcher (1995), 84–85. See also 50, 604; Thatcher (1993), 12–13, 618. On Ronald Reagan's embrace of Hayek, see Anderson (1988), 164.

[66] Hayek thus viewed the British welfare state, the New Deal, Soviet Communism and German Naziism as similar trends of the 1930s and 1940s: in each case the state was stepping beyond its legitimate sphere of action.

[67] Hayek (1994), 56.

[68] Hayek too claimed that Dicey had misunderstood Europe's 'administrative courts'. For him (basing his perspective on the *Rechtsstaat* structures of nineteenth-century Prussia and his native Austria) these were rule of law compliant, created specifically to guard against government discretion. See Hayek (1994), 80; Hayek (2006), 178–179.

Hayek, if collective action is channelled through the state, rather than through voluntary associations, some goals that everyone might agree on in principle, such as 'social justice', become problematic in practice, as there is no necessary or right way to achieve them.[69] Decisions about how best to achieve them must, as a result, be delegated to 'experts', whose choices will have distributive consequences.[70] The capacity to make decisions of this kind for a society in general 'presupposes ... the existence of a complete ethical code'.[71] But there is no such consensus, Hayek claims, and so decisions taken by 'experts' on behalf of others necessarily involve coercion.[72]

Market competition is the appropriate means for distributional decisions to be reached, in Hayek's view, for a number of reasons. First, markets are non-coercive – they are a voluntary meeting place for freely chosen exchange – and competition in markets involves freedom of individual choice rather than imposition from above. Moreover, markets produce and allocate goods and services more efficiently than governments, because each decision is made on the basis of the best possible information, which is already in the hands of each individual market participant. For any specific good, a vast amount of information is distilled and filtered by the market into a single clear signal: its price. By contrast, the collection and processing of the data needed for centralised production and allocation is expensive, inefficient, and, in any case, unachievable.[73] Centralised attempts to plan production, consumption and expenditure, to direct the availability or appropriate applications of labour, and to predict the investment needs, capital needs and energy needs of national industry must therefore fail.[74]

Hayek claimed not to be advocating laissez faire, which he characterised as 'leaving things just as they are'.[75] To the contrary, 'in order that competition should work beneficially, a carefully thought out legal framework is required'. The rule of law provides this framework. For Hayek, the rule of law means that 'government in all its actions is bound by rules fixed and announced beforehand – rules which make it possible to foresee with fair certainty how the authority will use its coercive powers in given circumstances and to plan one's individual affairs on

---

[69] Hayek (1994), 67–68.   [70] Hayek (1994), 72–75.   [71] Hayek (1994), 64.
[72] Hayek (1994), 78: 'planning leads to dictatorship because dictatorship is the most effective instrument of coercion and the enforcement of ideals and [is] as such essential if large-scale planning is to be possible.'
[73] Lal (2002), 128–129.   [74] See Lal (2002), 130–137.   [75] Hayek (1994), 41.

the basis of this knowledge.'[76] The rule of law is, in short, about the capacity of each individual to plan on his or her own behalf rather than have the state do it for them.[77] In a familiar formula, the rules should be general (that is applicable to everyone, not tailored to specific individuals or interests) and they should be promulgated for the long-term (that is, they should not alter with changing circumstances but, again, aim at general applicability). Like Weber, Hayek contrasts the 'formal' law of a rule of law system and the substantive justice of 'arbitrary government'.[78] Formal laws are 'merely instrumental', Hayek says, because, like signposts on the road, they tell people how to get to a variety of destinations, but do not tell people where to go. It is precisely this assumption of ignorance about individual goals, purposes and desires that distinguishes the rule of law, in Hayek's view, from state planning.[79]

Hayek identified welfare as a form of 'central planning' – that is, akin to predicting consumer needs and desires across entire populations – and charged that it was the form of planning most inimical to the rule of law:

[F]ormal equality before the law is in conflict, and in fact incompatible, with any activity of the government aiming at material or substantive equality of different people ... any policy aiming directly at a substantive ideal of distributive justice must lead to the destruction of the Rule of Law.[80]

The corollary is that the rule of law, so understood, will necessarily result in unequal distributions:

It cannot be denied that the Rule of Law produces economic inequality – all that can be claimed for it is that this inequality is not designed to affect particular people in a particular way.[81]

Critical legal studies

The realists had provided tools that challenged some of Hayek's basic assumptions. Hale in particular had queried the viability of the

---

[76] Hayek (1994), 80.
[77] In 1960, Hayek switched terms, to *dirigisme* 'since the word "planning" is so ambiguous': Hayek (2006), 203.
[78] Hayek (1994), 81: 'The distinction we have drawn before between the creation of a permanent framework of laws within which the productive activity is guided by individual decisions and the direction of economic activity by a central authority is thus really a particular case of the more general distinction between the Rule of Law and arbitrary government.'
[79] Hayek (1994), 83.   [80] Hayek (1994), 87-88.   [81] Hayek (1994), 88.

distinction between freedom and coercion upon which Hayek's writings depended.[82] According to Hale, echoing Weber, coercive state backing is *always* present in a modern state – including in the exercise of 'private rights' and civil liberties. The public monopoly on violence does not restrain *all* private coercion – to the contrary, as Hale remarks, it implicitly backs certain private actions and opposes others. Hale commented that 'much private power over others is in fact delegated by the state, and ... all of it is "sanctioned" in the sense of being permitted.'[83] Social relations, in this view, are inherently framed by force channelled through law. Individual liberty in any given sphere is simply the flipside of a state guarantee to use force to withhold the liberty of another from interfering in that sphere. On this reading, much talk about private freedom can be reframed as concerning private access to public coercion, practically the reverse of the 'freedom from' government indicated by Hayek.[84] On this view, a public coercive backdrop *enables* the market – where the law, far from acting merely as a 'signpost', actively structures the relative value of different skills and assets, magnifying the capacity of some and reducing others – with of course, the promise/threat of publicly backed coercion constantly in the background: 'the law endows some with rights that are more advantageous than those with which it endows others. It is with these unequal rights that men bargain and exert pressure on one another. These rights give birth to the unequal fruits of bargaining.'[85] Hale might counter Hayek thus: inequality, whether 'inevitable' or 'designed' (whatever the difference is) results not from rigorous legal proceduralism itself, but from substantive legal weightings.[86]

Although some critical legal scholars did develop critiques along these lines, the dominant CLS narrative that ultimately emerged about the rule of law was, instead, remarkably consonant with Hayek's own. A prominent CLS line reapplied the realist attack on 'formalism' to the contemporary notion of the rule of law. In this analysis, adherence to the rule of law disguises an existing policy bias embedded in law and legal interpretation. This line takes its impetus from realist concern that 'progressive' aims might be rendered unattainable by a too deep

---

[82] This paragraph summarises Hale (1923) and (1935). [83] Hale (1935), 199.
[84] Yet, as Hale notes, a dominant rhetorical tradition insistently privileges private freedom over public coercion, despite the conceptual inadequacy of this distinction: Hale (1923), 475–478.
[85] Hale (1943), 628. [86] See, for example, text at note 95 below.

entrenchment of property and 'freedom of contract' in precedential jurisprudence. The concern was that, under a governing judicial practice of formalist interpretation, existing property claims would necessarily predominate whenever they came into conflict with welfare. Morris Cohen, for example, compared the legal protections available to property owners in the early twentieth century to the sovereignty of a feudal medieval lord.[87] A formalist approach to adjudication was, on this argument, sufficient in itself to hold welfare goals at bay, regardless of the views or policy bias of judges.

In this CLS restatement, then, the rule of law is viewed as *itself* an ideological obstacle to social justice. Roberto Unger argued that 'the very "generality" and "uniformity" of the [rule of law] can ... secure, effectively and invisibly, established inequalities of wealth and power.'[88] Philippe Nonet and Philip Selznick claimed that the 'rule of law' was merely a stage on the way towards a more inclusive 'responsive law', that would benefit from the advances in the social sciences to achieve discretional legal application in line with principles of human dignity, supportive of fundamental social rights.[89] Morton Horwitz encapsulated the drawbacks associated with a rule of law principle according to this general view:

> [The rule of law] creates formal equality – a not inconsiderable virtue – but it *promotes* substantive inequality by creating a consciousness that radically separates law from politics, means from ends, processes from outcomes. By promoting procedural justice it enables the shrewd, the calculating and the wealthy to manipulate its forms to their own advantage. And it ratifies and legitimates an adversarial, competitive and atomistic conception of human relations.[90]

Such a stance precisely mirrors Hayek's claim that the rule of law is (i) necessarily inimical to welfare and (ii) necessarily embeds inequality. It assumes that rigorous proceduralism in law does, in fact, itself cause 'substantive inequality'. Welfare aims, for both Hayek and the critical scholars, must derail the rule of law, by removing redistributive decisions from private ordering (that is, taking them out of the realm of contract and the hands of judges) and/or removing formal equality in favour of a law responsive to social needs. Welfare is identified, for both,

---

[87] Cohen (1928), 12.
[88] Unger (1976), 55. (Unger's views have since changed). A similar view was laid out by Franz Neumann 40 years earlier: Neumann (1996), 115.
[89] Generally Nonet and Selznick (2001).   [90] Horwitz (1977), 566 (italics in original).

with a quasi-authoritarian *pater familias*. According to both, the rule of law and social welfare exist in an ultimately irresolvable conflict: the procedural safeguards of law serve to lock in an established economic status quo; welfare, by contrast, requires discretionary power specifically to right perceived economic and social 'wrongs'.[91] In both views, civil rights constitute protections *from* the state, social rights expand and so empower the state; the rule of law places a ring-fence around private interests to shield them from the state. By the 1980s, in short, the meaning of the terms 'rule of law' and 'administrative discretion' were no longer contested in and of themselves – rather they provided set terms for a more entrenched struggle: for all alike they represented respectively 'private' and 'public', 'individual' and 'community', 'right' and 'left', 'capitalism' and 'socialism'.[92]

Social rights within a rule of law framework

As noted above, an available realist lesson from *West Coast* through *Brown* was that articulations within an existing rule of law register need not always be incompatible with welfare claims. Even if the courts are not necessarily the best arbiters of welfare policy, they remain the privileged centre of legitimacy under orthodox rule of law conditions, as the final arbiters of legal interpretation.[93] At the same time, courts encourage the articulation of individual claims in the form of rights. It is unsurprising, then, that, faced with broad resistance to welfare articulated in the language of the rule of law, the same goals have been increasingly rearticulated in the language of *rights*. As a result much has subsequently hinged upon their 'justiciability'.

---

[91] See Horwitz (1998), 213–246.
[92] Perhaps unsurprisingly, fears of the 'death' of the rule of law in the United States resounded throughout the 1980s. Thus Theodore Lowi (1987), 57: '[T]here seems to be no interest group organized to support the rule of law. Academic lawyers consider it unrealistic. New political groups are more concerned with getting a favorable administrative environment. Conservative groups oppose national regulation for mainly economic reasons and actually favor broader administrative discretion at local levels, where the administrators in question are police, prosecutors and often protectors of the public order.'
[93] Having noted the courts' 'blindspot' when it came to the state's 'delegation' of its coercive power to private actors, Hale immediately added, the courts' myopia was probably a good thing, since the issue 'require[s] more comprehensive treatment than a court is capable of giving': Hale (1935), 199.

Again the realists showed the way. Much progressive realist critique aimed to show that small changes to the protections of property and the background rules governing contract, could have profound consequences for rights allocation. Hale, for example, writes:

> With different rules as to the assignment of property rights, particularly by way of inheritance or government grant, we could have just as strict protection of each person's property rights and just as little government interference with freedom of contract, but a very different pattern of economic relationships.[94]

The rulings from *West Coast* through *Brown* suggested how small doctrinal shifts could lead to significant distributional outcomes. The shape of a rights-based approach to welfare was intimated by Roscoe Pound in 1953, who foresaw the necessity of 'a reconciliation of planning with democratic principles of justice' that would require 'general legislative directives laying down principles of administrative action' to be 'enforceable by independent tribunals' and thus operate as 'controls of administrative discretion'.[95] Pound found that administrative agencies in the United States had not, by that time, generated an ethos of 'fairness' (the undeniably soft criterion by then common in the UK),[96] that might have respected individual freedom while yet pursuing 'social goals'. The work of achieving the correct 'balance' between 'planning' and 'freedom' presented, in Pound's view, a 'great opportunity' for the 'Anglo-American lawyer'.[97] Yet this approach never really caught on in the United States,[98] and it has since receded along with the public welfare structure itself.

CONCLUSION

This chapter has sought to give an account of the reception of the rule of law as a term of art in the twentieth century at the disciplinary

---

[94] Hale (1943), 628. See also Kennedy (1983), 96–104.   [95] Pound (1954), 33–34.
[96] Following *Local Government Board* v. *Arlidge* ([1915] AC 120) which established that administrative bodies do not have to follow court procedures but must operate strictly within their statutory mandate and are required to be 'fair'.
[97] The 1970 case of *Goldberg* v. *Kelly*, in William Simon's words, 'extended the rule of law to the welfare system', by recognising that the 'rule of law principle requires procedures that are practically accessible to the beneficiaries of the substantive rights': Simon (1990), 777.
[98] In 1981, the Supreme Court in *Schweiker* v. *Hansen* (450 US 785 (1981)) appeared to diminish the prospects of asserting welfare 'rights' meaningfully in US courts. See Simon (1990).

interface of law and economics. As in the rest of this Part, I have not set out to determine what the rule of law *is* – and so, whether it *is* compatible or not with welfare or 'social rights'. Indeed, the foregoing analysis would again tend to warn against confident declarations of the 'content' of the rule of law. A key realist insight, after all, concerned the inescapability of policy considerations in the performative act of adjudication. Hence the difficulty of choosing between the 'bias' of the *Lochner* court as against that of the *West Coast* court. The acknowledgement of indeterminacy of this kind tends to upset any fixed relation between the legal system and the possible policy objectives expressed through it. But it cannot support the conclusion that the mere neutral application of procedural norms must in itself reproduce inequality. The recognition of indeterminacy is both more and less destabilising than that. It is more so because *any* ruling or interpretation can be re-read as ideologically inflected – including, of course, those that lead to 'progressive' redistributive outcomes. But it is also less destabilising, because there is no *necessary* ideological content to any given interpretation; there is simply a need to recognise, as Holmes did, an unavoidable residual subjectivism in the act of interpretation. Realist indeterminism, in short, neither proscribes nor inscribes any given legal interpretation.

Nevertheless, as this chapter has shown, the rule of law register is in fact frequently burdened with expectations about the content of law or the appropriateness of the policies projected through it. A discursive genealogical process has tended to favour the protections of certain rights under the rule of law rubric: property, contract; the privileging of certain kinds of state action – 'signposting', economic non-intervention; and the privileging of certain approaches to judicial interpretation – formalism and, later, 'balancing' of rights. This framing is not absolute, and is not always on display: it is not, fundamentally, a demonstrated or assumed 'fact' about the rule of law; it is rather a contextual bound or penumbra that it carries in its train. Welfare is, as a result, not an easy subject to discuss in rule of law language and is habitually neglected. A rule of law register can thus prejudice against welfare without ever having to engage or attack it on the merits.

Even reframed as 'individual rights', however, welfare objectives are likely to encounter difficulty at the gate of the 'rule of law'. For one, the turn to a vocabulary of rights from one of welfare is onerous: it displaces its historical register of solidarity and collective action ('society') with the borrowed clothes of autonomy and liberty (the 'individual'). It must also contend with strong countervailing assumptions embedded in standard rule of law discourse. One is that the success of a given access-right to state coercion, in law and in the courts, depends upon the extent to which it can be *represented* as individual freedom rather than public coercion (hence Habermas's reframing of social rights as rights of autonomy).[99] It might reinforce an existing distributive status quo, given the embedded preference – rhetorical and illusory, perhaps, but forceful nevertheless – for a private sphere of inviolability over tolerance for public intervention.[100] Social rights claims struggle against a recalcitrant history to make their claim stick. The difficulty is not that 'social and economic' rights are incompatible with personal autonomy (on most accounts they are not). Nor is it that social rights require extensive state agency; so, on most accounts, do civil rights.[101] The difficulty is simply that social rights lack a firm historical foothold in the legal articulation of personal autonomy; they lack the buttressing fiction of the history of natural rights, and the more recent, but already entrenched, narrative of the rule of law – with its firm support for property protections against state action (from Magna Carta through the Glorious Revolution and on to Dicey and Hayek). Acceding to a rights language to express welfare aims ensures that the debate continues to centre precisely on a somewhat artificial construction of 'freedom' that Hale had exploded before Hayek exploited it.

All that said, there is little doubt that the prevailing understanding of the rule of law 'at home' – certainly among lawyers, certainly in Europe – does not preclude basic welfare provision, much less the many other attributes of modern administration. But, as we shall see in Part II, a narrower view overwhelmingly dominates in the field of rule of law promotion abroad. When the World Bank began to speak of the

---

[99] See Chapter 1, text at footnote 51.
[100] This argument has been made at length by Ran Hirschl (2004), 13, 15 in a review of countries with constitutional social rights: '[W]hereas their impact on advancing progressive notions of distributive justice is often overrated if not outright negligible, the constitutionalization of rights and the establishment of judicial review have a transformative effect on political discourse and the way fundamental moral and political controversies are articulated, framed and settled ... [This] framework serves to encourage the transfer to the courts [of] issues that ought, prima facie, to be resolved in the political sphere.'
[101] See generally, Holmes and Sunstein (1999).

rule of law in 1989, propelling this vocabulary into development policy, Hayek was the principal relevant authority (see Chapter 4 below). A flurry of policy documents swiftly tied the 'rule of law', so expressed, to a series of post-Hayekian developments in economics: public choice theory, the new institutional economists and, latterly, the 'law and economics' movement in the United States.[102] Briefly, a principal goal was to achieve increased economic growth by preventing governments from 'distorting' market signals.[103] Hayek, and the 'Austrian school' that followed him, concluded that the market function of channelling and filtering vast amounts of information into a single clear indicator – the price – was obstructed or distorted by state 'planning', itself a symptom of disrespect for 'the rule of law'. The Bank's exhortation to client countries to 'get the price right' (we shall look at this in Chapter 4) was further influenced by the writings of Ronald Coase, who suggested that the market's sorting and organising mechanisms relied on clear allocations of property rights and reliable enforcement mechanisms (both of which involve the state), and Douglass North, whose studies into economic history concluded, in the vocabulary of public choice theorists, that 'institutions matter'; that is, even a 'free' market has need of functional courts and enforcement (i.e. access to state coercion).[104]

In theory, the task then became one of building state institutions while ensuring their activity was restricted to 'policing' or 'signposting' the market. It was as though Weber had been quite forgotten and was only slowly (and partially) being remembered. Gradually, it was recalled that a rational disciplined bureaucracy is an essential element of a modern law-abiding state. But other corollaries of Weber's (and indeed the realist) analysis were still to be remembered: that encroaching bureaucratisation also characterises and drives private sector development, that increased public discipline does not therefore

---

[102] See Arrow (1951); Coase (1960); Friedman (2002); North (1990); Olson (1965); Krueger (1986); Lal (1983); Soto (1991).
[103] See, for example, Krueger (1986), 62–63: 'Once it is realised that individuals respond to incentives, and that "market failure" is the result of inappropriate incentives ... the separateness of development economics as a field largely disappears. Instead, it becomes an applied field, in which the tools and insights of labor economics, agricultural economics, international economics, public finance, and other fields are addressed to the special questions and policy issues that arise in the context of development.'
[104] See generally Coase (1960); North (1990).

equate with increased private freedom, and that growing rationalisation and formalisation produces counter-claims for special treatment, from both powerful and vulnerable groups. There was no scope for the expression, or even the recognition, of these stakes in the comparatively uncomplicated worldview of the new Hayekian rule of law register.

3 Sovereignty

With the expression 'government of laws not men', the rule of law promises the restraint of sovereign power. Its guarantee to bind government to law and keep tyranny at bay is arguably the rule of law's most compelling claim as a public good. Indeed, in the aftermath of September 11, 2001, discomfort with counter-terrorist measures 'at home' have been consistently articulated in rule of law language, while – as we shall see in Chapter 5 – similar measures undertaken abroad are described as 'rule of law promotion'.

In keeping with the overarching theme of Part I, I will not be seeking here to define the 'rule of law' as a known art of subjection of sovereignty to law; rather I will be inquiring into the historical and thematic shaping of this central element of the rule of law register. In a first section I will revisit the inaugural, but highly ambivalent, discussion of the 'sovereignty of law' in Aristotle's *Politics*, a treatise often said to lie at the origin of the modern rule of law. A second section will turn to a contemporary philosopher, Giorgio Agamben, who describes a relation between law and sovereignty that is rather mutually expansive than restraining.

ARISTOTLE: NOMARCHY (THE SOVEREIGNTY OF LAW)

The conception of the rule of law as prioritising or guaranteeing sovereign restraint is often traced back to a statement of Aristotle's, often translated as follows: 'The rule of law, it is said, is preferable to that of any individual.'[1] This supposed genealogical lineage to ancient

---

[1] *Politics*, 1287a19. Translation of *Politics* is from Saunders (1992), unless otherwise noted.

Greece, the 'original' democracy and font of western philosophy, has lent significant prestige to the rule of law as term of art, with Aristotle frequently referred to as its 'founding father'.[2] Yet Aristotle hardly seems a natural ally for today's rule of law crusaders, given his disdain for democracy, for commerce and for the judicial function, and his sustained endorsement of slavery in *Politics*.[3] In the following section I will investigate Aristotle's writings on the relation between law and government – which are rather more ambiguous than the standard vignette suggests – both to interrogate the claim to ancient lineage that Aristotle's paternity supposedly bestows, and to draw on Aristotle's nuanced analysis to further inform my own discussion of these issues.

First a little philology. Dicey's extended discussion in his *Introduction* essentially bestowed conceptual coherence on the term 'rule of law' in 1885; and whereas many of the principles he drew on were familiar, the term itself was not, having barely appeared in print before then.[4] That same year (coincidentally or not) his professor of classics at Oxford, Benjamin Jowett, published a translation of Aristotle's *Politics*, including the familiar line cited above ('the rule of law ... is preferable to that of any individual').[5] Translations of Aristotle through the twentieth century continued to reproduce a diversity of renderings for this particular expression,[6] until about the 1960s, when the term 'rule of law' became increasingly standard and, moreover, began to be applied liberally *throughout* the text of the *Politics* wherever Aristotle speaks of the primacy of law in government.[7]

This lack of uniformity, both within and between translations, is certainly due in part to the fact that 'rule of law' does not translate any Greek idiom. There is instead a range of relevant expressions, which together suggest a cluster of related principles. The Greek expression found in the sentence above is '*nomon archein*', which

---

[2] See, for example, Tamanaha (2004), 9; Orts (2001), 77; Johnson (2002), 43; Solum (1994), 120; generally Waldron (1990), Bentham (2002), 77–80, Thomas (2005).
[3] *Politics* 1278a3–9; see also Hansen (1989), 6, 16. On slavery, *Politics* 1249a9–1255b30.
[4] See Stewart (2004), 194.
[5] Jowett follows J. E. C. Welldon's 1883 translation, listed in the *OED* as the first extant modern use of the expression 'rule of law': 'The rule of law then ... is preferable to the rule of an individual citizen.'
[6] See Ellis (1928), Rackham (1944), Sinclair (1974).
[7] See Saunders (1992) revising Sinclair. See also Barker (1962), Robinson (1988), Everson (1996).

straightforwardly combines *nomos* (law) with *archē* (rule) into an unremarkable dictum ('that law should rule'), one that does not figure in lexicons of Greek political terminology and appears randomly in *Politics*, where the association between *nomos* and *archē* arises in a variety of permutations.[8] But Aristotle also uses other terms in comparable contexts, notably *kurios*: 'the laws, if rightly established, ought to be sovereign [*kurios*]'.[9] *Kurios* and *archē* are not synonymous. *Archē* can mean origin or beginning: *archōn* is a ruler, in the sense of premier, or, depending on the context, a magistrate (judge) or other public figure. *Kurios*, by contrast, is a private or domestic authority. Usually translated as lord, master, or sovereign, it signifies the head of a household, a woman's legal guardian, but also the power of ratification. Neither *archē* nor *kurios* is truly equivalent to 'sovereign' (derived from Latin *superanus*), with its special signification of an overarching *public* authority. The idea of an overarching public authority without equal was, according to Hannah Arendt, fundamentally alien to the Greeks, arising only with the Roman Empire.[10] There was, for example, no Greek equivalent of the Latin term *auctoritas*.[11]

A third expression Aristotle uses in this context is *kata nomon* – 'according to law'. Four types of king are identified that rule *kata nomon*.[12] But tyrants too can rule *kata nomon* if they have been duly elected and people consent willingly to their rule.[13] On this score, Aristotle says, democracy is even less law-constrained than the hereditary tyrannies of the barbarians and ancient Greeks.[14] Rather, he says, democracy is

---

[8] The following terminological discussion in this section (and throughout) owes much to the vast Classics library online at www.perseus.tufts.edu, Liddell and Scott (1940) and to the discussions in Rosler (2005), 112–115 and Barker (1962), lxiii–lxxvi.
[9] *Politics*, 1282b. See also *Politics*, 1281a; *Politics*, 1292a; *Politics*, 1291b–1292a; *Politics*, 1292b.
[10] Arendt (1993), 104.
[11] According to Mommsen cited in Arendt (1993), 289. But see Agamben (2005), 75.
[12] *Politics*, 1285a; *Politics*, 1292b.
[13] *Politics*, 1285a. Aristotle disapproves of lawful tyranny not so much because the ruler uses law to his sole advantage as because the ruled acquiesce against their own interests. Like 'natural slaves', they deserve no better than a master-slave state. Arendt writes: 'The difference between tyranny and authoritarianism is that…. even the most draconian authoritarian government is bound by laws. Its acts are tested by a code which was made either not by man at all, as in the case of the law of nature or God's Commandments or the Platonic ideas, or at least not by those actually in power. The source of authority in authoritarian government is always a force external and superior to its own power' (Arendt (1993), 97).
[14] *Politics*, 1292a27–31.

a form of unlawful tyranny, where the assembly 'makes its decrees (*psēphismata*) sovereign over the laws' merely to benefit a majority.¹⁵

Clearly Aristotle had something very specific in mind when he spoke of 'law'. What was it? As it happens, the term *nomos* was undergoing a profound transformation at the time Aristotle was writing, precisely because of the rise of democracy. Martin Ostwald traces the usage of *nomos* at this time from a descriptive term for 'the timeless, unchangeable pattern observable in religious usage, in the daily activities that people perform, and in the norms that determine or ought to determine their way of life' to an approximation of 'statute' in later Athenian democracy.¹⁶ It is, as we have seen, the latter usage that Aristotle disdains. He consistently elevates customary law (*ethos* – custom or habit) over the 'written law'; custom is 'more sovereign' than statute. Even the rule of man, he says, is 'less fallible' than rule by statute.¹⁷ Written laws exist to produce particular results and therefore cannot be trusted as a source of general law. The *nomoi* may nevertheless include codified customary law or legislation – if these frame, support and maintain the constitution (*politeia* – the polity in which an individual can live the good life).¹⁸

How is the *nomos* to 'rule'? This was a problem that, in Hannah Arendt's view, both Aristotle and Plato grappled with; each attempted to 'introduce something akin to authority into the public life of the Greek polis'.¹⁹ *Politics* includes some discussion of the appropriate model for the 'rule' that might be expected of law – public rule among free men versus domestic rule of the household.²⁰ The distinction matters: in the private domain, the realm of necessity, a man had absolute authority over women, children and slaves; the public realm was a space of equals, if only among heads of households. Rule in the public realm was consensual; rule in the private realm was domination.²¹ It is

---

[15] *Psēphisma* is literally a 'proposition carried by vote of the assembly', Liddell and Scott (1940), i.e. legislation. The *psēphismata* of the democratic assembly (*ekklesia*), in contrast to the general *nomoi*, are specific in nature, since the universal *nomoi* cannot cover every eventuality.
[16] Ostwald (1986), 85–93, 129–136.   [17] *Politics*, 1287b6-7.
[18] Aristotle mentions the reforms of the fifth-century Cleisthenes and the laws of Solon, the legendary lawgiver.
[19] Hannah Arendt writes: 'neither the Greek language nor the varied political experiences of Greek history show any knowledge of authority and the kind of rule it implies': Arendt (1993), 104, 120–124, 136.
[20] *Politics*, 1255b16–20.
[21] Compare Chapter 1 above, text at notes 61–62.

significant too that Aristotle avoids the term used by Plato in speaking of law as sovereign – *despotēs*, mastery over slaves – in favour of *kurios*, mastery over women.

Law's umpire

The problem of the 'rule of law', then – which, following the foregoing, might be better reframed as concerning the 'sovereignty of nomos' or perhaps, to coin a phrase, *nomarchy* – breaks down into two interrelated conundrums in *Politics*: source and agency. How is the law to be known at all? And who can be trusted to administer and preserve it? On both scores Aristotle considers 'man' deficient:

> [H]e who bids the law rule may be deemed to bid God and Reason alone rule, but he who bids man rule adds an element of the beast; for desire is a wild beast, and passion perverts the minds of rulers, even when they are the best of men. The law is reason unaffected by desire.[22]

These were concerns Plato had already raised in his *Laws*.[23] (Indeed, the passage of *Politics* that contains the ubiquitous citation – 'the rule of law, it is said, is preferable to that of any citizen' – appears to summarise Plato's discussion.[24]) In *Laws*, an Athenian advises would-be colonists on the best constitution for their future state. According to the Athenian, there are 'just a number of ways of running a state, all of which involve some people living in subjection to others like slaves, and the state is named after the ruling class in each case'.[25] Their model state, therefore, should be called after 'God [*theos*] who is the true ruler of rational

---

[22] *Politics*, 1287a (transl. Jowett). The last phrase is translated variously to give: 'intelligence without appetition [sic]' (Saunders); 'wisdom without desire' (Rackham); and 'reason free from passion' (Barker).

[23] Barker (1959), 184; generally Strauss (1975). Ernest Barker has drawn attention to the way in which Aristotle here as elsewhere 'systematises' Plato's thought.

[24] Taken as a whole, the passage to which these citations belong summarises – without obvious criticism or endorsement – the key arguments of Plato's *Laws*: the ideal lawgiver is God, law is equivalent to reason, men should be *servants* of the law. Translators habitually distance the passage from Aristotle's own views. Ernest Barker's translation, for example, gives: 'The rule of law is therefore preferable, *according to the view we are stating*, to that of a single citizen' (italics added). The passage is sprinkled with qualifiers – 'it is said'; 'according to some' – and does not present a single coherent view. One translator writes: 'the entire chapter is written rather confusingly ... ostensibly... it is an account of the arguments of certain anti-monarchical polemicists, and it is not clear precisely where Aristotle's own comments, if any, begin or end': Saunders (1992), 225.

[25] *Laws*, 713. Translation of *Laws* is by Saunders (1970), unless otherwise noted.

men'.²⁶ As Leo Strauss puts it, in *Laws* the rule of law *is* the rule of God.²⁷ Plato is unequivocal:

> Where law is subject to some other authority and has none of its own, the collapse of the state, in my view, is not far off; but if law is the master [despotēs] of the government and the government is its slave, then the situation is full of promise.²⁸

Plato offers the allegory of the shepherd and his sheep or the inhabitants of the mythic city of Kronus: the state should ideally be ruled by 'beings of a superior and more divine order – spirits':²⁹ the relation must be, as Hannah Arendt commented, one of 'glaring inequality'.³⁰ This would resolve the twin problems of source and agency in a single figure – the philosopher-king of the *Republic*, or, in *Laws*, a wise legislator (*nomothetēs*) or benevolent dictator: a man of surpassing virtue with 'absolute control' of the state.³¹ Aristotle does not endorse Plato's quasi-theocratic state, but he does return repeatedly to this figure of supreme authority, a man who himself will intuitively know, or even embody, the law:

> If there is one man ... of such superlative virtue [*aretē huperbolē*] that the capacity of statecraft and the virtue of all the rest are simply not to be compared ... we must reasonably regard such a one as a god among men. ... There is no law that embraces men of that calibre: they are themselves law. ... Men will not say that they ought to rule over him, for that would be like claiming to rule over Zeus ... It only remains therefore to let nature take its course: he will govern and all will obey him. Thus such men will be permanent kings in their states. ... There is therefore nothing for it but to obey such a man and accept him as sovereign, not in alternation but absolutely.³²

Absolute kingship of this kind is 'the first and most divine' constitution. However, Aristotle is unable finally to recommend the superlative man as the ideal ruler. There will always be the danger that, being human, he will allow passion to cloud reason, or – lacking equals

---

²⁶ *Laws*, 713 (trans. Bury).
²⁷ Strauss (1975), 58. Strauss describes *Laws* as a progress towards the unity of reason and law in God: Strauss (1975), 71. Saunders (1970), 170, n.15, suggests the term 'theocracy' for the state envisaged by Plato.
²⁸ *Laws*, 715d. Strauss notes that *Laws* opens with the single word *Theos*. Strauss (1975), 5.
²⁹ *Laws*, 713d.   ³⁰ Arendt (1993), 109.
³¹ *Laws*, 709.   ³² *Politics*, 1284a–b; 1288a32; 1289a; 1287b40.

with whom to discuss (for Aristotle repeatedly states that reason is reached through argument) – will reason poorly, or will become corrupted and act only in his own self-interest. Aristotle struggles with this figure, discarding him then circling back to him repeatedly, as though no other solution to the problem of authority presents itself.[33] Ultimately *Politics* does not resolve this aporia: godlike men cannot be found. Instead, for his 'middle' or 'mixed' constitution – part democracy, part oligarchy, in constant struggle – he recommends that the laws, once codified by 'the best men', be left untouched.[34] Leo Strauss glosses:

It would be absurd to hamper the free flow of wisdom with any regulations; hence rule of the wise must be absolute rule. [But since] it is extremely unlikely that the conditions required for the rule of the wise will ever be met, a wise legislator [must] frame a code which the citizen body, duly persuaded, freely adopts. That code, which is, as it were, the embodiment of wisdom, must be as little subject to alteration as possible; the rule of the law is to take the place of the rule of men, however wise.[35]

Aristotle does not, in this context, evaluate the Athenian lawgiving assembly or the complicated legislative arrangements that had evolved there.[36] Although lawgivers must frame the 'best laws', Aristotle never identifies how such a one is to be known or how they should identify these laws, indicating only that law is fundamentally beyond human creativity.[37] Also for this reason he suggests that the role of the judge should be as mechanical and non-discretionary as possible.[38] Rather, in *Politics*, Aristotle makes a stab himself at documenting the best laws (that is, the structure of the ideal polity), as Plato did before him in *Laws*.

In *Politics*, then, the *nomos* swings between two extreme poles, with humanity featuring as either pure source (a single man identical with the law) or pure agency (administrators of an immutable constant). In the process, the 'rule' or 'sovereignty' of law is recognised as dangerously tautological. Law cannot be dissociated from the ruler who must administer it, who must be human and therefore fallible. 'Law' (reason) exists in irresolvable tension with 'Man' (passion).

---

[33] See *Politics*, 1281a12; 1287b36; 1288a15–30; 1332b; 1292a7–38; 1295a25–1296b10.
[34] *Politics*, 1286b8–22; 1288b; 1292a7–38.   [35] Strauss (1971), 140–141.
[36] *Politics*, 1273b27–1274b28; 1301a19–1304b18. On contemporary Athens, see Ostwald (1986), 509–524. Aristotle discusses these in the descriptive *Constitution of Athens*.
[37] *Politics*, 1296b34.   [38] *Rhetoric*, 1354a–b.

The Aristotelian tradition

As noted above, Aristotle's 'rule of law' differs from current usage in stark and non-trivial ways. His ideal authority is, if anything, less accountable than contemporary Athenian democracy permitted.[39] This is reflected in his historical reception, which tends away from separation of powers. Jean Bodin would later ground his 'rights of sovereignty' on Aristotle's three 'parts of the state' (administrative, deliberative and adjudicative).[40] Montesquieu, on the other hand, finds an 'awkwardness' in Aristotle's treatment of constitutions: an inability to find appropriate criteria for evaluating monarchy and a general confusion of executive and judicial functions.[41]

The import of the latent undecideability in *Politics* between source and agent is perhaps best illustrated in the book's constitutional importance to medieval theories of kingship, where it consistently provides a justification for absolutism, albeit with the proviso (crucial in the firmly theocentric world of the middle ages) that monarchs channel God's law. The ambivalence in Aristotle's political vocabulary is elided in Aquinas's 1266 *On Kingship*, which largely repeats *Politics*, and in which the authority gap has simply disappeared: 'rule belongs to the king who is both God and man'.[42] Aristotle's superlative man resounds through Bracton's thirteenth-century characterisation of the King as *non sub homine sed sub deo et sub lege* ('not under man, but under God and under law') in his influential *On Laws and Customs*.[43] This complex construction makes possibly the late medieval conception of the 'king's two bodies' – a separate but conjoined 'body politic' and 'body natural', comprising a deathless king without imperfection who incorporates a physical persona at coronation, and who then exists *infra et supra legem*, both above and under the law.[44] The notion that the king represents God's law, then, has the king *both* as subject to higher law (God's law) *and* as subject to no law on

---

[39] Morrow (1993), 548; Ostwald (1986), 28–77; Hansen (1975). Hansen describes in detail the *nomos eisangeltikos*, a procedure in fourth-century Athens for impeaching generals and magistrates who do not follow the law. Morrow strives to show that Plato's *Laws* too includes a robust separation of powers. Morrow (1993), 548–551. See also Hansen (1989), 15–17.

[40] Bodin (2001), 47.   [41] Montesquieu (2004), 168–171.

[42] Aquinas (1988), 27.   [43] Nederman (1984), 61–67; Barker (1959), 502.

[44] Kantorowicz (1997), 7–23, 27, 149. The same notion is captured in the expression 'Le Roi est mort, Vive le Roi!'.

earth.⁴⁵ So in 1610, in his famous tussle with the jurist Edward Coke, it is the absolutist James I who calls on Aristotle as his authority.⁴⁶ Coke, by contrast, asserts limits on James's power by reference to a newer authority: that of the tradition of the 'ancient' English constitution.⁴⁷ In all cases, the 'law' that would 'rule' is natural law and/or God's law, it is decidedly not man-made law, however arrived at. The critical question then is not procedural (*how* is law made?), but, to use a Weberian category, charismatic (*who* is equipped to channel it?).

When Aristotle is called upon to lend authority to the contemporary rule of law, it thus turns out to be a largely aspirational, rather than truly genealogical, association. A newer rule of law 'tradition' seeks to derive prestige, longevity and momentum from this illustrious forefather, who provides an origin myth and a distinguished lineage, just as the Romans used the Greeks and the great nationalist narratives of the eighteenth and nineteenth centuries used ancient local stories of intrigue and rebellion.⁴⁸ A set of disparate yet cohering theses is extracted from their original historical context and put into the service of a felt contemporary need. Yet beyond this, an intriguing Athenian resonance echoes through contemporary rule of law promotion, in particular in its concern with state-building. Both Plato and Aristotle too are preoccupied with learning how to *construct* the ideal state. Aristotle extracts best practices from an empirical comparative survey of (reportedly – the text is incomplete) 158 constitutions of ancient Greece;⁴⁹ Plato imagines the colonial establishment of a new world from first principles. In each case, it is admitted that different states must vary, but in each there is also a central principle from which deviation is not acceptable – the sovereignty of law. Citizens are not assumed capable of discovering this principle or preserving it themselves. It is knowable through custom, practice, analysis and reason; it can be installed by force (Plato) or political manoeuvre (Aristotle) and maintained by pedagogical means, through the training and education of governors and of the citizenry.

---

⁴⁵ Remarkably, some recent rule of law articulations reinsert these claims into an evolutionary narrative, finding that the king, as representative of God's law on earth, prefigures a 'government of laws not men': Tamanaha (2004), 15–31; Reid (2004), 10–16.
⁴⁶ Zuckert (1994), 35–43. ⁴⁷ Zuckert (1994), 52.
⁴⁸ On the invention of tradition generally see Hobsbawm and Ranger (1992).
⁴⁹ See Everson (1996).

In its contemporary form, the mainstream rule of law claim appears to perform a classic confusion of 'is' and 'ought'. Where Aristotle describes the subjection of human sovereignty to law as a *desideratum*, desirable but potentially unachievable, the same claim is inverted in a recent rhetoric that posits a rule of law state as one in which the sovereign is *by definition* subjected to law. Such a claim is certainly unsupported by the argument of *Politics*, if only because the 'source' of law has shifted so drastically: the 'law' in question is no longer, even in principle, a timeless universal *nomos*. Rather, at least according to a theoretical consensus dominant since the mid-nineteenth century, the law is sourced in the will of the sovereign itself, a state of affairs which (democratic or not) is conceptually closer to Aristotle's feared tyranny than to his putative nomarchy. For how is the *nomos* to be sovereign if the actual sovereign is both source and agent of the law? The next section turns for guidance in this dilemma, and its relation to current rule of law language, to the contemporary philosophy of Giorgio Agamben.

AGAMBEN: THE LAW OF SOVEREIGNTY

As we saw, the notion of law as 'sovereign' was modelled, in *Politics*, on the private authority of a household head, property owner, or lord, *kurios* (or *kyrios*): a domestic authority dependent upon an inhering relation of unquestionable dominance, rather than one of coercion or persuasion.[50] The task was to bring private authority into the public realm (to achieve 'domination' of the state as Weber would later put it). The parent-child relation is the leitmotif for the authoritative political relation imagined by both Aristotle and Plato; the figure who might make law sovereign is like a father to the people.[51] The *identity* of law-god-sovereign-father is thus prefigured by Aristotle, not as the answer to the rule of law riddle, but as the irresolvable riddle itself. The Roman emperor, the Pope, the medieval monarch and the renaissance prince each provided an attempted response to this riddle. The modern rule of law appears as a contemporary response, one which attempts to take 'man' out of the equation altogether, at least in principle, fusing

---

[50] Arendt (1993), 91–93. See Just (1989), 23; Schaps (1979), 48–88. *Kyrios* is close to Latin *dominus*, or Lord, the title taken by Roman Emperors from Caligula on. *Kyrios* itself provides the etymological root of that other great medieval authority, the 'Church' (from *kyriakē oikia*, the Lord's house).
[51] *Politics*, 1332b12; 1332b26; *Laws*, 690; 714.

source and agency together in the law itself, as a locus combining tradition, discipline and authority. Does it succeed? To finish this chapter, and with it this Part, I will examine a contemporary doubter, Giorgio Agamben.

Sovereign exception

Agamben's 1998 study of states of 'exception' (or 'emergency') does not champion the rule of law as a counterbalance to executive discretion.[52] His inquiry concerns rather the systemic and ongoing expansion of law itself into every area of lived existence, and the coextensive capacity of legal regimes to embed zones of lawlessness within themselves. Agamben's problem might be restated as thematising the rise of a notional rule of law that is forever tied to a 'state of exception' as its other terrifying face. Agamben tracks two schools of thought on the legality of the exception. The first considers it 'an integral part of positive law because the necessity that grounds it is an autonomous source of law'.[53] This approach is today codified through the notion of derogation.[54] Treaties and constitutional provisions allowing for a (usually) limited suspension of certain rights, (usually) for limited periods of time have long been viewed as a 'concession' to the 'inevitability' of exceptional state measures during emergencies.[55] As such, derogation has been called 'one of the greatest achievements of contemporary international law'.[56] The mechanism creates, in Tom Hickman's words, 'a space between fundamental rights and the rule of law', amounting in effect to a 'double-layered constitutional system'.[57]

Yet the underlying implication – that necessity is, as Agamben puts it, an 'autonomous source' of law – has the potential to thoroughly destabilise any available notion of 'rule of law', for it would appear to mean that any 'limits' on derogation, codified or not, must remain arbitrary or provisional at best, there being no way of predicting in advance the full jurisgenerative reach of such an autonomous source. In such a case, we need never expect that law would be regularly or entirely

---

[52] For a more comprehensive account, see my essay, Humphreys (2006).
[53] Agamben (2005), 23.
[54] See, for example, the International Covenant on Civil and Political Rights (ICCPR; entered into force 1976), Art. 4; European Convention on Human Rights (ECHR; entered into force 1953), Art. 15; American Convention on Human Rights (ACHR; entered into force 1978), Art. 27.
[55] Hickman (2005), 657.   [56] Klein (1993), 134.   [57] Hickman (2005), 659.

'suspended' in the name of emergency, but rather that its application may be unstable, patchy or uneven, subject to diverse and complex subrules or *leges speciales* that vary according to the kind of relation construed between the sovereign and the individual (a situation Agamben describes in an earlier treatise, *Homo Sacer*, in which the treatment of 'terror suspects' and 'illegal immigrants' are examples of special, violent sovereign regimes).[58]

Agamben's second school understands the state of exception to be 'essentially extrajuridical', something prior to or other than law. For these writers, legalised states of exception do little more than recognise the practical limits of constitutional dominion: it is neither possible nor desirable to control executive action in times of emergency.[59] In Alexander Hamilton's words, '[t]he circumstances that endanger the safety of nations are infinite; and for this reason no constitutional shackles can wisely be imposed on the power to which the care of it is committed.'[60] A space must instead be opened for untrammelled state action in order to restore the constitutional order. Attempts to impose legal controls in such cases risk infecting ordinary rights protections with extraordinary elasticity because 'necessity knows no law'.

Agamben rejects both these approaches – 'the state of exception is neither internal nor external to the juridical order … the problem of defining it concerns precisely a threshold, or a zone of indifference, where inside and outside do not exclude each other but rather blur with one another.'[61] He traces the 'legal' state of exception back to the dawn of the modern state – the 1789 decree of the French constituent assembly, distinguishing a 'state of peace' from a 'state of siege' in which 'all the functions entrusted to the civilian authority for maintaining order and internal policing pass to the military commander, who exercises them under his exclusive responsibility.' The state of exception is gradually emancipated to cope with a range of sources of anxiety even in peacetime – natural disasters and famines as well as political disturbance.

Agamben makes two observations: first, 'the modern state of exception is a creation of the democratic-revolutionary tradition and not the absolutist one'; second, the state of exception almost immediately assumes a 'fictitious' or 'political' character, whereby a vocabulary of war is maintained metaphorically to justify recourse to extensive

---

[58] Agamben (1998).   [59] See, for example, Gross (2003), 1021–1024.
[60] Madison *et al.* (1987), 185.   [61] Agamben (2005), 23, 5.

executive powers. These points are demonstrated in Agamben's brief history of the state of exception in Europe and the United States – the invocation of emergency powers to deal with financial crises in Germany in 1923 and France in 1925, 1935 and 1937, union strikes in Britain, earthquakes in Italy, and, in the US, their invocation by Presidents Lincoln – to provide a basis for the abolition of slavery – and Roosevelt, to ensure passage of the New Deal in 1933.[62] Roosevelt's words are illustrative: 'I shall ask the Congress for the one remaining instrument to meet the crisis – broad Executive power to wage war against the emergency, as great as the power that would be given to me if we were in fact invaded by a foreign foe.'[63]

Sovereign extension

Agamben proposes that the state of exception is a constitutive element of any modern legal system, 'the preliminary condition for any definition of the relation that binds and at the same time abandons the living being to the law'.[64] The 'state of exception' answers an extreme instance of a general problem: how can a law that is formal, rational and general cope with the uniqueness and unpredictability of the irreducibly non-legal: 'life itself'. The state of exception is a recognition of law's outside, but it simultaneously prompts attempts to encompass that very outside within the law. Agamben finds this 'long battle over anomie' at the heart of Carl Schmitt's well-known definition of the sovereign as 'he who decides on the exception'.[65] In the moment of exception, the sovereign unites the legal and non-legal by means of an extra-legal decision 'having the force of law'. In this way, according to Schmitt, a legal system (or 'juridical order', in Agamben's language) is preserved even when (elements of) the law itself are suspended – indeed, extra-legal acts are themselves justified in the name of preserving the law or of establishing it (the latter is called 'constituent power'). An archetypal moment is, again, the immediate aftermath of the French revolution, but, in principle, wherever an old order is overthrown and a new one introduced (as, for example, recently in Iraq[66]) this moment is accompanied by an effective suspension of law, during which period only the sovereign decides on the existence and content

---

[62] Agamben (2005), 13–22.   [63] Cited in Agamben (2005), 22.
[64] Agamben (2005), 33–34.   [65] Schmitt (2006), 5.
[66] See, for a good discussion, Bhuta (2006).

of law. Or, to put it another way, following Schmitt, whoever decides on what law applies in such a context is, by definition, sovereign.[67] Sovereignty, in this reading, is not merely a legal construct, it is rather an inescapable demonstrated fact of political autonomy that draws legal recognition to itself. Autonomy defines sovereignty: to generate law is to be sovereign.[68]

According to Agamben, however, the state of exception cannot be 'annexed' to the law but must be understood instead as law's 'other': 'the state of exception is not a "state of law" but a space without law', a 'zone of anomie'.[69] It is not equivalent to a dictatorship, where laws continue to be made and applied, but a condition in which law tends rather to be voided of content. Agamben places Schmitt's paradigm in the context of a short 1921 essay by Walter Benjamin, 'Critique of Violence', in which Benjamin speaks of a 'pure' or 'divine' violence that is neither subject to nor preserving of law, and that may appear in a revolutionary flash.[70] Schmitt's state of exception, on this reading, is a legal edifice constructed to domesticate or eliminate non-state ('pure') violence.[71] In sum, Benjamin and Schmitt agree that anomic violence exists – but they treat it differently, either as the violence that 'neither makes nor preserves law, but deposes it' (Benjamin) or as the last frontier to be annexed by the sovereign by means of the state of exception (Schmitt). On this reading, the rule of law is an ideological bulwark against revolutionary violence itself – the rule of law absorbs and expresses the admonishment that protest is legitimate only when it remains within the law, that revolution is by definition illegitimate – a move that signals the end of a certain vision of political change common since the seventeenth century.[72] The legal category of the emergency, in this reading, is used to extend or complete law's reach

---

[67] Cf. Chapter 5 below. [68] See Bataille (1990). [69] Agamben (2005), 50–53.
[70] Benjamin (1986), 300. Benjamin opposes this 'divine violence' to the 'mythical violence' he associates with the machinery of the state: 'if mythical violence is lawmaking, divine violence is law-destroying': Benjamin (1986), 297.
[71] Benjamin (1969), 254–255.
[72] This issue is alive in international law, where, as of early 2010, progress on a Comprehensive Convention on International Terrorism has been stalled since 2002 on the issue of whether or not the convention should cover the acts of non-state actors in non-international conflicts (liberation or revolutionary struggles), the question being whether the latter, once effectively free of the law of the state, are subject to international humanitarian law or indeed to any law at all. The Terrorism Convention would seek to make them criminals, subject therefore to an overarching, apparently burgeoning, sovereign in the international sphere.

to encompass moments of revolutionary or anomic violence, which then become absorbed within and channelled through the sovereign. Agamben concludes that the state of exception is 'a *fictio iuris* par excellence which claims to maintain the law in its very suspension', but produces instead a violence that has 'shed every relation to law'.[73] It is not that revolutionary violence has disappeared; it is that it becomes harnassed to the sovereign arsenal, still sublimely violent, but no longer revolutionary.

Agamben implicitly opposes the positive law of the sovereign to a 'natural law' of 'life itself'. Positive law can never be assumed merely to state or codify natural law, but constantly threatens instead to displace, dethrone, colonise or absorb it, just as Aristotle feared that democratic *psēphismata* would depose *nomos*.

It is useful to follow Agamben as he extends this general argument forward, toward a theory of the relation between law and 'life itself'. Throughout *State of Exception*, Agamben reframes the relation between law and the court process as isomorphic to the Saussurean linguistic paradigm of *langue* and *parole*.[74] Just as any specific instance of speech (*parole*) requires the background existence of a self-sufficient universe of language, but reaches beyond that background to touch specific non-linguistic phenomena, so in a court trial, judges apply laws to specific cases that depend for their effect on the existence of a self-referential legal system. The application of law by judges is, like speech, a performative act that applies the general to the particular. But just as speech acts can fail to connect with actual phenomena, circulating instead in the abstract self-referentiality of *langue*, similarly, law can be applied without any necessary recognition of a reality outside its own abstract realm. And just as structural linguists once feared that the repetitive abstraction of language can make the physical world inaccessible per se, trapping us within a self-referential 'prisonhouse of language',[75] so too law can shape and limit our conception of the politically possible, rendering a world beyond sovereign domination unthinkable or unattainable. Attempts like Schmitt's to legislate for anomie – that is, to create closure within the legal system – amount to a denial of the existence of an extra-legal reality.

This suggestion of Agamben's amounts to an ominous assessment of the tendency, indeed the necessity, within derogation regimes, to

---

[73] Agamben (2005), 59.   [74] Agamben (2005), 36–40, 60, 70.
[75] The position is stated perhaps most clearly in Frederic Jameson's book of that name.

ceaselessly redefine and parse the legality of each given act taken in defence of the 'life of the state'. How many hours in a 'stress position' amounts to torture?[76] What combination of curfew, electronic tagging, and non-stop surveillance amounts to a 'deprivation of liberty', or as Baroness Hale put it in a 2007 House of Lords case, 'What does it *mean* to be deprived of one's liberty?'[77] Each definition and redefinition of the emergency powers of the state, and each blurring of emergency and non-emergency powers, by bringing certain of those acts within the law, further extends 'law's empire' over 'life itself'.

Sovereign expansion

Agamben grounds much of his thesis in the work of Michel Foucault.[78] Foucault, for his part, contrasts sovereign power with 'disciplinary' power, that is the systemic and self-reproducing normalisation of multiple mechanisms of self-control. Disciplinary power, as he describes it, functions through a variety of widespread techniques: the inculcation of disciplinary habits through close-quarter training, the increasing replication of surveillance mechanisms throughout public and private spaces, and the systematic generation of information, even in advance of specific uses or needs for it (the maxim that 'what measures matters').[79] Disciplinary techniques are not, according to Foucault, a means by which government wields control over populations; rather disciplinary power is already inherent in the habits of the inhabitants of a modern state. It is self-reproducing, with government as a primary, but not sole, vehicle, an analysis in line with Weber's description of and caution concerning the self-extension of modern bureaucracy.

According to Foucault, disciplinary power is 'impossible to describe in the terminology of the theory of sovereignty' and 'ought by rights have led to the disappearance of the whole grand juridical edifice created by

---

[76] See, in this regard the memorandum from US Secretary of Defense Donald H. Rumsfeld to General James T. Hill outlining 24 permitted interrogation techniques, dated April 16, 2003 (online at: www.gwu.edu/~nsarchiv/NSAEBB/NSAEBB127/03.04.16.pdf).

[77] *Secretary of State for the Home Department (Appellant) v. JJ and others (FC) (Respondents)* [2007] UKHL 45, para. 57. Emphasis in the original.

[78] Agamben grounds his own account of *homo sacer* – the man stripped of rights under a burgeoning sovereign – in Foucault's notion of biopolitics, a power grounded not in territory but in control over persons: Foucault (1981), 140–144. For a critique of Agamben's claim to 'complete' Foucault's biopolitics, see Fitzpatrick (2001).

[79] Foucault (2000), 211.

that theory'.⁸⁰ This has not happened, according to Foucault, because, on one hand, the language of sovereignty and right has provided an indispensable means of expressing an ideology that counterposes an (illusory) individual autonomy against restrained government, and because, on the other, the continued dominance of a legalist language of *right* tends to conceal the actual centrality of disciplinary power to modern government. Nevertheless, the techniques of disciplinary power 'invade the area of right' such that 'the procedures of normalisation come to be ever more constantly engaged in the colonisation of those of law'.⁸¹ The point is not that 'sovereignty' and 'disciplinary power' are opposites or inassimilable modes of the organisation of power; it is rather that an expansive disciplinary mode prevails, but is obscured, to a degree, by the language of sovereignty, with its assumptions of clear (and fixed) rights mediated through formal procedures. It is in this sense that the rule of law, by which is here meant, again, the ideology of explicit legal checks on public action to guarantee private freedom, cannot be understood *merely* as a restraint on state coercive capacity; for it also and equally extends that capacity.⁸²

Returning, then, to the notion of a rule of law that is a 'government of laws not men', two possible interpretations are available. On one hand, the rule of law, in this sense, is integral to a 'sovereign order' as the system of rights that defines and allocates mutual freedoms and restraints. On the other, as a vehicle of disciplinary power, it is the means through which a uniformity of objectives and norms is efficiently normalised and transmitted. These two roles exist in some tension, if not outright contradiction, with one another. Agamben's (and Foucault's) concern, however, is that the second continually drives out the first in practice, while retaining it in principle. Thus 'freedom' and 'right' become the terms through which disciplinary modes are advanced and constantly refined and attenuated. In either case, the rule of law might still be viewed as a locus of sovereign restraint – but only if 'restraint' is assumed less as a form of disabling and rather to refer to a set of predefined procedures and techniques – which do

---

⁸⁰ Foucault (1980), 105.   ⁸¹ Foucault (1980), 107.
⁸² By the same token, to draw a connection between Agamben's expansive sovereignty and Foucault's self-reproducing disciplinary power, as I have done here, is to assimilate two supposed opposites. If they are not, in fact, opposites, it is to Agamben's misappropriation of Foucault that we must look for explanation (see Fitzpatrick (2001), 94–97). My interest here is in the points of convergence between these two thinkers, however, not their many points of divergence.

not in themselves guarantee that certain areas of practice or kinds of behaviour are necessarily off-limits. 'Restraint', from this perspective, is in fact *enabling*, because it creates possibilities for actions and outcomes, not only by channelling behaviour and expectations into activities that *themselves* provide legitimacy for the resulting actions and outcomes, but also by harnessing and directing corporate (public or private) energy and force towards the accomplishment of specific goals.[83]

CONCLUSION

We saw, in discussing Aristotle, two problems that arise for a 'government of laws not men': source and agency – how the relevant 'law' is to be known, and how it is to be made to 'rule'. A reading of Agamben found that states of necessity or emergency – the paradigmatic scenarios by which the bind of law is loosened in order that apparently unlawful government action will remain formally lawful – cannot simply be regarded as zones of vacillation between lawlessness and lawfulness. The exception is a paradigmatic example of the positive law colonising, or being deployed to colonise, 'life itself', extending sovereign (per Agamben) or disciplinary (Foucault) power into previously a-legal ('autonomous') zones, positive law deposing, as it were, the *nomos*. For the modern polity, these views reflect Hannah Arendt's suggestion elsewhere that the separation of powers might be viewed not merely as a system of checks, but also as 'a kind of mechanism built into the very heart of government, through which new power is constantly generated'.[84] On such a view it would be incorrect to associate sovereignty with the executive alone, as has traditionally been the case in the rule of law register. Bodin's three 'parts' of the sovereign may provide a better guide to a situation in which law, and its authority and capacity to underpin 'rule', provides a generative as much as a constraining mechanism for sovereign power. Sovereignty in this sense would always be expansive, in much the way Agamben describes.

Foucault further nuances such an interpretation. Sovereignty is not so much the driver of expansion as a cover for it. The extension of law into new areas of life is itself the expression of an expanding disciplinary power – and so it is increasingly expressed through disciplinary

---

[83] See Loughlin (2004), 137, citing Stephen Holmes.   [84] Arendt (1990), 151–152.

forms. Indeed, the contrast between Agamben and Foucault maps onto the earlier contrast in Chapter 2 between Dicey and Weber. Like Dicey, Agamben understands expansive legalism as a challenge to 'freedom', a challenge that is itself expressed in the language of autonomy and rights, whose basis cannot be statutory but instead escapes the ordinary positive law, residing behind or before it. Weber and, in a different register, Foucault, by contrast, understand the language of freedom and right as largely obscuring a quite different function of law in modern society: the enhancement of discipline, productivity, formality and rationality. The rule of law ideal, then – and in particular its steady deployment in opposition to an equally idealised (or demonised) 'sovereignty' – encourages and foregrounds legal and judicial contests and decisions as concerning freedom and right rather than in terms of the truer stakes of modern law (in the view of Weber and Foucault): discipline and efficiency.

The remainder of this book will turn to the continuing advance of law as a mechanism for enhanced discipline and efficiency – these being the *explicit* objectives of both colonial law and rule of law promotion, the subjects respectively of the following Interlude and Part II.

***

At the outset, I noted that my purpose in Part I was to sketch the parameters of this term of art: to determine what falls within its ordinary purview and what without. Falling within, as we saw in Chapter 2, are themes of personal inviolability, property protection, private economic ordering and the notion of limited government through constitutional protections. Falling without are welfare, equity, substantive justice, social and economic rights and, at the extreme, revolutionary or violent reordering.

But it is also possible, following our overview, to identify a number of broader effects of the deployment of rule of law language. Primary among them is the degree to which the articulation of phenomena in rule of law terms has the effect of reordering the relevant normative and terminological landscape. A discourse of private right and freedom moves to the foreground, an appreciation of public powers and authority to the background. Assertions of formal equality under the law move to the foreground; questions of substantive and economic inequalities to the background. Notions of sovereignty and restraint move to the foreground; corollary ideas about discipline and expansionary authority move to the background. The state (now decoupled from the 'nation') moves to the foreground; international or transnational loci of authority and power (public or private) move to the background. In each case, while one set of issues appears to be of central importance, another set is diminished in importance or obscured altogether. The effect of the parameters of the rule of law is, in short, to set terms of debate of the social, political and economic.

Interlude
Precursors: colonial legal intervention

Whereas the language of contemporary rule of law promotion is new, its form – the active mobilisation of law across borders for economic and political ends – is not. Among the many precedents for the enactment of legal interventions abroad undertaken (at least nominally) to benefit the host country, one obvious and immediate precursor to contemporary rule of law reform is late colonialism.[1]

The colonial encounter illuminates contemporary rule of law promotion for two reasons. First, interventions from that time laid the foundations for much current rule of law reform. While this is true in much of the world, the African context is especially illustrative since the foundations were laid relatively late, distilling previous lessons and introducing political and legal structures in a comparatively systematic and thorough fashion. Today's reformers thus work with materials – the basic administrative apparatus of the state – largely constructed by and inherited from the colonial authorities.

---

[1] This section is based on readings of the following texts: Alexandrowicz (1973); Allott (1957a), (1957b), (1960a), (1960b), (1962), (1963); Anderson (1963); Ansprenger (1989); Benton (2002); Betts (1998); Boisdon (1956); Buell (1928); Chanock (1991), (1998); Colson (1981); Comaroff and Roberts (1981); Crocker (1949); Davidson (1992); Delavignette (1968); Duignan and Gann (1975) (and contributions therein); Elias (1961), (1962), (1967); Förster et al. (1988) (and contributions therein); Gann and Duignan (1981) (and contributions therein); Gavin and Betley (1973); Gifford and Louis (1971) (and contributions therein); Hailey (1938), (1957), (1979); Hall (1894); Hertslet (1896); Hooker (1975); Ilegbune (1976); Jèze (1896); Lindley (1926); Lugard (1893), (1926); Mamdani (1996); Mann and Roberts (1991); Manning (1998); Meek (1946); Milner (1969); Nicolson (1969); Nys (1903a–c); Omosini (1972); Pakenham (1991); Palley (1966); Perham (1937); Phillips (1989); Read (1969); Reeves (1909); Roberts-Wray (1960), (1966); Rolin-Jaequemyns (1889); Sarbah (1910); Sarr and Roberts (1991); Suret-Canale (1971); Twiss (1883), (1884a), (1884b); Westlake (1894).

Second, the techniques and practices associated with contemporary rule of law endeavours share many family resemblances with the colonial era. This is not to say that modern rule of law reform simply or simplistically repeats or continues colonial legal transplantations. To the contrary, very much has changed. The rule of law vocabulary is itself, as I shall suggest in Part II below, adopted in part precisely to highlight discontinuities (some very real, others rather more aspirational) with the colonial past. However, even a cursory comparison of rule of law promotion with the justificatory language of late colonial law reform, on one hand, and with its core areas of intervention, on the other, finds a broad and unmistakeable pattern of shared themes and conceptions – governance, development, humanitarianism, free trade – that cannot easily be dismissed as coincidental, much less as a wholesale reversal of policy.

The practice of colonial law export nurtured habits of thought and practice in home countries with regard to the optimal use and reception of law in countries characterised as 'primitive' and in need of 'development'. Many of these habits and practices are retained in modern rule of law reform even if much of the language and working methods have changed. Moreover, both colonial legal endeavours and contemporary rule of law reform reflect broader trends in the ways in which law's relation to policy is viewed. Superficially, the evolution of colonial law through the late nineteenth and early twentieth centuries reflects that of the rule of law at home, described in Chapter 2 – from 'formalist' laissez faire to what has been called the 'rise of the social' (with the announced 'welfare' of Africans ever more central as nationalist movements began to threaten from the end of World War Two), peaking in the immediate post-colonial years (as it also peaked in Europe), only to revert again to a nominal formalism from the early 1980s.[2]

Law was constitutive in, and responsive to, the construction of sub-Saharan African statehood in at least three ways.[3] First, international law provided the formal basis for intervention with a view to furthering goals of interest to the international community of the time (the 'Powers') in general. Second, under the aegis of European powers, steps were taken internally within the colonies to mobilise law to the actual

---

[2] For a broad account, see Duncan Kennedy's 'Three Globalizations of Law and Legal Thought, 1850–2000': Kennedy (2006c).
[3] Numerous state-like entities existed throughout the subcontinent prior to the 'scramble for Africa'. All succumbed to the newer order with the exceptions of Liberia, already colonised by freed African-American slaves under United States patronage, and Abyssinia (modern Ethiopia), a Christian kingdom largely left alone.

achievement of these ends. Third, throughout these endeavours, both an objective and a condition of success was the inculcation of 'legalism' in the relevant populations. I will look at each of these areas of legal intervention in turn.

International law: the legal context for the promise of administration

International law, the web of essentially contractual and conventional agreements existing between the 'Powers' in the late nineteenth century, evolved rapidly to incorporate Africa, the only significant landmass still mostly outside the international legal and political order at the time. New international priorities were set by agreement: freedom of trade, movement and religion, economic development and humanitarianism.[4] All of these placed sovereignty at the centre of a newly mappable international legal order, premised on formal territorial controls that were increasingly seamless. The fact that, after the agreement of the Berlin Act in 1885, effective control of territories was not necessary for the assertion of legislative and executive jurisdiction in the new colonies – the 'promise' of future 'government' was sufficient – altered the landscape of intervention dramatically from a colonial past that had been more circumspect.

An initial exercise of jurisdiction was foreseen to ensure that the 'promise' would translate into effective administration. And this in turn was motivated, at international level (at conferences in Berlin in 1885 and Brussels in 1890) by reference to three key emergent principles of international relations at this time – free trade, humanitarianism and development. All three were initially affirmed in relation to the enormous territory at the heart of the African continent that was to become Belgian Congo. The first concern of the 'family of nations', the latter day 'international community', was to ensure that the immense Congo river basin remained open for trade and free passage regardless of which European entity controlled it (it notoriously fell to the International Association of the Congo, a supposedly humanitarian organisation created, owned and run for profit by King Leopold II of Belgium). Freedom of trade is the subject of Articles I through V of the General Act of Berlin of 1885, which further guarantees free movement for the Powers on the Congo river.[5]

---

[4] See Anghie (1999).
[5] Thus Article IV: 'Merchandise imported into these regions shall remain free from import and transit dues'; Article V: 'No Power which exercises or shall exercise

A second motivating trope was humanitarian in nature: abolition of the slave trade.[6] This was the main topic of the 1890 Brussels conference: humanitarian exigency provided the basis for the further extension of a now preponderant 'foreign jurisdiction'.[7] Inter alia, the Brussels Act required '[p]rogressive organisation of the administrative, judicial, religious, and military services in the African territories'.[8] As the international lawyer W. E. Hall explained at the time, 'Evidently … acts of the nature contemplated and prescribed compel extensive interference with the internal sovereignty of a community, and involve a commensurate assumption of sovereignty by the protecting state.'[9] Thus the framing, at international level, of the colonial endeavour itself ensured a highly goal-oriented application of law and legal tools in the colonies.

Shortly afterwards the new European 'empires' began to take steps to 'develop the estates', to use the words of the zealous British Minister for the Colonies, Joseph Chamberlain.[10] And so we find three familiar principles driving colonial intervention in Africa by the end of the nineteenth century: free trade, humanitarianism and development.

---

sovereign rights in the abovementioned regions shall be allowed to grant therein a monopoly or favour of any kind in matters of trade.' See Miers (1988), 336, citing Pauncefote to Granville, November 7, 1884, and Minute by Hill, January 7, 1885.

[6] General Act of Berlin, Article IX: '[T]he Powers which do or shall exercise sovereign rights or influence in the territories forming the Conventional basin of the Congo declare that these territories may not serve as a market or means of transit for the trade in slaves …. Each of the Powers binds itself to employ all the means at its disposal for putting an end to this trade and for punishing those who engage in it.'

[7] The evolution of the Foreign Jurisdiction Act from 1843 to 1890 – initially intended to allow consular jurisdiction in foreign lands 'in the same and as ample a manner as if Her Majesty had acquired that jurisdiction by the cession or conquest of territory' (Foreign Jurisdiction Act 1843, Article 1) – mapped the changing needs of the era. Identical language appears in the Foreign Jurisdiction Act 1890; see Article 2 (1843; Article 3, 1890): 'Every act and thing done in pursuance of any jurisdiction of Her Majesty in a foreign country shall be as valid as if it had been done according to the local law then in force in that country.'

[8] General Act of Brussels Relative to the African Slave Trade, signed on July 2, 1890, Article 1.

[9] Hall (1894), 207.

[10] On August 22, 1895, Chamberlain told the House of Commons: 'I regard many of our colonies as being in the condition of undeveloped estates which can never be developed without Imperial assistance … I shall be prepared to … submit to this House any case which may occur in which, by the judicious investment of British money, those estates which belong to the British Crown may be developed for the benefit of their populations and for the benefit of the greater population which is outside.' Cited in Nicolson (1969), 17.

'Developing the estates': state-building in colonial Africa

The second moment of legal evolution in the African colonial encounter resides in the interventions themselves: internally, within these new and 'inchoate' territories, an administrative apparatus and, increasingly with time, the very social order itself were to be created and nurtured by legal means.[11] Law was projected onto territories conceived of as near blank screens. The legal techniques brought to bear upon colonial possessions aimed everywhere at facilitating and encouraging productive activity in the colonies.[12] A concomitant rearticulation of existing normative arrangements involving the restructuring and subordination, and in some cases invention, of 'customary' laws and institutions,[13] sought to avoid the feared dissolution of societal and institutional structures under the transformative pressures of colonisation.[14] The European powers moved quickly to reshape and redirect

---

[11] John Westlake described colonial title to territories acquired in the post-Berlin era as 'inchoate': Westlake (1894), 165. 'Government', Westlake noted, was 'the international test of civilisation.' And what was government? That political organization 'under the protection of which ['people of the European race'] may carry on the complex life to which they have been accustomed in their homes'. Ibid., 141.

[12] Thus John Kasson, the American delegate at Berlin: 'It is not sufficient for all our merchants to enjoy equally the right of buying the oil, gums and ivory of the [Congo], and to sell goods of an equivalent value which the natives receive in exchange. It would only be a paltry outlet for the vast productive forces of Europe and America. Productive labour must be seriously encouraged in the African territories, and the means of the inhabitants of acquiring the products of civilized nations be thus increased.' Annex No. 14 to Protocol No. 5 to the Berlin General Act, cited in Gavin and Betley (1973), 220.

Compare Lugard almost forty years later (Lugard (1926), 61): 'The democracies of to-day proclaim the right to work, and the satisfaction of that claim is impossible without the raw materials of the tropics on the one hand and their markets on the other. Increased production is more than ever necessary now, to enable England to pay the debts she incurred in preserving the liberties of the world [i.e. in World War I].'

[13] Mamdani writes (1996; 51): 'The bearer of custom was said to be the tribe. Defined and marked as a member of a tribe, the colonized African was more fully encapsulated in customarily governed relations than any predecessor or, for that matter, any contemporary in the colonized world. The more custom was enforced, the more the tribe was restructured and conserved as a more or less self-contained community – autonomous but not independent – as it never had been before. Encased by custom, frozen into so many tribes, each under the fist of its own Native Authority, the subject population was, as it were, containerized.'

[14] In response to the visible dissolution of communities in many parts of colonised Africa, attributed in particular to the widespread reliance on migrant and wage labour, Lugard wrote in 1926: '[H]ere, then, in my view, lies our present task in Africa. It becomes impossible to maintain the old order – the urgent need is for adaptation to the new – to build up a tribal authority with a recognised and legal

existing institutions ('chiefs' and 'native courts') towards the overarching colonial needs of enforcing peace, encouraging productive labour, mapping and managing the use of land, and facilitating trade and distribution within and across regions.[15]

The language of 'humanitarianism' itself characterised the polity of the new territories in such a way as to facilitate sweeping reorganisation. The 'native' was sharply distinguished from the (European) 'foreigner' and subjected to a different regime, both under international arrangements and increasingly uniformly, under the territorial arrangements of the different Powers.[16] Protection of the 'rights' of foreigners required the maintenance of judicial systems to protect private interests in commercial transactions and private property against the colonial state. Acts taken in furtherance of the 'preservation' of the 'native tribes', on the other hand, was left, as John Westlake (a leading international lawyer at the time) succinctly remarked, 'to the conscience of the state to which sovereignty is awarded'.[17] Both conceptually and legally, the colonial polity was always a dual state, with different rules applying for Europeans and for Africans.[18] Within their own spheres, commercial and civil transactions were governed by different laws: 'modern' law in modern courts for Europeans, 'customary' law applied through 'native courts' for Africans.[19] With time,

---

standing, which may avert social chaos': Lugard (1926), 217. See Chanock (1998), 12-13.

[15] Mamdani (1996), 8, 53-59, 74; Delavignette (1968), 85; Lugard (1926), 210, 539-564. On courts in British Africa see generally Allott (1960a), (1962); Elias (1962a), (1962b), (1967); Roberts-Wray (1966); in French Africa, Poirier (1956); Delavignette (1968); Manning (1998); Sarr and Roberts (1991); Lydon (2006), 8-9.

[16] The General Act of Berlin (1885), Article VI reads: 'All the Powers exercising sovereign rights or influence in the aforesaid territories bind themselves to watch over the preservation of the native tribes, and to care for the improvement of the conditions of their moral and material well-being.' Compare Article V: 'Foreigners, without distinction, shall enjoy protection of their persons and property, as well as the right of acquiring and transferring movable and immovable possessions; and national rights and treatment in the exercise of their professions.'

[17] Westlake (1894), 143-144.

[18] Anghie (2000), especially 275-290; Anghie, (2002).

[19] Delavignette (1968), 85 writes: 'In French West Africa there are magistrates who administer justice according to the French legal Code, and others who administer local Customary law; and those who come under their jurisdiction, like the magistrates themselves, are divided into two different classes. The Code applies to French citizens, whatever their colour; Customary law applies to native subjects, whatever their rank. And it is laid down that Customary law is applicable in so far as it is not contrary to the principles of civilization.'

the proper management and integration of native courts into a wider administration became an increasingly central component of colonial rule:

[I]f our aim be to raise the mass of the people of Africa to a higher plane of civilization, and to devote thought to those matters which ... most intimately affect their daily life and happiness, there are few [matters] of greater importance than the constitution of the native courts ... [I]t is only by the patient training of such a court that better tribunals can be evolved and real progress achieved. The close supervision of such a court, and the personal education of its members, will involve more labour and personal effort than direct administration, but it is surely worth the effort [if] the native courts are to become an integral part of the machinery of Government ...[20]

For purposes of land and labour requisition in particular, 'chiefs' – authority figures who were initially identified, but later increasingly appointed – acted as mediators between the two spheres: head of the native court, tax-collector, local authority. The chief may have, as Mahmood Mamdani put it recently, 'fused in a single person all moments of power: judicial, legislative, executive and administrative',[21] but he was nevertheless subject to a regime of colonial tutelage that endeavoured to inculcate the behaviour proper to governing, to eliminate corruption, and to encourage support for commercial endeavour. In effect, as a principal colonial architect, Frederick Lugard wrote at the time, the colonial officer *trains in* the chief:[22]

The task of educating them in the duties of a ruler becomes more than ever insistent, of inculcating a sense of responsibility; of convincing their intelligence of the advantages which accrue from the material prosperity of the peasantry, from free labour and initiative; of the necessity of delegating powers to trusted subordinates; of the evils of favouritism and bribery; of the importance of education, especially for the ruling class, and for the filling of lucrative posts under government; of the benefits of sanitation, vaccination, and isolation of infection in checking mortality; and finally, of impressing upon them how greatly they may benefit their country by personal interest in such matters, and by the application of labour-saving devices and of scientific methods in agriculture.

---

[20] Lugard (1926), 547–549.
[21] Mamdani (1996), 23. In Lugard's words, '[t]he first step ... is to endeavour to find a man of influence as chief, and to group under him as many villages or districts as possible.' Lugard, 'Report on the Amalgamation of Northern and Southern Nigeria' (1919), cited in Mamdani (1996), 53.
[22] Lugard (1926), 210–211.

Land, labour and crime were the three key relevant areas of intervention. With slavery and various other forms of compulsory labour gradually phased out (the institution of slavery, as opposed to the trade in slaves, was finally illegalised only in the 1920s, and requisitioning of labour only after the Second World War), tax and land policies became proxies for labour organisation.[23] Head and hut taxes forced Africans into the workplace.[24] As to the laws governing land policy, Malcolm Hailey, in a 1938 survey of colonial administrative arrangements throughout the African continent conducted with a view to determining next steps, summed up as follows:[25]

[At first], policy was determined primarily by the physical character and economic possibilities of the territory coming under control ... [A]reas held to be suitable for European settlement were everywhere liable to expropriation for that purpose and those which ... were not so suitable, were liable to be subjected to various systems of control designed to place Europeans in a position to exploit their production. It was only at a later stage that the recognition of native rights became a question of policy, and even at this stage the acknowledgement of such rights seems to have owed much to economic considerations, such as the possible benefit to the colonial power of encouraging peasant production as compared with plantations or other forms of capitalist enterprise.

Several approaches were tried. In the Gold Coast (modern Ghana), an initial attempt at applying formal principles of individual title and exchange was abandoned, having led to a barrage of conflicting and apparently irresolvable claims, on one hand, while, on the other, failing to create the kinds of conditions necessary for putting productive land to good use.[26] In modern Uganda, a large portion of the land was subdivided equally among members of the Buganda ethnic group, but that too created unexpected problems, effectively installing a landlord class who, by ratcheting up rents, pushed wages beyond what European employers were willing to pay local labour.[27] In the East and South African settler countries, much of the land was set aside as 'reservations',

---

[23] Phillips (1989), 28-33, 39-42; Gann and Duignan (1981), 241; Buell (1928), vol. 1, 1043-1044; Lugard (1926), 390-391.
[24] Phillips (1989), 43, 56; Hailey (1938), 594-596, 608.   [25] Hailey (1938), 713.
[26] See Phillips (1989), 61, 69-70. See generally Omosini (1972); Ilegbune (1976); Agbosu (1983); Wilson (1975); Nworah (1972); West African Land Committee Draft report 1916, Martin (1988), Elias (1962), Fenske (2006).
[27] Mamdani (1996), 142; Hailey (1938), 762 refers to the landlords as 'rent-farmers'; Lugard (1926), 237; Hogendorn (1975), 312-315.

to which native Africans, if they did not already live there, were moved from the more mineral-rich territories, and over which they could not exercise title. Ultimately, the approach adopted by Lugard in the Nigerian protectorates from 1900 was standardised: native land was acquired by the Crown, initially only where assignable as 'waste' or forest, but later comprising any 'public land'; it was then designated 'customary' and placed outside of the formal market: 'native title' and 'native rights' applied to transactions among Africans along 'customary' lines, unless the Crown exercised prerogative. Land cultivation and labour management was then left to these supposedly traditional structures, with chiefs fulfilling the role of middleman between the new 'peasants', the state and private traders. ('Native rights', as Hailey used the term, were 'communal' rights, effectively unenforceable in colonial courts.[28])

At the same time, an inexorable drive to homogenise the polity took place through the criminal law. The novelty and reach of substantive law, punishment regimes, and procedures and fora of enforcement softened or superseded existing notions of transgression and redirected the moral order everywhere towards a putative relation between individual and state. The jurisdictional cover of 'customary law' for normative transgression was set, under all colonial regimes, quite minimally, with appeals to colonial courts readily available. Although local notions of criminality, studied and articulated by anthropologists and gradually wending through the appeal courts, were not ignored, the shift was everywhere away from restorative and towards retributive notions of justice. The entire burden of sentencing policy tended to re-education, designed not merely to punish and deter, but also to advertise the very novelty and non-negotiability of the new normative order. Criminal sanctions were hedged by the ubiquitous 'repugnancy' clause[29] and increasingly Europeanised; hence imprisonment and fines, both virtually unknown in precolonial days other than in Islamic West Africa, were introduced across the continent.[30]

---

[28] '[I]ndividual ownership of land is quite foreign to native ideas. Land belongs to the community, the village and the family, never to the individual': *Amodu Tijani* v. *Secretary, Southern Nigeria* [1921] 2 AC 399, at 404, citing Rayner CJ, Report on Land Tenure in West Africa (1898). See also *In Re Southern Rhodesia Land* [1919] AC 211.

[29] Customary sanctions were permitted as long as they were not 'repugnant' to 'equity', 'humanity', 'good conscience', 'public morality' or '*ordre publique*', applied by colonial appeal courts according to the conscience of the administrator.

[30] Today commentators generally agree that, in the words of James Read, Africans 'knew no prisons': Read (1969), 103. Read adds: 'Forms of physical restraint were

Colonial criminal techniques did, of course, aim to protect the colonial order and the specific interests of Europeans, particularly settlers and employers, against recalcitrant or hostile Africans – and to maintain law and order in the face of a feared dissolution of society under colonial pressure. Yet they were also strategic interventions into the body politic, reconstructing morality, sociality and behavioural patterns. Eventually, entire bodies of criminal law were transposed wholesale across the continent. In British Africa a set of near identical Penal and Criminal Procedure Codes were applied in each country, the former deriving, directly or indirectly, from an 1878 draft based on the common law, the latter from an 1877 Gold Coast ordinance.[31] In no other area of law was British policy so conspicuously uniform across its possessions.

Throughout Africa, then, the move to remake social, political and economic conditions despite a minimal cultural interface attempted to position law as *constitutive of*, rather than responsive to, the political and economic. Although progress was often ad hoc and uncertain, the proliferation of ordinances, decrees and *arrêtés*, the structuring of court hierarchies and police administration, were all viewed not merely as instruments of policy, but also as the *premise* for policy-making. With 'native' political mechanisms generally annexed to the project, colonial law became an instrument for an attempted redefinition of the political, social and economic landscapes in their entirety. Although this ran quite counter to the idealised notions of the rule of law being promulgated at this time back home, there are remarkable structural similarities between the principles at work then and those we find in rule of law today. The notable elements of colonial rule

used, but normally only to detain an offender pending [sanctioning processes] and even then rarely; certainly detention in itself does not appear to have been regarded as a punishment.'

[31] See Morris (1974), Seidman (1966), 324–326. The Penal Code was drafted by Sir Fitzjames Stephen, and first adopted with slight amendments in Queensland, Australia. That code was subsequently introduced in Northern Nigeria in 1904 and extended to Southern Nigeria in 1916. A second code deriving from the Queensland, Code – the Cyprus Code of 1928 – was transposed to the Gambia, and Britain's East African colonies in the 1930s. A third derivation of the Stephen Code was adopted in St Lucia in 1889 and transposed thence to Gold Coast. Another source was the Indian Penal Code. This had been applied in East Africa and British Sudan between 1899 and 1907, and was transposed to Northern Nigeria in 1959, with certain elements of Muslim law added. The 1877 Gold Coast Criminal Procedure Ordinance, from which all subsequent procedure codes derived, was drafted by D. F. Chalmers on the basis of rules and procedures drawn up for Hong Kong and Fiji.

from the perspective of the present investigation is that it embodies an approach that seeks to use the law as a structuring device to signpost and guide the free acts and transactions of ordinary people according to their own lights, which is governed by trained and monitored overseers and containerised within the parameters of a strict moral criminal code.

Rising into law: the injection of legalism

The third broad contribution of colonial legal intervention is the effort to inject *legalism* – a characteristic, albeit insufficient, rule of law attribute, as we saw in Chapter 1 – into systems represented as lacking law: as 'primitive', despotic, or at best 'customary'. Where existing African political associations were conceived of as communal or tribal, the work of introducing the state repositioned existing structures of rule-following or adjudication as inferior, uncivilised, or 'repugnant', and sought to replace them with a law conceived of as state-centric, impersonal, rational and modern. The extension of state authority to new jurisdictional boundaries, together with the repositioning of these new jurisdictions within an interstate system under an international framework, required that the subjects of colonialism become subject to the impersonal law of the state – and thereby achieve membership of the polity. The 'native' was to be lifted into law. The overall objective was stated explicitly by successive governors from each of the European colonising powers. Here, for example, is French administrator Adolphe Messimy:

> We must make countries out of these empty spaces, we must make nations out of these agglomerations of half-civilized or barbarian peoples, we must organise new states, give them traditions, morals, a political and social organisation.[32]

For the individuals concerned, the process appeared to expect their self-reconstitution as subjects of these new states, a process that has been called *interpellation*: the colonial individual was to be 'hailed' as a concrete subject of an actual legal system, and thus required to reposition him- or herself as such.[33]

In effect, this process continued through decolonisation: constitutions initially written in the colonial metropoles entrenched the imperatives of self-government, economic development and rights

---

[32] Adolphe Messimy, *Notre oeuvre coloniale*, cited in Cohen (1971), 77.
[33] The term is Louis Althusser's. See Althusser (2001), 117–120.

protections, with a view to stabilising the transformations of recent decades and fixing the order embedded therein. And today we frequently find transnational rule of law reform at work in these same areas of law in the same territories, reshaping and aligning customary and communal law with 'constitutional' rights, formalising and enforcing property rights, extending state coercive capacity, or clarifying the appropriate limits of public intervention into processes and arenas that are increasingly conceived of as private.

That transnational law reform today promotes similar objectives to those of the colonial era indicates the continuing importance, as a matter of international policy, then and now, of building functional self-administering economically viable entities capable of dealing in a global environment. Far from rupturing with this larger goal, the aftermath of decolonisation has seen a consistent, if not inevitable, stage in its furthering. Rule of law literature acknowledges no explicit continuity with the colonial past, however, tending to place its origins in the post-independence era, triggered rather by the venality (corruption, conflict), incompetence (in failed or fragile states) or irrationality (outdated laws or economic models) of the post-colonial present, as we will see in Part II. Ultimately, the story told here resituates colonialism and its aftermath within a larger narrative with which it has always comported easily: modernisation. This is a story of statehood as the condition of modern political association – as artificial as it is inescapable – and law as the durable expression of statehood. But the same story additionally redirects attention from the state to the trans-statal that it assumes and sustains.

Thus, the narrative according to which contemporary rule of law reform 'started' with the 'law and development movement' in the late 1960s is inaccurate.[34] The 'law and development' techniques adopted by US agencies in the 1960s to promote systemic reform of the legal systems of (mainly) Latin American countries were not US innovations; even at the time they merely complemented an equivalent body of work being undertaken by former European colonial powers, both bilaterally and in concert. Legal education, the main 'law and development' technique had long been supported by the British in particular, both by funding law schools abroad and providing scholarships

---

[34] This assumption of rupture is deeply embedded in US accounts of the period; appearing not only in the writings of proponents, but also of critics; see for comparison contributions to Carothers (2006) and to Trubek and Santos (2006).

for Indian, Sri Lankan and African students of law at Oxbridge and SOAS, well before the US began to do something similar with scholarships for Latin Americans in the 1960s. Aid funding for courthouses and other infrastructure, 'technical assistance' in legal drafting, and police and military training, were likewise generally available from the colonial powers during and after decolonisation. And, of course, all of this work relied upon the legal constructions of the colonial regimes themselves: the fragile administrations of the post-colonial states.

PART II · THEATRE OF THE RULE OF LAW

4 Market

The present chapter focuses on market promotion in the strategic planning and project work of the United States Agency for International Development (USAID) and the World Bank. Having laid out the broad canvas of work undertaken by each agency, the chapter asks what benefits might be expected from applying a rule of law vocabulary, with its long-standing connotations of non-instrumentality and legal autonomy, to the explicitly goal-oriented work of economic development. In doing so it draws in particular on the Bank's explications of the rationale for its rule of law work.

US FOREIGN ASSISTANCE

About a decade after the end of the first US foray into legal intervention abroad, the 'law and development movement' of the 1960s–70s, the current wave of US rule of law work began, in the mid-1980s, with USAID-funded 'administration of justice' programmes in Central America and the Caribbean.[1] The earliest programmes were created to gain bipartisan congressional support for the Reagan administration's military policies in Latin America. They focused in the main on criminal justice and law enforcement. In some countries (notably El Salvador), they were accompanied by targeted efforts to reshape the legal infrastructure in support of a market economy, through trade liberalisation, privatisation, and the nurturing of a business sector.[2]

---

[1] On the first administration of justice programmes, see Carothers (1991); Orr (1996); Pastor (1992); Zagaris (1988); Blair and Hansen (1994); MSI (2002); USAID FY1986; USAID FY1986(III); USAID AOJ (1985).

[2] Orr (1996), 292.

These two prongs of what are now called 'rule of law assistance' – 'democracy promotion' and 'market promotion' – have traditionally been kept apart, both within the US policy-making apparatus and 'in the field'.[3] Today, USAID's 'rule of law' programme category refers to law reform support for 'democracy and governance', as distinct from 'economic growth', but in its wider strategic and project documentation, the term is strongly associated with each of these domains as well as support for 'peace and security' abroad (the subject of Chapter 5). A 1994 evaluation of USAID's early rule of law assistance reached a conclusion that appears to have been applied since:

> USAID can serve effectively in a pioneering or trailblazing capacity in the ROL [sic] field, acting as an experimental, risk-taking innovator to develop approaches that can, when proved, be taken over by multilateral donors willing to make substantial investments in this sector.[4]

There is no easy way to assess the full extent of US rule of law funding today, in part because foreign assistance sources, channels and processes are myriad and complex, in part because there are no fixed criteria to determine what qualifies as a rule of law project, and in part because the term carries such talismanic significance today that many agencies and departments use it aspiringly, to attract funding or credibility that might not otherwise be forthcoming.[5] The primary agents of this work are the Department of State ('State') and USAID, both aligned under the Secretary of State. In 2007, USAID's total budget was $13.5 billion; the total foreign assistance budget of USAID and State combined was $34.9 billion.[6] A significant fraction of this money is devoted, under the

---

[3] Orr (1996), 429: '[M]arket promotion and democracy promotion efforts in practice have been kept quite separate, both by the [host] governments and its US backers. In part this has been due to a fear that democratic-induced demands might "contaminate" the market model by undermining necessary fiscal discipline. On the US side this has been exacerbated by the almost total separation of the offices and people dealing with political development programs and those dealing with economic development programs.' On the shift to 'rule of law' terminology, see Blair and Hansen (1994), 10; GAO (1999b), 1, at note 1.

[4] Blair and Hansen (1994), 6.

[5] In the only attempt to date to assess total rule of law assistance, in 1999, the General Accounting Office identified 35 relevant agencies, but noted they 'did not have an agreed-upon definition of what constitutes rule of law activities'. See GAO (1999a), 2. The GAO therefore 'relied on each agency to provide us information for those activities it considered rule of law'. See also GAO (1999b), 3–4. For a recent attempt at tracking the totality of 'rule of law' assistance in Iraq, see OIG (2005).

[6] USAID DOS (FY2007), 3, 39. See also USAID FY2006, 218.

rule of law rubric, to state-building and security sector reform abroad, much of it channelled through the Department of Justice (DOJ) and supplemented by funding from the Department of Defense (DOD).[7] A separate source of funding is the Millennium Challenge Corporation (MCC), created in 2003 to manage the Millennium Challenge Account, which also funds projects with rule of law components both directly and through USAID.

US rule of law aid flows through multiple channels, including multilateral donors such as the World Bank and the agencies of the UN, and a large subgroup of US private and quasi-governmental organisations, who in turn supplement public funding with private sources. That list includes the National Endowment for Democracy (NED), which reports to Congress, and the quasi-governmental International Foundation for Electoral Systems (IFES), United States Institute for Peace (USIP) and International Rescue Committee (IRC) – each of which feature a robust rule of law focus.[8] USAID contracts most of its rule of law work out to private contractors, who in turn outsource to multinational and local consultants and NGOs.[9] Some of these are prominent rule of law actors in their own right. The American Bar Association, for example, houses a sizeable Rule of Law Initiative, that adds its own financing to USAID (and other) sponsorship to conduct rule of law 'indexing' in 20 countries and 'training' of judicial and other legal professionals.[10] Each agency also works with local private and NGO partners on site in host countries. In short, US-funded rule of law reform is today a global business, with all the complexity and interdependence of buyers, sellers and competing products that entails. As each agency mixes and matches different sources and uses different accounting methods and terminology, budgets cannot easily be parsed for consistent 'rule of law' components clearly distinct from other elements and objectives.

---

[7] See below, Chapter 5.
[8] The International Rescue Committee is the State Department's single largest recipient of funds.
[9] These include inter alia the American Bar Association (ABA), Chemonics International, DPK Consulting, Freedom House, Management Systems International, Democracy International Inc., Booz Allen Hamilton. See USAID DCHA (2007), 17–18, 27–28; USAID DCHA (2008), 24, 26.
[10] Concentrating in East Europe, ABA builds judicial associations and assesses judicial independence, prosecutorial 'reform' and legal professionalism. ABA also spearheads a 'global rule of law movement' through high level symposia. See online at: www.abanet.org/rol. For its most recent symposium, the World Justice Forum, see www.abanet.org/wjp.

The world according to USAID

Today, USAID divides all the world into five types of country: Restrictive, Rebuilding, Developing, Transforming and 'Sustaining Partnership'; these are the five rungs on the ladder of 'transformational diplomacy' which US support aims to help its 130 or so aid-recipient countries to climb.[11] That aid in turn serves five strategic objectives: Peace and Security; Governing Justly and Democratically; Economic Growth, Agriculture and Trade; Investing in People; and Humanitarian Assistance – which are further broken down into 24 programme areas, 96 programme elements, and 407 programme sub-elements ('no more, no less').[12] If we imagine each of these 407 programme sub-elements along one axis of a matrix, and each of the 130-odd recipient countries on the other axis the result is the 'F matrix' that today guides State and USAID policy.[13] A dollar amount in each cell of the matrix describes US commitments in a given country under a particular programme sub-element; in every case, the amount must be justified in terms of how it will help the recipient country 'transform' such that it will move up to the next rung.

'Rule of law and human rights' is one of the 24 programme areas; it is located under the strategic objective 'governing justly and democratically' (GJD), alongside three other programmes ('civil society', 'governance' and 'political competition'). Yet this modest position understates the centrality of rule of law reform in US foreign assistance. Apart from a frequently stated relevance within *each* of the other three GJD programmes, it is also central to two other of the five strategic objectives: Economic Growth, Agriculture and Trade (EGAT) and Peace and Security (a new objective as of 2007).[14] Indeed, the term is ubiquitous in project and agency documentation relating to each of these latter objectives, and also in the key strategy papers that determine

---

[11] This paragraph relies in particular on Hyman (2008). Gerry Hyman was a long-time head of the USAID's Office of Democracy and Governance, from where GJD programmes are run. This configuration of foreign assistance is comparatively new, although it builds on a model loosely in place since 1992; it is liable to rapid change.
[12] Hyman (2008), 7.
[13] A template of the matrix can be found online at: www.state.gov/documents/organization/115470.pdf, with an explanation provided at: www.state.gov/f/c23053.htm.
[14] The associations are made separately, in two consecutive USAID strategy papers. See USAID (2002a), 54–72 (on the rule of law and economic growth); USAID DOS (2007), 12–17 (on the rule of law and peace and security).

overarching foreign policy – the National Security Strategies of 2002 and 2006, the White Paper of 2004, the USAID strategy paper of 2002 and the joint USAID/State Strategic Plan for 2007–2012.[15] Below I sketch the core activities carried out under GJD and EGAT.

The main areas of USAID's law-related market promotion work are laid out on the agency's website:[16]

1. General Commercial Law Framework, including (i) legal reform of the most fundamental kind (ii) revision of national constitutions, commercial codes, and contract law, (iii) omnibus commercial law projects, and (iv) crosscutting initiatives (e.g. information technology and e-commerce);
2. Business Environment (business entry and exit, company law and bankruptcy, accounting rules, corporate governance, employment laws, including labor and pension benefits, and tax laws);
3. Financial Services (business finance, capital markets, and insurance);
4. Trade & Investment (foreign direct investment, WTO accession and compliance, customs rules, public procurement, anti-trust laws and consumer protection, competitiveness, and foreign exchange rules);
5. Commercial Dispute Resolution (adjudication mechanisms for commercial disputes and enforcement mechanisms, including judicial training, court administration, docket control, arbitration, mediation, and training for bailiffs and marshals);
6. Institutional Reform (transparency, accountability, efficiency and effectiveness of institutions; anti-corruption);
7. Property Rights (laws establishing and defining all forms of property, registration, collateralization or mortgaging; both intellectual and real property).

The focus, as will be immediately apparent, is on the construction of a facilitative environment for business. Persistent efforts are made to gauge the 'impact' of interventions in each of these areas. According to government indicators, for example, an operational budget of US$385.5 million (of a total EGAT budget of US$ 3.2 billion) in 2007 contributed to 41 laws being passed in 12 national jurisdictions relating to the 11 'core legal areas' that 'constitute the framework for a healthy

---

[15] See generally, NSS (2002); NSS (2006); USAID (2004a); USAID (2002a); USAID DOS (2007).
[16] 'Legal and Institutional Reform: Legal Areas Where USAID is Active', online at: www.usaid.gov/our_work/economic_growth_and_trade/eg/lir_where_active. htm. Reforms of this kind were ubiquitous in Latin America in the 1980s, in Central Europe in the 1990s, and are still undertaken today in most countries of USAID engagement.

business climate'.[17] Yet market rule of law promotion extends well beyond 'technical assistance' – that is, helping draft the laws deemed necessary for modern capital markets and business transactions. It also requires nurturing the multiple interlocking constituencies who will cumulatively ensure that the law comes to life. Business groups and lawyers must be shown how to activate these laws to their benefit; 'civil society' to lobby for them; parliamentarians to draft them; officials to respect them; and judges to apply them.[18] As a matter of practice, then, this area of assistance is indissociable from 'governing justly and democratically'.[19]

Through its GJD programmes, USAID promotes laws, institutions and public attitudes in support of elections, women's and children's rights (in particular through mechanisms to tackle domestic violence),[20] civil society (not merely financial but also through training in fundraising and 'sustainable budgeting', and refining niche areas of activity),[21] parliamentary politics, judicial independence and 'alternative dispute resolution'; and against corruption and human trafficking.[22] USAID has published 'handbooks' in these areas aimed at project implementers, consultants and other donors.[23] According to the Department of State, US$ 532 million was spent in 2007 on the GJD sub-programme entitled 'rule of law and human rights' (from a total programme expenditure of US$ 2.1 billion).

In this area too, USAID seeks representative indicators to permit measurement of the impact of its funding under as many sub-programme elements as possible. For example, in 2007 USAID claims

---

[17] CBJ FY2009, 790–791. The twelve countries are Armenia, Azerbaijan, Egypt, Georgia, Indonesia, Kosovo, Macedonia, Montenegro, Nicaragua, Pakistan, Senegal and South Africa. The eleven legal areas are: 1. company law; 2. contract law and enforcement; 3. real property; 4. mortgage law; 5. secured transactions law; 6. bankruptcy law; 7. competition policy; 8. commercial dispute resolution; 9. foreign direct investment; 10. corporate governance; 11. international trade law.

[18] See for example, USAID LIME (2005); USAID LIME2 (2006); USAID Croatia (2004). On USAID's nurturing of a business lobby (FUGADES) in El Salvador, see Orr (1996), 405–419.

[19] See for example, USAID Madagascar (2006).

[20] See for recent activities, USAID Trafficking (2008); USAID Egypt (2008); USAID Philippines (2008a).

[21] See, e.g., USAID Kosovo (2008); USAID Romania (2008).

[22] In 2007, USAID trained over 100,000 'justice sector personnel' worldwide. USAID DOS (FY2007), 3.

[23] See, for example, USAID (1999a); USAID (1999b); USAID (1999c); USAID (2000); USAID (2002b); USAID (2002c); USAID (2003).

that 110,041 'justice sector personnel' ('judges, magistrates, prosecutors, advocates, inspectors, and court staff') in 31 countries received US government training and 350 courts in 19 countries received case management assistance.[24] The case management indicator is explained as follows:

> Improved case management leads to a more effective justice system by decreasing case backlog and case disposition time, reducing administrative burdens on judges, increasing transparency of judicial procedures, and improving compliance with procedural law. For these reasons, tracking the number of courts receiving U.S. Government assistance is a solid indicator of improvements to the overarching objective of improving the quality of the rule of law in host countries.

To read the above in reverse: evidence that the 'quality' of the rule of law has 'improved' can be gleaned by 'tracking' the 'number of courts receiving US government assistance', since money spent on improving 'case management' leads to a 'more effective justice system'. This is so because the latter expenditure can be assumed to speed up 'case disposition time', increase 'transparency of judicial procedures', reduce the time judges spend on administration and, improve 'compliance with procedural law'. Thus are the grandiose claims made for the rule of law reduced to hard measurable data.

THE WORLD BANK

World Bank spending on rule of law projects is currently growing faster than total disbursements.[25] In 2006, the Bank reported delivering US$4.6 billion on 'governance and rule of law programs', two of the Bank's eleven core themes, amounting to 19 per cent of its total

---

[24] CBJ FY2009, 752–754. Justice sector personnel were trained in: Angola, Armenia, Azerbaijan, Bolivia, Bosnia and Herzegovina, Cambodia, China, Colombia, Democratic Republic of the Congo, Dominican Republic, Egypt, El Salvador, Guatemala, Haiti, Honduras, Indonesia, Kazakhstan, Kosovo, Liberia, Macedonia, Mexico, Mongolia, Nepal, Nicaragua, Pakistan, Panama, Philippines, Serbia, Timor-Leste, Ukraine and Vietnam. The training target for 2009 was 60,000 persons; 600 courts were targeted for case management assistance. These figures include some security sector reform (SSR) work described below.

[25] The 'World Bank' here refers to the International Bank for Reconstruction and Development (IBRD) and the International Development Authority (IDA). A third member of the World Bank Group, the International Financial Corporation (IFC) has also played a significant role in rule of law promotion, particularly through its annual flagship publication *Doing Business*.

loans and grants.[26] Bank expenditure on these themes almost doubled between 2001 and 2006, during which time total disbursements increased rather less: by around a third. Still, given the ubiquity of the legal and institutional environment to project work of every kind, these figures might not seem impressive. Indeed, only 577 of the 11,500 projects launched since 1990 included a 'rule of law' component.[27] This comparatively low figure is due in part to the Bank's sectoral approach to its project work, which treats the 'justice sector' in isolation from others.[28] Yet, partly as a result of this narrow framing, the rule of law theme is heavily weighted at the Bank. Small-bore amendments to the legal or institutional environment of a kind that many projects entail are not billed as 'rule of law' projects. Instead, with titles such as 'Justice and Integrity Project' and 'Judicial Modernization Project', these projects are explicitly intended to effect root shifts in the role, impact and public understanding of law, judiciaries, legal institutions and arguments as a whole, and to mobilise entire legal systems in the interests of profound and structural economic and social reform.

After 1989: governance and PSD

Explicit World Bank interest in shaping the legal systems of client countries dates from the end of the 1980s, and is closely associated with two reorienting policy foci emergent at that time – the promotion of 'governance' and of 'private sector development' (PSD in Bank parlance) in client countries.[29] In the intervening decades, the Bank has insistently repeated and clarified the link between a particular configuration of laws and legal institutions, called 'rule of law', and a market economy. In countries of Bank engagement, the alleviation of poverty is said to depend on economic growth; this is said in turn to depend on the nurturing of a market economy and integration in the global market; both of which ultimately depend upon the rule of law, or so the Bank has been claiming repeatedly since the late 1980s. By

---

[26] World Bank (2006f), 14. Spending on governance and rule of law was down slightly in 2007, to US$ 3.8 billion (15 per cent), World Bank (2007h), 23, 57.
[27] According to the Bank's project database as of June 2008. Of 2,325 active projects today, 163 are tagged with the rule of law theme (the Bank's assigned themes are not exclusive).
[28] See World Bank (2005f), 2. For a definition of the 'justice sector', see World Bank (2007d), 8.
[29] See World Bank (1989b); World Bank (1989c); Shihata (1990).

upholding and respecting the rule of law, a state cultivates an 'enabling environment' for private sector confidence, foreign investment, and thus growth, which in turn creates wealth and employment. The rule of law, in short, is central (on this account) to the Bank's mission of poverty eradication. That, at least, is the stated reason for its promotion in client states. The rest of this section briefly sketches the policy imperatives at the turn of the 1990s that provide the context for this claim.

Governance

The rule of law first arises as a Bank term in response to a 'long-term perspective' study on sub-Saharan Africa that identified 'governance' as 'a basic issue in the development strategy for that region'.[30] The study was concerned in particular with a claimed slide in quality of African bureaucracies since independence. The relevant passage is worth citing at length:

Deteriorating Governance. At independence Africa inherited simple but functioning administrations. They were managed largely by expatriates and were not geared to the development role assigned to them by African leaders. The responsibilities of the state were enormously expanded. But at the same time the rapid promotion of inexperienced staff and the gradual politicization of the whole administrative apparatus led to declining efficiency. A combination of administrative bottlenecks, unauthorized 'fees' and 'commissions', and inefficient services imposed costs on businesses that have progressively undermined their international competitiveness. The gradual breakdown of the judicial systems in many countries left foreign investors doubtful that contracts could be enforced.... Authoritarian governments hostile to grassroots and nongovernmental organizations have alienated much of the public. As a result economic activity shifted increasingly to the informal sector. Too frequently ordinary people see government as the source of, not the solution to, their problems.[31]

In 1989, the idea that colonialism was a golden era of faceless efficient civil servants ran counter to the recent narrative of the triumph of African nationalism and self-determination. Indeed, the storyline of

---

[30] Shihata (1990), 54–56. Shihata sought to situate 'governance' within the Bank's mandate, to 'explain the legal framework' and 'clarify the legal limits' of relevant Bank policy.

[31] World Bank (1989b), 30. The World Bank President at the time, Barber Conable, wrote in a foreword: 'Private sector initiative and market mechanisms are important, but they must go hand-in-hand with good governance – a public service that is efficient, a judicial system that is reliable, and an administration that is accountable to its public': World Bank (1989b), xii.

the report flatly contradicted the still dominant independence narrative of young African nations, in which a coercive and extractive colonial state had finally been vanquished. The Bank suggested, by contrast, that 'ordinary people' had lost confidence in a post-independence state that, *since colonialism*, had become predatory. Where the colonial state had been trustworthy, on this account – to locals and foreigners alike – the independent African state no longer was. First among its problems was its transfer from 'expatriates' to 'African leaders', who had redirected the state, expanded (for they surely did not invent) its 'development role', promoted 'inexperienced staff' (given the post-independence flight of 'expatriates'), 'politicized' the administration, and introduced bottlenecks and bribes. In the background familiar colonial themes arise – the 'breakdown' of law and order, the hostility to the free passage of foreigners. 'The state has an indispensable role in creating a favorable economic environment' according to the report: 'This should, in fact, be its primary concern.' This had, indeed, been the primary concern of the colonial state. Instead, 'far from promoting the private sector, the state often actively curbed private initiative, including cooperatives and grassroots organizations.'[32]

The report concluded that the independent African state's hostility to the private sector, rather than being a reaction against the recent colonial past, resulted from the absence of structured communication between private investors and the state, which, in the passage above, is now attributed to the impotence of civil society and the 'alienation of the public'. 'Because countervailing power has been lacking, state officials in many countries have served their own interests without fear of being called to account … at worst the state becomes coercive and arbitrary.'[33] Here we see an early articulation of 'development' in the terms of an active and interested public sphere that will be familiar from Chapter 1 above. In sum, what had been a condition of the colonial state's very existence – the absence of a 'public' to hold the government to account – was now redescribed as an affliction of the post-independence state. This pessimistic post-colonial scenario 'can be resisted', however, through 'a systematic effort to build a pluralistic institutional structure, a determination to respect the rule of law, and vigorous protection of the freedom of the press and human rights'. 'It is of the utmost importance', the study asserted, 'for the state to establish a predictable and honest administration of the regulatory

[32] World Bank (1989b), 54.   [33] World Bank (1989b), 60–61.

framework, to assure law and order, and to foster a stable, objective, and transparent judicial system.'³⁴

The Africa study came at a time of changing strategic priorities at the Bank, because donors had 'clearly not [been] getting value for their money'.³⁵ The state was from now on to be wrenched around from 'planner' to 'enabler' in keeping with the structural adjustment policies introduced in the 1980s to ensure that interest payments on debt could continue from countries undergoing steep recession.³⁶ Structural adjustment involved a general rollback of state expenditure, with a particular emphasis on privatisation. Donor funding would, henceforth, be used to promote 'public policy for the private sector', as a Bank periodical title had it. Additionally, 'NGOs should be used more intensively for channeling ODA.'³⁷ It is in the context of this new policy focus that the language of 'governance' and the 'rule of law' arose at the Bank.³⁸

Private sector development

In 1988, the World Bank established a Private Sector Development Review Group, whose report the following year became the basis of the Bank's 'PSD action program'.³⁹ The report began by noting the 'growing recognition that the distortions caused by government regulations, taxes, subsidies, and budget deficits and the poor performance of public enterprises place limits on the legitimate role that governments can play in supporting development'.⁴⁰ With 'private sector initiative and competitive markets' emerging as the 'dominant themes

---

³⁴ World Bank (1989b), 61, 55.   ³⁵ World Bank (1989b), 180, 14.
³⁶ On the debt crisis and structural adjustment, see Roett (1992); Pastor (1992); contributions to Pastor (1987), especially Canavan (1987); contributions to Kahler (1986), Kahler and Cohen (1986); contributions to Claudon (1986); Lal (2002) ('Postscript'); Masson (2007); Handelman and Baer (1989); Krueger (1986); WDR 1979, WDR 1985, WDR 1987, WDR 1988 and WDR 1989.
³⁷ World Bank (1989b), 180.
³⁸ In this context see, Shihata (1997); Shihata (1999); Sureda (1999), 11; Morais (2004).
³⁹ In a 1991 paper, Ibrahim Shihata predicted that PSD would become the 'hallmark of Bank Group activities in the nineties', having taken on 'special importance' in the 1980s due to the debt crisis, the fall of communism and the fact that 'many influential members of the World Bank Group, prompted by strong beliefs in the importance of market forces and the virtues of private initiatives also advocated these beliefs in the Bank suggesting that they be followed by its developing members'. Article 1 of the IBRD's Articles of Agreement, he noted, required it 'to promote private foreign investment by means of guarantees or participations in loans and other investments made by private investors': Shihata (1991d), 46.
⁴⁰ World Bank (1989c), v.

in development thinking today', the action programme recommended four priority areas for Bank action: (i) improving the business environment for the private sector; (ii) restructuring or privatising public enterprises; (iii) developing the financial sector, particularly to improve the operation of financial intermediaries and the transfer of resources; and (iv) undertaking research and policy analysis to lay the basis for future operations.[41] By 1990, according to a progress report, 150 out of 228 Bank operations 'included identifiable PSD components'.[42]

All this, it became quickly clear, meant a renewed focus on law as an instrument of policy, which had before then only received 'erratic treatment in Bank operations'.[43] The Bank's new 'deep involvement in PSD' made it, in the words of Ibrahim Shihata, its Legal Vice President at the time, 'important, in fact, inevitable, for [the Bank] to focus more critically on legal and institutional framework issues'.[44]

> The laws governing property rights – the rules of the game for ownership and exchange – also govern the working of markets and thus profoundly affect the efficiency of the private sector. Clear, simple laws, effectively applied, are essential for generating expectations of a stable and supportive business climate, both for domestic and foreign investors. Shortcomings are common, however. Surveys have shown that uncertainty about the rules of the game has been a major concern for foreign investors … Lack of clear laws governing commercial liability, bankruptcy, and liquidation may have been one of the factors limiting the responsiveness of many developing countries to changes in the international environment.[45]

Shihata's 'opinion' (an informal expression of Bank policy) to the Bank's executive directors listed typical problems facing private actors in Bank client countries: 'unenforceability of contract or property rights, doubts about land tenure, difficulties in establishing, restructuring or liquidating firms, inflexible labor laws, excessive taxation, poor regulation or over-regulation of investment and banking activities are all typical examples.'[46] Laws inherited from the colonial era were gapped,

---

[41] World Bank (1989c), v–vi. See also Shihata (1990), 209.
[42] World Bank (1991c), 2. See Shihata (1990), 211.
[43] World Bank (1989c), 11. Shihata writes (1991b), 223: 'The shift to a market environment requires considerable adaptation of the legal environment and thus a particularly important part of the Bank's technical assistance in such circumstances is of a legal nature.'
[44] Shihata (1991b), 230.   [45] World Bank (1989c), 11.
[46] 'The Role of Law in Private Sector Development: Implications for the Bank's PSD Action Program'. Reproduced as part III of Shihata (1991b), 226. On Shihata's 'opinions' see Shihata (1997); Shihata (1999); Sureda (1999), 11; Morais (2004).

reflecting the cut-off moment of independence and, as a result, often 'out of date' (see Chapter 6 below). Post-independence state-led development policies meant the legal systems 'may be generally unresponsive to the needs of important parts of the community, including the business community'. In contrast, Shihata provided the ideal scenario:

> In the abstract, a sound legal and institutional framework includes a comprehensive, well-defined body of laws and regulations, a cadre of able and honest public administrators, a court system to enforce property and contractual rights and to resolve competing claims, legal and accounting professions to provide a basis for checks and balances and a general willingness on the part of society to be bound by those laws and to respect the institutions which implement and enforce them.[47]

On this basis, Shihata laid out a work schedule for the Bank: to focus on land tenure, the financial sector, labour laws, family and inheritance laws, administrative law, tax laws and investment codes. All these potential areas of activity, Shihata emphasised 'have to be considered in the context of the privatization process in order to ensure that the transfer of ownership solves the problems of low efficiency and productivity generally associated with public sector enterprises'. The Bank cannot, he stressed, achieve large in-country alterations on its own: 'However committed to structural adjustment or private sector development, governments ultimately decide what is politically feasible in their societies.'[48] The Bank can, however, offer 'comparative experience' and 'legal technical assistance' that might help mitigate the 'sociopolitical issues' that law reform could otherwise raise.[49] Finally, Shihata observes, 'practically all developing countries' have now realised that the policies of the past had failed, bloating the public sector 'at the expense of the private sector', breeding inefficiency and corruption. Countries worldwide were now moving generally towards privatisation and private sector development, but 'workable privatization has to be preceded or at least accompanied by a serious attempt to create a new environment where private business can thrive'.[50]

---

[47] Shihata (1991b), 226, 228–230.
[48] Shihata notes that this new 'major approach … should not be seen as a politically motivated, ideological commitment on the part of the Bank, even though such commitment does exist among many Bank members': Shihata (1991b), 233.
[49] Shihata (1991b), 231–232, 233–234.
[50] Shihata (1991b), 234. In a coda, Shihata added some 'personal reflections'. In addition to a 'legal and regulatory framework', other desiderata of 'an attractive and stable investment environment' include 'adequate infrastructure', environmental

The rule of law was described, in this context, as that 'aspect' of the legal system in client countries that falls within the Bank's ordinary sphere of intervention, comprising a set of systemic norms that are 'a basic requirement for a stable business environment; indeed for a modern state'.[51] The Bank *must* have a legitimate interest in safeguarding the rule of law in member states since its absence 'could render meaningless any process of economic reform'.[52] According to this rationale, rule of law at the Bank refers to 'economic', rather than 'political' interventions (as the latter are deemed to be off-bounds).[53]

THE ECONOMY OF LAW

Whereas USAID and the Bank carry out similar projects in market promotion, only the Bank offers a sustained justification for this kind of work and for rule of law terminology, as we have seen. In this section I examine this framing language – concentrating in particular on the

---

regulation, and a 'generally favourable attitude among bureaucrats and the public at large towards private investment'. Countries 'should be given adequate time for the adoption of the new laws and regulations that suit them most [and these should be] discussed at length before their adoption by those most affected by them and by the public at large.' Additionally, private investors 'must also be characterized by responsibility', including attention to the 'public interest'. 'Interestingly', Shihata comments, 'almost all of these factors require government involvement': Shihata (1991b), 235–236.

[51] Shihata (1990), 85. Shihata defined the rule of law as a system wherein '(a) there is a set of rules which are known in advance, (b) such rules are actually in force, (c) mechanisms exist to ensure the proper application of the rules and to allow departure from them as needed according to established procedures, (d) conflicts in the application of the rules can be resolved through binding decisions of an independent judicial or arbitral body and (e) there are known procedures for amending the rules when they no longer serve their purpose.'

[52] Shihata (1990), 86.

[53] Shihata (1990), 86. Interventions on behalf of the rule of law are 'not political' as they merely 'address the process of the formulation and application of rules rather than their substance'. The 'process' serves what Shihata calls 'the economic objective' (among others), whereas the substance 'will of course reflect the policies of each government and should be based on its choices and convictions'. For the 'prohibition' on 'political' interventions, see Shihata (1990), 65–67, 81; IBRD Articles of Agreement, Article III, Section 5(b), Article IV, Section 10 and Article V, section 5(c). Section 10 provides: 'Political Activity Prohibited. The Bank and its officers shall not interfere in the political affairs of any member; nor shall they be influenced in their decisions by the political character of the member or members concerned. Only economic considerations shall be relevant to their decisions, and these considerations shall be weighed impartially in order to achieve the purposes [of the Bank].' Identical provisions appear in the IDA Articles of Agreement.

Bank's usage – in the light of my discussions in Part I of the parameters of the rule of law.

At the heart of contemporary rule of law reform at the Bank is the notion that the configuration of law in a given context can encourage or obstruct economic growth and that law reform is therefore a relevant and necessary tool for optimising economic growth. According to the Bank:

> [D]evelopment experience [shows] that the rule of law promotes effective and sustainable economic development and good governance. Lack of the rule of law significantly hinders economic growth and corruption regressively taxes the poor. The developing countries' transition toward market economies necessitated strategies to encourage domestic and foreign private investment. This goal could not be reached without modifying or overhauling the legal and institutional framework and firmly establishing the rule of law to create the necessary climate of stability and predictability.[54]

The 'rule of law' in Bank parlance is thus today shorthand for the optimal legal configuration for growth. It is explicitly promoted and established, not (or not primarily) as an end in itself, but *in order* to achieve economic growth. This frank instrumentalism has been a consistent aspect of Bank-promoted law reform since it first addressed the theme in 1989. Today, project documents on 'legal and judicial reform' reflexively reference the importance of 'establishing an effective "rule of law" needed for further development of a market economy'.[55] At the same time, the Bank touts the rule of law's economic merit at every opportunity – here, for example, is Bank President Robert Zoellick speaking in September 2008 in Geneva: 'The most fundamental prerequisite for sustainable development is an effective rule of law, including respect for property rights.'[56]

Although increasingly ubiquitous, there is nothing self-evident about this linguistic turn. To refer to 'legal institutions for a market economy', or plain 'legal and judicial reform' – two expressions common at the Bank – as 'rule of law promotion' may appear somewhat grandiose, but it is also counter-intuitive. Traditionally, as we saw in Part I above, the rule of law has been conceived in opposition to 'legal

---

[54] WB LVP (2004), 2. [55] WB Armenia (2007a), para. 4.
[56] Daniel Dombey, 'World Bank Chief Calls for Rethink over Failed States', *Financial Times* (September 12, 2008). 'Yet', Zoellick continued, 'the international security and development communities have let the task of building justice and law enforcement systems fall between the cracks.'

instrumentalism'. As explained there, 'rule of law' narratives have generally celebrated the *autonomy* of law, its non-subordination to other demands than those of the law itself.[57] The notion that law is autonomous expresses the idea that legal reasoning and legal development are subject to a logic and process peculiar to the history and discipline of law.[58] Law, on this view, should not be subject to extra-legal pressures. To 'politicise' or 'instrumentalise' the law is therefore to violate the rule of law – for if law is answerable to something other than law, it presumably does not 'rule'.

Law's autonomy, as it has been characterised over the years, may derive from many possible sources – God, nature, 'reason', history, culture or even just the learned normativity of a disciplinary milieu. Few today would argue that the autonomy of law is inevitable or natural, but even if widely understood as socially constructed, many legal professionals nevertheless regard law's autonomy as an appropriate horizon or ideal guiding legal activity.[59] The Bank (and USAID) depart from this tradition when they frankly invoke the rule of law as a means to an end, and when they undertake to mobilise political pressures of various kinds to bring about the legal architecture sought to this end.

This counter-intuitive usage can be explained in a number of ways. One explanation is that rule of law language was introduced into the Bank by economists, who simply do not 'get' the rule of law (or not, at least, in the way lawyers do).[60] Another is that the peculiarities of the Bank's institutional and interpretative mechanisms have led it into this register, arrived at primarily in order to avoid the *appearance* of doing 'political' work.[61] Third, it could also be that the rule of law is an ideal umbrella term for the Bank's diffuse and diverse purposes: sufficiently broad and time-honoured to unite many differing aims and perspectives both within the Bank and between it and its donor partners, vague enough to avoid obvious ideological bias, yet still narrow enough to occlude certain social visions that the Bank might view as

---

[57] See in particular the discussion of Aristotle's dilemma in Chapter 3 above.
[58] See Chapters 1 (on Michael Oakeshott) and 2 (on Max Weber and Oliver Wendell Holmes).
[59] See the discussion of the realists above, Chapter 2. See Bourdieu (1987); Fitzpatrick (1992), 3–8, 147–149.
[60] As suggested occasionally by lawyers at the Bank. See, for example, World Bank (2005f), 2.
[61] As described in Shihata (1990). See Newton (2006).

undesirable.⁶² All of these suggestions have been made, and all are no doubt partly true. I will not attempt here to choose between them or to offer an alternative solution to this conundrum, but I believe it is nevertheless useful to flag briefly a number of *effects* this deployment of the rule of law register may be expected to accomplish for Bank projects.

First, the Bank's legal reform work stands to gain in *legitimacy* if it is understood as connected with the rule of law. This is an obvious but important point. Because the rule of law is universally seen as a public good, potential Bank collaborators are more likely to wish to be associated with projects under this label, while possible critics may be less willing to attack it. Framing Bank law reform work as rule of law promotion stands to bestow legitimacy upon the Bank among several different constituencies. In donor countries, the vocabulary reassures legal and other professionals, whom the Bank will need to approach as project consultants, about the motives and overall orientation of work they might collaborate on. Different groups can furthermore be left to make their own associations. Lawyers and judges will think of procedural rights and the public good that the law itself represents; economists will focus on property rights and contract; bankers, investors and other donors, who rely on Bank contracts and guarantees for investments in developing countries, will be reassured that steps are being taken to protect their assets.⁶³ Human rights advocates and other potential critics of the Bank may recognise its rule of law goals as valuable to their own goals and advocacy.⁶⁴ To speak of the 'rule of law' might therefore reach and build a wider support constituency than 'justice sector reform' alone. Ultimately, career movement within this transnational constituency can broaden and spread the ethos of reform.⁶⁵

---

⁶² Santos (2006).
⁶³ The Bank itself is an important source of contracts and opportunities for businesses in donor countries. See for example, US Dept. of Commerce, DOC (2008): 'The [World Bank] lends $18–25 billion annually to developing country governments to fund projects designed to spur sustainable economic growth and development and poverty alleviation. This funding generates roughly 40,000 contracts each year for private companies to supply a wide range of goods, equipment, services, and civil works. Contracts range from several hundred million to a few thousand dollars, representing significant export opportunities for a broad range of U.S. companies large and small.'
⁶⁴ See, for example, HRW 2001, Introduction: 'the World Bank in particular has begun to change [its] sorry legacy. Under the leadership of James Wolfensohn, the bank's efforts to combat corruption, reduce poverty, and promote good governance and the rule of law have led it, in some countries, to show greater sensitivity to human rights.'
⁶⁵ On this point, see generally Bourdieu (1987); Dezalay and Garth (1996) and (2002).

In host countries too, a rule of law focus may carry much weight. It presumptively distinguishes the Bank from external actors of the past – colonials on one hand, communists on the other – who have intervened in national legal systems. In principle, the rule of law can be packaged to represent a reversal of the experience and policies of that period. It is likely to be an object of veneration among educated classes in host countries – particularly among legal professions – and so its deployment stands to gain their 'buy-in', ordinarily thought vital to the success of any law reform project. The fact that the rule of law is also promoted by many or most other donor and development actors, and by local 'civil society' groups, may increase the Bank's own prestige in recipient countries. At the same time, the rule of law has underdog associations not normally available to the Bank, of equality under the law and as a bulwark against the powerful. (Stories from donor countries of opposition, in the name of the rule of law, to anti-terrorism excess can no doubt add to its appeal in host countries, provided the Bank itself escapes association with its primary funders.)

Second, the rule of law register tends to legitimise a certain view of the legal system and its relation with the economy, and to naturalise a particular kind of economic structure. The insistent association of the rule of law with growth, development, a 'market economy', a good 'investment climate', an 'enabling environment for business', and so on, does enormous work to this end. The association is relentless and repeated through multiple channels, benefiting from the immense publicity resources of the World Bank (and USAID, inter alia). These include not only the project documents – and the circuit of meetings, briefings, mentoring, training and sundry pressures that accompany project implementation – but also an outpouring of policy research and working papers, trade journals, and the many reports listing 'rule of law' and 'governance' indicators and ranking governments accordingly, which are aimed not only at the governments themselves but also at the 'business community' and, of course, for the perennial amplification of the international and local media.[66]

This association draws selectively on certain of the lodestars in the rule of law's conceptual past – cherry-picked from among the influences I have laid out in Part I – in order to promote, through Bank

---

[66] See note 21 to the Introduction. Also WDR 2005; Doing Business 2005, 2006, 2007, 2008; Governance Matters III; IV and VI. On the ubiquitous 'public awareness' component of rule of law projects see below, Chapter 6.

work, a certain view of the purpose of a legal system, the appropriate shape of an economy and the relation between the two. The background theoretical framework that informs the Bank's specific usage is widely acknowledged though rarely alluded to: it draws in particular on the work of Friedrich Hayek (see above, Chapter 2) and the line of economists whose work is indebted to him, the public choice school that derives partly from his work, and the newer discipline of 'law and economics'.[67] Few members of this loose family of ideas are well captured by the term 'rule of law', but all have left an imprint upon the standard Bank deployment of the term.

A related presumptive effect of a rule of law framing is to prejudice against certain policy options at national level. As discussed in detail in Chapter 2, certain policy approaches are simply more difficult to communicate through a rule of law register. Where Bank documents speak about 'poverty reduction' and 'poverty eradication', as they insistently do, these are associated rather with the economic growth expected to flourish in a rule of law environment than with active redistribution of any kind.[68] Poverty, on this argument, will be alleviated by a flourishing private sector that will lift populations into paid labour and deliver better services to them. It cannot be associated with redistributive measures by the state, regarded suspiciously both as disincentives to productive work and saving and as probable sources of price distortion and public sector expansion and discretion. A rule of law discourse presumes against redistribution of this sort and expects the absence of such measures from the policy map. Occasionally, such as in the IFC's *Doing Business* reports, welfare measures of any kind (and indeed taxation) are explicitly associated with the 'regulation' that is actively and consistently berated as a disincentive to foreign investment and thus an obstacle to growth that developing nations simply cannot afford.[69] Paradoxically, to help the poor is presented, in rule of law literature, as damaging to the poor; rather the poor are to be helped by helping the rich.[70]

---

[67] See Chapter 2 above, references at note 100.
[68] In claiming that the Bank cannot support civil and political rights in a client country because they are 'political', Shihata argued that the Bank's work was, by contrast, geared towards the fulfilment of social and economic rights. See Shihata (1989), 109–120, especially 113–115.
[69] See, for example, Doing Business 2006, 26, 51.
[70] On the role of 'the poor' in Bank documentation, see Chapter 6 below.

Traditional development goals such as health and education and the provision of infrastructure do not disappear from donor work – far from it – but they are reframed within a discourse that has already ruled against certain kinds of intervention on their behalf (robust social security) and in favour of others (incentives to private initiative). Moreover, where Poverty Reduction Strategy Papers (PRSPs) – the national policy documents that record a promise to the Bank and other donors of actions to be taken as a condition for debt relief – prioritise social goals, as they frequently do, these coexist in uneasy tension with the exigencies of a PSD legal architecture.[71] So, for example, where Uzbekistan's 2008 PRSP predicts a shortfall of 6,000 housing units per year and a waiting list of 265,000, the following 'instruments' are suggested as remedy: development of a primary mortgage market, development of a real estate market, 'providing the legal framework', providing tax breaks for families with children, and the completion by 2010 of flats 'built in 1990 but privatized without any further renovation'.[72] Under 'providing the legal framework', the document states:

> Measures will be taken to increase awareness of the population about the state of the real estate market, prices for housing and new construction, based on assessments by independent assessment agencies and realtors. National legislation will be passed that would allow the issuing of mortgage bonds and securities guaranteed with mortgages. International standards of property evaluation and brokerage operations with property will be ensured.

The result is a curious invention. There is, after all, nothing new about mobilising law to economic ends; this was a feature of colonialism and is, indeed, an aspect of policy implementation everywhere. But of course, per Chapter 2 above, it is precisely a suspicion of the latent authoritarianism of the state as a policy engine – with perhaps the colonial state as a pre-eminent example – that gave rise to the

---

[71] PRSPs are 'nationally-owned' documents representing a policy pact with the Bank and the IMF; debt relief under the Heavily Indebted Poor Countries (HIPC) initiative is tied to progress on their fulfilment. PRSPs detail rule of law-type reforms and regularly include levers for assistance that subsequently reappear in the preamble of rule of law project documents. The US-funded International Development Law Organization has launched a project to scan PRSPs for rule of law reform opportunities (see: www.idlo.int/ROL/external/ROLPRS.asp). See IMF IDA (2006), IMF IDA (2007), IMF (2007a). For examples of PRSPs IMF Albania (2006), IMF Cameroon (2008), IMF DRC (2007b), IMF Gambia (2006).

[72] IMF Uzbekistan (2008), 90–91. A footnote remarks: 'This section draws from material prepared with World Bank technical assistance within the framework of the project "Development of Housing Financing in Uzbekistan".'

private-centred 'rule of law' register of restraint in the first place. The Bank's innovation has thus been to continue this long tradition of legal instrumentalism in practice while rejecting it in principle. It has done so by harnessing the old English ideal of the rule of law – an ideal that rejects policy per se – to drive what is in fact a centrally managed and widely implemented policy.

This brings me to a third possible effect of rule of law language in the project context, which is to downplay the extent to which rule of law promotion is, in fact, a policy at all, and to elide, to a degree, the central role of the Bank itself (and of other donors) in driving such a policy. Since 1990, over 500 rule of law projects have been initiated by the Bank in 113 countries, supplemented by hundreds of similar projects in the same countries by USAID and other actors. This is, in short, a large-scale, highly motivated enterprise; one that is inconceivable without a well-resourced and centralised administration, such as that which pertains at the Bank (and indeed at USAID), with country offices in most states, each in regular contact with a central bureau in Washington, DC, from where policy is made and disseminated.[73] But neither this institutional arrangement nor the policy-making process that flows through it is self-evident or easily understood; the Bank makes little effort to foreground or explain the fact that policy is set not by Bank staff, nor by its army of researchers, nor least of all by its 'clients', but by its 'shareholders', a tiny group of *government* actors, with votes weighted according to their contribution of funds.[74]

Add to this the peculiar status of the Bank itself as an institutional actor. The universe imagined by rule of law language is peopled by individuals and states; transnational actors such as the Bank are not easily visible within it. Furthermore, a rule of law world is made up of hard and bright lines – rights, obligations and accountability. The jurisdictional status of actors like the Bank is, however, uncertain and the authority of their norm-generating role obscure. If rule of law promotion is a policy, it is not obvious where such a policy originates or who is responsible (or accountable) for it. Moreover, if it is a *global* policy, and/or a policy intended to nurture and support a global market (as project

---

[73] Bank country offices have less freedom of action than those of USAID, although in recent years the latter too have been brought more closely into alignment with central policy. Hyman (2008).
[74] The five largest shareholders to the IBRD each appoint one of 24 Executive Directors to the Bank's Board of Directors (the rest are elected); Bank policy is determined by the Board, with voting rights allocated according to each 'shareholder's'

and strategy documents frequently indicate), this too is obscured in a discourse that refers predominantly and reflexively to the relationship between the state and the individual. It is not that the global economic 'benefits' of state-centric rule of law promotion are concealed (rather they are trumpeted), nor that this global function appears merely as a fortuitous side-effect of a policy pursued primarily for other reasons; it is rather that the concentration on national-level rule of law tends to obscure the preponderance of transnational or non-national actors in the global schema. The relationship between state policies, transstatal policy-makers and transnational beneficiaries remains obscure because a focus on national legal systems has little to say about transnational constraints and dynamics.

The choice of a 'rule of law' framing for what is, in fact, a global policy, has curious effects. For one it deflects the burden of responsibility for actions undertaken onto the state. Indeed, once the rule of law is problematised at all, the fault lies – it can only lie – with the state. The state must, as it were, fix itself, seeking outside help if necessary. Project documentation typically responsibilises the state at every step. Thus, states are faulted and penalised for their ranking on the myriad indicators of the rule of law.[75] But beyond seeking to improve these scores, or simply requiring a better 'investment climate', reform looks to national processes for legitimacy: constitutional guarantees that remain unfulfilled, treaty provisions that carry national obligations, or country-level strategy documents such as PRSPs. Obligations under international treaties – themselves frequently acceded to as project objectives – become in turn facilitative levers for further reform.[76] Project documents regularly refer to the 'opportunities' created through reforms achieved, or pressures imposed, by other donors.[77]

---

contribution. In December 2007, the top five shareholders/contributors commanded almost 40% of the Bank's voting powers (they were: France (4.3%), Germany (4.49%), Japan (7.86%), the United Kingdom (4.3%) and the United States (16.38%)). See the Bank's website (http://go.worldbank.org/11PWB3RTM0 and http://go.worldbank.org/O9S0U0IOA0). The Boards of the Bank and the IMF meet yearly to coordinate policy (http://go.worldbank.org/UVCJX4BN00).

[75] On rule of law indicators see Introduction, text at note 20.

[76] See, in this regard, the section entitled 'Denouement: global integration' in Chapter 6 below.

[77] For example, 'Throughout the World Bank's Europe and Central Asia region, the EU's mandate in addressing overarching political and constitutional issues provides an opening for the World Bank to engage at the implementation level': WB Albania (2006), 19.

The generation of hooks of this sort is an ordinary task in the operational strategy of transnational actors, who ceaselessly look out for 'windows of opportunity' for reform.[78] With policy initiatives habitually framed and claimed at national level, and encouraged as such, the prior transnational intervention and coordination that engineers a reform-friendly environment remains undisclosed, unnoticed and ultimately deniable.

At the same time, and for similar reasons, however, rule of law projects are also difficult to associate with state-level policy. A rule of law framing typically establishes a reform timeframe beyond the lifespan of a single elected government, and instantiates a set of transformational activities that will generally transcend any particular party line. Beyond this, rule of law is, as we have seen, an anti-policy policy, so to speak, aiming to rescind policy levers from the state – a point I will turn to in more detail in Chapter 6 – and, indeed, denying its own policy significance. In fact, of course, not all relevant policy levers reside with the state at the outset. Transnational rule of law mobilises both private and non-national agents towards its implementation, and is thus best viewed at the supranational level. As a *policy*, in short, both globally and locally, the task of identifying the *policy-maker* responsible for rule of law promotion is elusive. The Bank thus avoids another value ordinarily associated with the rule of law – accountability and a facility of assigning responsibility.

CONCLUSION

This chapter has laid the ground for an assessment of contemporary rule of law assistance programmes aimed at market promotion. I will undertake more detailed project-level analysis in Chapter 6. The chapter quickly glosses the background to and rationale for rule of law assistance through US foreign assistance bodies and the World Bank.

---

[78] See, for example, World Bank (2000d), 34: 'All too often Bank resources have been used to promote reforms in countries that are locked into dysfunctional political equilibria. Sometimes it may be more effective to postpone reform efforts until a genuine 'window of opportunity' is evident – and to focus Bank resources on countries with a more favorable environment. As an intermediate step when windows of opportunity appear small, it may be possible to focus Bank efforts on certain activities (such as workshops or private sector surveys) that help educate key stakeholders, build constituencies for reform in the future, and keep the Bank engaged in policy dialogue without a major commitment of resources.' See also World Bank (2006c), 9.

A preliminary analysis of the Bank's stated rationale for adopting the rule of law register noted that its deployment in an explicitly instrumental policy-oriented context is innovative, given the term's long association with conceptions of legal 'autonomy'. The chapter then described three possibly expectable effects of such a deployment: to provide legitimacy for the Bank's law reform work, in both home and host countries; to naturalise a certain view of the economy and the role of law within it, and thus prejudice against certain policy options; and to elide the policy-making centrality of the Bank and other transnational actors at global level.

The Bank's (and other donors') relentless promotion of a particular legal configuration, insistently described as itself constituting 'the rule of law', to achieve particular economic ends is, no doubt, reshaping the very notion of the rule of law as a term of art. Regardless of whether economists 'get' the rule of law or not, in other words, the rule of law 'ideal' is likely to retain the associations the Bank bestows upon it. This is pre-eminently the case in Bank target countries, many of which lack strong competing rule of law traditions and are relentlessly bombarded from numerous sources with a vision largely derived from and at a minimum compatible with the Bank's. In home countries, on the other hand, the relation is complex: a richer tradition of the rule of law competes with the narrower view shared by the Bank, which is itself sustained in the field of law and economics that has flourished in many (primarily US-based) law schools in recent years. At the same time, Bank and other work is providing an immense amount of data for scholars in those schools to further refine a theoretical architecture that might describe more precisely the legal framework best suited to achieving 'growth'. Increasingly it is the results and policy directives of that work that are signified by the term 'rule of law'.

5 State

Rule of law literature distinguishes between 'economic' and 'political' rule of law assistance – between market promotion, on one hand, and state-building in the interests of 'peace and security', on the other. Both deployments are now in wide circulation among a broad series of actors, though there is a disciplinary divide: those who mean market-structuring by 'rule of law' rarely use the term in reference to 'peace and security' and vice versa. This chapter looks at the latter phenomenon, comprising law enforcement and institution building: police and prison systems, crime prevention, the creation of judiciaries and protection of human rights.[1] In a first section I will lay out 'peace and security'-related rule of law assistance of, first, the United States, followed by the United Nations. In a second section, having laid out the main activities, I will examine some implicit questions raised by this deployment of the language of the rule of law.

THE UNITED STATES

Since 1985, the United States has supported criminal justice and 'security sector reform' (SSR) throughout the world. This work – which involves training investigators and prosecutors, building and equipping prisons, helping draft laws against terrorism, transnational crime and corruption, and training police and military officers – has traditionally fallen to entities other than USAID.[2] Three key actors are the

---

[1] These are tasks the Bank claims are foreclosed to it by its mandate. See Chapter 4, text at note 53.
[2] USAID undertook police training from 1961 until 1973, through the Office of Public Security, closed down by Congress after reports that it was providing torture and

Department of Justice's International Criminal Investigative Training Assistance Program (ICITAP) and Office of Overseas Prosecutorial Development, Assistance, and Training (OPDAT) and the State Department's Bureau of International Narcotics and Law Enforcement Affairs (INL), initially created to run 'counternarcotics' programmes in Latin America.[3] A recent creation, the Anti-Terrorism Assistance Program (ATA), also undertakes special training for foreign law enforcement officials in targeted counter-terrorism techniques.[4] The budgets for this work are hard to pin down, but cumulatively reached well over a billion dollars in 2008.[5] The sheer scale of vision is extraordinary. The State Department's budget request to Congress for fiscal year 2009 includes plans to train police forces in over 100 countries.[6] The work of the principal institutions overlaps globally (INL in 150 countries, ICITAP in 50, OPDAT in 20), particularly in Afghanistan and Iraq, where the Department of Defense is their principal funder.[7]

assassination techniques to death squads. As a result, in 1985, USAID refused responsibility for this component of the AOJ programme undertaken in Central America (see Chapter 4 above, text at note 1). See Carothers (1991), 213–215; Orr (1996), 371–372; GAO (1992), 1; generally Donziger and Fine (1989); Rockwood and Simpson (2001); Cottam and Marenin (1989); Cranston (1992).

[3] INL's largest programme remains the Andean Counterdrug Initiative in six Latin American countries (Bolivia, Brazil, Colombia, Ecuador, Panama, Peru). See INL FY2008, 44.

[4] On the ATA, see CBJ FY2009, 130–131. ATA undertakes training 'in critical GWOT ['global war on terror'] and Presidential Initiative countries, such as Afghanistan, Pakistan, Jordan, Indonesia, the Philippines and Colombia', as well as in Liberia and Kenya, and 'regional strategic initiatives' in the Horn of Africa, South Asia, and the Maghreb. 'During FY 2009, approximately 270 ATA training courses or events are expected to be delivered to over 70 participating Partner Nations'. Their expertise is in training special elite forces in tasks such as protecting high-level officials from assassination attempts.

[5] In Afghanistan INL spent US$ 399 million in FY 2007 on 'civilian law enforcement' (police training and related programmes) and US$ 40 million on 'administration of justice' ('justice sector training' and 'corrections reform and infrastructure'). For FY 2008, US$ 68 million was requested for 'administration of justice' (no figure is supplied for criminal law enforcement as funding is expected from DOD, not DOS). In Sudan, US$ 23 million was requested for police training and 'criminal justice development' in FY 2008, up from US$ 8.7 million in 2007. In Iraq, US$ 234.8 million is requested for FY 2008, for 'corrections services' and 'criminal justice development' (including a 'supplemental' request of US$ 159 million): INL FY2008, 317, 195, 276.

[6] See generally CBJ FY2009.

[7] 'More than 239,000 Iraqi police have been trained in courses developed and/or delivered by ICITAP ... and ICITAP-trained Iraqi instructors, with more than 24,000 Iraqi police having participated in specialized and advanced training.' DOJ (2008), 2.

While this work is not new, it received a significant boost after 2001. The US National Security Strategies (NSS) of 2002 and, in particular, 2006, emphasised an association between the rule of law abroad and security at home. Viewed as part of the 'infrastructure of democracy', the 'rule of law' moves to the centre of the 2002 NSS as a condition for access to aid, a policy subsequently implemented through the new Millennium Challenge Account.[8] This carrot-and-stick approach to the rule of law was reiterated in the 2006 NSS, where it was joined by a more explicit national security focus, particularly in the context of the war in Iraq, 'the front line in the war on terror'.[9] The administration promised to 'build Iraqi Security Forces and the capacity of local institutions to deliver services [and] advance the rule of law'. Poor rule of law in foreign countries, it is said, creates conditions for terrorism. In response, 'by helping to strengthen the rule of law and law enforcement capacity in foreign countries, ICITAP helps strengthen the security of the United States'.[10] 'Peace and security' became a 'strategic objective' for USAID in 2006, with 'rule of law assistance' tagged under four of its six 'strategic priority' subheads (the four are: counter-terrorism, security sector reform, conflict prevention, and transnational crime).[11]

A tight linkage emerges in these documents between security cooperation (with 'rule of law' as its objective), development assistance (with rule of law as its condition) and (as I shall pursue in Chapter 6) trade liberalisation (with rule of law as both condition and consequence). The cluster is further glued and imbued with, on one hand, 'tough love' (aid

---

[8] NSS (2002), 9, 10, 28. Indonesia's respect for the rule of law 'guaranteed' increased US assistance. Conversely, *if* Palestinians 'embrace' the rule of law, 'they can count on American support for the creation of a Palestinian state'.

[9] NSS (2006), 13.

[10] From ICITAP's website www.usdoj.gov/criminal/icitap. The idea is to 'enhance the ability of foreign governments to prevent terrorism, or disrupt it before it passes through their borders to threaten the United States'. DOJ (2006), 17.

[11] Thus: 'Our national strategy for combating terrorism appropriately stresses the advancement of democracy, the rule of law, and a global environment inhospitable to violent extremism'; 'Security sector reform enhances governments' ability to deliver adequate security and responsive, transparent, and accountable government through the rule of law'; 'We will promote international cooperation and coordination on combating international criminal activities, and provide training and technical assistance to build institutional capacity to uphold the rule of law.' As to implementation: '[The] Department of Justice ... leads on international legal assistance and implements some criminal justice and rule of law programs in conjunction with the Department [of State] and USAID.' See USAID DOS (2007), 12, 13, 14, 16.

providers must be cruel to be kind – that is, they should withhold funding if states are not demonstrating progress in the rule of law), and, on the other, the background threat of pre-emptive force, should terrorism become entrenched in a non-rule of law environment.[12] References to the rule of law reappear with the regularity of a pulse throughout these documents.

Rule of law language has thus seeped gradually into strategic thinking on a range of leading US foreign policy objectives, wherever they involve cooperation with, or training of, security forces in other parts of the world. Relevant policies are those addressing drug and human trafficking, cybercrime, transnational organised crime, money laundering and corruption. INL, for example, 'builds capacity ... where weak justice sectors are vulnerable to terrorist threats' and strengthens 'rule of law institutional capabilities [to] build up the law enforcement and criminal justice sector capacity of foreign governments'.[13] Similar themes and goals are steered through multilateral agencies where large-scale US funding brings agenda-setting influence, such as at the OSCE, OECD, and various UN agencies (notably the reworked Office on Drugs and Crime) and in each of which rule of law language quickly flourished.

Nevertheless, the tenor of US government documents on security assistance, which are today saturated in the rule of law motif, is *sui generis*. Some examples will illustrate. According to the strategy of the Department of Justice for 2007–2012, the 'primary mission' of its agencies, including ICITAP and OPDAT, is the prevention and eradication of terrorism, including inter alia the following objectives:[14]

Improve the skills of foreign prosecutors, investigators, and judges; encourage legislative and justice sector reform in countries with inadequate laws; and promote the rule of law and regard for human rights. OPDAT has developed highly complex and politically sensitive legal technical assistance programs targeting terrorist financing in more than 20 of the Department's priority countries. OPDAT coordinates

---

[12] USAID (2002a), 51: '[O]nly with a comprehensive, consistent, "tough love" approach from the international community is political will for governance reform likely to emerge and to be sustained. Once there is evidence of such political will, assistance for democracy and governance must work on many fronts to develop the institutions that fight corruption and defend the rule of law.' On pre-emption, see NSS (2006), 18. Where the NSS made a case for pre-emptive military action, development assistance too, according to USAID, would serve to 'pre-emptively' head off 'threats and disasters'. See USAID (2002a), iv, 2.

[13] INL FY2008, 2 ('Program Objectives').   [14] DOJ (2006), 18–19 (italics in original).

and implements bilateral training programs for prosecutors, investigators, and judges that present international standards and best practices in the areas of money laundering and terrorist financing.

Improve host-nation law enforcement agencies that are on the front lines of terrorism in an effort to control indigenous crime and reduce the proliferation of related transnational crime ... ICITAP's strategy is to deliver programs and products that focus on developing sustainable law enforcement institutions to combat the terrorist threat.

Prepare foreign counterparts to cooperate more fully and effectively with the United States in combating terrorism and related transnational crime ... OPDAT will provide assistance to foreign counterparts to improve the skills of foreign prosecutors, investigators, and judges; encourage legislative and justice sector reform in countries with inadequate laws; and promote the rule of law and regard for human rights.

INL has a special mandate to 'establish rule of law in post-conflict societies', where it builds, trains and equips police forces, courts and 'corrections facilities'; it 'currently deploys more than 1,000 police and corrections advisors and justice experts in eight countries'.[15] In Afghanistan, INL manages 'police and justice programs designed to ... train 62,000 police'. It has trained and equipped the 7,300-member Kosovo Police Service, the 3,000-member East Timor Police Service and the 3,500 members of Liberia's police service, as well as supporting Liberia's 'struggling court system'.[16]

Iraq is the paradigmatic example, where all three leading agencies are active. ICITAP claims to have trained, or facilitated the training of, 239,000 police officers in Iraq alone.[17] A Central Criminal Court of Iraq (CCCI) in Baghdad and associated provincial criminal courts were constructed under US supervision; OPDAT provides 'resident legal advisors' (RLAs) to advise the Iraqi magistrates in each province.[18] INL 'seek[s] to support twin goals through our rule of law and corrections programs: to help the Iraqis develop the institutional and societal frameworks on which the rule of law rests while simultaneously

---

[15] INL FY2008, 13.

[16] INL FY2008, 13. 'Rule of law is a keystone for the continued stability, security, and future development of Liberia' (INL FY2008, 176).

[17] DOJ (2008), 2. In addition, 'more than 24,000 Iraqi police having participated in specialized and advanced training.'

[18] DOJ (2008), 2. See also DOJ (2006), 23: 'CT ['counter-terrorism'] RLAs develop technical assistance programs for prosecutors, judges, and investigators to help enhance skills development and to implement new money laundering and terrorist financing laws and procedures. Most importantly, the RLA CT program strengthens bilateral relations and cooperation on criminal justice matters.'

addressing more immediate problems that impede the effective functioning of justice'.[19] Among its accomplishments INL lists having done the following: trained 100 judicial investigators; advised in the training of 7,535 'corrections personnel'; 'mentored dozens of Baghdad judges'; supported the CCCI in conducting 'over 1,800 trials and gain[ing] over 1,200 convictions to date'; and finally 'created a pilot database capable of tracking an accused individual from time of arrest or detention through adjudication to acquittal, conviction, incarceration and/or release; proved the database viable; trained Iraqi personnel from the police, courts, corrections, and juvenile justice sectors in [the] use of the automated database'. So extensive is all this activity that in March 2007 a 'Rule of Law Coordinator' was appointed in Iraq to oversee 'all civilian and law enforcement efforts to support the rule of law'.[20]

Beyond this, the US military undertakes its own 'rule of law promotion' in war zones, training foreign soldiers and setting up rudimentary tribunals.[21] Courses in 'military rule of law' are offered to foreign as well as US troops, including UN peacekeepers, through the US military's Defense Institute of International Legal Studies.[22] US soldiers, though they rarely take a lead role in UN peacekeeping missions, will frequently have trained peacekeepers from other armies (such as from Senegal and Pakistan). The US also funds security sector training courses through International Law Enforcement Academies in five countries, which have the following mission:

[To] protect American citizens and businesses through strengthened international cooperation against crime[;] buttress democratic governance through the rule of law; enhance the functioning of free markets through improved legislation and law enforcement; and increase social, political, and economic stability by combating narcotics trafficking and crime.[23]

[19] INL FY2008, 273-274 ('program justification: Iraq').
[20] DOJ (2008), 1. The coordinator oversees 300 personnel and advises the US Ambassador on justice-related issues.
[21] For instance, in Iraq, '[t]he U.S. military and other coalition forces ... have assumed a major, albeit somewhat unorthodox, role in advancing rule of law. This reflects the fact that most U.S. government assets in Iraq are military, including soldiers doing tasks that might normally fall to civilians, and indicates the sheer numbers of those in uniform and the budgets available to them': OIG (2005), 25.
[22] According to its website brochure, the institute 'provides expertise in over 320 legal topics of Military Law, Justice Systems, and the Rule of Law, with an emphasis on the execution of Disciplined Military Operations.' 'Participants from 126 nations' have taken part in DIILS programs. See online: www.dsca.mil/diils.
[23] See the ILEA website: www.state.gov/p/inl/ilea/c11242.htm.

This clearly amounts to a massive and influential exercise in shaping law enforcement structures and capacity around the world. It also inaugurates a new weighting for the rule of law rubric that differs substantially from the old ideal, as I shall explore, following a short overview of the UN's 'rule of law' work in this same general arena.

THE UNITED NATIONS

Today the UN has a firm rule of law niche in conflict and post-conflict contexts – or 'rule of law vacuums', in former Secretary-General Kofi Annan's words – where a handful of agencies (DPKO, UNODC, OHCHR, and UNDP) contribute expertise to what is generally referred to as its 'restoration'. Although by far the widest ranging and most resource-intensive area of UN rule of law interest, it is not the only one. In recent years, the General Assembly has flagged 'the rule of law at the national and international levels' for discussion, and invited member states and UN agencies, including the International Law Commission, to contribute views to that end.[24] Submissions to this process to date set a quite different tone to the determinedly criminal justice-focused work currently underway at the UN, which has largely been arrived at through communications between the Secretary-General and the Security Council in the context of 'peacebuilding'.[25] These recent efforts in member-state-dominated fora of the UN to expand the penumbra of rule of law language follow on reports such as 'A More Secure World' (2004) and the 2005 World Summit Outcome, which expressed concern about, inter alia, the 'international rule of law', an expression that is wholly absent from the domain of rule of law promotion. The multilateral push to raise the US- and UK-led invasion of Iraq as itself a rule of law issue might be viewed as a sign of unease with mainstream 'rule of law' discourse. However, these efforts remain very much at the margins of UN rule of law activity.

The overwhelming predominance of security and criminal justice concerns in mainstream UN work can be traced back to 1993, when the then new Office of the High Commissioner for Human Rights was mandated to provide, on request, 'technical and financial assistance to national projects in reforming penal and correctional establishments, education and training of lawyers, judges and security forces in human

---

[24] A/RES/62/70. [25] See A/62/121 and A/62/121/Add.1.

rights, and any other sphere of activity relevant to the good functioning of the rule of law'.[26] OHCHR's subsequent 'technical cooperation', conducted from field offices in post-conflict countries – notably Rwanda from the mid-1990s – remained relatively limited in terms of budgets and expertise, but nevertheless provided the occasion for annual reports from the Secretariat on the UN's role in 'strengthening the rule of law'.[27] Around the same time, with the UN peacekeeping mandate greatly expanding in the early to mid-1990s, the new Department of Peacekeeping Operations too began to talk up the importance of the rule of law in post-conflict scenarios. On its (re)launch in 1997, the United Nations Office on Drugs and Crime was another voice raising rule of law concerns in the context of transnational crime, responsibility for which was frequently attributed to weak or 'fragile' states. Given that these agencies worked closely with other donors where the rule of law register had long been adopted, their embrace at this time is unsurprising. (During the mid-1990s, UNDP, for example, began to register concern about rule of law, corruption and governance in development, quite some time after the language had become dominant at the World Bank, though it too would soon shift its focus primarily to post-conflict scenarios.[28])

Rule of law moved towards the centre of UN peacekeeping with the 2000 'Brahimi Report', which recommended 'a doctrinal shift in the use of civilian police and related rule of law elements in peace operations', by which was meant explicit recognition of a mandate to build and reinforce law enforcement institutions.[29] The report suggested the creation of a dedicated rule of law unit within DPKO with criminal law expertise that would help reform police in post-conflict countries and ensure that peacekeepers and police reformers were themselves

---

[26] The Vienna Declaration recommended a 'comprehensive programme ... to help States in the task of building and strengthening adequate national structures which have a direct impact on the overall observance of human rights and the maintenance of the rule of law': A/CONF.157/23, para. 69. The point of departure was a preambular reference in the UDHR: 'Whereas it is essential, if man is not to be compelled to have recourse, as a last resort, to rebellion against tyranny and oppression, that human rights should be protected by the rule of law.'

[27] See for example, A/50/653, para. 4. See also A/55/177, para. 5: 'The number of States requesting assistance for fortifying and consolidating the rule of law has increased significantly in recent years and can be considered an indicator of the growing awareness of the importance of the rule of law.' See also A/RES/50/179; A/RES/51/96. For an assessment, Flinterman and Zwamborn (2003), 75.

[28] See, for example, UNDP (1997).   [29] A/55/305-S/2000/809, ix.

informed about 'local law'.³⁰ At this time, UNDP received a new rule of law mandate (adopted by its equally new, and streamlined, Executive Board), which was likewise stolidly conflict-focused:

> UNDP will leverage its trusted status as a development partner to assist ... countries ... in the sensitive area of the rule of law. [V]iolent conflict often arises when respect for the rule of law breaks down ... Conversely, conflicts arising for other reasons may result in the collapse of the rule of law. A society where the rule of law is absent will ... be prone to conflict and will lack the enabling environment ... for sustainable development and poverty eradication.³¹

A turning point came in late 2003 when, under the British presidency, the Security Council held two high-level meetings on the 'rule of law and justice'. At ministerial level, the Security Council agreed with the Secretary-General on the need for 'a comprehensive approach to justice and the rule of law', one that 'should encompass the entire criminal justice chain – not just police, but lawyers, prosecutors, judges and prison officers, as well as many issues beyond the criminal justice system.'³² That such an agenda appeared to broaden ('not just police'³³), rather than narrow, the parameters of rule of law work is explicable only in the context of evolving and competing institutional mandates. Police training had been identified as an inadequate focus of peacekeeping. Indeed, the perceived failures of the past provided the rationale for the advertised expansion of rule of law activities:

> The United Nations ... has learned that the rule of law is not a luxury and that justice is not a side issue. We have seen people lose faith in a peace process when they do not feel safe from crime, or secure in returning to their homes, or able to start rebuilding the elements of a normal life, or confident that the injustices of the past will be addressed. We have seen that without credible machinery to enforce the law and resolve disputes, people resort to violent or illegal means. And we have seen that elections held when the rule of law is too fragile seldom lead to lasting democratic governance.³⁴

---

³⁰ A/55/305–S/2000/809, paras. 224–225.   ³¹ DP/2001/4, para. 39.
³² S/PV.4833, 2.
³³ See also S/PV.4835, 4, remarks of Jean-Marie Guéhenno, Under-Secretary-General for Peacekeeping Operations: 'the establishment of the rule of law requires more than just a focus on policing. It requires that all components of the criminal justice chain – the police, the judiciary, the defence bar, prosecutors and corrections – be included and funded.'
³⁴ S/PV.4833, 3.

The new rule of law emphasis coincided with a shift of vocabulary at the UN from 'peacekeeping' to 'peacebuilding'.[35] When the Secretary-General recommended the establishment of a 'Peacebuilding Commission', the rule of law became an inevitable centrepiece, quickly coming to stand in generally for a set of operational SSR guidelines.[36] The S-G proposed 'concrete actions' to permit the UN to 'support domestic reform constituencies, help build the capacity of national justice sector institutions, facilitate national consultations on justice reform and transitional justice and help fill the rule of law vacuum evident in so many post-conflict societies.'[37] The key notion of a 'rule of law vacuum', a *social* void disclosed as conflicts recede, provided the UN with a new role: 'restoring' the rule of law with the rudimentary building blocks of the state.[38] To that end, a 'division of labour' was established within the UN, 'in which designated lead entities would assume clearly defined coordination and other responsibilities for specific areas of rule of law activity'.[39] UN's Office of Legal Affairs (OLA) had responsibility for international and hybrid criminal tribunals; OHCHR was given the 'overall lead for transitional justice and monitoring'; DPKO was to lead on 'police and law enforcement, on prison system reform [and] on strengthening legal and judicial institutions' in peacekeeping contexts.[40] UNDP was initially allocated court administration and civil

---

[35] The notion of 'peacebuilding' too was channelled through the Brahimi report (A/55/305–S/2000/809, para. 13), as an adjunct to 'peacemaking' and 'peacekeeping': 'Peace-building ... includes but is not limited to reintegrating former combatants into civilian society, strengthening the rule of law (for example, through training and restructuring of local police, and judicial and penal reform); improving respect for human rights through the monitoring, education and investigation of past and existing abuses; providing technical assistance for democratic development (including electoral assistance and support for free media); and promoting conflict resolution and reconciliation techniques.'

[36] On the Peacebuilding Commission, see A/59/2005, paras. 114–119.

[37] S/2004/616, para. 65; summary.

[38] See also A More Secure World (2004), para. 229: 'Along with establishing security, the core task of peacebuilding is to build effective public institutions that, through negotiations with civil society, can establish a consensual framework for governing within the rule of law. Relatively cheap investments in civilian security through police, judicial and rule-of-law reform, local capacity-building for human rights and reconciliation, and local capacity-building for public sector service delivery can greatly benefit long-term peacebuilding. This should be reflected in the policies of the United Nations, international financial institutions and donors, and should be given priority in long-term policy and funding.'

[39] A/61/636–S/2006/980, para. 39.

[40] Secretary-General's Decision on the Rule of Law (Decision No. 2006/47 of 24 November 2006), cited in DPKO Primer, 11. UNICEF and UNHCR too produced tools for transitional contexts. See A/61/636–S/2006/980, para. 26.

law in post-conflict scenarios, in part because the 'inventory' of skills upon which allocations were first made had concluded that UNDP 'lacks a clear conceptual framework for JSSR' (justice and security sector reform).[41] Since then, however, UNDP's Bureau for Crisis Prevention and Recovery (BCPR) has published a three-year 'global programme', aiming at 'integrated and coherent UN system-wide assistance and coordination on Rule of Law/JSSR'.[42]

Rule of law 'tools' have, as a result, spilled forth from UN agencies. UNODC produced a 'criminal justice assessment toolkit', covering policing, judiciaries ('Access to Justice'), corrections ('Custodial and Non-Custodial Measures') and 'cross-cutting issues' such as victim protection and juvenile justice.[43] It also examined how 'strengthening the rule of law' (meaning, in this case, crime reduction) would aid development in Africa.[44] DPKO and OHCHR refined their operational guidelines in the post-conflict arena. In 2006, OHCHR produced a series of 'Rule of Law Tools for Post-Conflict States', covering five areas: Mapping the Justice Sector, Prosecutions, Truth Commissions, Vetting (personnel in the justice sector) and Monitoring (of legal systems).[45] DPKO published a 2006 'United Nations Primer for Justice Components in Multidimensional Peace Operations: Strengthening the Rule of Law', intended as a practical guide for peacekeepers.[46] UNDP added its own series of handbooks, guides and policy documents.[47]

Rule of law 'units' and other advisory bodies also flourished, starting with internal focal points, task forces and working groups devoted to developing UN policy on the rule of law.[48] Advisory and coordination

---

[41] EOSG (2006), 27.
[42] UNDP (2008). UNDP is also eking out a niche in DDR ('disarmament, demobilisation and reintegration'), where it works with DPKO and other donors. See also UNDP (2003); UNDP (2002). The US Congressional Budget Justification for FY 2009 sought US$ 76.4 million for UNDP (by way of comparison, OHCHR was allocated under $1 million): CBJ FY2009, 123.
[43] See online at: www.unodc.org/unodc/en/justice-and-prison-reform/Criminal-Justice-Toolkit.html; UNODC (2006b).
[44] UNODC (2005).
[45] OHCHR, Rule-of-Law Tools for Post-Conflict States: OHCHR (2006a), (2006b), (2006c), (2006d), (2006e).
[46] DPKO (2006). For background see Carlson (2006).
[47] A/61/636–S/2006/980, para. 26.
[48] These include a Task Force for the Development of Comprehensive Rule of Law Strategies for Peace Operations under the UN's Executive Committee on Peace and Security (one of four committees established to advise on UN reform). The Task Force created a Rule of Law Focal Point Network, bringing together eleven UN departments

units followed, foremost among them the Office of Rule of Law and Security Institutions (OROLSI) established within the DPKO in 2007 (a much discussed 'rule of law assistance unit' at the Peacebuilding Commission not yet having come into being[49]) whose frankly security-centred mandate captures the particular application of rule of law language in this register:

> [OROLSI] was created ... to provide an integrated and forward-looking approach to United Nations assistance in rule of law and security entities. OROLSI unifies police, judicial, legal, correctional units, and mine action, disarmament, demobilization and reintegration [DDR], as well as new security sector reform functions, primarily in support of United Nations peacekeeping operations. [It also operates] globally ... in the context of countries with no peacekeeping missions...[50]

As a result of all this activity, the Secretary-General could report in December 2006 that the UN is 'consistently integrating rule of law and transitional justice issues into the strategic and operational planning of new peace operations'.[51] And too, 'the Security Council is more prepared than previously to include human rights, policing, judicial and legal systems and prison system responsibilities in mandates.'[52]

---

and agencies (Office of Legal Affairs (OLA), Department of Political Affairs (DPA), DPKO, OHCHR, UNDP, UNESCO, UNICEF, UNIFEM, UNFPA, UNODC, UNOPS) 'to facilitate coordination on rule of law issues and to strengthen [the UN's] support to rule of law aspects of peace operations'. See S/2004/616, para. 57; also EOSG (2006), 45; ECPS (2002); Oswald (2002). A Rule of Law Coordination and Resource Group was also created, as well as a Working Group on Rule of Law and Justice, chaired by an Assistant Secretary-General and consisting of OLA, DPA, DPKO, OHCHR, UNODC, UNDP and UNHCR. See A/61/636–S/2006/980, paras. 27, 33, 46.

[49] On the Rule of Law Assistance Unit see, for example, A/59/2005, para. 137, and A/RES/60/1, para. 134.

[50] See: www.un.org/Depts/dpko/dpko/orolsi.shtml. 'All relevant [DPKO] entities have been brought together into OROLSI: the Police Division; the Criminal Law and Judicial Advisory Section; the Disarmament, Demobilization, and Reintegration Section; the United Nations Mine Action Service; and certain Security Sector Reform functions.'

[51] A/61/636–S/2006/980, para. 7. 'Member States now almost universally recognize the re-enforcement of the rule of law as an important aspect of peace missions in order to achieve sustainable peace and security.'

[52] In June 2006, the Danish Presidency of the Security Council called another meeting on 'justice and the rule of law', again centring on post-conflict states. See S/2006/367, Letter dated 7 June 2006 from the Permanent Representative of Denmark to the United Nations addressed to the Secretary-General (7 June 2006). The agenda asked 'How should the Council approach developing a policy on what United Nations peacekeeping missions could do in cases of rule-of-law vacuums, including on the need for United Nations forces to take on detention powers? What

Peacekeeping operations today regularly incorporate rule of law units, tasked with demilitarisation and the establishment of criminal justice and other legal institutions within post-conflict states. They typically work closely with transitional governments on the legal and institutional architecture to that end.[53] UNMIL in Liberia and MONUC in the Democratic Republic of Congo both have such units, whose mandate includes training police, magistrates and corrections officers, building and equipping prisons, courts and police stations and DDR.[54] UNMIL now boasts a Rule of Law Implementation Committee and recently appointed a Deputy Special Representative of the Secretary-General for Rule of Law. The definition of the rule of law supplied in DPKO's 'principles and guidelines for operations' (the 'Capstone Principles'), codifying best practices, describes a set of activities that cumulatively bear little obvious relation to the rule of law ideal described in Part I:

[T]he rule of law in the context of conflict and post-conflict settings includes the following sectors: transitional justice; strengthening of national justice systems and institutions, including police and law enforcement agencies and prisons; and other priority areas such as victim and witness protection and assistance, anti-corruption, organized crime, trans-national crime, and trafficking and drugs.[55]

The Capstone Principles reserve and isolate the term 'rule of law' from other management 'tasks' in post-conflict states, such as 'economic governance', with the former a task for UN peacekeepers, the latter for the World Bank (see diagram below). The 'division of labour' introduced at the UN thus appears to replicate a larger division of labour within which the UN is merely one of a number of transnational institutional

---

role could the Peacebuilding Commission play in advising the Council on rule-of-law issues?'

[53] This renewed rule of law focus coincided with a 'surge' in peacekeeping operations In the month of August 2006 alone, the number of peacekeepers deployed by the UN increased by almost 50 per cent: Security Council Report, 'Twenty Days in August: The Security Council Sets Massive New Challenges for UN Peacekeeping', Special Research Report No. 5 (8 September 2006). See DPKO Surge 2006. See Security Council resolutions 1701, 1704 and 1706 on Lebanon, Timor-Leste and Darfur respectively, involving a cumulative increase of personnel from 78,413 to 115,655. The total deployment of police officers almost doubled, from 8,713 to 15,621.

[54] In the case of MONUC, the preferred term is DDRRR ('disarmament, demobilization, repatriation, resettlement and reintegration'), the extra terms signifying the fact that the armed groups are often foreign; they are repatriated by the UN to their home countries where, in principle, their governments are expected to assist in their 'resettlement and reintegration'. See www.monuc.org/news.aspx?newsID=712.

[55] DPKO (2008), 42 (note 12).

162   THEATRE OF THE RULE OF LAW: STATE

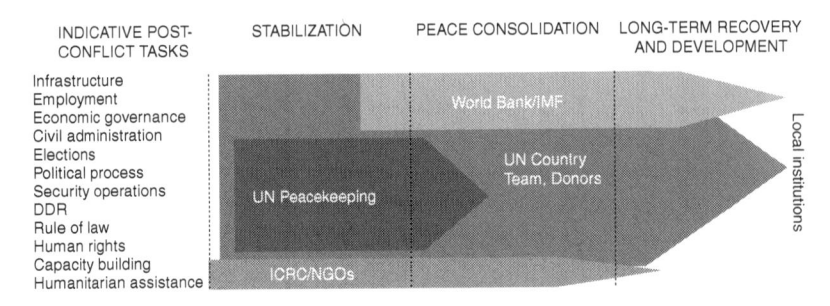

Figure 1: The core business of multi-dimensional United Nations peace-keeping operations
Source: DPKO, United Nations Peacekeeping Operations: Principles and Guidelines (the 'Capstone Principles') (2008)

actors skilled in rule of law specialisations of various kinds. UN bodies appear in the main today as the 'implementers' of a *certain kind* of rule of law valued under conditions of (global) instability and insecurity.

THE RULE OF LAW AND ORDER?

Law enforcement capacity dominates the vision of the rule of law put forward in the documents of the INL, ICITAP and OPDAT, on one hand, and of the DPKO, UNODC and (increasingly) UNDP, on the other, to the near exclusion of other themes. Yet the fixation, in this exceedingly widespread deployment of rule of law vocabulary, on what amounts to good old-fashioned 'law and order' is surely jarring. Rule of law enthusiasts habitually distance themselves from 'mere law and order'. 'Rule *of* law', it is often claimed, 'is not the same as rule *by* law', where the latter is associated with authoritarian regimes that operate through strict law enforcement, while yet disrespecting that more precious and nuanced ideal, the 'rule of law'.[56] Nevertheless, the expression 'rule of law' appears to have quite supplanted the old 'law and order' in recent literature – the latter appears extremely rarely in project documents; when it does, it is downgraded (to 'basic' or 'baseline' law and order), restricted to contexts, such as refugee camps, where the state is entirely absent, or, more often, assigned wholly negative connotations.[57]

---

[56] The distinction between 'rule of law' and 'rule by law' is a staple of recent rule of law accounts. See for example, Carothers (2006), 5; Tamanaha (2005), 4; Belton (2005), 9. See also the discussion of Aristotle in Chapter 3 above.
[57] UNDP's rule of law 'global programme' for 2008–2011 offers a typical example: 'Armed actors tend to be the principal agents of "law and order", often at the cost

And whereas criminal justice has frequently constituted a mainstream rule of law concern, the focus has generally been on the rights of the accused, a theme that fits easily into a favourite rule of law genealogy from Magna Carta through habeas corpus. It is odd, then, to find so little attention devoted to 'due process' in rule of law as a criminal justice export, and so much devoted instead to yearnings for a more capable coercive state such as, for example: numbers of prisons constructed; police and prison officers trained; prosecutions launched and convictions achieved, and to the publicising of achievements such as the arming of police (a recent 'rule of law milestone' in Liberia).[58] It is not that the desiderata of a strong state are incompatible with the (hitherto) mainstream doctrine of the rule of law. It is rather that such topics – the expansion of prisons and police forces – have always had a marginal place (or indeed none at all) within rule of law narratives and sit strangely at its centre. Many of the attributes and tensions that usually mark, or even define, the rule of law, as per Chapter 1, have quite vanished from view in these accounts; historical/cultural contingency, organicism, free acquisition, and parliamentary autonomy, are all absent. The elements that remain – state-centricism, legalism, discipline and (presumably) pluralism – on their own sketch a very different, if still related, animal to the rule of law described above: its centre of gravity has shifted dramatically.

How has such an impoverished vision of the rule of law become so widespread and readily deployed in international assistance? A number of possible answers present themselves. One is that it may be merely incidental, a convenient marriage between, on one hand, a response to pressing security needs in post-conflict environments and, on the other, the ready availability of a language already shared by the principal donors. This would be the rule of law in talismanic mode, a motivating language familiar to all that engenders a sense of shared purpose. Even if a theoretical basis for a 'hard' rule of law register is lacking, on this view, it may be thought useful to introduce the language throughout

---

of basic human rights and customary practices': UNDP (2008), 29. The term is rarely used even as a synonym. CBJ FY2009, for example, detailing police, military and other assistance in over 100 countries, has 267 iterations of the term 'rule of law' as against 7 of 'law and order'.

[58] 'The fifth class of 33 Corrections Officers, including six females, graduated in May, adding momentum to the ongoing efforts to strengthen Liberia's Rule of Law institutions': 'More Corrections Officers Graduate', UNMIL (2008), 16. See also, 'Police Rearmed', UNMIL (2007b), 14. Similar examples can be found throughout the archives of UNMIL's *Focus* and MONUC's website.

the state-building process: a blunter deployment during a cruel-to-be-kind law-and-order phase to begin; a more nuanced articulation waiting in the wings until 'stabilisation' is complete. Thematising the rule of law at *each* stage might be good practice on this view; to do so injects continuity and structure into a long-term process and prepares target populations for a fuller denouement in a later act. If this were so, the saturation of post-conflict law enforcement in rule of law themes would, perhaps, be somewhat self-consciously disingenuous to start with, expected to come into its own over time.

Alternatively, a second, perhaps stronger, argument might be made that an effective state is a *necessary* prerequisite of the rule of law which must therefore be constructed sequentially. One cannot (this argument would say) be overly concerned with limiting the state until there is an effective state to limit. The message is of overriding imperatives: building the rule of law must begin with the nuts and bolts of functional legal coercion; we can worry about the frills later. Thinking along these lines appears to underpin the Capstone Principles cited above: law enforcement is the hard face of the rule of law, economic opportunity its soft underside. The disciplined security-centred rule of law would then be a necessary but insufficient first step required before reformers could turn to the niceties of economic 'freedoms'.[59]

And yet, although there is robust theoretical backing for the notion that strong authoritative control is a pre-requisite of statehood (see Weber in Chapter 2; a comparable tradition derives from Hobbes), the standard rule of law narrative has classically resisted – indeed it has generally constituted a term of resistance to – this 'Leviathan'. The authors examined in Part I do not suggest that a hard law-and-order state must prefigure the rule of law; to the contrary, the mainstream genealogy running from Dicey through Hayek to the Bank is profoundly Lockean (rather than Hobbesian) in this respect, viewing liberty, property and exchange as *natural*, and introducing the state only as a servant or coordinator of this natural order, not its progenitor. (The latter notion, however, underpinned colonial approaches to the management of land in the colonies, as we saw above in the Interlude.)

---

[59] At the extreme, such an approach would see in conflict an *opportunity* for future rule of law reform, a thought articulated at the World Bank (2006e), 19: 'In the post-conflict context, there appears to be a window of opportunity for reform because the system has often collapsed, and there are few actors remaining that have institutional incentives to oppose reform, in contrast to rule of law reform in weak but entrenched legal systems.'

In any case, rhetoric aside, it is doubtful that rule of law interventions are, in fact, pursued sequentially: the introduction of market-friendly legal structures generally takes place simultaneously – and often, where post-conflict countries are resource-rich, urgently.[60] The World Bank frequently acts as a coordinator of disarmament, demobilisation and reintegration (DDR) programmes – which themselves often involve multiple donors – both because of the large volumes of finance involved and because such projects shift financing directly from security into 'development'.[61] The Bank often involves itself simultaneously in re-engineering the legal environment for private sector development even during ongoing conflict. With war still underway in the DRC, for example, the Bank responded in early 2008 to a government request for private sector financing with a proposal to, instead, reorder the 'legal and judicial environment for private sector development'.[62] (Components of the proposed project include the establishment of commercial courts, the promotion of arbitration, a review of land laws and labour laws, and 'drafting of new laws and regulations in the financial sector'.)

Some interventions advertised as 'rule of law promotion' in this register appear to run quite contrary to fundamental conceptions of the rule of law in its standard 'home' narrative. For example, training foreign security officials in US counter-terrorist techniques as part of that country's 'war on terrorism' (see the ATA Program above, text at note 4) appears to run counter to the dominant strain of rule of law critique outlined in Chapter 3: a number of the collaborative exercises undertaken between US and other security actors have been identified by observers as violating conceptions widely associated with 'the rule of law'.[63] Rule of law promotion in this mode thus offers an illustration

---

[60] See, for example, Rebecca Bream, 'Stability Tempts Mining Companies back to Congo', *Financial Times* (February 21, 2007) [reprinted on MONUC website].
[61] See, for example, WB DRC (2007); IMF DRC (2007a).
[62] WB DRC (2008), 3–5. The proposed project will also facilitate 'dialogue' between the private sector and the government. Separately, a large 'governance' project involves restructuring the public sector and mining industry, and decentralising government. Co-donors include DFID, UNDP, the EU and the Belgian government. See also IMF DRC (2007b).
[63] Perhaps the best-known examples involve the practices of 'extraordinary rendition', administrative detention, and coercive interrogation. See, for examples, PACE Doc. 11302 rev. Marty (June 2007) (para. 14: 'The fight against terrorism must not serve as an excuse for systematic recourse to illegal acts, massive violation of fundamental human rights and contempt for the rule of law'); E/CN.4/2006/120 ('the legal

of the suggestion in Chapter 3 above that sovereign enablement may reside within disciplinary restraint.

This last consideration returns us to the awkward conundrum with which we began: how come the rule of law, used in this register, looks so unmistakeably similar to 'law and order'? How can it comport with the wholesale invitation to a public policing power to ownership and control of the public space, as a matter of both stated principle and practice? This chapter's final section will examine this question of discipline and enablement further with a view to identifying some themes that might have encouraged or facilitated the term's apparent passage.

The lure of law

As in the previous chapter, it is not my intention here to provide definitive answers to these questions, or to determine *why* the rule of law register has achieved this curiously preeminent status in the context of transnational police training and criminal justice assistance. But again, I will try to identify a few expectable effects of such a choice, some similar to those in the previous section, others peculiar to this context. Again the intention is not to capture what rule of law promotion has or has not achieved *in fact*, but to identify some of the background expectations that may reside within the choice of its rhetorical deployment in a particular context. Four such possible expectations follow.

First, the rule of law plays a deactivating function. What does the rule of law in peacekeeping and criminal justice exclude? An entire rich vocabulary of peacemaking and reconciliation – forgiveness, mercy, compassion, amnesty – is rendered difficult or unavailable where a rule of law vocabulary is successfully enacted in post-conflict settings.[64] *Impunity* is frequently the lead motif introducing a rule of law culture in post-conflict scenarios.[65] Story after story tells how a

---

regime applied to these detainees seriously undermines the rule of law', para. 17); A/HRC/10/3; Mark Danner, 'US Torture: Voices from the Black Sites', *New York Review of Books*, Vol. 56, No. 6 (April 9, 2009) (citing US Senator Patrick Leahy: 'our detention policies and practices … have seriously eroded fundamental American principles of the rule of law').

[64] For thoughtful discussion, see Sarat and Hussain (2007).
[65] For example, immediately after the invasion of Iraq, the United States Institute of Peace produced a policy paper entitled 'Establishing the Rule of Law in Iraq', that

'culture of impunity' flourished during war or in a previous regime, and must now be uprooted or eradicated. The DPKO Primer contrasts a 'culture of impunity' with a 'culture of the rule of law', illustrating en route the many obstacles that may stand in the way of establishing the latter:

Lack of Rule of Law Culture: The rule of law presupposes a basic culture of legal accountability and faith in state institutions. Parts of the society in a post-conflict environment may have limited experience with the underlying concepts of democracy and human rights. A whole generation might be born and raised in an environment of violence and may have little experience with formal nonviolent mechanisms for resolving disputes. Moreover, there may well be cultural or social factors that impede the establishment of pluralistic democratic institutions that protect human rights. Local counterparts also may have strategic interests opposed to the establishment of independent rule of law institutions, and a lack of political will for reform ...[66]

Victims of violence, we are assured, seek 'justice'; the 'rights of victims' must be prioritised in the criminal justice process.[67] The task of a rule of law regime, then, is to channel that 'desire for justice' away from 'revenge' and towards judicial process.[68] In the backdrop, the machinery of international ad hoc and hybrid criminal tribunals dramatises these motifs in, as it were, a global rule of law theatre. Thus the Secretary-General, in his pivotal 2004 report, writes of the ad hoc tribunals:

They have proved that it is possible to deliver justice and conduct fair trials effectively at the international level ... More significantly still, they reflect a growing shift in the international community, away from a tolerance for impunity and amnesty and towards the creation of an international rule of law.[69]

This shift in the application of rule of law language in the criminal justice sphere from a traditional concern with the 'rights of the accused' to its new focus on the 'rights of victims' constitutes a remarkable turnaround in rule of law discourse.

---

outlined the stakes: 'Establishing the rule of law will require a two-track process, involving: (1) administering justice for past atrocities and ridding the Iraqi government of those implicated in the abuses of the regime, and (2) rebuilding the justice system': USIP (2003a), 7.

[66] DPKO (2006), 4. See also, Carlson (2006), 2.
[67] See for example, OHCHR (2007); DOJ (2006), 91; in an Annex, DPKO (2006) lists 16 international soft-law instruments under the title 'rights of victims'.
[68] DPKO (2006), 4.   [69] S/2004/616, para. 40.

Second, reflecting its economic deployment, rule of law in this second register also naturalises a certain kind of social order, albeit with a very different emphasis. Whereas in its market promotion context, the rule of law speaks of freedom, the rule of law here is rather about discipline – or rather, the disciplinary face of the rule of law that remains largely implicit in discussions of the market here becomes explicit. Nevertheless, this is not simply a complementary register; it does not describe merely the restraints on the public sector that frame and support the freedom of private individuals. Rather, the disciplinary themes that run throughout this mode, or code, of practice, aspire to all equally, private and public alike. The rule of law in this register is disciplinary in (at least) three senses.[70]

The immediate disciplinary subjects are the state's newly trained security forces and judicial personnel, who are disciplined primarily in regard to their hierarchical superiors, and to their trainers and 'mentors' in the 'international community'. The latter are not merely the positive source of rules, methods and procedures, but also constitute the normative source of the disciplinary apparatus itself. This is also, therefore, discipline with regard to the law (a literal 'rule of law'), an obedience that applies even if the ultimate source of the particular law in question is distant, unknown or inaccessible.[71] Beyond the pedagogy of 'training', the human rights component of most programmes prescribes a further layer of disciplinary restraint and normative orientation, reaffirming the superiority of the universal order over what had prevailed locally ('chaos' or 'custom').[72] In post-conflict settings, where officers and officials must first abandon allegiance to

---

[70] Michel Foucault distinguishes between 'government' and 'discipline'. The former is concerned with the big picture – the welfare of the population at large, 'the improvement of its condition, the increase of its wealth, longevity [and] health'. It operates (in Tania Li's succinct summary) 'by educating desires and configuring habits, aspirations and beliefs'. Discipline, by contrast, seeks to reform specific groups through detailed supervision. While rule of law promotion as a whole might be described as 'government', I am here concerned with the more precise category of 'discipline'. See Foucault (2000), 218–219; Li (2006), 3.
[71] So, for example, at the closing ceremony following a joint four-day US–UN training session for Congolese officials conducted by DIILS and MONUC, the provincial governor 'underlined the importance of the knowledge gained from the training in capacity building, respect for law and good discipline to the military justice officers, in order to maintain law and order within the army': MONUC (2008).
[72] Police reform is 'never easy' in post-conflict scenarios, where security forces will themselves 'have often perpetrated human rights violations,' changing the institutional 'ethos' to a 'rights-respecting' culture: O'Neill (2005), 1–2.

previous disciplinary regimes, reform involves a host of disciplinary mechanisms:

> Effective and sustainable institutional reform is a complex and challenging task. Institutional reform measures may include, for example, the creation of oversight, complaint and disciplinary procedures; the reform or establishment of legal frameworks; the development or revision of ethical guidelines and codes of conduct; changing symbols that are associated with abusive practices; and the provision of adequate ... equipment and infrastructure.[73]

A term now commonly used to distinguish the role of the police under new universal regimes from whatever role they may have had under various authoritarianisms is 'democratic policing'.[74] Its model systems are those of South Africa and Northern Ireland, where mixed ethnic police 'services' have gradually replaced ethnically-biased and/or authoritarian 'forces'. Democratisation not only signifies that minorities are better represented, but also that human rights and ethics codes are known and respected, that internal disciplinary mechanisms exist, and that the officer 'on the street' views their role as to 'serve and protect' the law-abiding citizen, while nevertheless retaining the authority to make an initial determination as to who might or might not be 'law-abiding'.[75] The officers' submission to the new disciplinary order brings rewards in the form of equipment (uniforms, but also weapons), tangible authority and the lure of a prestigious career path.[76] While augmenting their coercive capacity, including through improved coordination techniques, democratic policing repackages public control as the actualisation of the public's own freedom.

The target population in the host country are, then, a second relevant group, both vital spectators and participants in the drama of discipline.

---

[73] OHCHR (2006d), 4.   [74] See generally, for example, Bayley (2001).

[75] UNMIL asked members of the general public what they wish from their new police force. One featured reply: 'I would like to see a disciplined and tolerant new Liberian police focused on the rule of law. Those now being trained should take the public as a friend and not an enemy. I want to see a refined police which will serve the interest of the masses; where those in trouble and distress can run to and not run from. Yes, a police that can protect and defend the public': UNMIL (2007a), 38.

[76] According to the OHCHR, 'Internal disciplinary mechanisms, if fair and objective, encourage good behaviour since they directly influence an officer's career'; 'Successful police or judicial reform is every bit as much about personnel management, established career paths and transparent disciplinary procedures as it is about human rights training and awareness campaigns or about improved crime-fighting equipment or computerized case management systems': OHCHR (2006a), 33, 38.

Indeed, this is the flipside of the steady excoriation of impunity in rule of law literature. For victims to receive 'justice', perpetrators must be punished. Prisons are an early and central aspect of post-conflict rule of law, in both UN and US work, in what appears to be a direct descendant of colonial era criminal law interventions. Rule of law reformers assist in drafting criminal laws, building criminal courts and training magistrates and investigators. An entire criminal justice machinery is built and set in motion by reformers. The United States, for example, measures the progress of its transnational crime assistance by the number of prosecutions and convictions obtained annually (5,808 prosecutions for human trafficking were initiated with US help in 2007, resulting in 3,150 convictions; the target for 2008 was 6,098 prosecutions and 3,308 convictions, rising, in 2009, to 6,403 and 3,473 respectively).[77]

The rule of law in this mode not only reconstructs the normative environment, it also creates and sharpens a line between legitimacy and illegitimacy, in order to highlight and police (both figuratively and literally) the boundaries between acceptable and unacceptable social, moral, cultural and economic behaviours. In this area, rule of law and human rights oppose not only the atrocious habits of wartime, but also the residual or revived 'traditional' practices of peacetime. The rule of law response (a contemporary recycling of the colonial 'repugnancy' motif[78]) is to seek distinct lines – although they may not be immediately available – to assess customary practices in the light of human rights norms, reshape or reform them when judged incompatible with constitutional rights, and realign and universalise them when judged compatible.[79]

The discipline of the rule of law is, thirdly, a source of efficiency and productivity. In principle, it contributes to the extension of

---

[77] CBJ FY2009, 748–749. This indicator is used as a proxy by the US government to 'assess a host government's progress in instituting rule of law and criminal justice sector improvements'. The transnational crime budget is rising rapidly, from US$ 51 million spent in 2007 to over US$ 99 million requested for 2009.

[78] In European colonies in Africa, 'customary' law was to be recognised as long as it was not 'repugnant to natural justice, equity, and good conscience' (in British Africa) or to 'the principles of civilization' (in French Africa), prompting A. O. Elias to ask whether customary law is, in fact, really law at all, given its 'constitutional dependence upon principles that could only be found elsewhere': See Delavignette (1968), 87–88.

[79] Thus a UNDP rule of law project in Darfur 'entails support to traditional and tribal conflict resolution mechanisms, dialogue and the alignment of customary laws and structures with basic universal standards, while harmonizing these with statutory justice mechanisms': UNDP (2007), 20.

transformative potential across the span and resources of a territory, and throughout populations.⁸⁰ The capacity to implement policy effectively throughout territories depends both on the efficiency and obedience of public servants – a functional bureaucracy in the Weberian sense – and also on the shared signalling system of an overarching normative and instructive language. From this perspective, the rule of law training of officials is a natural ally of the international community's 'governance' objectives (see below, Chapter 6).

So far, I have identified two possible functions that the introduction of rule of law language might be expected to achieve: a deactivating and a disciplinary function. A third expectable function of rule of law language in the peacekeeping context is to manage the terms of debate. Regardless of the existence of consensus or otherwise on the need for 'law and order' in a post-conflict context, that vocabulary carries colonial overtones that the rule of law register manages to avoid. 'Law and order' brings with it an abandoned vocabulary from an undignified past that has not always been forgotten in target countries, and that might obstruct reform.⁸¹ Marginal distinctions thus run right through contemporary peacekeeping language cumulatively painting a quite different picture from past practice. Where 'pacification' in that past kept recalcitrant populations in check, 'peace and security' today expresses the collective will of the world's states. Where colonial armies put down 'skirmishes' and checked mischief-makers and 'ringleaders', today's interveners are peacemakers in the midst of 'civil unrest' – no longer caused by the rapaciousness of foreign powers, but by the 'greed or grievance' of local 'warlords' struggling over scarce resources.⁸² Where the root problem in the past was training sufficient 'native administrators' today it is the 'fragility' of the state itself.⁸³

These worrying associations of the past that might be revived in a language of law and order do not, however, accrue to the 'rule of law'

---

⁸⁰ In August 2007, then Special Representative of the Secretary-General Coordinator of United Nations Operations in Liberia, Alan Doss, wrote how 'important [it is] to expand the presence of the LNP [Liberian National Police] in the rural areas to ensure that the rule of law prevails throughout the country': UNMIL (2007a).

⁸¹ A police reform document notes, 'Not wanting to be perceived as neocolonialists, CIVPOL [civilian police trainers] personnel may become too deferential and not press hard enough for important reforms': Bayley (2001), 59.

⁸² Collier and Hoeffler (2002).

⁸³ The shortage of trained native administrators in Africa forms a main theme of Malcolm Hailey's influential report on 'Native Administration and Political Development in British Tropical Africa': Hailey (1979).

register. To speak of the rule of law is, in short – as it is in the economic context – to reach for a language of legitimacy. Reformers might speak of 'rule of law' even where 'law and order' would be accurate and adequate precisely *because* the rule of law is thought to be 'more than' law and order (or 'rule by law'). This 'more' potentially matters for everyone in the process – donors, peacekeepers, and beneficiary trainees and officials – all of whom are thus embarked upon a grand state-building project rather than mere policing and corrections. It is a 'more' that is, however, regularly betrayed in the project literature itself, which, in the pursuit of definable targets and measurable impacts, persistently returns donor efforts to, precisely, policing and corrections.

Fourth, and finally, much as observed in the case of market promotion, in its 'peace and security' register too rule of law language serves to elide the primacy and responsibility of an international *policy* in determining the institutional and legal structures and infrastructures of the state. On one hand, the 'international community', consisting of a broad range of actors, is the explicit source of the authority that underwrites as well as implements the work.[84] Project documents frequently refer to 'international consensus' and international law and 'standards' as the lead motivation, or obligation, for 'local reform'. The international framework is thus facilitative of national-level restructuring. On the other, however, the state-centric language of the rule of law – together with its regular constellational companions, democracy and human rights – reflects these activities and relations back onto the screen of the state-individual (or rather putative state and citizen).

In such cases the primary agent, the congeries of international agencies, are deresponsibilised while the nascent state is burdened with immediate responsibilities: obligation moves to the state, which takes on a debt both to the citizenry and the international 'community', while the lead agents, by contrast, do not incur a debt (to state or citizenry) but are rather *owed* (thanks, responsibility, peace, market access). For example, where training relationships exist between local trainees and international mentors, the rule of law register (and its contractual basis) restructures the same relation as mediated through

---

[84] Today, the Council of the European Union is a significant funder of and participant in this work. Others include DFID, and the French, Belgian and Dutch governments, as well as the US and UN agencies already mentioned. See the press releases on EULEX and EUJUST Themis on the Council's website (http://consilium.europa.eu/), and recent efforts in DRC and Kosovo.

the state, even though the state in question remains, so to speak, a mere promise dependent upon the successful outcome of the training itself (and other related efforts). Although these supposed agents of the state are *in fact* agents of (that is, paid by and acting on behalf of, and according to the directives of) the 'international community', that relation is deliberately subordinated to a national state's notional sovereignty. As these national administrators become, in the course of time, the instruments of the new state, the state itself effectively becomes the administrative face of an apparent international will. This involves a curious reversal of the standard international law account of the relation between the state and the international sphere, with the former a product of the latter, rather than vice versa.

Such an arrangement raises complex questions about sovereignty. On one hand, the capacity for a sovereignty that would inhere in the state must derive from control over its coercive arms. On the other, the capacity, legitimacy and disciplinary reflexes of these same instruments are unequivocally produced by another apparent or de facto sovereign, one that inheres in the nebulous constituent power of the 'international community'. Actual sovereignty, the capacity or freedom to act in the international sphere, is deferred back and forth between, on one hand, a state that, if often little more than a promise or product, is nevertheless close at hand and nominally 'in power', and, on the other, an international community that is rather distant and veiled but nevertheless recognisably and authentically authoritative. The state appears essentially as a proxy for some larger sovereign; it is precisely the transnational source and substance of the 'rule of law' that displaces sovereignty in this manner.

CONCLUSION

This chapter has sketched the main rule of law programmes undertaken to promote 'peace and security' abroad by US and UN agencies. This large volume of work includes training of police, prosecutors, judges and investigative judges, prison officers and soldiers. The work extends from training officials and officers in international law and the law of human rights to inter-governmental collaboration in counter-terrorism and counter-narcotics activities and the amendment of national laws to facilitate information exchange to the same end. It also extends to the physical construction and equipment of prisons, court houses, police stations and the like. Although the reach of this work extends far beyond 'fragile' and 'post-conflict' states, the latter provide the occasion for mobilising and elaborating a rule of law response. Project literature responds to 'rule of law vacuums' with a desire to 'restore' it (echoing the colonial claim to 'preserve' traditional systems while in effect thoroughly reshaping them).[85]

In this chapter I questioned the now ubiquitous deployment of rule of law language to describe these activities and indicated four expectable effects that recourse to this language might have. First, it might be expected to structure the relevant field of justice activities in a certain way – steering discussion away from forgiveness and/or amnesty, and towards retribution and/or punishment. Second, it might be expected to propagate certain disciplinary norms among state actors and, through them, among an imputable 'general public'. Third, in doing so, the rule of law register might be thought to displace an alternative available disciplinary terminology of the past, that of colonialism, displacing an outmoded language of law and order and pacification, with a normatively dissimilar but substantively familiar vocabulary of rule of law and peacebuilding. Fourth, the state-centric emphasis of the rule of law might be expected to obscure, or mystify, the international sources of authority and legitimacy that underlie the construction of the new state.

As in Chapter 4, this chapter too has tracked the rise of a competing signification of the rule of law that appears capable of displacing its hitherto mainstream significations. So widespread and consistent is the deployment of the rule of law in this register that it surely risks occupying the space of the term. Where the rule of law comes to signify the coercive capacity of the state and its disciplinary structures and effects, rather than its constraints; when it signifies the rights of the victim, rather than the accused; when it is measured in convictions and boots on the ground, rather than in the texture of the social fabric (as the authors cited in Chapter 1 would have presumed), something has surely been lost. When such an effect is promoted consistently, country-by-country at global level, through numerous channels, that loss begins to look irrevocable.

---

[85] See generally, on this subject, Mamdani (1996).

6 Public

The rule of law narrative that emerges from a close examination of the project literature resembles a stylised drama, peopled by familiar actors performing from a limited and well-known repertory. The following chapter examines the themes and actors that habitually reappear on the rule of law stage. The motivating theme is modernisation, providing a distinctive setting and consistent background motif. This setting posits a *relation* between donor and recipient countries, with the latter aspiring to the conditions in the former, but also intended to further their mutual association to their mutual benefit. The action, which takes place in the host country, takes the form of a morality play dramatising the complementary, if contrasting, obligations of public and private actors: the former must be bound in order that the latter might be free. The plot comprises a series of set ordeals illustrating the virtues of modern government: moral rectitude (anti-corruption), self-discipline (governance) and self-abnegation (privatisation).[1] Other characters central to plot development are the judiciary, civil society and the media – who in different ways reinforce and refine the public–private divide. The stock character of the 'reform constituency' in the host country mediates the action; significantly more complex character development is expected of 'the poor'. The drama's projected ending looks forward to the integration of the state in the global community, having assumed an enabling environment for investment, judicial protections of assets and of political and economic freedoms, without discrimination, and obligations towards other international actors.

---

[1] See, for a resonant set of themes from 1930, Weber (1992).

These themes and actors are so basic to the rule of law narrative that their appearance here may seem banal to those familiar with the field. Still, by revisiting them in a spirit of naiveté – that is, by setting aside the presumptions and foreknowledge that typically accompany their invocation – my aim is to allow them to serve as windows onto the heart of contemporary transnational rule of law promotion. Throughout I will refer back to materials gathered earlier, in each of the previous chapters, to help illuminate contemporary practices.

THE THEME: MODERNISATION

Rule of law project documents regularly introduce modernisation as a motivating theme. The term is not defined in the literature: rather its rhetorical function is to provide an intuitive rationale for systemic interventions.[2] That rationale hinges on three notions of modernisation, one chronological, another topographical, a third technological.

Chronologically, the notion of modernisation counterposes 'state of the art' laws and institutions against those that are or have become 'outdated'. A project in Russia, for example, claims to address something 'universally recognized as among the most pressing problems in transition countries: the incomplete, out of date, and contradictory legal framework'.[3] Kazakhstan, according to one USAID project document, has had 'no experience with ... the modern rule of law'.[4] A key constraint to Zambia's 'long term development program', on the Bank's assessment, is the country's 'outdated policies and legal framework'.[5] The implication is that much of the apparatus of the state in target countries was made for a different era and is not suited to the present. In many countries, this is a plausible notion; the laws and judicial

---

[2] Twenty-three World Bank rule of law projects thematise 'modernization' in their titles; others, focusing on 'development' and 'reform', introduce the theme through their methodologies and assessments.
[3] WB Russia (2006), 4.   [4] USAID Kazakhstan (2007), 3.
[5] WB Zambia (2008), 46. A 'key priority' in a West Bank project: 'Many laws were in urgent need of modernization to enable local firms to compete regionally and internationally... [T]he judiciary was plagued by concerns as to its independence, outdated procedures and management systems, inadequate facilities and a shortage of funding resources': WB West Bank (2004), 2. A subcomponent of a project in Armenia: 'Based on national priorities, existing technical regulations/standards would be rationalized, eliminating those that are excessive, outdated, or redundant. To fill the regulatory gaps, international standards would be adopted and adapted as appropriate': WB Armenia (2004), 53.

institutions were indeed constructed or shaped during periods of colonialism or communism, with particular purposes in view that may since have vanished or altered. With the recession of the colonial/communist apparatus, state laws and institutions need to be 'overhauled' to suit a new political/economic configuration. So reflexive is this approach that it is even applied in many Latin American countries, despite the comparative remoteness of the colonial era.[6] USAID (among many) observes that misuse and/or underuse over decades of dictatorial and authoritarian leadership had allowed an (already inadequate) inherited European judicial system to fall into disrepair.[7] By extension, a command economy, or indeed economic planning in any form (certainly outside the industrial countries), harks back to a pre-1989 era, is outmoded and needs updating.

By foregrounding modernisation, donors thus effectively distance themselves from their colonial or communist forerunners, and invite partner governments to do likewise. Specificity of historical circumstance is easily elided in the common failure of different countries to achieve rule of law.[8] In practice, the implications differ somewhat for post-colonial and post-communist countries. In the former, the fact that laws and courts are 'outdated' is associated with a lack of investment and/or under-utilisation of the formal machinery of justice.[9] A common implication, as we saw in Chapter 4, in the Bank's pivotal 1989 'governance' report on sub-Saharan Africa, is that post-independence

---

[6] See World Bank (1995d), especially contributions to Part VIII. Assessments on these lines were already common during the first wave of law and development; see for example Rosenn (1971).

[7] 'In the LAC [Latin American and Caribbean] region ... the civil code system had generally failed to modernize; codes had largely become antiquated and anachronistic; and abuses stemming from the opacity of the inquisitorial system had been allowed to develop': MSI (2002), 4 (also 3, 58, 66, 77). The authoritarian governments of the 1980s are less often targets of this rhetoric, perhaps because they often facilitated market reforms. See generally Carothers (1991), Dezalay and Garth (2002); on El Salvador, Orr (1996); on Chile, Valdés (1995).

[8] See, for example, MSI (2002), 25, noting that, despite, their differences, Bangladesh, Egypt, the Philippines, Mongolia and Nepal 'share the common experience of dominance by authoritarian, repressive regimes [who] systematically weakened the courts and marginalized the rule of law'.

[9] In Guinea Bissau 'the legal system is antiquated and constraining, as most of the legislation in force today dates back to the early colonial period': WB Bissau (2002), 8. In Gambia, 'Private sector development is hindered by: (i) lack of good legal, regulatory and incentive frameworks to support investment; (ii) inadequate enforcement of laws for economic processes – laws are outdated and performance of the judicial system is ineffective': WB Gambia (2001), 3.

governments are to blame if once-functional laws and institutions have fallen into desuetude or disrepair or have become dysfunctional due to incoherent policies and legislation or corruption in the intervening years.[10] Post-colonial countries in turn drifted into a 'suffocating' developmentalism: an over-involved state, these narratives indicate, itself breeds corruption and stifles creativity. For post-communist countries, on the other hand, the laws and institutions were never really acceptable even when first instituted. There, overhaul was always needed, but is only now possible. Everywhere, though, the implication is that while the *world*, or *society* has moved inexorably forward, the *state* has failed to keep up (or to 'update'). It is the state's job now to meet the more sophisticated needs of a contemporary national/global/cosmopolitan society. Even while it assaults the government, in short, such a language is designed to appeal to 'modernisers' within government, a 'reform constituency' framed as representing the 'progressive' sectors of 'public opinion': to pull the country forward out of the 'backwardness' of the past.[11]

Modernisation is, second, a topographical concern in that 'modern' societies are distinct from traditional, rural, or customary ones.[12] Modern in this sense is equivalent to 'developed' or 'industrial', and historically correlated with 'western', but as a cultural (rather than an income) category. The *modern state* (a Weberian notion which is, it will be recalled from Chapters 1 and 2, a rule of law requisite, a view

---

[10] Thus in Ghana, 'The intractable land problems and disputes ... cannot be resolved without the streamlining and harmonization of the prevailing contradictory policies and legislation and reforming the non-collaborating and inefficient public sector land agencies': WB Ghana (2003), 15.

[11] One of the earliest sustained expositions of the contemporary reform model, the World Development Report 1991 on 'The Challenge of Development' ('A consensus is forming in favour of a "market-friendly" approach to development': WDR 1991, 1), overlays an inherited pre-colonial backwardness with a newer post-independence backwardness. On one hand '[w]hen many developing countries achieved independence, their leaders were concerned with both political and economic development. Their primary economic goal was the rapid structural transformation of backward agrarian economies into modern industrial ones': WDR 1991, 33. On the other, '[d]uring the 1980s, the backwardness of the command economies contrasted sharply with the rapid technological advance in the market-oriented economies of Asia and the West': WDR 1991, 19.

[12] For example: 'Although substantial military and technical assistance was provided [to Yemen's] government, its governance remained traditional in character, and the size of its public sector was small. Many of the institutions of modern governance were absent and public administration and financial management systems were only partly developed': WB Yemen (2008), para. 1.1.

reiterated verbatim by the Bank[13]) is one in which the state commands unrivalled dominance throughout its territory and has a monopoly over the legitimate use of force; it is a state which has surpassed the parochialism of the community, and replaced it with a pluralist 'tolerance' among strangers who need not share the same backgrounds and belief systems. The 'traditional', by contrast, retains just these elements – communal, shared belief systems (ethnic or religious), parochialism. Since such a system cannot perform statehood, it survives under the wing of a protecting state or remains residually dominant where the supposedly authentic state is absent, weak, or illegitimate. A predominance of 'traditional' justice sectors outside the 'formal' structures of the state is, then, prima facie evidence of weak rule of law. Afghanistan's 'traditional' justice mechanisms have, for example, attracted intense donor interest since efforts commenced, after the 2001 invasion, to establish the rule of law there:

> The 'informal justice sector' or 'customary law sector' covers a wide variety of clusters of norms and practices, often uncodified and orally transmitted, usually combined together in varying mixes. This includes customary law ... local understanding of Islamic legal traditions ... and even some modern laws ... The only thing these methods have in common is that they reflect a level of fairness and justice broadly accepted by the majority of the population and they are all outside the scope of the formal state justice system. Whereas the authoritative purveyors of this decision making and dispute resolution system may enjoy some degree of state endorsement of their authority, including the enforcement of their judgments by the state, the sources of their authority are invariably based in their communities and in local power structures.[14]

In this context, reference to the 'modern' activates and accentuates the difference between donor and recipient countries primarily in terms of the relative capacity of the state. Of particular importance in post-conflict settings – but of insidious significance wherever the capacity of the state is at issue – it sets up a quasi-paternal relation, in which the donor is the bearer of a knowledge and expertise that the recipient cannot be expected to match.

Both colonial and communist states were 'modernising' in this sense; both characterised the 'traditional' as 'backward', 'primitive' or 'childlike' and sought to protect and develop it at once.[15] Paternalist

---

[13] Shihata (1990), 85 (see Chapter 4 above).
[14] USAID Afghanistan (2005), 3–4. See also UNDP (2005); USIP (2003b); USIP (2003c); USIP (2007).
[15] See, for example, Reyes (1995), 192, 195–196; World Bank (2005d), 4.

modernisation of this kind involves nurturing and shaping rather than merely rejecting or overruling the 'traditional'. Legal intervention during the colonial era had as a principal project the cultivation of 'native courts'. It sought to capitalise upon and reshape 'customary' law to fit modern ends.[16] Contemporary rule of law reform too retains gentler reform overtones in the traditional context than it does with regard to (post-communist or post-colonial) positive law. Law reformers speak of 'formalising' or merely 'clarifying' traditional land tenure systems, not replacing them outright, and of 'integrating' traditional or customary legal systems into the 'formal' system to ensure they are in line with constitutional or 'international human rights' norms: as with colonial 'repugnancy' clauses, it is the subordination of 'traditional authorities' to the state's overarching authority – not their elimination – that is desired.[17] In this sense of 'modernisation', then, contemporary rule of law reform is recognisably descended from, if not identical with, a colonial forebear that too sought to preserve but reshape the traditional without actively destroying it. Even though the 'customary', in many post-colonial settings, will often itself be a colonial product, it is generally treated as an 'authentic' traditional inheritance and handled with a mix of respect and reform.[18]

Finally, 'modernisation' is about technology. Modern here refers back to its Enlightenment signification, the reliance on science to dispel myth and superstition and to engender progress. Technology has always constituted evidence of that progress: in any given environment, access to and application of technologies that replace labour, increase efficiency and productivity, and track, monitor and order reality are a sign of the achievement of modernity. In project documents, 'modernisation' translates into numerous technological objectives; indeed, rule of law projects consistently bring technology.[19] Furthermore, the transmission of the *technē*, the know-how, of modern policing, prison,

---

[16] See, for example, Lugard (1926), 547–549, and the 'Interlude' above, text at note 19.
[17] See World Bank (2005d); WDR 1996. In Ethiopia, '[s]trengthening traditional courts, while holding them accountable to constitutional principles, could alleviate the current burden of the formal system on the state': WB LVP (2004), 13. On 'repugnancy' clauses, see Chapter 5, note 79.
[18] See, for example, WB Ghana (2003).
[19] So, in Azerbaijan, a World Bank project involves 'creating new courts and upgrading court facilities, training and evaluating judges, applying new technologies, increasing system efficiency, improving legal assistance, and boosting citizen trust'. WB Azerbaijan (2006), 1–2.

and judicial systems is a recurrent theme. The earliest US-funded administration of justice projects in Latin America brought training in forensic techniques for government investigators, who were using 'long outdated methods'.[20] Electronic database techniques featured in USAID projects throughout the 1990s.[21] In addition to staples – computers, fax machines and photocopiers – projects put video recording equipment in courtrooms and new weapons in the hands of police, introduced 'automated' case-management, workflow and 'enforcement service management' systems, installed databases of legislation and case law, software for land registries and case-tracking, and so forth.[22] Projects even fund the building of 'state of the art' prisons and courthouses.

Hardware interventions are sometimes dismissed by observers as of minor consequence compared with the loftier questions of justice and the public good that rule of law reform raises. Nevertheless, hard technologies alter the physical and psychological context of judicial work and engender soft technological complements. They require training programmes (generally provided through the projects) in which future users familiarise themselves with and adjust to their new technological environment, join socially with their peers as the acolytes of a new enterprise, and acquire fresh habits of thought and practice.[23] The extent to which judges, lawyers, police, prison officers, civil servants and others become 'users' of technology steers them away from what are regarded as old unproductive mindsets and into the new 'communities of practice' that are growing up alongside the technologies, which are themselves transnational. So, for example, in Kazakhstan after the trial introduction of video cameras in courts, USAID claims, 'Judges and lawyers ... reported that all trial participants were generally better prepared for trial – and acted

---

[20] Blair and Hansen (1994), 10, 47. The objective was to prosecute the murderers of three American nuns in 1980.
[21] See the extensive 'grant program status report', provided in Annex C of USAID Central Asia (2007).
[22] Technology inputs are a central component of the great majority of USAID and Bank rule of law projects. See, for prominent examples, USAID Croatia (2004); WB Colombia (2001); WB Albania (2006); WB Morocco (2004); WB Bissau (2002); WB Pakistan (2006).
[23] In Armenia, the World Bank reports in 2007, 'an automated case management system was developed and introduced in seven pilot courts, and efforts are currently underway to extend the system to all courts': WB Armenia (2007b), 14.

more appropriately during trial – when they knew the video recording system would be used.'²⁴

Technological standardisation has other advantages for donors, in that they permit cross-national comparisons, such as aligning tracking of cases – and indeed of the movements of individuals – between states. This is especially relevant to criminal justice projects. A USAID-financed project in Mongolia, for example, 'automated' 14 prosecutor's offices with 117 computers, and photocopiers, telephones and faxes, as well as introducing 'automated fingerprinting identification systems', an 'automated mugshot system' and fully automated case management software, to allow easier exchange between offices and with other agents, including presumably in international collaboration when needed.²⁵

All that said, there is a clear distinction between 'modern' or 'modernity' and 'modernisation'. The rule of law, as noted, has consistently been associated with the 'modern state'. But modernity is not merely a chronological, topographical or technological attribute; rather it is cultural or social. As we saw in Habermas's account in Chapter 1, modernity is understood to involve the inauguration of society's self-awareness *as* society, and its self-propelled role in managing or orchestrating the state in its own (that is, the general) interest. The 'modern state' is, in principle, precisely a state that is subjected to the controls of a given society.²⁶ This control is arrived at through a form of self-reflection, or 'self-reflexivity', to use Anthony Giddens's term – the quality of rational inquiry into social and political process that he describes as the 'quintessential modern trait'.²⁷ Inquiry and critique – the public use of reason, as Kant put it – has thus traditionally been understood as the basis for a 'modern state', or for that quality of the state that qualifies it as 'modern'.²⁸ Clearly 'modernisation', as it appears in rule of law programming, describes a very different process, apparently substituting the epiphenomena of modernity – a smorgasbord of laws

---

²⁴ USAID Kazakhstan (2007), 6.
²⁵ USAID Mongolia (2008), 12–13, 20, 33–34.
²⁶ Foucault traces a similar progression in the term 'government', beginning from self-control (government of the self), continuing through to control of the state. Foucault (2000), 202. See also the discussion of Oakeshott in Chapter 1.
²⁷ Giddens (1991). Self-reflexivity in modernity is traced back to Descartes' *cogito* – the moment of self-recognition that places doubt and self-critique at the heart of a progressive process of disquisition.
²⁸ Kant (1983), 42. See Chapter 1 at note 68.

and technologies, and an insistent delineation of and pressure on the 'traditional' – for the social processes that, in existing accounts of the origins of modernity, are generatively inextricable from these phenomena. No theoretical account is offered in the rule of law literature as to why such reverse engineering might be expected to work. (And indeed there is little evidence that it does work.)

It might presumably be argued that modernity may emerge in reverse, so to speak, itself produced through the conscious introduction of the phenomena that ordinarily characterise its prior existence. If so, rule of law reform, as a modernisation project, would end up looking uncomfortably like its colonial – and indeed communist – forebears, each of which relied on engineered processes of modernisation to produce modernity (and each of which is reflexively derided, within the rule of law literature, for having failed). However, as we shall see in a moment, rule of law promotion takes the modernisation project a step further than its progenitors – into the attempted construction of the very public sphere itself that, on most accounts, is the proper locus and vehicle of the modern.

The reform constituency

An arresting theme that recurs throughout rule of law project documentation is the conviction that in order to 'push through' reform, donors will need to work with a small 'reform-minded' minority in government, sometimes in disregard of the formal legislative process. 'Without reform-minded and active leadership in the Government of Egypt', one project report notes, 'USAID and ATR [Assistance for Trade Reform] efforts would have been futile. This point cannot be overemphasized.'[29] The importance of working through a 'reform constituency' was flagged early on in rule of law work: the first of four 'essential needs', according to a 1994 evaluation of USAID's rule of law work, is 'host country political leadership in support of ROL [sic] reforms'.[30] In practice, donors frequently rely on close links with key figures in government to accelerate reform processes and avoid

---

[29] USAID ATR (2006), vi.
[30] Blair and Hansen (1994), 3. If this support is lacking, 'donors will need to support constituency and coalition building strategies to strengthen political and public pressure for reform.' Coalition-building is, in fact, a significant rule of law activity. One project document puts it thus: 'Skills training not only develops skills but also develops a cadre of change agents': USAID Croatia (2004), 6.

lengthy public or parliamentary debate. USAID, for example, explains the advantages of grant-making over loans in these terms:

> Even highly concessional loans typically require ratification by the legislature, whereas grants can be implemented by the executive branch. The process of legislative approval can stretch the gap between initial project agreement and the start of implementation into months or years. In the meantime conditions may change – a dedicated minister is replaced by one less committed to reform, or the conditions necessary for the passage of a key law or regulation are no longer in place. USAID's grant funding helps avoid this problem.[31]

The World Bank observes that, in practice, successful reforms often avoid the 'process of legislative approval' altogether:

> Macroeconomic reforms are often carried out in times of crisis by a stroke of the pen – achieved by administrative decree and a few key actors. The benefits are usually immediate, visible, and spread across the population, with losers or potential losers often too dispersed or too small in number to be of political importance.[32]

Project documents are replete with references to key legislative hooks introduced by decree, which often turn out to be instrumental in allowing relevant projects to take place at all.[33] Indeed, these begin with the shaping of constitutions, an area where USAID was extremely active in the early 1990s in former communist countries.[34] Delivery of the appropriate legislative environment is typically a core project output; the process through which it is achieved remains secondary. Donors not only 'assist' in drafting legislation, they frequently pre-draft it.[35]

---

[31] USAID (2008), 12.   [32] World Bank (2006c), 2.
[33] See, for example, WB Azerbaijan (2006), 1; WB Indonesia (2003), 8.
[34] MSI (2002), 12 recounts USAID aid in drafting the constitutions of Albania, Armenia, Bulgaria, Georgia, Russia and Ukraine. The general spirit is well captured in the following comment on Macedonia, where USAID did *not* help: 'Macedonia accordingly went about drafting its new constitution, adopted in 1991, and many of the new basic laws, mostly on its own and without technical assistance. And, most observers would say, it did a reasonably good job. The new constitution, for example, recognizes freedom of speech, freedom of religion, and the right to privacy. There is a right to own and inherit property and a guarantee for "freedom of the market and entrepreneurship".'
[35] For example, in Cape Verde, 'Although Mr. David Weinstein did not come to Cape Verde, he provided excellent short term assistance in drafting a modern, comprehensive Industrial Property Law, and suggested revisions to the Cape Verde Copyright Law. Mr. Weinstein also reviewed draft responses to intellectual property questions raised by the European Union and the United States': USAID Cape Verde (2005).

Indeed, even where the work remains local, donor influence is often very hands-on. Here, for example, is the description provided by a USAID consultant on inserting WTO-friendly language into Tajikistan's Civil Procedure Code:

> Specifically, the project carefully and successfully guided the development of the draft [Code] so that each now contains preliminary relief provisions as required for WTO accession ... We argued most loudly for these provisions in the Civil Procedure Code, and were not successful until the eleventh hour, when [project staff] met the Minister of Justice and urged inclusion of these provisions. The project helped draft the necessary language, translated it into Tajik, and worked with the Minister and his colleagues on the reasons for which the provisions were important for Tajikistan's future.[36]

An implicit assumption in much of the literature, as the above citations indicate, is that the beneficiaries of reform are not necessarily apprised of their own best interests – which in turn increases the value of the reform constituency. If they lose ground, projects can suffer or be abandoned.[37] There is thus a constant concern in rule of law reform circles with 'political will', its presence or absence, its inducement and encouragement:

> How can the political will to bring about basic, systemic reform be generated? Such political will is generated from three directions: from below, from within, and from outside. Organized pressure from below, in civil society, plays an essential role in persuading ruling elites of the need for institutional reforms to improve governance. There may also be some reform-minded elements within the government and the ruling party or coalition who, whether for pragmatic or normative reasons, have come to see the need for reform but are reluctant to act in isolation. Finally, external actors in the international community often tip the balance through persuasive engagement with the rulers and the society and by extending tangible rewards for better governance and penalties for recalcitrance.[38]

---

[36] USAID LIME2 (2006), 45.

[37] Thus the World Bank withdrew support for a follow-up to its 'legal and judicial development project' in Yemen after '[t]he implementation of the Judicial Development Component, in particular, was compromised in mid-2001 by the replacement of a reform-minded minister with a significantly more conservative minister' which 'sent a message that modernization of the judiciary was not a priority': WB Yemen (2003), 6. The project's objectives were 'to assess the impact of targeted training of judges and arbitrators on the effectiveness of the judiciary and to enhance the ability of the Ministry of Legal and Parliamentary Affairs to prepare and advise on business and economic legislation'.

[38] USAID (2002a), 48.

The reform constituency is not, however, to be confused with 'the elite'. The latter term, which appears regularly throughout rule of law literature, carries the consistently negative connotation of status quo power-brokers with the most to lose from reform.[39] Corrupt and collusive, the elite – defined as 'any economic, political, ethnic, social or other group trying to promote their interests at the expense of the interests of non-elite members' – are often assumed to have 'captured' the state.[40] Reformers are thus pitted against the elites, as the following 'assessment' of reform prospects in Nigeria illustrates:

> The champions of reform are many but varied, and they tend to lack the resources commanded by those who benefit from the status quo. However, [two] elements ... bode well for reform. The first is that those elites with vested interests in the informal networks of patronage are increasingly divided ... Secondly, the increasing demands placed upon the political elite by the population means that the frailties of the existing political system have become raw and exposed, and threaten to cast the political order into conflict and turmoil.[41]

On this account, the true protagonists in the drama are the 'population' against the 'elite', with the 'reformers' valiantly standing up on behalf of the general interest. Since the elite can manipulate the resources at their disposal, including the media, to capture popular acquiescence, reformers must struggle against popular reticence or misunderstanding. Reform is thus frequently presented as a heroic endeavour, pursued in the face of populist opposition, by a handful of far-sighted and selfless reform-minded politicians or bureaucrats, idealistic civil society agitators, the 'business community', often mobilised in chambers of commerce (who play frequent cameos in rule of law project scripts) and other 'stakeholders'.[42] (Needless to say, 'stakeholders' include

---

[39] An early USAID paper put it thus: 'In developing countries, elite segments of society (which often include the civil service) may use the state as an instrument to pursue their own narrow interests, setting aside the legitimate needs and aspirations of the majority': USAID (1991), 9.
[40] World Bank (2005f), 4. 'Elite capture' is a term of art in Bank literature, extending to the judiciary ('Corruption and elite capture within judicial systems are among the obstacles to development to overcome through legal and judicial reform': World Bank (2005e), 66). See especially, Hellman *et al.* (2003).
[41] USAID Nigeria (2006), v. Other examples: USAID Senegal (2007); Bonicelli (2007).
[42] Rule of law projects frequently work closely with local Chambers of Commerce, but the role of local business is ambiguous in these projects; generally viewed as poorly equipped to themselves constitute a 'reform constituency', the 'business community' is usually rather a target *audience* for public education (see further below).

non-nationals. Thus, a World Bank project in Georgia cites among its target audiences 'international investors': 'the international business community should be aware of the efforts undertaken in Georgia to set in place a competent and fair judiciary and ensure the rule of law.'[43])

LEAD ROLES: PUBLIC AND PRIVATE

Rule of law literature does not offer a theoretical account of the public-private distinction, yet both terms recur with the regularity of a muezzin: we hear much about public accountability and private development, about public policy and private choices; the public and private *sectors* are each supported in different ways. The distinction is treated as natural – it is assumed rather than explained – and the private is consistently privileged over the public, often implicitly: a primary role of the public is to facilitate the freedom of the private. Finally, the legal system's role in the upkeep of this distinction too is implicitly treated as axiomatic in rule of law writing. The law sharpens the distinction even if it rarely articulates it: each sector has its own legal discursive properties and relations between the two are subject to a specific form of regulation.

In Chapter 1, I introduced Jürgen Habermas's account of the rise of the public sphere in Europe during the eighteenth and nineteenth centuries. Where Habermas described the constitutional guarantees introduced to preserve the integrity of the public sphere in Europe, I remarked on their inextricability from contemporary notions of the rule of law. The account was intended not only to reiterate the genealogy, and thus historical and cultural contingency, of contemporary rule of law notions, but also to describe the particular social conditions that had allowed this particular idea or ideal of the public sphere to flourish in the first place. Among these, one necessary condition was the cultural and social development of technologies, notably communication technologies (printing presses, newspapers, the theatre), supportive of concrete and differentiable public and private activities. A consolidating notion of 'privacy' applying to individuals 'in their own

---

The ambiguity is captured in a World Bank project in Zambia: '[The] weakness of domestic lobbies, such as the business community, which might otherwise pressure the state to improve services or infrastructure, promotes inertia in the system': WB Zambia (2008), 2.

[43] WB Georgia (1999), 25.

homes' – accessing information, 'culture' and 'news' in private – soon extended to economic independence (from the manor, the community, the family, the village) and this in turn provided a basis for stepping forward into a notional public sphere. There, as members of civil society – in debating halls and coffee salons, at public events and in the pages of newspapers and journals – private individuals debated among themselves with a view to determining the public interest, eventually transmitted (as 'public opinion') to a state that was increasingly constrained (through constitutional safeguards) to act upon it. The public/private divide is thus classically conceived as a *tripartite* distinction between (i) private persons as such (the private sphere), (ii) a public sphere of private persons and economic actors (civil society and the private sector), and (iii) a public sector, the state.[44]

It is helpful to remember that account in the present context, because contemporary rule of law programmes assume these structural conditions and largely aim to replicate them in countries of implementation. Rule of law and associated language provides a conceptual armoury that places the consolidation of the distinction between public and private at the heart of institutional reform work. Governance, corruption, privatisation, civil society, judicial independence – and other keywords associated with rule of law promotion – together provide an interdependent framework for nurturing the distinction in part by emphasising an ontological non-identity between public and private (as a matter of principle) and insisting upon the desirability of achieving their complete separation (as a matter of practice). Rule of law activities aim largely at the liberation of the private from the public, by holding the two apart and introducing multiple disciplinary controls over the public realm, while encouraging freedom of action and 'enterprise' in the private.[45]

The interconnected terms that have come to dominate international rule of law promotion since 1989 redefine the roles of public and private actors with a view to recreating and reinforcing the relationship between them. They do so by assuming that the relevant

---

[44] The tripartite distinction picks up the Hegelian description of the polity as composed of the family, civil society and the state. See Chapter 1, text at notes 80–81.

[45] The private space, too, of course, is a space of enforced discipline, as we saw in discussions of the realists, Weber and Foucault in Chapters 2 and 3. Yet, precisely because the disciplinary force of the private space is delegated by the public realm to the private, it is concealed within public law discourse, which instead treats private actors as 'free' without distinction.

constituencies (entrepreneurial private sector, civil society and media, on one side; state bureaucracy on the other) already exist, but have become submerged or displaced; they must be helped to re-emerge and equipped to take their proper place in a recognisably 'modern' theatre of public life. From the bloated bureaucracies of the developmental state, a disciplined and efficient public sector is to be sculpted. The private sector and civil society must be awakened and unleashed to match, challenge and constrain the state. There is an apparent paradox here: these actors are to be activated from without in a *self*-actualising manner as though they already exist in latent form within, simply awaiting ignition.[46] So whereas the public realm – the new or survivor or residual state inherited from some past process – is an object of explicit shaping, disciplining and pruning, the private is to be coaxed and seduced; incentives (including direct funding, but generally premised on the reorganisation of the public) are to be placed appropriately to call it forth from its supposed slumber, extending, ideally, to a regulatory environment open to everyone, national and foreign alike. The assumption that appropriate incentives will simply call forth private and civil society sectors appears much less presumptuous when it is remembered that these actors do, in fact, already exist transnationally, fully formed outside the states in question, ready to mobilise under the right circumstances.

Reform also extends to the 'private sphere', the family, by way of the long-running donor interest in 'gender'. Gender is USAID's leading 'human rights' theme, has been 'mainstreamed' through UN work, and is common even in Bank rule of law projects.[47] Gender interventions appear to reinforce public access to the private sphere, but in fact this is only true if 'private' is associated with the patriarchal family rather than with the individual. Since privacy in either case is structurally maintained by public guarantees, public intervention in the family, need not necessarily assail privacy per se (as it is sometimes characterised), but may rather displace and refocus it, prioritising individual private interest over communal/family interests and encouraging women into the workforce. On behalf of a public interest comprised of private

---

[46] A similar paradox is captured in Nikolas Rose's description of a cognate phenomenon, 'government through community'. According to Rose, in this model of government, the community 'is to be achieved, yet the achievement is nothing more than the birth-to-presence of a form of being which pre-exists': cited in Li (2006), 4.

[47] See, for example, WB Ghana (2003).

interests, the state thus opens the 'traditional' private sphere (the family) in order to liberate the modern private interest (the individual). In a move reminiscent of Aristotle's *kyrios* conundrum (see Chapter 3 above), the individual's allegiance/protection shifts from the head of the family to the state, the latter thus increasing its 'domination', to employ a Weberian register.

I will examine these themes through the deployment of certain keywords in the project and strategy-level documentation of the World Bank, USAID and the UN. The following section briefly examines three of these terms – governance, corruption and privatisation.

Governance

Governments determine how well, or how poorly, markets function. This simple truth explains the current concern with 'governance' as the world shifts toward an overwhelming endorsement of markets as the base of economic activity.[48]

Governance has come, over time, to define the boundaries and scope of the public sector.[49] The International Development Association – the World Bank's grant arm for the poorest countries – defines it as 'the way the state acquires and exercises the authority to provide and manage public goods and services – including both public capacities and public accountabilities,' further broken down as follows:[50]

1. Property rights and rule-based governance ['the extent to which the legal system and rule-based governance structure and facilitate private sector activity by enforcing property and contract rights'];
2. Quality of budgetary and financial management;
3. Efficiency of revenue mobilisation;
4. Quality of public administration;
5. Transparency, accountability, and [lack of] corruption in the public sector;
6. Quality, reliability and transparency of procurement administration.

At root, these principles of a functional bureaucracy, similar to those identified by Weber, supply a disciplinary category, the boundaries that

---

[48] World Bank (1991a), 1. See also World Bank (1989c), and for a more recent example, World Bank (2007i).
[49] Nine definitions are supplied in World Bank (2002a).
[50] WB IDA (2006), 1, 6.

circumscribe the activities of public officials. They are the 'economic governance' functions of the state, those initially managed by the Bank and other financial institutions as distinct from the rule of law platform ('baseline law and order') provided by DPKO and other UN actors. In the latter interventions, the 'international community' acts as 'mentor' to a generation of responsible public officials, demonstrating the correct activation and deployment of the coercive machinery of the state. However, once control of that coercive machinery is in the hands of local officials, they have an incentive to 'free-ride' (in public choice jargon) to benefit disproportionately from the public wealth. 'Governance' thus describes the parameters of *legitimate* state coercive activity, that is, it describes the 'legitimate' in Weber's formula of a state 'monopoly on legitimate violence'. Its disciplinary character is reinforced by donors (including the IDA) who measure it as a basis for dispensing funds.[51] To assess 'governance' is to determine whether the public sector has deviated from its core function (creating an 'enabling environment' for investment, as per Chapter 4 above), and to take punitive steps if so.

Corruption

Corruption is the flipside of governance: its absence or infringement. Usually defined as 'the abuse of public office for private gain', the term focuses on the boundary between public and private and provides criteria for policing that boundary.[52] The 'private gain' in question may refer to the private interest of *others* in transaction with the public official, but more precisely refers to the public official's *own* private interest, which is strictly illegitimate. Wherever the boundary between public and private (even, or especially, as that boundary exists within a specific person) is transgressed, ignored or misperceived, the result is termed 'corruption':

> [U]naccountable and nontransparent public governance can lead to a blurring of the lines between the public and private sectors and to ... excessive government interference, corrupt capital market or utility regulation, or government 'capture' by private interests, as in 'crony capitalism'.[53]

---

[51] WB IDA (2006), 1; 6. See also the Millennium Challenge Account: MCC FY2007, MCC FY2008.
[52] For one of many examples, World Bank (2007j), para. 3.
[53] World Bank (2000d), 14.

Corruption is thus effectively twinned with 'governance' as its other – the confusion of public and private realms is to be criminalised.[54] The problematisation of corruption is an occasion for intensive scrutiny of the appropriate boundaries between public and private, as witness the United Nations Convention Against Corruption, with its meticulous and sometimes tortuous refinement of the relevant actors in each listed instance of possible corruption.[55] Steps to address corruption further explicate and reinforce these roles, by creating private pressures and public obligations. Thus there has been, on one hand, a significant (and largely privately funded) push to create an 'anti-corruption movement' by replicating human rights techniques of civil society monitoring and 'naming and shaming'; hundreds of NGOs globally receive funding to this end.[56] On the other, the repeat *source* of information on corruption is the private sector. By soliciting the perceptions, rather than monitoring the behaviour, of private actors, corruption indicators such as Transparency International's well-known Corruption Perceptions Index effectively assume the latter as members of the 'movement'. The expected effect of all this is to turn the cosy relationship between public and private interests that corruption indicates into a relation rather of hostility or correction: the public and private as foes or co-surveillants.

So while privately-funded anti-corruption work responsibilises the public *sphere* – mobilised to police the boundaries – Bank work places the burden of correction on the public (rather than private) *sector*. At project level, anti-corruption work involves the inculcation of criteria for recognising and activating the boundary between public and private: codes of ethics; reporting and other transparency procedures; public information campaigns, intended to encourage (or initiate) exposure to public scrutiny. In principle, then, the achievement of governance necessarily involves the elimination of corruption, so the latter goal appears to add merely rhetorical (and 'moral') weight to the former. Anti-corruption work is therefore an exercise in hygiene – indeed, in *moral* hygiene.

---

[54] See in this context, the UN Convention Against Corruption (UNCAC), Arts. 15–42.
[55] See, for example, UNCAC, Art. 2(a).
[56] Forging an association with NGOs between human rights and corruption has proved difficult for donors, perhaps because the primary 'victims' of corruption are perceived as wealthy.

Privatisation

The tremendous enthusiasm for the self-abnegation of the state – the obligatory ritual of renouncement that constitutes privatisation – at the Bank, within USAID, and elsewhere, was (and is) driven in part by the clarity it introduces between the private and public sectors, attentive to their differing roles (entrepreneurship, on one hand, governance, on the other).[57] On one hand, the massive transfer of assets from nominally public to private hands, with the number of annual privatisations growing apace since 1989, clearly signals the central importance of their mutual differentiation and relative privileging.[58] On the other, a perhaps more crucial effect is the *clarification* of control over assets, with the assumption that ownership is in fact more sharply defined as well as more efficiently allocated in private than in public hands. (For example, a World Bank project in Romania was 'geared to strengthening financial discipline in the state enterprise sector, liquidating nonviable loss-making enterprises, privatizing most remaining state enterprises and cutting overall losses and subsidies in the state enterprise sector by 22 percent'.[59]) According to a fiercely defended discourse, privatisation of state-run enterprises permits the costs of inefficiencies and the rewards of efficiencies to be properly allocated to, and so felt by, the responsible individuals, rather than being absorbed into an amorphous and unaccountable leviathan.[60]

There is thus a clear ideational linkage between 'governance', 'corruption' and 'privatisation', a linkage that assumes that productive resources are a priori best left in private hands, which, in order to be meaningful, further requires that private and public actors are definitively distinguished, that the role of the latter is minimised and monitored, and that the boundary between the two is carefully policed. Privatisation reduces the scope for corruption (an informal tax on the private sector), not only by altering incentive structures, but also by merely recategorising revenues.[61] Thus 'corrupt' payments to a public

---

[57] The World Bank's privatisation database records 1,425 privatisations valued at over US$1million each between 2000 and 2006. Online at: rru.worldbank.org/privatization.
[58] Privatisations in 2006 were valued at US$ 105 billion in total, increasing to US$ 133 billion in 2007, 'a record in nominal terms'. World Bank (2008a), 1 and World Bank (2008c), 1
[59] WB Romania (2005a), 5. 'These objectives were all met and this component can be rated as satisfactory.'
[60] See generally, Hayek (1994), Coase (1960), Lal (2002), Krueger (1986), Friedman (2002).
[61] The point was made early on: 'Privatization, or the reduction of government controls and regulations and the sale of public enterprises to the private sector,

official for a public service reappear as profit to a service provider once the service is privatised: but in the process income from the service is formalised and rationalised, the 'profit' moved from a public gatekeeper to a private owner who might reinvest it 'more efficiently' (which may also mean expatriating it, as investment too is always potentially transnational).

The extensive theoretical baggage that aligns privatisation, governance and anti-corruption with economic growth all moves in and around the edges of the ordinary rule of law penumbra as it has come down to us in association with the discipline of economics (see Chapter 2 above). As a limitation of public interference with private rights (or assets), a strong associative presumption links privatisation and the rule of law in Bank and other literature. On any account, as we have seen, the rule of law assumes a clear distinction between public and private and reinforces the boundary between them; accounts differ, however, on where precisely the boundary should be drawn. But a strong association with privatisation, such as that adopted by the Bank, USAID and others, will tend to redirect rule of law language toward the most parsimonious delineation possible. And this assumption is easily compatible with most accounts of the rule of law in the Hayekian and post-1989 tradition, even if, as we have seen, it has little traction with its classical normative scope.

A public sphere of private ... investors?

It should already be clear that this account of the public sphere differs from Habermas's in some crucial respects. Whereas both privilege private over public, the contemporary account does so in a manner that is at the same time narrower and broader than the Habermasian ideal. It is narrower in that it consistently privileges a mere slice of private activity – commercial entrepreneurship – above all others: the private sector, and even more, the private investor, are fetishised to the point that they occupy almost the entire space of 'the private' in rule of law literature. 'Civil society' in this account appears not only secondary in importance to, but ultimately parasitic upon, the private sector. Characterised in the diminished guise of advocacy-oriented

has potential to increase transparency and reduce corruption abuses': World Bank (1991a), 24.

NGOs, rather than as the cumulative product of rational exchange in the public domain, civil society is (as we shall see in more detail below) expected to turn to private funding for sponsorship, and to launch 'public awareness' campaigns to jostle and compete in the media with commercial advertising.[62]

The scope of the private in rule of law activity is also *broader* than usually conceived, however, in that it abandons the implicit rootedness of the private realm within the bounds of the nation-state. Private investors, and the private sector, are transnational from the outset, with no necessary relation to a given 'public sector', except as incidental (and fundamentally interchangeable) locus of protection/regulation. The same is true of civil society and the media, both of which are conceived of as *essentially* transnational, even if nationally inflected in a given context. Much as specific projects focus on national actors, the beneficiaries are also always transnational. The public sphere and public sector no longer map onto one another in the form assumed in the Habermasian model: an implicit symmetry between public and private, or state and society, that underpins relevant models from Kant through Weber is discarded in contemporary rule of law discourse. The 'society' that is to 'control' the state turns out itself to be trans-statal.

And yet, both 'public' and 'private' are imagined throughout this literature in a highly attenuated and idealised manner. On one hand, the selfless civil servant or functionary, efficient and productive, and differing from the Weberian bureaucrat only in his special regard for the market economy. On the other, the private individual in one of two guises: as latent entrepreneur ready to 'unleash market forces' or as active member of 'civil society'. The 'public' actor is to be produced through self-discipline, through sharp delimitation of a field of activity, and through policing of the boundaries by 'civil society'; the 'private' actor is to be seduced into existence by the appeal of the market itself (with experienced foreign investors leading the way). I will examine this set of relations in more detail in the next section.

SUPPORTING ROLES

If 'governance' describes the proper limited role of a public sector clearly separated from the private realm and 'corruption' describes

---

[62] See USAID Romania (2008). See also part two of Habermas (1994).

a condition whereby these spheres or the boundaries between them become blurred or confused, the rule of law is introduced as a means to hold public and private apart. This role of the rule of law is so deeply embedded in the literature's self-representation – so self-evident – that it is easily overlooked. So whereas the rule of law comprises basic civil controls over the public realm, thus *presupposing* two distinct realms – as we saw in Chapter 1 – the corollary evidenced in contemporary reform is that the rule of law and the public/private distinction are mutually constitutive. In states where the rule of law is said to be weak or absent, it is, in effect, the distinction between public and private itself that is weak, blurred, collapsed, or underdeveloped. To 'strengthen the rule of law' in such circumstances means to provide clarity and definition between distinct public and private realms, to supply mechanisms for negotiation between them, and to reinforce each in its own role. Rule of law culture relies on three such mechanisms: the disinterested figure of the judge, the interested figure of the private citizen (civil society) and the passive beneficiary ('the poor').

The judiciary: autonomy and prestige

In the ideal rule of law configuration, the judiciary is the key guarantor of the divide between public and private, but only insofar as it is independent of both. Its multifold remit is well captured in the following citation from an Armenian project document:

Both domestic and foreign investors were expected to benefit from an efficient, independent and impartial judiciary thus promoting private sector development and economic growth in Armenia. Judges and court personnel were expected to benefit in terms of enhanced professional training, administrative independence and security, improved working conditions and better access to legal information. The general public and legal professionals would benefit from improved access to the courts and legal information, and impartial and professional functioning of the judiciary.[63]

---

[63] WB Armenia (2007b), 3, citations omitted. The project included the objective of a constitutional amendment to improve judicial independence, which, according to the project report, 'was a challenging task for the authorities. After the first unsuccessful attempt in 2003, the government was able to secure a successful outcome in November 2005. The revised Constitution brought full constitutional independence to the COJ [Council of Justice]': WB Armenia (2007b), 8.

The Armenian project in this citation – and the wider literature to which it belongs – claims that three groups are expected to 'benefit' from judicial 'independence': foreign and domestic investors, legal professionals and the 'general public'. I will return to the second and third of these in a moment. The first, however, might be thought surprising, as we might expect that if a judiciary is truly 'independent' it would not benefit any one group more than any other; in a rule of law world everyone, after all, is equal under the law, at least in theory. What appears to have happened is that the literature has identified the public interest with 'domestic and foreign investors' and the rule of law itself – the guardianship of the law – with the courts. I will take these two themes in order.

First, a judiciary that is independent of the public sector – that is, unanswerable to political imperatives (project documents on former socialist countries speak disparagingly of 'telephone justice'[64]) – provides public recognition of the legitimacy and authority of private interests as the proper content of the public sphere. An independent and impartial judge disentangles the 'public interest' from the 'public realm' and (re)associates it with the private realm. It is this association of the public interest with the supposed totality of private interests that comprise it that is expected to bring economic dividends (i.e. growth/development). The key point here is not, of course, who might win in any specific case; an independent judiciary does not guarantee the success of any particular private interest. Indeed, that is precisely the point: where a fuzzy or bloated public realm had, in practice (so the narrative runs), provided special protection to select private interests (variations on 'crony capitalism'), a rule of law culture will instead treat all equally under the law. Judicial independence dissociates the law from the public realm – *and* from particular ('favoured', 'national champion') private interests – and associates instead with the 'general interest' of cumulative private interests.

There are two further implicit claims here. One is that in Armenia in the past (and other communist and developmental states), foreign

---

[64] See USAID Kazakhstan (2007), 3. A Russian project appraisal describes the phenomenon thus: 'whereby judges allegedly prefer to get instructions from the *prokuratura*, higher courts or extrajudicial authorities (e.g. governors) rather than risk having their decisions reversed': WB Russia (2007), 2. In Romania, for example, 'Interference of the executive and prosecutors with judicial decision-making was common, and so-called "telephone justice" was widespread': WB Romania (2005b), 27. See also on Russia, MSI (2002), 119.

investors were discriminated against, by means of subsidies, tariffs and other forms of economic nationalism; by lifting that discrimination, equality under law is returned and development is furthered.[65] This claim further relies on the machinery of trade liberalisation and the internalisation of WTO principles into national law (an area of significant rule of law reform activity, as we shall see below). The second claim is that investors are in some way particularly representative of the public interest. This claim is indissociable from the particular economic view that runs from Mandeville through to de Soto, that by reallocating resources to where they will be most efficient, investors perform the ultimate public good (the bees in Mandeville's Fable of the Bees; see Chapter 1).[66] The notion that 'foreign and domestic investors' are viewed as personifying, or at least adequately representing, the general interest will come as a surprise to many. Yet that implicit claim is a staple of contemporary project literature, rooted in the particular attenuated vision of the rule of law whose genealogy I investigated in Chapter 2.[67]

Second, if law is to rule, its priests and guardians must be tended. An important background theme in rule of law projects has been to increase the prestige of the judiciary.[68] Judicial independence derives from many sources, mostly of a structural nature.[69] Among these, the

---

[65] The World Bank (2005h), 95: 'Multilateral, reciprocal, nondiscriminatory trade liberalization offers the best means for realizing the development promise of trade': NSS (2006), 27: 'While most of the world affirms in principle the appeal of economic liberty, in practice too many nations hold fast to the false comforts of subsidies and trade barriers. Such distortions of the market stifle growth in developed countries, and slow the escape from poverty in developing countries. Against these short-sighted impulses, the United States promotes the enduring vision of a global economy that welcomes all participants and encourages the voluntary exchange of goods and services based on mutual benefit, not favoritism.'

[66] For example, at project level, the World Bank claims for one project that it 'would benefit the entire population of Georgia, and in particular, the business community and foreign investors through the establishment of an independent and competent judicial system, leading to the enforcement of more secure property rights and contractual obligations and an environment conducive to the establishment of the rule of law': WB Georgia (2007), 3 (citing WB Georgia (1999)).

[67] See Chapter 2, text at notes 67–82 and 'Conclusion'.

[68] MSI reports on USAID's support for judicial associations in Eastern Europe that 'the need for such professional associations has been particularly important in post-communist societies because their judiciaries have typically been accorded less power, prestige, and resources than their western counterparts. USAID has made a very important contribution in helping develop judicial associations throughout the region': MSI (2002), 16.

[69] For an overview of the ingredients of judicial independence, see USAID (2002b), 12–41. Among the priority areas identified are: selection processes, security of tenure,

literature agrees that good remuneration and working conditions are essential.[70] Prestige further depends upon the inculcation among legal actors of professional pride in their unique guardianship of the rule of law. Project literature is full of examples of demoralised, underpaid and unprofessional judicial actors. In Georgia, one project notes: 'Judges received poor remuneration, and held little if any prestige. For these reasons, the judiciary was staffed with individuals who were often unwilling or incapable of providing independent, professional judicial decisions.'[71] Courthouse rehabilitation, new computers, better wages, professional training, according to project documents, all of these elements contribute to the prestige of the judiciary. The World Bank thus describes two lessons derived from its 'depth of experience in the reform and development of legal and judicial institutions, particularly in transition countries':

The first is that judicial independence relies as much on the constitutional empowerment of the judiciary to self-governance as it does on the capacity of the judiciary to manage and administer its own resources – human, financial, informational, technical and physical. The latter [is] sometimes called operational independence ... The second lesson is that the effectiveness of a judiciary lies in its ability to deliver efficient services to the public as much as in its role as a check and balance on the executive. As such, developing effective service delivery mechanisms through IT systems, courthouse modernization, training, and public education are essential corollaries to strengthening independence.[72]

Funding judicial associations and supporting regular conferences on themes such as the role of judges in society, or the importance of the rule of law, are all intended to address these shortcomings, to nurture professional pride, and to sensitise the courts to their public

---

length of tenure, and structure of the judiciary (including budgets). For increasing 'judicial capacity', recommendations include training programmes, access to legal materials, codes of ethics, increasing the status of judges, and creating judicial associations.

[70] USAID (2002b), 31: 'The question is: How to increase the self-respect of judges? ... In terms of affecting the attitude of the judges themselves, salaries and benefits are key factors.'

[71] WB Georgia (1999), 3. In Russia it was believed that increased prestige will help the courts 'attract the better graduates from law schools': WB Russia (2007), 10. In Ethiopia, 'the deplorable conditions of service and lack of training are seen to contribute to the lack of prestige and authority judges command in the eyes of the general public'. WB Ethiopia (2004), 20.

[72] WB Armenia (2007a), 2.

role.⁷³ If legal professionals and judges are themselves persuaded of the importance of their calling, the logic goes, they will better serve as impartial arbitrators. In a virtuous cycle, this will lead to greater 'societal respect' (the term used in one USAID document for 'legitimacy'), which will in turn boost their capacity to apply the law independently.⁷⁴ If the judge is gradually prodded in the appropriate direction, other good things follow:

> [In the Dominican Republic] USAID facilitated a dialogue that led to placing the role of the judiciary in the proper perspective. For the first time, objectives for fair and efficient court performance were established. These included a Supreme Court mission statement, which informs judges and court administrators what is expected of them by the public. Court staff and judges were made aware that court performance and judges' and administrators' actions should facilitate access to justice, expeditious procedures, impartiality and integrity, political independence, accountability, and public confidence in the judicial system.⁷⁵

In the ideal horizon, judicial integrity would be entirely governed by internal disciplinary mechanisms, such that neither public imperatives nor private incentives can claim the allegiance of the judge. Allegiance is instead transferred to a body of norms characterised as 'the rule of law', the source of which is removed from ordinary politics and returned, in theory, to the discipline of legal practice itself, now universalised. Just as judicial independence affirms the independence of the law itself, so a prestigious judiciary brings dignity to the law. In rule of law culture, then, a primary role of the courts and the figure of the judge is iconic – to *symbolise* the gravity, stolidity, prestige of law; its capacity to rule and its fittedness to do so. The judge evokes and advertises the autonomy of law, a role she can play even if that autonomy itself is in fact ultimately

---

⁷³ See for example, USAID Karelia (1998); Program of the 2nd Annual IBA Bar Leader's Conference, 16–17 May 2007, Zagreb, Croatia ('How Can Bar Associations Promote the Rule of Law'): 'Promoting the rule of law has two very different aspects. One might be called "public education". More often than not, it is a country's government itself which is most in need of education. However, educated support for the rule of law among the population at large is essential if the rule of law is to become embedded in a society. The other aspect involves concrete steps to build legal capacity ...'

⁷⁴ USAID (2002b), 36, *'Promoting Societal Respect for the Role of an Impartial Judiciary ...* the most important [factor] affecting judicial independence [is] the expectations of society. If a society expects and demands an honest judiciary, it will probably get one. If expectations are low, the likelihood that the judiciary will operate fairly is equally low.'

⁷⁵ MSI (2002), 58.

untraceable or illusory, and even if her own role in doing so derives primarily from a series of funded initiatives hailing from a handful of institutions mostly based in Washington, DC.

Accountability

By corollary, however, the judge in this picture cannot fall back on opinions or interpretations not firmly grounded in the relevant normative context. A judge cannot, for example, substitute a personal opinion for a legal directive whose apparent consequences may not chime with her own ethical outlook. As one document puts it, 'no judiciary in the world is completely free to act according to its own lights; nor should it be.' Judicial independence is not unlimited. Bank and USAID projects are also, therefore, concerned with the flipside of 'judicial independence' – 'judicial accountability' – which involves buttressing the disciplinary environment such that individual judges are kept within certain professional boundaries.[76] Where property rights have been tightened, judges are constrained to rule against squatters, for example, even in post-communist countries where a substantive right to housing had previously prevailed, regardless of their views on rising homelessness. They must uphold newly 'flexible' labour laws, even if it may leave families destitute. In each case, to do otherwise would be to protect special private interests in the face of the wider general interest embedded in the law. How is an 'independent' judge to be kept 'accountable'? The ultimate court in contemporary rule of law literature turns out to be the same as that located by Dicey in the nineteenth century, and, retrospectively, by Habermas in the eighteenth – the court of public opinion:

> Although a court must be free to decide cases impartially, if its opinions begin to stray too far from public sentiment, a correction will usually be called for, whether by demands for changes in the law or more subtle pressures on the judicial system to select judges deemed more responsive to popular opinion.[77]

Here too, however, rule of law reform is at work, shaping the environment and process by which public opinion is formed, transmitted and received, as we shall see in a moment.

---

[76] 'Judicial accountability' features in projects on Albania, Armenia, Azerbaijan, Georgia and Russia and is the focus of a project in Honduras. See WB Honduras (2005). See also USAID (2002b), 39–41.
[77] USAID (2002b), 39.

Alternatives

Despite – or perhaps, given the associated difficulties and expense, because of – its fetishisation of the judiciary, rule of law reform has also long supported alternative dispute resolution (ADR), and commercial arbitration in particular.[78] The initial promise of ADR is 'to bypass court systems that are frequently unresponsive to reforms'.[79] Where courts are slow or overburdened, ADR can save time and money, and where they lack independence ADR can provide a specialised arbitrator (or somewhat less specialised mediator) better attuned to investors' needs and priorities.[80] Published manuals by both USAID and the World Bank's International Finance Corporation (IFC) on ADR promotion demonstrate the Apollonian perspective required for this work:

> Before deciding whether to begin a mediation project in a country, and what the project should look like, a detailed analysis must be conducted of the country's needs and its legal and business environments. The following questions must be addressed in this assessment phase: What are the problems with the resolution of commercial disputes in the country? Can these problems at least partly be ameliorated by introducing mediation or other ADR methods?[81]

Project implementation involves assessing the adequacies and gaps of entire judicial systems, designing models addressing the needs of particular groups who are ill-served by the existing regime, and getting 'buy-in' from other powerful groups (including legal professionals) who may feel threatened.[82] But if ADR programmes may serve the private sector by insulating them, to a degree, from the capriciousness,

---

[78] For example, World Bank projects in Albania, Colombia, Georgia, Honduras, Malawi, Philippines, Peru, Russia, West Bank and Gaza; USAID projects in Argentina, Bangladesh, Bolivia, Croatia, El Salvador, Mexico, Mozambique, Philippines, Sri Lanka, Ukraine. On the international dimension of this work, Dezalay and Garth (1996). World Bank (2005c).

[79] Blair and Hansen (1994), 4, 40. After initial experiments, USAID suggested that 'ADR should have a more central role in USAID's ROL development planning' (Blair and Hansen (1994), 56).

[80] WB IFC (2006), 81; USAID (1998), 5.   [81] WB IFC (2006), 7; USAID (1998), 34.

[82] USAID (1998), 25: 'Judges, lawyers, and interest groups that benefit from current institutional biases may all be sources of strong opposition to ADR programs.' WB Honduras (2005), 8, speaks of 'a widespread skepticism among professionals about the benefits of ADR mechanisms.' See also USAID Croatia (2004), 4, 6 (opposition of Bar Association); WB IFC (2006), 21. MSI (2002), 35: 'In 1990, mediation was virtually unknown in Argentina[;] USAID has had an extraordinary impact in changing this situation.'

costs and delays of a not-yet-reformed judiciary, they also have a second supplemental role at the far end of the spectrum, providing 'access to justice' for the poor.[83] The two goals are, in fact, mutually supportive:

> In Bolivia ... the USAID mission supported the first ADR program (commercial arbitration and conciliation) for the benefit of a politically influential sector (small business), and implemented it through a politically powerful ally, the Chamber of Commerce. Once the legal foundations for this program were established, other programs, such as community justice centers for disadvantaged parts of the population could be planned.[84]

'Community justice centres' are one of a variety of expressions for local systems of justice, gathered neatly in the umbrella term ADR, that generally aim to build upon 'customary law' systems, those that in many cases colonial rule had left behind as 'native courts'.[85] It is to these that donors will now turn as possible platforms for ADR, rather than continuing or attempting further integration into the formal system, as many post-colonial governments had (a move later blamed for delays and exorbitant caseloads).[86] In marked similarity to their colonial forebears, ADR systems are informal, apply 'equity rather than the rule of law', and do not set precedent.[87] Also, a large part of the task is to ensure a functioning coherence with the formal justice system, that the village or community 'leaders' (a figure that replaces the 'chiefs' of colonial times) are selected appropriately and adequately trained, and that they remain impartial.[88] With its inherent limitations acknowledged from the outset, the erstwhile 'native courts' and other customary and 'communal' systems need not offend against the rule of law, but rather complement it.[89]

---

[83] WB Honduras (2005), 13. [84] USAID (1998), 25.
[85] Thus, in Bangladesh: 'The program design builds on the traditional (*shalish*) system of community dispute resolution, which has much greater legitimacy than the court system': USAID (1998), Appendix B, 1. In Ghana, 'ADR mechanisms ... in many cases, already exist within the customary system': WB Ghana (2003), 26. On 'native courts' in British Africa see generally Lugard (1926), 539–564; Allott (1960a), (1962); Elias (1962a), (1962b), (1967); Roberts-Wray (1966); in French Africa see Poirier (1956); Delavignette (1968); Manning (1998); Sarr and Roberts (1991); Lydon (2006), 8–9. For a good analytical overview, Mamdani (1996).
[86] See for example WB Ghana (2003), 10.
[87] USAID (1998), 21–23. Compare Lugard (1926), 547–549.
[88] USAID (1998), 37–47. Again compare Lugard (1926), 210–211, 539–540 and Mamdani (1996), 23, 53–59, 74.
[89] USAID (1998), 3: 'ADR programs can support not only rule of law objectives, but also other development objectives, such as economic development, development of a

Civil society: public education

The public sphere as such generally appears in project literature in the guise of 'civil society'. In project documentation, civil society today is freighted with an attenuated reconstruction of its role in the classical public sphere. Where for Habermas (and Hegel before him), civil society signified the collective and active body of private individuals acting in the public interest,[90] in today's rule of law world it is synonymous with CSOs (civil society organisations) or NGOs ('non-profit' as well as non-governmental), specific niche mediators between public and private realms. NGOs have three main roles in rule of law projects. They are, first, representatives of the general public; a relevant audience or constituency for project outputs, who are counted on to activate the project's wider goals. Here is an example from a World Bank Philippines 'judicial reform support project':[91]

> *Improvements in information provided to the public and greater collaboration with civil society.* The public has little understanding of how the courts operate and what their rights are under the law. This has profound implications for access to justice, especially by the poor. It also contributes to a situation where the courts are extremely vulnerable to graft and corruption and political pressures. There is a need to improve public information and collaboration with civil society, organized groups, the legal profession and media, in order to improve access, improve the utilization of judicial services, and enhance accountability of judicial personnel.

Second, they are themselves a vehicle for project activities – project funding is channelled through them to 'monitor' the public sector and 'hold it accountable'.[92] Third, as a constituent part of a modern polity, rule of law projects aim themselves to build and nurture civil society.[93] In the rule of law vision, civil society actors effectively constitute the public sphere; as private citizens, they monitor and pressure the public

---

civil society, and support for disadvantaged groups, by facilitating the resolution of disputes that are impeding progress toward these objectives.'

[90] See Chapter 1, text at notes 80–81; 91–99.   [91] WB Philippines (2003), 6.
[92] The task of promoting civil society organisations as monitors or watchdogs is not a priority for the World Bank, but is actively pursued by other donors, including USAID and the EU and private rule of law funders.
[93] For example, the 'Romania Civil Society Strengthening Program' was implemented between September 2005 and December 2007, involving a USAID grant of US$ 4.8 million, of which US$ 2.4 million was allocated as grant support for Romanian NGOs that agreed to partner with USAID's contractor, World Learning for International Development (WLID): USAID Romania (2008).

sector to act in the public interest. They are not themselves subject to the discipline of 'governance'; rather they police its boundaries. A sharpened public/private distinction does not therefore need to result in mutual isolation; but to provide a platform for interchange, itself the basis of 'public policy in the private interest' (the title of a Bank publication). Once properly distinct, contact between public and private spheres is encouraged through 'civil society consultation' and 'public-private dialogue'.[94] The consciously constructed nature of 'civil society' in this vision is well outlined in the following activities of a USAID 'civil society strengthening' project undertaken in Romania:

> Organizational and financial sustainability grants [were] provided [to] watchdog and public policy NGOs with specific opportunities to develop products and systems that made them potentially more attractive to donors and to their members, supporters and constituents while providing opportunities to develop local funding bases ... NGOs established and put into operation realistic business plans ... and introduced new mechanisms for revenue generation; staff training and appropriate systems of remuneration were introduced so as to retain staff ... and finally, they tapped increasing volunteerism and expanded their volunteer base to enjoy the benefits of this human resource ... Financial sustainability was enhanced by the NGOs' better documentation of the impact that their advocacy activities had for marketing purposes and for increasing the credibility of the watchdog and public policy NGO sub-sector; citizen and organizational membership schemes were developed to assist in creating identifiable constituencies as well as to enhance local fundraising strategies ...[95]

Indeed civil society, in this construction, faces both ways – not only do CSOs monitor and pressure the government (the public *sector*), they also monitor and pressure the public *sphere*, albeit in the vein of agitation rather than accusation. As CSOs agitate for reform and to mobilise the public, they must rely upon a functional media. 'Public information' and 'public awareness' are of immense significance to rule of law projects. Judicial independence projects combine 'judicial transparency' with public information components, designed to increase the prestige of the judge in the public eye, to habituate judicial personnel to the public sphere, to generate 'judicial accountability', and to 'raise awareness about the project and its themes.[96] Another favourite

---

[94] Many projects include mechanisms for public-private and civil society 'dialogue'. On public-private dialogue, see USAID Bulgaria (2005) and WB Malawi (2007). On civil society consultation, USAID Romania (2008) and WB Philippines (2003).
[95] USAID Romania (2008), 2–3.   [96] USAID (1998), 33–36.

area of 'awareness raising' concerns rights – the injunction to 'know your rights' repeatedly arises as a vehicle of public mobilisation, and a concretisation of the public/private separation, with 'human' or 'civil' rights both held against the state and enforced through it. In one fascinating case in Armenia, a TV programme funded by the World Bank as part of a justice sector reform project, *My Right*, became the most popular show on Armenian television:[97]

Public Awareness and Education. The image of the judiciary, as an open, fair and accessible institution, was improved as a result of several project activities. The main output of the Public Awareness component was the 'My Right' television show, which was developed and broadcasted on Armenian Public Television starting September 2004. By 2006 the show had been rated number one by the Public Television of Armenia for two consecutive years making it a real success. The show also has an official website that provides useful legal information and opportunities for the public to ask questions. In response to the large number of citizens requests for legal information, the MOJ organized a number of free consulting sessions where the 'My Right' TV judge and Ministry legal experts provided advice. Some activities of this component, such as journalism training and publication of brochures were dropped due to the Government's view that they were relatively ineffective and the availability of other donor resources for such activities.

The example of *My Right* succinctly illustrates the dislocation between the classical public/private distinction, as it appears in the writing of Habermas and others, and the contemporary distinction promoted through rule of law projects. The show popularises the primary theme of the public sphere according to the rule of law – enforceable rights held against the state – and no doubt increases and mobilises faith in the capacity of that public sphere to self-mobilise. And yet while it appears to instantiate a Habermas-like collective of private interests, it is in fact wholly a creature of the public sector itself; the product of an agreement between the World Bank and the government, implemented with public funding and projected into the public sphere to help in the latter's self-consolidation or emergence, in a process that not only relies upon government support for its success but defers to government suggestion in its execution. The secret paradox disclosed by this remarkably controlled projection of the rule of law – its managed consolidation of a public/private distinction so attenuated as to have effectively vanished – is the inescapability of the public in the construction of

---

[97] WB Armenia (2007b), 17.

the private; precisely the reverse of the process described by Habermas in Chapter 1. We might call the production of these pseudo-adversarial public and private figures, a pedagogy of the rule of law.[98]

'The poor': investors in waiting

Ostensibly, the principal 'stakeholder' of rule of law reform is 'the poor'. This amorphous group-noun recurs with extraordinary frequency in the documentation of the Bank in particular, whose mission, of course, is to 'eradicate poverty'. The vocabulary of poverty does enormous work for the Bank. First, in aid-recipient countries, 'the poor' generally comprise a large part of the population – they are therefore the relevant 'public' who are to benefit from reform. However, second, 'the poor' are not really a public at all, in that they do not possess the attributes of a public sphere. Indeed, if (as we have seen) a 'private person' is ideally an autonomous educated property owner, 'the poor' of the Third World are uniquely unqualified (or disqualified) prima facie. In corollary, 'the poor' do not comprise 'civil society'; although 'grassroots movements' can and do appear, the poor *cannot* constitute a public among publics 'lobbying' for certain interests, because, defined merely by the absence of wealth, they do not form an 'interest group' – they are rather the negative of civil society, a 'class'. Nevertheless, third, the poor appear to donors as a natural 'constituency for reform', since the quality that defines them – the absence of wealth – itself constitutes the undesirability of the status quo; the poor are the *raison d'être* of development. Fourth, as such – a constituency for reform that does not in itself constitute a public – the poor need protection or representation. As their home elites, in rule-of-law deficient countries, do not protect or represent them adequately, the role is left to others. The Bank supplies this representation unstintingly; Bank documents on every topic reflexively note the benefits for 'the poor' of recommended measures:

Poverty reduction: rule of law reform is considered essential to poverty reduction as the poor suffer more from crime, the impact of crime on their livelihood is greater, and they are less able to access the justice systems.[99]

[98] A Philippines project provides a literal example: to develop 'community outreach programs ... for children in primary schools to inculcate an understanding of the rule of law and the role of judges, in partnership with the department of education': WB Philippines (2003), 36.
[99] World Bank (2006e), 3. Similar language appears in project documents, such as this objective from a rule of law project in Colombia: 'contribute to poverty alleviation

Reducing trade protection generally promotes exports and raises the incomes of the poor by supporting labor-intensive activities.[100]

Especially in poor countries, the scope for improving the welfare of the poor through redistribution is extremely limited ... Evidence is also mounting that, where income distribution has worsened with growth, much of the fault has been due to inappropriate incentive policies.[101]

Improving access to financial services such as savings, credit, insurance, and remittances is vital to enabling the poor to take advantage of economic opportunities and guard against uncertainty.[102]

The World Bank Group's focus on Governance and Corruption is based on its mandate to reduce poverty – a capable and accountable state creates opportunities for the poor.[103]

Weak governance and corruption often mean that the resources that should fuel economic growth and create opportunities for the poor to escape poverty instead go to enrich corrupt elites.[104]

Corrupt bureaucracies and biased enforcement of contract and property rights inhibits the poor from making investments in physical and human capital that could raise their incomes.[105]

Corruption is an especially regressive tax, with the poor hit hardest by even small demands for bribes or fees when they want public services.[106]

A key feature of successful workfare programs is the ability to target participants through self-selection processes. In Argentina [a workfare] program kept the wage rate below the minimum wage, encouraging the poor to self-select into the program. Kenya, Malawi, Mali, and Senegal ... paid wages above the market wage rates, undermining the self-targeting design and diverting jobs away from the very poor.[107]

A recurrent motif that runs through many of the above quotes and through a preponderant section of the Bank's voluminous writing on poverty associates its relief with 'opportunities' in a liberated economy, and occasionally pairs 'the poor' with 'small and medium enterprises'.[108]

---

since an improved rule of law should specially protect and benefit the poor which [sic] are most affected by violence': WB Colombia (2001).

[100] WDR 1991, 10.   [101] Krueger (1986), note 14.   [102] World Bank (2006f), 21.
[103] World Bank (2007j), 2.   [104] World Bank (2007i), 2.   [105] World Bank (2004), 40.
[106] WDR 2002, 5. This common refrain is counter-intuitive. Since bribes, unlike value added taxes (which are, of course, regressive), can be modulated to match individual capacity to pay, it is surely more likely that corruption would be a progressive tax on the wealthy.
[107] WDR 2005, 155.
[108] Thus, for example, World Bank (2007f), 2: 'the abolishment of such barriers [to banking] and financial development disproportionately benefit the poor and small businesses.'

The recurrent interest in micro-business and micro-financing evinces a similar conviction that an enabling environment for private sector development suits 'the poor' just as well as the foreign investor precisely because the poor are themselves merely investors-in-waiting. As the final quote above shows, even as providers of labour – inevitably the role which the overwhelming majority of the 'poor' are or will be assigned in a successful rule of law economy – they are still viewed as entrepreneurial. (In practice, the Bank has little to say about 'labour'.)

Yet a large Bank survey into the conditions for 'the poor' in twenty-three countries reported that most of the tens of thousands interviewed, far from uncovering new opportunities and investments, were instead struggling in deteriorating circumstances, and attributed their new hardships to the measures the Bank had claimed should help.[109] In general, the report found that 'households are crumbling under the stresses of poverty' and the 'social fabric, poor people's only "insurance," is unraveling'.[110] Despite its 1,000-page length, the study does not investigate the underlying causes of the malaise it describes – the authors explain that it 'was not designed to disentangle and evaluate the effects of specific economic policies or trends on the lives of poor people', but merely to 'present the analyses of those who are currently poor, who recount the negative impact that certain economic policies and market changes have had on them and on their households and communities'.[111] It is to the 'voices of the poor' themselves, then, at least as channelled through the Bank, that we must turn for an empirical picture of the effects of rule of law promotion:[112]

> Poor people from several countries expressed deep concern over the economic upheavals and policy changes that are buffeting their lives ... Depending

---

[109] In the Introduction to the third report in the series, the authors provide some insight into the response at the Bank to these presumably unwelcome findings. World Bank (2002b), 8: 'Several reviewers of draft chapters were upset by the "negative", "exaggerated", or "emotional" tone of poor people's reports. Some of the strongest feedback was expressed by reviewers who work in the Europe and Central Asia region, who reacted to poor people's expressions of hopelessness and to their "distorted nostalgia" for the secure jobs and public services that they had in the past ... Regardless of the validity of these reviewers' points, open-ended participatory methodology is designed to elicit people's views. Trained researchers probe without leading, cross-check information with others, and record poor people's interpretations of their own experiences. Hence, to assume that people are remembering incorrectly when their memories do not fit our biases would be a violation of the basic tenet of the open-ended participatory approach.'

[110] World Bank (1999c), 7. World Bank (2000c).

[111] World Bank (2002b), 471.   [112] World Bank (2002b), 471–476.

on the country, poor people mentioned privatization, factory closures, the opening of domestic markets, currency devaluation, inflation, reductions in social services, and other related changes as having depleted their assets and increased their insecurity.

Cynicism and anger over this abandonment [of public services] are evident everywhere but are especially prominent in countries of the former Soviet Union, where people once experienced effective delivery of basic services and now face both high state capture and widespread corruption.

In the wake of the transition to market economies in the four countries visited in Eastern Europe and Central Asia, people reported steep drops in living standards. Especially hard hit were the 'one-company towns' and villages that once revolved around large state farms.

In all countries visited in this region, poor people connected extensive unemployment and underemployment to the dismantling of the state before functioning markets were in place.

In all four countries of Latin America and the Caribbean, people described the economic and social devastation of their communities in the wake of macroeconomic crises and policy reforms.

Poor men and women in the four European and Central Asian countries described the wrenching effects created by the elimination of free medical services. Participants related frightening experiences of going without needed medical services and medications and of receiving surgery without anesthesia.

Thus we appear to have come full circle. Where, as we saw at the outset of our investigation in Chapter 1, Dicey premised the rule of law precisely upon its role in binding the 'social fabric', the promotion of the rule of law today leads to the unravelling of the 'social fabric' wherever it is introduced. Where the rule of law had been organic, an expression of existing rights handed down through history, it has become, in its promotion, mechanical, the imposition of a uniform imported paradigm that aims specifically to undo any relationship between rights and locality – culture, history or existing relations – and to redistribute them towards a specific constituency, 'foreign and domestic investors' (recast as a universal public).

Despite these observations, *Voices of the Poor* concludes that the key 'challenges' for the Bank concern the relative weakness of national-level institutions. Institutional state failures, the report says, create and exacerbate problems for the poor: corruption; clientelism and patronage; lawlessness, crime, and conflict; discriminatory behaviour.[113] In

---

[113] World Bank (2002b), 477–480. A fourth is 'alienation and hopelessness'.

response, the report urges tweaks on existing orthodoxy: 'pro-poor' economic policies; investing in poor peoples' assets; supporting partnerships with poor people; addressing gender inequities; and protecting poor peoples' rights.[114]

It would appear, then, that faced with the spectre of 'social chaos' (as, indeed, colonial law reformers were in the past[115]), the choice has been to soldier on.[116] This is apparent in a recent attempt to address the apparent dissonance, at the Bank and elsewhere, between the rhetoric of 'pro-poor growth' and the observed experience, in much of the world, of the reverse. In response to this conundrum, a new term was added to the rule of law lexicon: 'legal empowerment'. In its initial formulation, this term signified a shift in process and focus, rather than in the content, of rule of law work. Still frankly instrumental, law reform would abandon some of the formal pretensions of a 'rule of law orthodoxy', while nevertheless remaining broadly within the field's mainstream themes.[117] Legal empowerment meant using the law to alleviate poverty; although it would be 'rights-based' and concerned with enforcing existing protections already 'on the books', the initial focus on 'paralegals' (that is, legal help from trained non-lawyers) and using law to address poverty indicated an apparently substantivist orientation.[118]

When a 'Commission on Legal Empowerment of the Poor' was created in 2005, however, the focus shifted towards more, rather than less, formalism. The Commission's 2008 report opens with the astonishing claim that 'four billion people around the world are robbed of the chance to better their lives and climb out of poverty, because they are excluded from the rule of law'.[119] The central premise of the two main

---

[114] World Bank (2002b), 487–493.
[115] See Lugard (1926), 217; Chanock (1998), 12–13. See Interlude above, note 14.
[116] Concomitant with this, the Bank pursues a gradual policy of promoting individual titling with regard to customary tenure which, since the post-independence state took over regulation from the colonial state, is no longer regarded as efficient. See for example WB Ghana (2003), 5: 'Because of the insecurity surrounding land rights, land figures very little in the valuation of residential and commercial property, thus minimizing its value in the economy and as collateral for loans as well as for tax assessment by both local and national governments. Furthermore, it undermines both national and international investor confidence in land and other sectors of the economy.'
[117] Upham (2006).   [118] Golub (2006), 161–165.
[119] Empowerment Commission (2008a), 1. 'At best', the report adds, 'they live with very modest, unprotected assets that cannot be leveraged in the market due to cumulative mechanisms of exclusion': Empowerment Commission (2008a), 19. A note on the Commission's composition is given in the Introduction, at note 1.

reports is that poverty is in part due to and exacerbated by exclusion from the (formal) legal system per se – and that inclusion in some form is thus, in itself, a step to curing poverty.[120] The Commission's response is to call for the formalisation of labour, property and 'business' rights, and to ensure greater 'access to justice' and court processes.[121] The assumption implicit in many Bank materials that 'the poor' are in fact embryonic entrepreneurs awaiting only a formally secure system to incentivise them to creativity is embraced by the Commission:

> For all these people, protection of their assets is fundamental. But protection of what they have is not enough, for they are poor and their possessions meagre. They deserve a chance to make their business operations, no matter how small or even micro they are, more productive, and they are entitled to decent working conditions. Reforms of the institutions they relate to are essential for their empowerment. Only through such systemic change will the poorest be able to take advantage of new opportunities and be attracted to joining the formal economy.[122]

It is not clear here or elsewhere whether the authors are aware that formalising the 'property rights' of the poor may open the way to dispossession as much as to investment;[123] that 'business rights' can be

---

[120] With regard to property rights, the report says: 'Both state and market have indeed been neglecting or harming the poor, but in the fight against poverty there is no alternative to the dynamic relation between a reformed and more legitimate state and a functional market that includes the poor in the value chains': Empowerment Commission (2008b), 75. The writings of Hernando de Soto, a chair of the Commission, are associated with formalisation of property to encourage debt and investment by the poor. See de Soto (1980) and (2000). The report nevertheless counsels against too swift disruption of customary tenure.

[121] According to the report, '"Business rights" need not yet be regarded as a new term in law, but rather as derived from existing rights related to doing business of the individual, newly bundled together under this term on the basis of their vital instrumentality in the livelihoods of the poor': Empowerment Commission (2008b), 5.

[122] Empowerment Commission (2008a), 20. See also, at 8: 'Access to basic financial services is indispensable for potential or emerging entrepreneurs. Just as important is access to protections and opportunities such as the ability to contract, to make deals, to raise investment capital through shares, bonds, or other means, to contain personal financial risk through asset shielding and limited liability, and to pass ownership from one generation to another.'

[123] The relevant passage is ambiguous: 'The possibility is opened for the poor to use property as collateral for obtaining credit, such as a business loan or a mortgage … Property records unify dispersed arrangements into a single legally compatible system. This integrates fragmented local markets, enabling businesses to seek out new opportunities outside their immediate vicinity, and putting them in the context of the law where they will be better protected by due process and association

mobilised by well-resourced actors against poorer ones; or that 'labour rights', if reduced to 'job opportunities' with 'social protection' languishing as a mere aspiration, need not provide more security for workers than the informal market (which can also be, for example, kin or clan based).[124] By confusing the identities of 'the poor' with investors-in-waiting, the Commission's authors appear to miss the possibility that, absent strong and specific protections of a kind they do not suggest, the former stand to lose at least as much as they gain, or that the gains might need to be weighed against losses, and that a functional legal framework may facilitate loss.

Such impoverished analysis is facilitated by the report's frankly ideological embrace of the entire edifice of rule of law economics, now washed in a newly utopian abstraction:

> The law is the platform on which rests the vital institutions of society. No modern market economy can function without law, and to be legitimate, power itself must submit to the law. A thriving and inclusive market can provide the fiscal space that allows national governments to better fulfil their own responsibilities. The relationship between society, the state and the market is symbiotic. For example, the market not only reflects basic freedoms such as association and movement, but also generates resources to provide, uphold, and enforce the full array of human rights. It is processes such as these, in which the poor realise their rights and reap the benefits of new opportunities, which enable the fruition of citizenship – in short, legal empowerment.[125]

In this passage, and in the report from which it is taken, the rule of law subject finally appears in all her glory: as a market-citizen for whom fundamental rights are market rights, in a state dedicated to upholding those rights.

DENOUEMENT: GLOBAL INTEGRATION

Rule of law literature speaks often of 'global integration', holding out the promise to poorer countries to 'join the club'. While the expression

---

of cause': Empowerment Commission (2008a), 7. However, the point receives little support in the working group study: 'State of the art analysis reveals only a modest positive effect of land titling on access to mortgage credit, and no impact on access to other forms of credit': Empowerment Commission (2008b), 85.

[124] See especially Davis (2004); Faundez (2000).
[125] Empowerment Commission (2008a), 3.

usually arises in reference to trade liberalisation, which I shall concentrate on here, there are other relevant rule of law modes of 'integration' too, notably the growing transnational security network mentioned in Chapter 5 above, constructed through shared judicial and criminal methodologies, shared information gathering and disseminating techniques, and a shared narrative of conflict (previously centred on narcotics; currently, and more successfully, on terrorism) providing a normative context for these activities. These two themes, trade and security, meet most seamlessly in the US National Security Strategies of 2002 and 2006. The latter, having discussed the importance of the rule of law in contributing to peace and security turns to trade:

> We will continue to work with countries such as Russia, Ukraine, Kazakhstan, and Vietnam on the market reforms needed to join the WTO. Participation in the WTO brings opportunities as well as obligations – to strengthen the rule of law and honor the intellectual property rights that sustain the modern knowledge economy, and to remove tariffs, subsidies, and other trade barriers that distort global markets and harm the world's poor.[126]

The Strategy has among its nine overarching goals, to 'ignite a new era of global economic growth through free markets and free trade'.[127] This translates into USAID policy commitments to pursue 'bilateral investment treaties that open new markets, support job creation in the United States, and provide important protections to U.S. investors' as well as 'state-of-the-art free trade agreements that open new markets for U.S. agriculture, goods, and services and extend strong U.S. investment, transparency, and intellectual property protections abroad'.[128] The World Bank shares these goals. 'Trade and integration' is one of three Bank 'metathemes' and one of five 'global public goods priorities' the Bank endeavours to further throughout its activities.[129] In the literature of both the Bank and the US government, free trade benefits everyone, but it is particularly good for poorer countries – and, within

---

[126] NSS (2006), 28: 'Opening markets and integrating developing countries'.
[127] NSS (2006), 25–30.
[128] See USAID (2006c), 11, 27–28. In 2008, the State Department requested the (comparatively tiny) sum of US$ 950,000 towards a WTO Global Trust Fund 'to demonstrate the concrete commitment of the [US Government] to trade liberalization by supporting developing countries' efforts to actively engage in WTO trade negotiations': CBJ FY2009, 120.
[129] The Bank's two other metathemes are 'Corporate Advocacy Priorities' and the Millennium Development Goals.

them, for their poorest members.[130] USAID's 2008 'economic growth strategy' claims that 'the current world trading system provides the greatest opportunity for global integration and poverty reduction the world has ever seen.'[131]

The rule of law lies at the heart of these visions in a two-way relation. On one hand, rule of law is considered a necessary precursor for a country's integration into the global economy; on the other, joining free trade regimes itself helps entrench the rule of law in signatory states.[132] This purported interdependence between trade liberalisation, internal legal transformation, market expansion and private sector development is well illustrated by the State Department's request for funding trade liberalisation in Vietnam:

> A top U.S. priority in Vietnam is to support a dynamic and expanding economic environment conducive to reform, legal transformation, and development of a vibrant private sector. USAID programs will assist Vietnam's World Trade Organization (WTO) and Bilateral Trade Agreement (BTA) implementation, comprehensive reform of laws and policies related to trade and investment, and creation of a business enabling environment that fosters private sector development and enhances competitiveness ... Expanding technical assistance is imperative to develop institutional capacity and human resources for implementation of reforms and best practices, and to ensure that regulatory oversight keeps pace with integration into the global economy.[133]

To encourage 'integration' – touted as a repository of investment and employment opportunities, and of heightened productivity standards, as well as a harbinger of pluralism and tolerance in recipient countries – certain groundrules must be in place. Foreign investors must be reasonably confident about what to expect (so we are told).[134] Barriers to trade, both direct and indirect, must not only be removed but their removal must be enforceable and enforced.[135] Judicial independence in

---

[130] 'As the world moves into the twenty-first century', a World Bank strategy document on Africa proclaimed, 'the consensus is greater than ever that markets, private initiative and integration into the global marketplace are the cornerstones of economic success': World Bank (1998a), vii.

[131] USAID (2008), 9.

[132] These themes were repeatedly raised during China's WTO accession preparations. See Orts (2001); Peerenboom (2002); Stephenson (2006); Dam (2006).

[133] CBJ FY2009, 394.

[134] WDR 2005, 36: 'Uncertainty about the future affects whether and how firms choose to invest. Governments need to provide clear rules of the game, but approaches that lack credibility will fail to elicit the intended investment response.'

[135] The State Department lists the following target indicators for FY 2008: 'Free Trade Agreements (FTAs) with South Korea, Malaysia, Thailand, Panama and United Arab

this light also involves freedom from nationalist pressures and protectionist bias. The courts must understand and respect private and commercial rights and interests in host countries, and must be familiar with the relevant international law. Global integration requires that a host state's legal institutions are in synch with the outside markets; that a shared procedural framework governs the handling of goods and processes; that partners on both sides of a given transaction are acquainted with the procedures; and that they can be reasonably confident that transactions will follow expectations.[136] These 'rules of the game' (as 'rule of law institutions' were commonly termed through the 1990s) reflect the World Bank's earliest definition of the rule of law: there are rules, the rules are known, they are actually enforced, independent adjudication exists in cases of dispute, and there are known procedures for changing the rules.[137]

It is thus a common objective of rule of law reform to 'assist', as one USAID project put it, 'development of the legal framework necessary to support Tajikistan's accession to the World Trade Organization and its participation in the global economy'.[138] Reformers therefore promote accession to international trade mechanisms and use accession processes to further rule of law goals. According to a World Bank study:

Trade and product market reforms proved to be a major driver of other reforms in virtually all our case studies. By increasing competition, such reforms helped shift the incentives of incumbents once opposed to reform while creating new constituencies for change. In Mexico trade liberalization through the North American Free Trade Agreement (NAFTA) induced business associations to lobby the government for reductions in the regulatory burden to help them compete ... And in Colombia greater openness and competition led employers

---

Emirates enter into force. Two additional Bilateral Investment Treaties (BITs) enter into force; initiate additional BITs. Enter into Open Skies civil air transport agreements with Libya, Brazil, South Africa and Australia': DOS FY2008, 99.

[136] USAID's 2002 strategy paper says 'Over time it has become clear that successful globalization requires more than just liberalizing trade: other essential efforts include liberalizing domestic commodity and capital markets, establishing the rule of law to enforce property rights, and implementing effective regulation': USAID (2002a), 61.

[137] Shihata (1991), 85 (see Chapter 4 above). According to the Bank: 'Differences in the quality of economic institutions – broadly understood as the "rules of the game" – have been found to be the most significant source of sustained economic growth in both cross-country research and case studies': World Bank (2004), x; generally, USAID (2000d); see also World Bank (1996), 105; World Bank (1995a), 1. The term is from North (1990), 4.

[138] USAID LIME2 (2006), 2–3. See too USAID Cape Verde (2005).

to become vocal supporters of reforms aimed at increasing labor market flexibility ... That an economy's openness is significantly associated with institutional change is among the main findings of the IMF's *World Economic Outlook, September 2005*.[139]

The theme of global commercial integration drives a vision of a global legal architecture, provided and maintained by monadic public actors, along which (certain) private actors can move as frictionlessly as possible. The optimum arrangement is outlined in numerous Bank documents, and comprise the main subject of the 2005 World Development Report ('A Good Investment Climate for Everyone') and the IFC's *Doing Business* reports: the elimination of constraints on the movement of goods and capital, the minimisation of taxes on capital and investment, regulative ease of starting and closing businesses and flexible labour laws.[140]

This architectural vision in turn guides rule of law promotion in-country: the protection of the rights and property of foreign investors, the elimination of discriminatory practices favouring domestic investors and the secure enforcement of property and contract.[141]

CONCLUSION

This chapter has sketched the primary themes and characters that inform and guide the drama of rule of law promotion. It has looked at the overarching theme of modernisation, which has three aspects – chronological, topographical and technological. Each of the three serves to indicate the need of the recipient country for aid and the capacity of the donor to provide it; the form in which modernisation

---

[139] World Bank (2006c), 11.
[140] WDR 2005. Its contents are: 'Stability and security (Verifying rights to land and other property; Facilitating contract enforcement; Reducing crime; Ending the uncompensated expropriation of property); Regulation and taxation (Regulating firms; Taxing firms; Regulating and taxing at the border); Finance and infrastructure (Financial markets; Infrastructure – connecting firms and expanding opportunities); Workers and labor markets (Fostering a skilled and healthy workforce; Crafting interventions to benefit all workers; Helping workers cope with change); International rules and standards (International arrangements and the investment climate; Enhancing credibility; Fostering harmonization; Addressing international spillovers).'
[141] Background shaping documents at the Bank include: Knack and Keefer (1995); La Porta *et al.* (1998); Djankov *et al.* (2000); World Bank (2000f); Djankov *et al.* (2002); World Bank (2003a); Botero *et al.* (2004); World Bank (2005i); World Bank (2006g).

is described further distinguishes the relationship from previous modernising efforts, those of the communist and the colonial powers. A 'reform constituency' in host countries facilitates entry. The reform cadre need not be in government; their necessarily minority status and their constitutive opposition to 'elites' and 'vested interests' both permit and require that the ordinary legislative process be bypassed. The chapter then described how rule of law promotion thematises and reinforces the distinction between public and private actors, how it submits the public sector to a disciplinary regime ('governance'), imbued with ethical significance ('corruption') and requiring self-abdication ('privatisation').

I then turn to the other key actors in the drama: first, the judiciary, whose independence and prestige are a primary theme of rule of law reform, with a view to symbolising and elevating the 'autonomy' of law, securing a view of the public interest as the aggregate of private interests, and ensuring non-discrimination between foreign and domestic investors; second, civil society, which in the rule of law story appears much diminished from its heyday in the eighteenth century, now represented in various NGOs, who are often themselves little more than an amplifier of the will of the donors upon whom they depend for funding. A lead actor, on paper at least, is 'the poor', who are to benefit from rule of law reform, in particular through the formalisation of their rights in land and labour, which are seen as providing them with the capacity to activate their potential assets and thus promote investment. There is, however, little evidence that rule of law reform does in fact benefit the poor – and much that it does not. To finish, the chapter considered the overarching context of 'global integration', which provides a destination and unifying theme for rule of law reform, drawing a thread between uniform activities in multiple country environments and an international architecture within which they operate.

Conclusion

Not long into the twenty-first century, the world looks very different from 1989, when international development policy turned so sharply towards the 'rule of law' paradigm. War seemed very distant then: today it is a persistent and apparently unshakable element of the political landscape. Climate change had just been recognised as an international concern; but it is only now beginning to expose the defects of international policy.[1] Despite the wealth-generating boom of the last two decades, prosperity has not spread: by 2010, more people lived in slums and more were exposed to hunger than at any time in the past.[2] The easy optimism of the early 1990s has, it now seems, long since dissipated into threat, risk and insecurity.

To what extent has insistent promotion of the 'rule of law' model sketched above contributed to the shape of developments over two decades? A study like the present cannot answer this question. It does show, however, that the rule of law policy mix has been more concerned with the generation than the distribution of wealth, that it does not lend itself to broad big-picture policy orientations of a kind presumably indispensable to managing large-scale problems like climate change, and that it is clearly designed to assist and facilitate resource transfers, to minimise labour costs and to reduce tax revenues, all of which might be expected to produce the kind of precariousness that might in turn be expected to underpin conflict.

No doubt, over time, the intensity with which 'rule of law' language is systematically reproduced at present will wane. Other talismanic

---

[1] The Intergovernmental Panel on Climate Change was founded in 1988.
[2] World Food Programme, 'Number of World's Hungry Tops a Billion', Press Release (June 19, 2009), online: www.wfp.org/stories/number-world-hungry-tops-billion. See too Davis (2006).

terms will move to the fore. But even so, the set of principles that reside beneath current usage are here to stay. As the foregoing has shown, these are ideas and associations with a long pedigree and with deep roots in Western political and economic theory. Rule of law rhetoric, if it has often failed to achieve its stated objectives, has nevertheless been successful in globalising that set of ideas, and associating them closely with certain constructions of the legal, the social and the economic. Although the rhetoric may evolve, therefore, it is unlikely to disappear soon. With that in mind, in this conclusion I will glance at some of the broader issues raised by the recent dominance of this register, and of the communities of practice that have formed around and through its invocation. I will do so after first revisiting and synopsising the main arguments and expanding shortly on some of the broader points indicated by them.

The picture in brief

The foregoing chapters have laid out two quite distinct yet fundamentally interrelated themes: the parameters of the rule of law as term of art and the contemporary practice of rule of law promotion abroad. They are interrelated not only in that the activities examined in Part II draw and depend upon the concepts and language examined in Part I for their coherence, legitimacy and, to a degree, content and direction. They are also interrelated in that rule of law promotion is currently a primary generative engine of discourse about 'the rule of law', and is thus, presumably, itself reshaping the parameters of the term going into the future. In this sense, it is not only the extent to which the deployment of the term today extends or diminishes past usage that matters, what also matters is the extent to which *activities* under the rule of law rubric today fit both with past usage and with the claims made on their behalf.

In Part I, I dwelt less on the many familiar narratives that have served over time to reassure us of the merits of the rule of law, seeking instead to identify some concealed assumptions or counternarratives that might flesh out a fuller picture. In doing so, I aimed to burrow beneath the familiar list of rule of law attributes that has characterised much recent writing on the subject. Versions of what Thomas Carothers once called (with deliberate irony) the rule of law 'standard menu' have played an important role in concretising a vision of law and its institutions stripped of historical, local, cultural or social peculiarities: an easy universalism is instead constructed in these visions (laws are known and internally consistent, they are applied to all equally by independent judiciaries, and so on), which in turn translates quickly, when we look abroad, into a register of presence and absence, without needing to open questions of cultural specificity or historical cause.[3] Part I showed that this easy universalism is neither a necessary nor even an obvious attribute of the rule of law. One might thus ask, what does it mean for the expression 'rule of law' to shift from signifying the 'peculiar colour' of the English legal system, as Dicey had it, to indicating instead the optimal desiderata of *any* legal system, the *sine qua non* for a state to *be* a state, regardless of local or cultural history or circumstance?

Part I drew attention to a number of elements that appear to be generally embedded within rule of law discourse though rarely acknowledged. Whereas the rule of law seems to signal reticence towards state policy intervention or capacitation generally, it has in fact generally inaugurated a discourse saturated with specific policy desires, underpinned by a secure and coercive state apparatus. Despite a language generally couched in the register of renouncement of state intervention, the rule of law ideal also embeds a vision of *what* policy should treat and *how* state capacity should be directed. On inspection, the rule of law ideal is less concerned with the question of whether the state should or should not intervene; more with how it should intervene and on behalf of whom.

There would thus appear to be an *inherent* tension between the private freedom celebrated in Dicey's rule of law ideal, on one hand, and the 'iron cage' of modern 'formal, rational' legal arrangements that Weber disparages on the other. The second appears necessary to the first. The analysis of the rule of law ideal could thus be taken further than it was in Part I. As Weber commented, the burgeoning state capacity channelled through a dissemination of legalism (whether 'organic' or motivated), while conducive to an expansive market-based economy, may restrict as well as expand personal freedoms, and may empower as well as constrain the state.[4] So where a common vein of rule of law adulation, following Dicey, speaks of private (economic) freedom and

---

[3] Carothers (1999), 96. The 'menu' commonly comprises a list of desirables, from Lon Fuller's eight elements (Fuller 1969) to the World Bank's five (Shihata 1990, 85); Lord Bingham's eight 'sub-rules' (Bingham 2006) or the World Justice Forum's five (ABA 2008).

[4] See Chapter 2, text at notes 12–30.

public (political) constraint, these claims must be set against the significant economic *restraints* the same register imposes, on one hand (as we saw in Chapter 2 and, somewhat differently, in Chapter 4), and the political capacities it *enables*, on the other (as we saw in Chapter 3 and, again differently, in Chapter 5). And if this concomitant and apparently contrary effect is often missed, that may be because, as Foucault had noted, the rule of law register directs us towards a certain kind of vision – emphasising sovereignty, right and restraint – and away from others through which the expansion of disciplinary power might better be expressed and so rendered available for analysis.[5]

In turning to the actual implementation of rule of law promotion abroad in Part II, it is relevant to bear in mind the concrete disciplinary mechanisms upon which this body of work sits, related briefly in the Interlude: the legal interventions of the colonial era. The link is made for us throughout the early post-colonial period by such as Sir Kenneth Roberts-Wray of the Colonial Office, who wrote in 1960 that 'British administration in overseas countries had conferred no greater benefit in overseas countries than English law and justice', which he further characterised as 'the rule of law, the independence of the judiciary, the writ of habeas corpus, freedom of speech and a fair trial'.[6] When Martin Chanock refers to this widely disseminated notion as the colonials' 'last surviving myth', it is not merely because these 'benefits' were conferred only patchily or not at all.[7] Rather, as Chanock puts it, 'the legacy of justice bequeathed is one of the most stubborn fantasies about British colonialism, perhaps because it derives from one of the most stubborn of fantasies about British life itself.'[8]

The immense drive through the early decolonisation period to represent colonial rule precisely as a colonial gift of the rule of law to Africa and elsewhere – in post hoc interpretations such as Roberts-Wray's and Anthony Allott's (as well as the heroic consensus-building efforts of the International Commission of Jurists) – today appears deeply contingent upon contemporary political realities.[9] Retrospectively, other benefits of these discourse-shaping efforts are clear; the aura of the rule of law seems intended to bestow legitimacy and permanence on a legal order about to fall out of its progenitors' hands, and so to preserve colonial

---

[5] See Chapter 3, text at notes 69–74.   [6] Roberts-Wray (1960), 66.
[7] Chanock (1998), 5.   [8] Chanock (1998), 5.
[9] Allott (1960a), Allott (1960b), Allott (1962), Allott (1963), Elias (1961), ICJ Declaration of Delhi, 1959.

legal engineering intact. At the same time, the rights of large residual settler minorities – especially in property but also in the supposition of basic freedom from the interference of the new post-independence states – were to be preserved. Talk of the rule of law legacy thus seemed deployed to fix or freeze a certain legal (and so, political and economic) order in place through a period of social and political upheaval.

The historical threads that intertwine in Part II, therefore, are numerous and varied. Contemporary rule of law promotion shares certain features with the ideal of the rule of law, on one hand, and with colonial legal interventions on the other. Like the rule of law ideal, its stated economic preference is for incentives over policy; it opposes redistribution and substantive justice with formalism; it foregrounds individual rights and judicial processes; it privileges private over public; it represents itself as *modern*. At the same time, contemporary transnational rule of law promotion deviates from the classical rule of law often dramatically – and in the ways in which it resembles colonial legal engineering: it is motivated and instrumental; it constitutes a centralised (global) policy; it is universal or abstract rather than local and particular; it ignores or reviles tradition and local culture, nurturing while reshaping them specifically as containment mechanisms; it assumes its own unproblematic transplantation by fiat; it is oriented to global integration; it is *modernising*. In many ways, indeed, the rule of law register might be thought of as standing in for the old language of 'civilisation' – the mark of accomplishment of the modern; something *we* have but *they* do not; that we must help them achieve; and whose presence or absence is itself the determinant and mobilising criterion for a body of other interventions. Certainly, at a minimum, the rule of law has become today a key term of a new language through which the old goals of 'developing the estates' are continued and managed.

What is becoming of the rule of law?

It is tempting to conclude from all this that, its self-representations notwithstanding, the body of work with which the present thesis has been concerned is not primarily about the rule of law at all, so many and significant are its deviations from the rule of law ideal. The rule of law has signified a non-instrumental understanding of law – law as 'autonomous' from political or economic goals; yet it is today frankly promoted as a means to achieve a range of other public goods and fix an expanding series of ills. The rule of law has signified the limits to or outside of policy and the pre-eminence of signposting over commandeering;

yet today rule of law *is* public policy, breaking down into a set of identifiable prescriptions that states everywhere are exhorted, and often required, to implement. The rule of law has signified the centrality of the state as the modern political unit; yet today a burgeoning arsenal of incentives, indicators and coercive measures view the state rather as a carrier of policies elaborated elsewhere, a driven and uniform transnational policy with which target states must contend throughout domestic policy-making processes. The rule of law has signified that lawmaking processes, to be legitimate, must be sourced in the polity that is subject to the relevant law; yet rule of law promotion subverts or bypasses the ordinary legislative process, instead shaping domestic law through elite agreement at transnational level. Finally, the rule of law had from the outset been conceived as a cultural or societal product, something arrived at, spontaneously and voluntarily, by a society in congress with itself; so thoroughly does this view of the rule of law jar with contemporary practice that it is doubtful whether it continues, in fact, to be an attribute of the rule of law at all.

And therein lies the rub. For to query what is or is not 'rule of law' today is to run immediately into the complex reality of a term of art that saturates contemporary political life and accommodates increasingly broad political desires. The rule of law is an open-ended concept subject to a barrage of motivated deployments, many of which, as we have seen, are disseminated globally from capable centres of global norm-generation and discourse-shaping. The term has always been evolving, never more so than today: the question is not whether a given constellation of claimed 'rule of law' effects are 'in fact' the rule of law; rather it is: what is becoming of this ideal known as 'rule of law'?

Some assessment of the term's ongoing evolution might be gleaned from the foregoing account. Its loose association with a certain form of market essentialism has certainly tightened and deepened. Also, the rule of law – that, in the writings of Dicey and Oakeshott and others, provided a mainstay against a 'teleocracy' or 'technological conception of the state' – has taken on an increasingly instrumentalist tenor. The old opposition between purposive and autonomous law might then break down, resulting in a kind of synthesis: law in the service of, and inextricable from, an economic ideal. The notion of legal autonomy might, one would expect, be irreversibly undermined or transformed beyond recognition, or the illusion of autonomy finally exploded. Law would then appear, in a rule of law description, as it frequently does already within the school of law and economics – a schema of incentives that are combinable and adjustable in differing permutations to secure rewards for efficiency, punishment for inefficiency and an optimisation of productivity across fields and sectors. This sounds like a very different proposition from Dicey's, despite the common themes and antecedents.

It may be that the new capaciousness of rule of law language may yet stretch to accommodate quite different associations from those channelled forcefully through it in recent years; certainly the illustrative examples cited in my Introduction appear to indicate a conceptual looseness that quite undoes any remaining precision of meaning.[10] Yet even if the policy pendulum were to swing away from the objectives currently driven through rule of law promotion – if, as seems increasingly likely today, this relentless framing of economic life were eventually to generate its own opposition – the term's very ubiquity and gravitational pull would still no doubt continue to shape discourse and set terms of argument, privileging certain notions of the public good and visions of the social, channelling discipline through (apparent) freedoms of sovereignty and right, naturalising and legitimising certain economic and legal forms, concealing family resemblances with colonial law export, and likewise obscuring certain policy options or complicating their appearance or justification. If, in short, it is difficult to state precisely what is becoming of the rule of law, it is not difficult to predict that its deployment will continue to privilege market solutions over other possible articulations of the public good.

What law is to rule?

In Chapter 3 I referred to Italian philosopher Giorgio Agamben, to ground a suggestion that rigorous insistence on the law, far from constraining sovereign power, may instead extend that power. Such a claim rests on an opposition (implicit in Agamben) between the positive law, which is the product and prerogative of sovereignty, and a natural or divine law (or, perhaps, *nomos*) that is constantly threatened or displaced by the positive law of the sovereign. Each exercise of sovereignty, on this reading, will tend to encroach upon the hitherto non-

---

[10] Not for the first time. Judith Shklar wrote in 1987: 'It would not be very difficult to show that the phrase "the Rule of Law" has become meaningless thanks to ideological abuse and general over-use': Shklar, (1987), 6; Raz (2001), 290–291.

legal, the domain of 'life itself', which is thus increasingly 'colonised' by sovereignty, as Agamben puts it. As in Aristotle, the key question buried in the 'rule of law' preoccupation would then be not 'does law rule?' but rather 'what law rules?': how are we to *know* or legislate the *best* law and how are we to bind authority to it?

So what 'law' is to 'rule' in this brave new rule of law world? Or, to sharpen the terms: is the rule of law better conceived as premised on 'natural' or 'positive' law? As the law *of* the sovereign or the law that *opposes or constrains* sovereignty? In practice, of course, the term 'rule of law' is used to both ends: *both* to assert rigour in and obedience regarding the (positive) law in place *and* as a normative desideratum against which to compare and challenge existing laws and institutions and through which to seek their 'reform'. On one hand, the rule of law is said to be violated when the laws are inconsistent, unpredictable, non-transparent, retroactive and so on, or when they infringe certain substantive norms, such as non-discrimination or human rights. On the other, it is also said to be violated when there is persistent disobedience to or disregard for the law in force. In the former usage, the rule of law constrains the state. In its latter deployment it reinforces the state.

This ambiguity appears to be inherent, given that 'rule of law' appeals to both positive and natural conceptions of law. Once acknowledged, it quickly becomes clear that indeterminacy on this question – on whether the appropriate source of the law that is to rule is 'natural' or positive – is central to the successful mobilisation of the rule of law as a rhetorical device. For any given actor, where existing law reflects their set of preferred substantive orientations, the rule of law can be relied upon for its proceduralism: the emphasis is on *obedience to the law*.[11] But where the positive law deviates from a desired substantive orientation, calls to abide by 'the rule of law' can become, instead, a basis for seeking *reform of the law*.

Movement between these positions recurs regularly in the mobilisation of the rule of law in its transnational export context. On one hand, 'reform' of the law in a given country is sought by appeal to a (natural law) order that is universal and external in contrast to the

---

[11] So, for example, Gen. Ray Odierno, the US commander in Iraq described a court decision to release five private military contractors due to procedural technicalities as 'a lesson in the rule of law' for Iraqis: see Timothy Williams, 'Iraqis Angered as Blackwater Charges Are Dropped', *New York Times*, January 1, 2010.

existing positive order. On the other, this same supposedly universal order *is* fixed in the positive law: it is found in international law, in the 'best practices' of rule of law poster-states, and in the bromides of rule of law donors. The appeal to 'reform' – the stirring call to stand against the status quo – turns out on inspection to be an appeal on behalf of another status quo, a profoundly conservative mobilisation in the name of an abstract, yet exceedingly active, 'international' or supposedly 'universal' *source* of law (a global sovereign? is there such a thing?). Rule of law language, then, with its focus on state and society, appears to obscure the trans- or supra-statal from view. There is a divergence between the state, the supposed Leviathan and subject of rule of law reform, on one hand, and the actual source of the law that is to rule – in the universal and general mode preferred by a rule of law register – on the other: an inchoate or diffuse *transnational* authority. The reform that is sought from the state, in a classic rule of law register, turns out, then, to be not only a (natural law-based) resistance to the sovereign from below, but also a (positive law-based) expression of sovereign authority and will from above.

With natural law in abeyance, it is the rule of law as disciplinary mechanism (see Chapters 3 and 5 above) that comes to the fore in this reading – a mechanism that, rather than limiting and constraining sovereignty, expands and extends it. Or rather, since the only available premise for the authority of 'the rule of law' is a 'natural' order historically produced and transposed into international law, rule of law claims must habitually redirect respect for natural law into obedience to the positive law. Rule of law claims would then be the reverse of what they appear: conservatism as opposed to 'reform', discipline as opposed to 'liberty'. The rule of law, then, would be one of many disciplinary mechanisms originating from a cognisable prescriptive authority that burrows into the normative imperatives of society at large: the colonisation of the world by means of the replication of the state form globally. Can this be right?

A transnational public?

A second observation from the foregoing analysis concerns the rule of law's overflow, in its current deployment, of the national boundaries that had determined its referential scope in the classic rule of law ideal – explicitly and necessarily in Dicey and Oakeshott, but implicitly in most or all accounts of the rule of law, or indeed of modern law generally – whose mooring in the sovereign state necessarily assumes a state-based and -bounded model of the public and private and their interrelation. Today's rule of law, by contrast, spills over or around the state's borders. Not only is its promotion a transnational enterprise, but as we have seen it also assumes a transnational 'public sphere' as its relevant audience, the source of its legitimacy, and the benefactor of its engineering. What is this transnational polity? Contemporary theorists identify increasingly dense networks of private cross-border actors that appear to indicate either an existing or consolidating transnational 'public authority' (that would underpin and guarantee that activity), or at least a shared system of norms and values that would be associated with a rising 'public sphere'.[12] The transnational rule of law plays – or sets itself – a significant role in entrenching the background conditions within which such a densification of transnational private activity can take place, by explicitly embedding comparable legal norms everywhere and bringing institutions into line across different countries. From the perspective of transnational rule of law, public actors are necessarily and exclusively national (indeed by definition), whereas private actors are not.

What would it mean to speak of a transnational public sphere in the context of extensive cross-border rule of law promotion? A quick recap of Habermas's account will help here. According to Habermas, the public sphere ideal performed a series of interrelated functions in European societies of the eighteenth and nineteenth centuries. It provided *both* an explanatory framework for the institutional reform of the state *and* an ideal towards which many members of civil society aspired. But (third), on Habermas's account, the public sphere also comprised an ideology; in other words, once it is generally accepted that the public is the proper locus of justification and legitimation of political action, it becomes possible and convenient to attribute responsibility to it for policy decisions. Talk of public opinion, rational debate, transparency and so on, might, in other words, be engineered, and might distract from a set of very different, perhaps more profound or decisive, political goals and aspirations that are more truly determinative of legal and political outcomes. Finally (fourth), the public sphere was and is a complex phenomenon, different aspects of which can be stressed to differing effect. The observer's focus can shift between, say, the conditions of entry, the characteristics of actual participants, the

---

[12] See generally, Dezalay and Garth (1996); Teubner (1997); Steinhardt (1991); Michaels and Jansen (2006); Caruso (2006).

nature and procedures of argument, the means by which arguments circulate within the public sphere and recede or dominate, the kinds and purposes of protections of entry and argumentation, the detail of the institutional structures needed to maintain it, and so on. In each case the phenomenon will appear very different or may serve a variety of purposes, some of which may even be contradictory (thus its *ideal* function of channelling public reason into the political sphere may exist in irresolvable tension with its *ideological* function of shaping public opinion to serve political or private ends).

Habermas treats the public sphere in all these ways: as an explanation for existing political and legal institutions; an ideal worth striving for; a justificatory ideology that eases governance and often misleads; and ultimately as an irreducible and unascertainable sociocultural phenomenon.

Much of Habermas's account is re-enacted in rule of law reform, as we have seen. The expansion of the public sphere beyond property owners through expanding franchise (first to unpropertied men, later to women) is reanimated today through the promotion of democracy abroad that invariably accompanies rule of law reform.[13] Insofar as contemporary rule of law actively strives to ignite the ideal of the public sphere, Habermas's account provides much of the historical background, political context and intellectual logic that inform present processes. So, for example, the history of the ideal of the public sphere may explain why rule of law accounts of the developmental state veer inexorably towards the identification of tyranny and absolutism regardless of whether the state in question is post-communist, post-colonial, post-conflict, weak or corrupt. More pertinently, this history may explain why government everywhere can always be judged against the universal public good ensconced in private freedom, rather than according to any local legitimating processes. The latter tend to disappear from consideration wherever they do not obviously contribute to a public good articulated in terms of private autonomy.

Nevertheless (still according to Habermas), back in Europe, this expansion of the public domain took place side by side with a retreat of the public sphere from its ideal, and especially its critical, function. The nominal public sphere became a zone of contestation for competing political forces or interests, where, on one hand, the state intervened

---

[13] See generally Marks (2003), Carothers (1999).

to generate public legitimacy for its actions while, on the other, private actors sought to shape and reflect public opinion in their own interests.[14] Rather than an arena of critical debate, the public sphere had, by mid-twentieth century, split in two directions. Rational critical debate took place mainly in the academy, but was rarely truly 'public'. The sphere of *publicity*, by contrast – the media – had essentially become a zone of passive consumption of pre-digested ideas and commodities, involving little rational-critical discussion. Habermas's own later work is concerned largely with taking the kernel of the ideal or aspiration of the public sphere – of deliberative participation in political governance – and subjecting it to a barrage of reality tests and theoretical reformulations.[15] In doing so, the model's fundamental *failure* to describe actual conditions, both as a matter of fact and as a formula for reform in response to publicly initiated normative demands, comes to the fore. This diagnosis should, in turn, condition an attitude of further critique, the very attitude that characterises the public. In its ideal form, then, the public is always a horizon, an aspiration, rather than an accomplishment. The public can truly become a public only in response to the recognition that it is not yet a public, and through an awareness of its fragility and vulnerability to manipulation.

The critical difference when we turn to the transnational rule of law is the contrast with just this aspect of Habermas's writing. In rule of law discourse, the complexity disappears: the public sphere is made to appear in radically simplified form, as a systematic set of axioms about the public good (summed up in the incontestable 'rule of law' good itself). Any awareness of a possible ideological function too disappears; the assumption throughout is that this ideal is achieved or achievable everywhere, in principle – and the relevant process of getting there is simply a matter of 'reform', the content and direction of which are not only knowable, but already known. The failure of the transnational rule of law is thus more acute than that identified by Habermas in the European public sphere, and this failure is most clearly seen in the poor or partial correspondence between its physical locus and its site of action.

---

[14] This argument constitutes the 'structural transformation' of his title. Habermas's own description of the public sphere as a battleground of organised public and private concerns is very much in keeping with Hegel's 'corporatively reintegrated' public, with which, Habermas says, 'Hegel has definitively left liberalism behind': Habermas (1992), 120. See also Hegel (2005), paras. 236, 243–245, 314–318.

[15] The main relevant works are two volumes laying out his 'theory of communicative action' as well as Habermas (1998). On this theme generally, see McCormick (2007), especially, 34–47 and 126–175.

Where is this 'public'? Although its domain is the (expected or solicited) public of the particular state wherein reform is enacted, the transnational rule of law itself is not *of* the public: it overspills the bounds of state and of society. In its configuration through the mediation of rule of law programming, an imputed transnational public sphere marks (or assumes) a breakdown of the territorial coextension and identity of state and society. The private persons whose rational opinions and conclusions are channelled through transnational funding make up societies that are not bound to a given state and they express ideals that are likewise freed from any dependency on national society or culture, and may rather oppose them. The rule of law is thus frequently signalled as the desire of a presumptive 'global civil society', a loosely knit agglomeration of local, regional and international groups that together comprise the echo chambers of a supposed critical-rational discussion that takes place beyond the state – embracing broad networks, such as chambers of commerce or human rights groups, which themselves function through multinational chapters.[16] Thus, transnational 'societies' loop around the world like octopi, with their bulk firmly in the 'north' but a presence running through myriad other hubs.

Indeed, the agents of rule of law promotion might themselves be described as constituting a (transnational) public among publics. Thus gatherings such as the World Justice Forum, cited in the Introduction, might best be thought of as assemblies of a particular public, with its own codes, goals and values.[17] Given their shared convictions and groundrules, and their self-conscious sense of their own reforming role, this public aligns apparently readily with Habermas's rising bourgeois public of the late eighteenth century. The comparison is instructive: the politics, legal norms and state principles they propose and promote self-consciously replicate those attributed to their European forebears. On a generous reading, this apparent identity might be read as indicative of a transnational 'moment' that reflects the 'national' moment of two centuries ago – the coextensive consolidation of a modern state with a modern society, but at global level. On this model, the group's

---

[16] Keane (1998); Keane (2001).
[17] A forerunner to the Forum, ABA's 2006 'International Rule of Law Symposium' 'brought together representatives from the bar, business, government, media, philanthropy and NGOs to discuss ways to strengthen the Rule of Law movement': 'As our world and profession grow smaller and more connected, the responsibility we have to provide lawyers around the world with the information and the tools to promote the Rule of Law becomes greater. This conference addressed this need.' See online: www.abanet.org/rolsymposium/.

self-interest as a private (bourgeois) sector would be the authentic voice of a global society-in-waiting – the harbingers of progress along classic Enlightenment lines, but beyond the state. It seems likely that this is indeed how the transnational rule of law public, if we may so name this small coterie of international professionals, thinks of itself, or that it is encouraged to do so, at least, by its patrons.

And yet, on inspection the parallel seems flawed. Given this public's elite composition – and in particular the heavy dose of public funding that propels it – the agents and direct beneficiaries of the transnational rule of law clearly do not square with an idealised 'global civil society'.[18] The essentially interventionist cast of rule of law reform, regardless of whether it is funded by public or private monies, gives it rather the guise of public, than private, ordering. Indeed a distinctive trait of rule of law reform is its widespread support among a specific group of global actors that *cannot* properly be characterised as 'non-governmental': rich country governments, a multinational private sector, developing country elites, the international 'public' arms of the UN, and so on. Indeed these actors cannot even be described as engaged in reformative combat with an overarching sovereign. By contrast, the targets of their reforming zeal – the governments and recalcitrant populations of recipient countries – have relatively little sway over the content of transnational rules; they are rule-takers rather than -shapers. The 'reformers' themselves thus appear much more as the agents, than the opponents, of some larger 'sovereign'.

Viewed as a public among publics, a community of funders, it is immediately clear how little this public shares with Habermas's ideal public sphere, and how much more it has in common, in paradoxical point of fact, with the co-infection of public and private spheres characteristic of the mid-twentieth century and generally represented as the rule of law's contrary.[19] In the theatre of the rule of law, however, these actors comprise not the public, but the spectacle. The public is, instead, to be interpellated, imported, or, at the limit, assumed: a public of upwardly and geographically mobile private persons, a self-consciously 'civil' society, expected to recognise, absorb and apply this newly narrow rule of law, performed under tutelage by a local public sector for a transnational public-in-waiting.

---

[18] See Habermas (1992), 432.   [19] See Chapter 1 above, text at note 100.

Bibliography

I. ARTICLES AND MONOGRAPHS

Afrika Instituut-Studiecentrum-Leiden (1956), *The Future of Customary Law in Africa*, Papers from a symposium held in Amsterdam 1955, Universitaire Pers Leiden

Agamben, G. (2005) [2003], *State of Exception*, University of Chicago Press
  (2002) [1998], *Remnants of Auschwitz: the Witness and the Archive*, Zone Books
  (1998) [1995], *Homo Sacer: Sovereign Power and Bare Life*, Stanford University Press

Agbosu, L. K. (1983), 'The Origins of Forest Law and Policy in Ghana during the Colonial Period' 27 (2) *Journal of African Law* 169

Ajayi, J. F. A. (1981), 'Colonialism: An Episode in African History', in Gann and Duignan (1981)

Alexandrowicz, C. (1973), *The European-African Confrontation: A Study in Treaty Making*, Sijthoff

Allan, T. R. S. (2003), *Constitutional Justice*, Oxford University Press

Allen, T. (1973), *The Right to Property in Commonwealth Constitutions*, Cambridge University Press

Allen, F., Jun Qian and Meijun Qian (2005), 'Law, Finance, and Economic Growth in China' 77 *Journal of Financial Economics* 57

Allott, A. (1957a), 'Native Tribunals in the Gold Coast 1844–1927. Prolegomena to a Study of Native Courts in Ghana' 1 *Journal of African Law* 163
  (1957b), 'The Judicial Ascertainment of Customary Law in British Africa' 20 *The Modern Law Review* 244
  (1960a), *Essays in African Law*, Butterworth
  (1960b), 'The London Conference on the Future of Law in Africa' 3 *African Studies Bulletin* 13
  (1962), *Judicial and Legal Systems in Africa*, Butterworth
  (1963), 'Legal Development and Economic Growth in Africa', in Anderson (1963)

Allott, P. (2002), *The Health of Nations*, Cambridge University Press

Althusser, L. (2001), 'Ideology and Ideological State Apparatuses', in L. Althusser, *Lenin and Philosophy*, Monthly Review Press

Anderson, A. (1988), *Revolution*, Harcourt Brace Jovanovich
Anderson, J. N. D. (1963), *Changing Law in Developing Countries*, George Allen & Unwin
Anghie, A. (1999), 'Finding the Peripheries: Sovereignty and Colonialism in Nineteenth-Century International Law' 40 *Harvard International Law Journal* 1
   (2000), 'Time Present and Time Past: Globalization, International Financial Institutions, and the Third World' 32 *New York University Journal of International Law and Politics* 283
   (2002), 'Colonialism and the Birth of International Institutions: Sovereignty, Economy and the Mandate System of the League of Nations' 34 *New York University Journal of International Law and Politics* 513
   (2005), *Imperialism, Sovereignty and the Making of International Law*, Cambridge University Press
Anon. (1982), 'Round and Round the Bramble Bush: From Legal Realism to Critical Legal Scholarship' 95 *Harvard Law Review* 1669
Ansprenger, F. (1989), *The Dissolution of Colonial Empires*, Routledge
Aquinas (1988) [1266], *De Regimine Principum* [On Kingship], in Paul Sigmund (ed.), *St. Thomas Aquinas on Politics and Ethics*, Norton
Arden, The Rt Hon Lady Justice (2005), 'Human Rights in the Age of Terrorism', University of Essex and Clifford Chance Lecture (January 27, 2005)
Arendt, H. (1958), *The Human Condition*, University of Chicago Press
   (1990) [1963], *On Revolution*, Penguin
   (1993) [1956], 'What is Authority?', in Hannah Arendt, *Between Past and Future*, Penguin
Arrow, K. (1963) [1951], *Social Choice and Individual Values*, Wiley
Baker, J. H. (2002), *An Introduction to English Legal History*, Butterworths
Barker, E. (1959), *Political Thought of Plato and Aristotle*, Dover
   (1962) [Aristotle, *Politics*, trans. E. Barker], *The Politics of Aristotle*, Oxford University Press
Bataille, G. (1991) [1949], *The Accursed Share* (Vol. 3: Sovereignty), Zone Books
Belton, R. K. (2005), 'Competing Definitions of the Rule of Law: Implications for Practitioners', Carnegie Endowment for International Peace, Rule of Law Series No. 55
Benjamin, W. (1969) [1942], 'Theses on the Philosophy of History', in *Illuminations*, Schocken Books
   (1986) [1921], 'Critique of Violence', in *Reflections: Essays, Aphorisms, Autobiographical Writings*, Schocken Books
Bentham, H. (2002), *Constitutional and Administrative Law* (4th edn), Cavendish
Benton, L. (2002), *Law and Colonial Cultures: Legal Regimes in World History, 1400–1900*, Cambridge University Press
Betts, R. (1998), *Decolonization*, Routledge.
Bhuta, N. (2006), 'A New Bonapartism?', in A. Bartholomew (ed.), *Empire's Law*, Pluto Press

Bingham, Tom (2007), 'The Rule of Law' 66 *Cambridge Law Journal* 67
Bodin, J. (2001) [1583], *On Sovereignty*, Cambridge University Press
Boisdon, D. (1956), 'Note sur les conflits entre le statut civil français et les statuts civil coutumiers dans les pays d'Outre-Mer dépendant de la République Française', in *Afrika Instituut*
Botero J. C., S. Djankov, R. La Porta, F. Lopez-de-Silanes, and A. Shleifer (2004), 'The Regulation of Labour' November 2004 *The Quarterly Journal of Economics* 1339.
Bourdieu, P. (1987), 'The Force of Law: Toward a Sociology of the Juridical Field' 38 *The Hastings Law Journal* 814
Buell, R. (1928), *The Native Problem in Africa* (2 vols.), Macmillan
Burke, E. (2000), *On Empire, Liberty, and Reform: Speeches and Letters of Edmund Burke*, David Bromwich (ed.), Yale University Press
Calhoun, C. (1992), 'Introduction' in Craig Calhoun (ed.), *Habermas and the Public Sphere*, MIT Press
Canavan, T. C. (1987), 'The Threat to the International Banking System', in Pastor (1987)
Carothers, T. (1991), *In the Name of Democracy: US Policy towards Latin America in the Reagan Years*, University of California Press
  (1998), 'The Rule of Law Revival' *Foreign Affairs* (March/April 1998), reproduced in Carothers (2006)
  (1999), *Aiding Democracy Abroad*, Carnegie Endowment for International Peace
  (ed.) (2006), *Promoting the Rule of Law Abroad: In Search of Knowledge*, Carnegie Endowment for International Peace
Caruso, D. (2006), 'Private Law and State-Making in the Age of Globalization' Boston University School of Law, Working Paper Series Public Law & Legal Theory, No. 06-09
Channell, W. (2005), 'Lessons Not Learned: Problems with Western Aid for Law Reform in Postcommunist Countries' Carnegie Paper No. 57, Carnegie Endowment for International Peace (March 2005)
Chanock, M. (1991), 'Paradigms, Policies and Property: A Review of the Customary Law of Land Tenure', in Mann and Roberts (1991)
  (1998), *Law, Custom and Social Order: The Colonial Experience in Malawi and Zambia*, Heinemann
Chong A. and C. Calderon (2000), 'Causality and Feedback Between Institutional Measures and Economic Growth' 12 *Economics and Politics* 69
Chowdhury, S. R. (1989), *The Rule of Law in a State of Emergency: The Paris Minimum Standards of Human Rights Norms in a State of Emergency*, St Martin's Press
Clarke, D. C. (2003), 'Economic Development and the Rights Hypothesis: The China Problem' 51 *American Journal of Comparative Law* 89
Claudon, M. P. (ed.) (1986), *World Debt Crisis: International Lending on Trial*, Ballinger Publishing Company
Coase, R. (1960), 'The Problem of Social Cost' 3 *Journal of Law and Economics* 1
Coby, P. (1986), 'Aristotle's Four Conceptions of Politics' 39 *The Western Political Quarterly* 480

Cohen, B. (1986), 'International Debt and Linkage Strategies: Some Foreign-Policy Implications for the United States', in Miles Kahler (ed.), *The Politics of International Debt*, Cornell University Press

Cohen, F. (1935), 'Transcendental Nonsense and the Functional Approach' 35 *Columbia Law Review* 809

Cohen, M. (1928), 'Property and Sovereignty' 13 *Cornell Law Quarterly* 8

Cohen, W. B. (1971), *Rulers of Empire: The French Colonial Service in Africa*, Hoover Institution Press

Collier, P. and A. Hoeffler (2002), 'Greed and Grievance in Civil War' CSAE WPS 2002-01

Colson E. (1981), 'African Society at the Time of the Scramble', in Gann and Duignan (1981)

Comaroff, J. and S. Roberts (1987), *Rules and Processes: The Cultural Logic of Dispute in an African Context*, University of Chicago Press

Cook, W. W. (1918), 'Privileges of Labor Unions in the Struggle for Life' 27 *Yale Law Journal* 779

Cottam, M. and O. Marenin (1989), 'Predicting the Past: Reagan Administration Assistance to Police Forces in Central America' 6 *Justice Quarterly* 589

Courcel, G. de (1988), 'The Berlin Act of 26 February 1884', in Förster *et al.* (1988)

Craig, P. (1997), 'Formal and Substantive Conceptions of the Rule of Law: An Analytical Framework' [1997] *Public Law* 467

Crawford, J. (1979), *The Creation of States in International Law*, Clarendon Press

(2006), *The Creation of States in International Law*, Oxford University Press

Crocker, W. R. (1949), *Self-Government for the Colonies*, George Allen and Unwin

Dam, K. (2006a), 'China As a Test Case: Is the Rule of Law Essential for Economic Growth?' John M. Olin Law & Economics Paper No. 275, University of Chicago Law School

(2006b), *The Law-Growth Nexus: The Rule of Law And Economic Development*, Brookings Institute Press

Davidson, B. (1992), *The Black Man's Burden: Africa and the Curse of the Nation State*, James Currey

Davis, K. (2004), 'What Can the Rule of Law Variable Tell Us About Rule of Law Reforms' 26 *Michigan Journal of International Law* 141

Davis, M. (2006), *Planet of Slums*, Verso

Davis, K. E. (2008), 'The Relationship Between Law and Development: Optimists versus Skeptics' 56 *American Journal of Comparative Law* 895

Davis, K. E. and M. Kruse, 'Measuring Regulation: A Review of the *Doing Business* Project' New York University School of Law (unpublished, April 2006)

Delavignette, R. (1968) [1946], *Freedom and Authority in French West Africa*, Cass

Derrett, D. M. (1963), 'Justice, Equity and Good Conscience', in Anderson (1963)

Derrida, J. (1992), 'Force of Law : the "Mystical Foundation of Authority"', in D. Cornell, M. Rosenfeld and D. G. Carlson (eds.), *Deconstruction and the Possibility of Justice*, Routledge (2002)

Dezalay Y. and B. Garth (1996), *Dealing in Virtue: International Commercial Arbitration and the Construction of a Transnational Legal Order*, University of Chicago Press

(2002), *The Internationalization of Palace Wars: Lawyers, Economists, and the Contest to Transform Latin American States*, University of Chicago Press

Dicey, A. V. (1962), *Introduction to the Study of the Law of the Constitution* [1885], Macmillan

(1959), *Introduction to the Study of the Law of the Constitution* (10th edn), Macmillan, introduction by E. C. S. Wade

(2008), *Law and Public Opinion in England During the Nineteenth Century*, Liberty Fund

Djankov, S., R. La Porta, F. Lopez-de-Silanes and A. Shleifer, 'The Regulation of Entry', Harvard Institute of Economic Research Discussion Paper No. 1904 (September 2000)

Djankov S., R. La Porta, F. Lopez-de-Silanes and A. Shleifer, 'Courts: The Lex Mundi Project' Revised Draft (March 2002) [funded by the World Bank]

Donziger, S. and G. W. Fine (1989), 'Police Aid and Central America: The Reagan Years' 2 *Harvard Human Rights Journal* 197

Douglas, W. (1965), 'The Rule of Law in World Affairs' 13 *University of Kansas Law Review* 473

Duignan, P. (1988), 'The USA, the Berlin Conference, and its Aftermath', in Förster *et al.* (1988)

Duignan P. and L. Gann (1975), *The Economics of Colonialism*, Cambridge University Press

Dyzenhaus D. (2005a), 'An Unfortunate Outburst of Anglo-Saxon Parochialism' 68 *Modern Law Review* 673

(2005b), 'The Rule of (Administrative) Law in International Law' 6 *Law & Contemporary Problems* 127

Eley, G. (1992), 'Nations, Publics and Political Cultures: Placing Habermas in the Nineteenth Century', in Calhoun (1992)

Elias, T. O. (1961), 'General Report', in International Commission of Jurists, *African Conference on the Rule of Law, Lagos Nigeria January 3–7, 1961*, ICJ (1961) [symposium]

(1962), *Ghana and Sierra Leone: the Development of their Laws and Constitutions*, Stevens

(1967), *Nigeria: the Development of its Laws and Constitution*, Stevens

Ellis, W. (1928) [Aristotle, *Politics*, trans. W. Ellis], *Politics: A Treatise on Government*, J. M. Dent & Sons

Everson, S. (1996) [Aristotle, *Politics*, trans. Stephen Everson], *Aristotle: the Politics and the Constitution of Athens*, Cambridge University Press

Faundez, J. (2000), 'Legal Reform in Transition Countries: Making Haste Slowly' (unpublished, 2000)

Fenske, J. (2006), 'The Emergence (or not) of Private Property Rights in Land: Southern Nigeria, 1851 to 1914' (unpublished)
Fisher, W., M. Horwitz and T. Reed (eds.) (1993), *American Legal Realism*, Oxford University Press
Fitzpatrick, P. (1992), *The Mythology of Modern Law*, Routledge
  (2001), 'Bare Sovereignty: Homo Sacer and the Insistence of Law' 5(2) *Theory and Event* 82
Flint, J. (1988), 'Chartered Companies and the Transition from Informal Sway to Colonial Rule in Africa', in Förster *et al.*
Förster, S., W. Mommsen and R. E. Robinson (1988), *Bismarck, Europe and Africa: The Berlin Africa Conference 1884–1885 and the Onset of Partition*, Oxford University Press
Foucault, M. (1977), *Discipline and Punish*, Penguin
  (1980), 'Two Lectures', in Foucault, *Power/Knowledge, Selected Interviews and Other Writings 1972–1977*, Colin Gordon (ed.), Pantheon
  (1981), *The History of Sexuality: 1*, Penguin
  (1990), *The Use of Pleasure: The History of Sexuality Vol. 2*, Vintage
  (2000), 'Governmentality', in Foucault, *Power*, James Faubion (ed.), The New Press
Friedman, B. (2000), 'The History of the Countermajoritarian Difficulty, Part Four: Law's Politics' 148 *University of Pennsylvania Law Review* 971
Friedman, M. (2002) [1962], *Capitalism and Freedom*, University of Chicago Press
Fuller, L. L. (1934), 'American Legal Realism' 82 *University of Pennsylvania Law Review* 429
  (1969), *The Morality of Law*, Yale University Press
Gann, L. (1988), 'The Berlin Conference and the Humanitarian Conscience', in Förster *et al.* (1988)
Gann, L. and P. Duignan (1981), *Colonialism in Africa 1870–1960, Vol. 1*, Cambridge University Press
Gavin R. J. and Betley, J. A. (1973), *The Scramble for Africa, Documents on the Berlin West African Conference and Related Subjects, 1884/1885*, Ibadan University Press
Gellhorn, E. and R. Levin (1997), *Administrative Law and Process* (3rd edn), West Publishing Co.
Geuss, R. (2001a), *History and Illusion in Politics*, Cambridge University Press
  (2001b), *Public Goods, Private Goods*, Princeton University Press
Giddens, A. (1991), *Modernity and Self-Identity*, Polity
Gifford, P. and W. R. Louis (1971), *France and Britain in Africa: Imperial Rivalry and Colonial Rule*, Yale University Press
Goerner, E. (1983), 'Letter and Spirit: The Political Ethics of the Rule of Law Versus the Political Ethics of the Rule of the Virtuous' 45 *The Review of Politics* 553
Golub, S. (2006), 'The Legal Empowerment Alternative', in Carothers (2006)
  (2007), 'The Rule of Law and the UN Peacebuilding Commission: a Social Development Approach' 20 *Cambridge Review of International Affairs* 47

Greenberg, K. (2006), *The Torture Debate in America*, Cambridge University Press

Greenberg, K. and J. Dratel (eds.), *The Torture Papers: The Road to Abu Ghraib*, Cambridge University Press

Gross, O. (2003), 'Chaos and Rules: Should Responses to Violent Crises Always be Constitutional?' 112 *Yale Law Journal* 1011.

Habermas, J. (1992), 'Further Reflections on the Public Sphere', in Calhoun (1992).

(1994) [1962], *Structural Transformation of the Public Sphere*, Polity Press

(1998), *Between Facts and Norms: Contributions to a Discourse Theory of Law and Democracy*, MIT Press

Hailey, M. (1938), *An African Survey: A Study of Problems Arising in Africa South of the Sahara*, Oxford University Press

(1957), *Native Administration and Political Development in British Tropical Africa, Report by Lord Hailey, 1940–42* (Confidential), Kraus Reprint

(1979), *An African Survey: A Study of Problems Arising in Africa South of the Sahara* [rev.], Oxford University Press

Hale, R. (1923), 'Coercion and Distribution in a Supposedly Non-Coercive State' 38 *Political Science Quarterly* 470

(1935), 'Force and the State: A Comparison of "Political" and "Economic" Compulsion' 35 *Columbia Law Review* 149

(1943), 'Bargaining, Duress, and Economic Liberty' 43 *Columbia Law Review* 603

(1946), 'Prima Facie Torts, Combination, and Non-Feasance' 46 *Columbia Law Review* 196

Hall, W. E. (1894), *A Treatise on the Foreign Powers and Jurisdiction of the British Crown*, Frowde and Stevens

Handelman, H. and W. Baer (1989), 'Introduction: The Economic and Political Costs of Austerity', in H. Handelman and W. (eds.), *Paying the Costs of Austerity in Latin America*, Westview Press

Hansen, M. (1975), *Eisanglia: The Sovereignty of the People's Court in Athens in the Fourth Century BC and the Impeachment of Generals and Politicians*, Odense University Press

(1989), *Was Athens A Democracy?*, The Royal Danish Academy of Science and Letters

Hart, H. L. A. (1997), *The Concept of Law*, Oxford University Press

Hatchard, J. (1998), '"Perfecting Imperfections": Developing Procedures for Amending Constitutions in Commonwealth Africa' 36 *Journal of Modern African Studies* 381

Hayek, F. (1973), *Law, Legislation and Liberty, Vol. 1: Rules and Order*, University of Chicago Press

(1977), *Law, Legislation and Liberty, Vol. 2: The Mirage of Social Justice*, University of Chicago Press

(1981), *Law, Legislation and Liberty, Vol. 3: The Political Order of a Free People*, University of Chicago Press

(1994) [1944], *The Road to Serfdom*, University of Chicago Press

(2006) [1960], *The Constitution of Liberty*, Routledge Classics
Hegel, G. W. F. (2005) [1871], *Philosophy of Right*, Dover
Hellman, J., G. Jones, and D. Kaufmann (2003), 'Seize the State, Seize the Day: State Capture and Influence in Transition Economies' 31 *Journal of Comparative Economics* 751
Hendrix, S. (1998), 'Innovation in Criminal Procedure in Latin America: Guatemala's Conversion to the Adversarial System' 5 *Southwestern Journal of Law & Trade in the Americas* 365
Hertslet, E. (1896), *The Map of Africa by Treaty* (3 vols.), Harrison and Sons
Hickman, T. (2005), 'Between Human Rights and the Rule of Law: Indefinite Detention and the Derogation Model of Constitutionalism' 68 *Modern Law Review* 655
Hiebert, J. (2005), 'Parliamentary Review of Terrorism Measures' 68 *Modern Law Review* 676
Hirschl, R. (2004), *Towards Juristocracy: The Origins and Consequences of the New Constitutionalism*, Harvard University Press
Hobsbawm, E. and T. Ranger (1992), *The Invention of Tradition*, Canto
Hogendorn, J. S. (1975), 'Economic Initiative and African Cash Farming: Pre-Colonial Origins and Early Colonial Developments', in Duignan and Gann (1975)
Hohfeld, W. (1913), 'Some Fundamental Legal Conceptions as Applied in Judicial Reasoning' 23 *Yale Law Journal* 16
Holmes, O. (1894), 'Privilege, Malice, and Intent' 8 *Harvard Law Review* 1
(1897), 'The Path of the Law' 10 *Harvard Law Review* 457
Holmes, S. (2003a), 'Lineages of the Rule of Law', in J. M. Maravall and A. Przeworski, *Democracy and the Rule of Law*, Cambridge University Press
(2003b), Conference Transcript, 'Constitutions, Democracy and the Rule of Law: Do Constitutions Constrain?' (October 16, 2003)
Holmes, S. and C. Sunstein (1999), *The Cost of Rights: Why Liberty Depends on Taxes*, Norton
Hooker, M. B. (1975), *Legal Pluralism: An Introduction to Colonial and Neo-Colonial Laws*, Clarendon Press
Horwitz, M. (1977), 'The Rule of Law: An Unqualified Human Good?' 86 *Yale Law Journal* 561
(1978), *The Transformation of American Law 1780-1860*, Harvard University Press
(1992), *The Transformation of American Law 1870-1960*, Oxford University Press
Humphreys, S. (2006), 'Nomarchy: On the Rule of Law and Authority in Giorgio Agamben and Aristotle' 19 *Cambridge Review of International Affairs* 331
Hurwitz, A. and R. Huang (eds.) (2008), *Civil War and the Rule of Law: Security Development, Human Rights*, Lynne Rienner Publishers
Hutchinson, A. and P. Monahan (1987), 'Democracy and the Rule of Law', in Hutchinson and Monahan (eds.), *The Rule of Law: Ideal or Ideology*, Carswell
Ikime, O. (1988), 'Nigerian Reaction to the Imposition of British Colonial Rule, 1885-1918', in Förster *et al.* (1988)

Ilegbune, C. U. (1976), 'Concessions Scramble and Land Alienation in British Southern Ghana, 1885–1915' 19(3) *African Studies Review* 17

International Commission of Jurists (ICJ) (1959), *Declaration of Delhi*, International Commission of Jurists

  (1993), *States of Emergency: Their Impact on Human Rights*, International Commission of Jurists

Jameson, F. (1972), *The Prisonhouse of Language*, Princeton University Press

Jansen, E. and T. Heller (eds.) (2003), *Beyond Common Knowledge: Empirical Approaches to the Rule of Law*, Stanford Law and Politics

Jansen, N. and R. Michaels (2007), 'Private Law and the State: Comparative Perceptions, Historic Observations, and Basic Problems' 71/2 *Rabels Zeitschrift fur ausländisches und internationales Privatrecht* 345

Jayasuriya, K. (1999), 'Introduction: A Framework for the Analysis of Legal Institutions in East Asia', in K. Jayasuriya (ed.), *Law, Capitalism, and Power in East Asia: The Rule of Law and Legal Institutions*, Routledge

Jennings, I. (1959), *The Law and the Constitution* (5th edn), University of London Press

Jèze, G. (1896), *Etude théorique et pratique sur l'occupation comme mode d'acquérir les territoires en droit international*, Giard et Brière

Johnson, G. R. (2002), 'The First Founding Father: Aristotle on Freedom and Popular Government', in Tibor Machan (ed.), *Liberty and Democracy*, Hoover Institution Press

Jowett, B. (2000) [1885], Aristotle, *Politics* (trans. B. Jowett), Dover

Just, R. (1989), *Women in Athenian Law and Life*, Routledge

Kahler, M. (1986), 'Politics and International Debt: Explaining the Crisis', in Miles Kahler (ed.), *The Politics of International Debt*, Cornell University Press

Kant, I. (1983) [1784], 'An Answer to the Question: What is Enlightenment?', in *Perpetual Peace and Other Essays*, Hackett

Kantorowicz, E. (1997), *The King's Two Bodies*, Princeton University Press

Katz, S. and M. Ocheltree (2006), 'Intellectual Property Rights as a Key Obstacle to Russia's WTO Accession' Carnegie Paper No. 73, Carnegie Endowment for International Peace (October 2006)

Keane, J. (1998), *Civil Society: Old Images, New Visions*, Stanford University Press

  (2001), 'Global Civil Society', in H. Anheier, M. Glasius and M. Kaldor (eds.), *Global Civil Society 2001*, Oxford University Press

Kennedy, David (1991), 'Turning to Market Democracy: A Tale of Two Architectures' 32 *Harvard International Law Journal* 373

  (2006a), *Of War and Law*, Princeton University Press

  (2006b), 'The "Rule of Law", Political Choices and Development Common Sense', in Trubek and Santos (2006)

Kennedy, Duncan (1982), 'Distributive and Paternalist Motives in Contract and Tort Law, with Special Reference to Compulsory Terms and Unequal Bargaining Power' 41 *Maryland Law Review* 565

  (1993), 'The Stakes of Law, or Hale and Foucault!', in *Sexy Dressing Etc.*, Harvard University Press

(2004), 'The Disenchantment of Logically Formal, Legal Rationality, or Max Weber's Sociology in the Genealogy of the Contemporary Mode of Western Legal Thought' 55 *Hastings Law Journal* 1031

(2006c), 'Three Globalizations of Law and Legal Thought, 1850–2000', in Trubek and Santos (2006)

Kirchheimer, O. (1996a) [1932], 'Legality and Legitimacy', in Scheuerman (1996)

(1996b) [1933], 'Remarks on Carl Schmitt's *Legality and Legitimacy*' [1933], in Scheuerman (1996)

Kirk-Greene, A. (1955), 'Le Roi est mort! Vive le roi! The Comparative Legacy of Chiefs after the Transfer of Power in British and French West Africa', in Kirk-Greene and Bach (1995)

Kirk-Greene, A. and D. Bach (1995), *State and Society in Francophone Africa since Independence*, St Martin's Press

Klein, C. (1993), 'Jaime Oraa, Human Rights in States of Emergency in International Law' (Book review) 4 *European Journal of International Law* 134

Knack, S. and P. Keefer (1995), 'Institutions and Economic Performance: Cross-Country Tests Using Alternative Institutional Measures' 7 *Economics and Politics* 207

Koskenniemi, M. (2001), *The Gentle Civilizer of Nations: The Rise and Fall of International Law, 1870–1960*, Cambridge University Press

Koskenniemi M. and P. Leino (2003), 'Fragmentation of International Law? Postmodern Anxieties' 15 *Leiden Journal of International Law* 553

Kossick, R. (2004), 'The Rule of Law and Development in Mexico' 21 *Arizona Journal of International and Comparative Law* 715

Krueger, A. (1986), 'Aid in the Development Process' 1 *Research Observer* 57

La Porta, R., F. Lopez-de-Silanes, A. Shleifer and R. W. Vishny (1998), 'Law and Finance' 106 *The Journal of Political Economy* 1113

Lal, D. (2002) [1983], *The Poverty of 'Development Economics'*, The Institute of Economic Affairs

Landis, J. M. (1938), *The Administrative Process*, Yale University Press

Lauterpacht, H. (1947), *Recognition in International Law*, Cambridge University Press

Lewis, V. B. (1998), 'Politeia kai Nomoi: On the Coherence of Plato's Political Philosophy' 31 *Polity* 331

Li, T. M. (2006), 'Neo-Liberal Strategies of Government through Community: The Social Development Program of the World Bank in Indonesia' IILJ Working Paper 2006/2

Liddell, H. G. and R. Scott (1940), *A Greek–English Lexicon*, Clarendon Press

Lindley, M. (1926), *The Acquisition and Government of Backward Territory in International Law*, Longmans, Green and Co.

Lindsey, T. (1991), 'The "God-Like Man" versus the "Best Laws": Politics and Religion in Aristotle's Politics' 53 *The Review of Politics* 488

Llewellyn, K. (1930), 'A Realistic Jurisprudence – the Next Step' 30 *Columbia Law Review* 431
  (1931), 'Some Realism About Realism' 44 *Harvard Law Review* 1222
Loughlin, M. (2000), *Sword and Scales*, Hart
  (2004), *The Idea of Public Law*, Oxford University Press
Louis, R. (1971), 'The Berlin Congo Conference', in Gifford and Louis (1971)
Lowi, T. (1987), 'The Welfare State, the New Regulation', in Hutchinson and Monahan (eds), *The Rule of Law: Ideal or Ideology*, Carswell
Lugard, F. (1893), 'Treaty Making in Africa', *Geographical Journal* (January 1893)
  (1926), *The Dual Mandate in British Tropical Africa*, William Blackwood & Sons
Luhmann, N. (1998), *Observations on Modernity*, Stanford University Press
Madison, J., A. Hamilton and J. Jay (1987), *The Federalist Papers*, Penguin
Magen, A. (2004), 'EU Democracy and Rule of Law Promotion: The Enlargement Strategy and Its Progeny' Center on Democracy, Development, and the Rule of Law, Stanford Institute for International Studies, Working Paper No. 27
Maini, K. (1967), *Land Law in East Africa*, Oxford University Press
Mamdani, M. (1996), *Citizen and Subject*, James Currey
Mann, K. and R. Roberts (1991), *Law in Colonial Africa*, James Currey
Manning, P. (1998), *Francophone Sub-Saharan Africa 1880–1995*, Cambridge University Press
Mansell, W. (1991), 'Legal Aspects of International Debt' 18 *Journal of Law and Society*, 381
Marks, S. (1999), 'Guarding the Gates with Two Faces: International Law and Political Reconstruction' 6 *Indiana Journal of Global Legal Studies* 457
  (2003), *The Riddle of All Constitutions: International Law, Democracy, and the Critique of Ideology*, Oxford University Press
Martin, S. (1988), *Palm Oil and Protest: An Economic History of the Ngwa Region, South-Eastern Nigeria, 1800–1980*, Cambridge University Press
Masson, P. (2007), 'The IMF. Victim of its Own Success or Institutional Failure?' 62 *International Journal* 889
Mattei, U. and L. Nader (2008), *Plunder: When the Rule of Law is Illegal*, Wiley-Blackwell
McCormick, J. P. (2007), *Weber, Habermas, and Transformations of the European State*, Cambridge University Press
McHugh, P. (2004), *Aboriginal Societies and the Common Law: A History of Sovereignty, Status and Self-Determination*, Oxford University Press
McPetrie, J. C. (1963), 'Survey of Constitutions drafted at the Colonial Office since 1944', in Anderson (1963)
Mednicoff, D. (2005), 'Legalism Sans Frontières? U.S. Rule-of-Law Aid in the Arab World' Carnegie Papers No. 61, Carnegie Endowment for International Peace (September 2005)
Meek, C. K. (1946), 'A Note on Crown Lands in the Colonies' 28 *Journal of Comparative Legislation and International Law* 87

Mensch, E. (1998), 'The History of Mainstream Legal Thought' [1982], in David Kairys (ed.), *The Politics of Law: A Progressive Critique*, Basic Books

Merryman, J. H. (1977), 'Comparative Law and Social Change: On the Origins, Style, Decline and Revival of the Law and Development Movement' 25 *American Journal of Comparative Law* 457

Meyler, B. (2007), 'Economic Emergency and the Rule of Law' 56 *DePaul Law Review* 539

Michaels, R. and N. Jansen (2006), 'Private Law Beyond the State? Europeanization, Globalization, Privatization' 54 *American Journal of Comparative Law* 845

Miers, S. (1988), 'Humanitarianism at Berlin: Myth or Reality?', in Förster *et al.* (1988)

Milner, A. (1969), *African Penal Systems*, Routledge & Kegan Paul

Montesquieu, C. (2004) [1748], *The Spirit of the Laws*, Cambridge University Press

Morais, H. (2004), 'Testing the Frontiers of Their Mandates: The Experience of the Multilateral Development Banks' 98 *American Society of International Law Proceedings* 98

Morris, H. F. (1974), 'A History of the Adoption of Codes of Criminal Law and Procedure in British Colonial Africa, 1876-1935' 18 *Journal of African Law* 6

Morrow, G. (1993), *Plato's Cretan City: A Historical Interpretation of the Laws*, Princeton University Press

Murell, P. (ed.) (2001), *The Value of Law in Transition Economies*, University of Michigan Press

Nader, L. (2007), 'Promise or Plunder? A Past and Future Look at Law and Development' 7 *Global Jurist*, Article 1

Nederman, C. (1984), 'Bracton on Kingship Revisited' 5 *History of Political Thought* 61

  (1997), 'Nature, Ethics and the Doctrine of "*habitus*": Aristotelian Moral Psychology in the Twelfth Century', in *Medieval Aristotelianism and its Limits*, Variorum

Neumann, F. (1996), 'The Change in the Function of Law in Modern Society', in Scheuerman (1996)

Neumayer, E. (2003), *The Pattern of Aid Giving: The Impact of Good Governance on Development Assistance*, Routledge

Newton, S. (2006), 'The Dialectics of Law and Development', in Trubek and Santos (2006)

Nicolson, I. F. (1969), *The Administration of Nigeria 1900-1960: Men, Methods, and Myths*, Clarendon Press

Nonet, P. and P. Selznick (2001) [1978], *Law and Society in Transition: Toward Responsive Law*, Transaction Publishers

North, D. (1990), *Institutions, Institutional Change, and Economic Performance*, Cambridge University Press

Nworah, K. D. (1971), 'The Liverpool "Sect" and British West African Policy 1895-1915' 70 (281) *African Affairs* 349

Nys, E. (1903a), 'L'état indépendant du Congo et les dispositions de l'Acte Général de Berlin concernant la liberté commerciale et la prohibition des monopoles et des privilèges en matière commerciale' *Revue de Droit International*, Vol. 2, Tome 5, 315

(1903b), 'L'état indépendant du Congo et le droit international' *Revue de Droit International*, Vol. 2, Tome 5, 233

(1903c), 'La doctrine de la reconnaissance des états. Les prétendues conditions mises à la reconnaissance. Les cases historiques. L'état indépendant du Congo' *Revue de Droit International*, Vol. 2, Tome 5, 292

Nzemeke, A. D. (1988), 'Free Trade and Territorial Partition in Nineteenth-Century West Africa: Course and Outcome', in Förster *et al.*

O'Neill, W. (2005), 'Police Reform in Post-Conflict Societies: What We Know and What We Still Need to Know' International Peace Academy

Oakeshott, M. (1999), *On History and other Essays*, Liberty Fund

(2003), *On Human Conduct*, Clarendon Press

(2006), 'The Character of a Modern European State', in T. Nardin and L. O' Sullivan (eds.), *Lectures in the History of Political Thought. Selected Writings*, Vol. 2, Imprint Academic

Ohnesorge, J. (2003), 'The Rule of Law, Economic Development and the Development States of Southeast Asia', in Christoph Antons (ed.), *Law and Development in East and Southeast Asia*, Routledge

Olson, M. (1971) [1965], *The Logic of Collective Action: Public Goods and the Theory of Groups*, Harvard University Press

Omosini, O. (1972), 'The Gold Coast Land Question, 1894–1900: Some Issues Raised on West Africa's Economic Development' 5(3) *The International Journal of African Historical Studies* 453

Orr, R. (1996), 'Paradigm Lost? United States Approaches to Democracy Promotion in Developing Countries' (Dissertation Manuscript), UMI

Orts, E. (2001), 'The Rule of Law in China' 34 *Vanderbilt Journal of Transnational Law* 44

Ostwald, M. (1986), *From Popular Sovereignty to the Sovereignty of Law: Law, Society and Politics in Fifth-Century Athens*, University of California Press

Oswald, B. M. (2002), 'The Rule of Law on Peace Operations: A Cornerstone of Effective Peace Operations', in H. Langholtz, B. Kondoch, A. Wells (eds.), *International Peacekeeping: The Yearbook of International Peace Operations*, Vol. 8

Pakenham, T. (1991), *The Scramble for Africa*, Abacus

Palley, C. (1966), *The Constitutional History and Law of Southern Rhodesia, 1888–1965: with Special Reference to Imperial Control*, Clarendon Press

Pastor, R. (ed.) (1987), *Latin America's Debt Crisis: Adjusting to the Past or Planning for the Future*, Lynne Rienner Publishers

(1992), *Whirlpool: US Foreign Policy Toward Latin America and the Caribbean*, Princeton University Press

Peemans, J.-P. (1975), 'Capital Accumulation in the Congo under Colonialism: The Role of the State', in Duignan and Gann (1975)

Peerenboom, R. (2002), 'Let One Hundred Flowers Bloom, One Hundred Schools Contend: Debating the Rule of Law in China' 23 *Michigan Journal of International Law* 471
Perham, M. (1937), *Native Administration in Nigeria*, Oxford University Press
Phillips, A. (1989), *The Enigma of Colonialism*, Indiana University Press
Pierce, R., S. Shapiro and P. Verkeuil (2004), *Administrative Law and Process* (4th edn), Foundation Press
Plato (1967), *Laws* (trans. R. Bury), *Plato in Twelve Volumes, Vols. 10 & 11,* Harvard University Press
  (1975), *Laws* (trans. Trevor Saunders), *The Laws*, Penguin
Pound, R. (1910), 'Law in Books and Law in Action' 44 *American Law Review* 12
  (1931),'The Call for a Realist Jurisprudence' 44 *Harvard Law Review* 697
  (1954), 'The Rule of Law and the Modern Social Welfare State' 7 *Vanderbilt Law Review* 1
Purvis, T. (2006), 'Looking for Life Signs in an International Rule of Law', in Amy Bartholomew (ed.), *Empire's Law*, Pluto Press
Rackham, H. (1944) [Aristotle, *Politics*, trans. H. Rackham], *Aristotle in 23 Volumes, Vol. 21, Politics*, Harvard University Press (1944)
Ranelagh, J. (1991), *Thatcher's People: An Insider's Account of the Politics, the Power, and the Personalities*, Harper Collins
Rawls, J. (1999), *A Theory of Justice* (rev.), Belknap Press
Raz, J. (2001)[1979], 'The Rule of Law and Its Virtue', in D. Dyzenhaus and A. Ripstein (eds.), *Law and Morality*, University of Toronto Press
Read, J. (1969), 'Kenya, Tanzania and Uganda', in Milner (1969)
Reeves, J. (1909), 'The Origin of the Congo Free State, Considered from the Standpoint of International Law' 3 *American Journal of International Law* 99
Reid, J. (2004), *Rule of Law: the Jurisprudence of Liberty in the Seventeenth and Eighteenth Centuries*, Northern Illinois University Press
Reimann, M. (2004), 'From the Law of Nations to Transnational Law: Why We Need a New Basic Course for the International Curriculum' 22 *Penn State International Law Review* 397
Roberts, W. (2004) [Aristotle, *Rhetoric*, trans. W. Roberts], *Rhetoric*, Dover
Roberts-Wray, K. (1960), 'The Adaptation of Imported Law in Africa' 4 *Journal of African Law* 66
Roberts-Wray, K. (1966), *Commonwealth and Colonial Law*, Stevens
Robinson, R. (1995) [Aristotle, *Politics*, trans. R. Robinson], *Aristotle: Politics III and IV*, Oxford University Press
Rockwood, L. and A. Simpson (2001), 'Training the World's Police' *Foreign Policy in Focus* Vol. 4(3)
Roett, R. (1992), 'The Debt Crisis and Economic Development in Latin America', in J. Hartlyn, L. Schoultz and A. Varas (eds.) (1992), *The United States and Latin America in the 1990s: Beyond the Cold War*, University of North Carolina Press
Rolin-Jaequemyns, G. (1889), 'L'année 1888 au point de vue de la paix et du droit international' XXI *Revue de Droit International* 167

Rosen, E. (2005), 'The Wal-Mart Effect: The World Trade Organization and the Race to the Bottom' 8 *Chapman Law Review* 261

Rosenfeld, M. (2005), 'Constitutional Adjudication in Europe and the United States: Paradoxes and Contrasts', in G. Nolte (ed.), *European and U.S. Constitutionalism*, Council of Europe Publishing

Rosenn, K. S. (1971), 'The Jeito: Brazil's Institutional Bypass of the Formal Legal System and its Developmental Implications' 19 *American Journal of Comparative Law* 514

Rosler, A. (2005), *Political Authority and Obligation in Aristotle*, Oxford University Press

Sachs, J. (1996), 'The Transition at Mid Decade' 86 *The American Economic Review* 128
  (1998), 'Globalization and the Rule of Law' remarks delivered at Yale Law School on October 16, 1998

Sachs, J. and K. Pistor (eds.) (1997), *Rule of Law and Economic Reform in Russia*, Westview Press

Salomon, C. (1889), *L'occupation des territoires sans maître*, Giard, et Brière

Samuels, W. (1973), 'The Economy as a System of Power and its Legal Bases: The Economics of Robert Lee Hale' 27 *University of Miami Law Review* 262

Sandoz, E. (ed.) (1993), *The Roots of Liberty: Magna Carta, Ancient Constitution and the Anglo-American Tradition of Rule of Law*, University of Missouri Press

Santos, A. (2006), 'The World Bank's Uses of the "Rule of Law" Promise in Economic Development', in Trubek and Santos (2006)

Sarat, A. and N. Hussain (n.d.), 'Toward New Theoretical Perspectives on Forgiveness, Mercy and Clemency', in Sarat and Hussain (eds.), *Forgiveness, Mercy and Clemency*, Stanford University Press

Sarbah, J. M. (1910), 'Maclean and the Gold Coast Judicial Assessors' 9(23) *African Affairs* 349

Sarr, D. and R. Roberts, 'The Jurisdiction of Muslim Tribunals in Colonial Senegal', in Mann and Roberts (1991)

Saunders, T. J. (ed.) (1992) [Aristotle, *Politics*, trans. T. A. Sinclair], *The Politics*, Penguin

Schaps, D. (1979), *Economic Rights of Women in Ancient Greece*, Edinburgh University Press

Scheuerman, W (1996) *The Rule of Law Under Siege: Selected Essays of Franz L. Neumann and Otto Kirchheimer*, University of California Press

Schmitt, C. (2004a), *The Concept of the Political*, University of Chicago Press
  (2004b), *Legality and Legitimacy*, Duke University Press
  (2006), *Political Theology: Four Chapters on the Concept of Sovereignty*, University of Chicago Press

Schwarzenberger, G. (1939), 'The Rule of Law and the Disintegration of International Society' 33 *American Journal International Law* 56

Seidman, R. (1966), *A Sourcebook of the Criminal Law of Africa*, Sweet and Maxwell

Shapiro, I. (ed.) (1994), *Nomos XXXVI: The Rule of Law*, New York University Press

Shapiro, M. (1988), *Who Guards the Guardians?, Judicial Control of Administration*, University of Georgia Press

Shelley, L. (1995), 'Post-Soviet Organized Crime and the Rule of Law' 28 *John Marshall Law Review* 827
Shihata, I. (1997), 'The Role of the World Bank's General Counsel' 91 *American Society of International Law Proceedings* 217
  (1999), 'The Creative Role of the Lawyer – Example: The Office of the World Bank's General Counsel' 48 *Catholic University Law Review* 1041
Shklar, J. (1986), *Legalism: Law, Morals, and Political Trials*, Harvard University Press
  (1987), 'Political Theory and the Rule of Law', in A. Hutchinson and P. Monahan (eds.), *The Rule of Law: Ideal or Ideology*, Carswell
  (1990), *The Faces of Injustice*, Yale University Press
Simon, W. H. (1990), 'The Rule of Law and the Two Realms of Welfare Administration' 56 *Brooklyn Law Review* 777
Simpson, A. W. B. (2001), *Human Rights and the End of Empire*, Oxford University Press
Sinclair, T. A. (1974) [Aristotle, *Politics*, trans. T. A. Sinclair], *The Politics*, Penguin
Singer, J. A. (1988), 'Legal Realism Now' 76 *California Law Review* 465
Skinner, Q. (1998), *Liberty Before Liberalism*, Cambridge University Press
Smith, A. (1904)[1776], *The Wealth of Nations*, edited by E. Cannan, Methuen and Co.
Solum, L. (1994), 'Equity and the Rule of Law', in I. Shapiro (ed.), *Nomos XXXVI: The Rule of Law*, New York University Press
Sorum, P. C. (1977), *Intellectuals and Decolonization in France*, University of North Carolina Press
Soto, H. de (1980), *The Other Path: The Invisible Revolution in the Third World*, Perseus Books
  (2000), *The Mystery of Capital: Why Capitalism Triumphs in the West and Fails Everywhere Else*, Basic Books
Spence, M. J. (2005), 'The Complexity of Success: The U.S. Role in Russian Rule of Law Reform' Carnegie Paper No. 60, Carnegie Endowment for International Peace
Steinhardt, R. (1991), 'The Privatization of Public International Law' 25 *George Washington Journal of International Law and Economics* 523
Stephenson, M. (2006), 'A Trojan Horse in China?', in Carothers (2006)
Stewart, I. (2004), 'Men of Class: Aristotle, Montesquieu and Dicey on "Separation of Powers" and "the Rule of Law"' 4 *Macquarie Law Journal* 187
Strauss, L. (1971), *Natural Right and History*, University of Chicago Press
  (1975), *The Argument and Action of Plato's Laws*, University of Chicago Press
Stromseth, J., D. Wippman and R. Brooks (2006), *Can Might Make Rights? Building the Rule of Law after Military Interventions*, Cambridge University Press
Sureda, A. R. (1999), 'The World Bank and Institutional Innovation', in E. B. Weiss, A. R. Sureda and L. B. de Chazournes (eds.), *The World Bank, International Financial Institutions and the Development of International Law (A Symposium Held in Honor of Dr. Ibrahim F. I. Shihata)*, Studies in Transnational Legal Policy No. 31, American Society of International Law

Suret-Canale, J. (1971), *French Colonialism in Tropical Africa 1900–1945*, Hurst and Company
Tamanaha, B. (2004), *On the Rule of Law: Politics, History, Theory*, Cambridge University Press
  (2006), *Law as a Means to an End*, Cambridge University Press
Teubner, G. (1997), 'Global Bukowina: Legal Pluralism in the World Society', in G. Teubner (ed.), *Global Law Without a State*, Dartmouth
Thatcher, M. (1993), *The Downing Street Years*, Harper Collins
  (1995), *The Path to Power*, Harper Collins
Theberge, A. (1999), 'The Latin American Debt Crisis of the 1980s and its Historical Precursors' (unpublished, 1999)
Thomas, C. (2006), 'Max Weber, Talcott Parsons and the Sociology of Legal Reform: A Reassessment with Implications for Law and Development' 15 *Minnesota Journal of International Law* 383
Thomas, M. (2007),'What do the Worldwide Governance Indicators Measure?' School of Advanced International Studies, Johns Hopkins University
Tierney, S. (2005), 'Determining the Exception: What Role for the Parliament and the Courts?' 68 *Modern Law Review* 668
Todd, S. (1993), *The Shape of Athenian Law*, Oxford University Press
Trubek, D. (1972a), 'Towards a Social Theory of Law: An Essay on the Study of Law and Development' 82 *Yale Law Journal* 1
  (1972b), 'Max Weber on Law and the Rise of Capitalism' 1972 *Wisconsin Law Review* 720
  (2006), 'The "Rule of Law" in Development Assistance: Past, Present and Future', in Trubek and Santos (2006)
Trubek, D. and A. Santos (2006), *The New Law and Economic Development: A Critical Appraisal*, Cambridge University Press
Twiss, T. (1883), 'La libre navigation du Congo' XV *Revue de Droit International* 437–442; 547–563
  (1884a), *The Law of Nations Considered as Independent Political Communities*, Part I, Clarendon Press, 2nd edn
  (1884b), 'La libre navigation du Congo' XVI *Revue de Droit International* 237
Unger, R. M. (1976), *Law in Modern Society: Toward a Criticism of Social Theory*, The Free Press
  (2006), 'The Universal Grid of Philosophy', in *The Self Awakened: Pragmatism Unbound*, Harvard University Press
Upham, F. (2006), 'Mythmaking in the Rule of Law Orthodoxy', in Carothers (2006).
Valdés, J. G. (1995), *Pinochet's Economists: The Chicago School of Economics in Chile*, Cambridge University Press
Wade, E. C. S. (1957), 'Administration under the Law' 73 *Law Quarterly Review* 470
Waldron, J. (1990), *The Law*, Routledge
Walker, G. de Q. (1988), *The Rule of Law*, Melbourne University Press
Warner, M. (2002), *Public and Counterpublics*, Zone Books
Warren, K. (2004), *Administrative Law in the Political System*, Westview Press

Watson, A. (1974), *Legal Transplants: An Approach to Comparative Law*, Scottish Academic Press

Weber, M. (1978)[1922], *Economy and Society* (2 vols.), University of California Press
(1992)[1930], *The Protestant Ethic and the Spirit of Capitalism*, Routledge
(1994)[1919], 'The Profession and Vocation of Politics', in P. Lassman and R. Speirs (eds.), *Weber, Political Writings*, Cambridge University Press

Weingast, B. (1997), 'The Political Foundations of Democracy and the Rule of Law' 91 *American Political Science Review* 245

Welldon, J. (1883), *Aristotle's Politics* (1883), cited in *Oxford English Dictionary* (2nd edn), Oxford University Press

Westlake, J. (1894), *Chapters on the Principles of International Law*, Cambridge University Press

Wilson, C. (1975), 'The Economic Role and Mainsprings of Imperialism', in Duignan and Gann (1975)

Zagaris, B. (1988), 'Law and Development or Comparative Law and Social Change – the Application of Old Concepts in the Commonwealth Caribbean' 19 *University of Miami Inter-American Law Review* 550

Zuckert, M. (1994), *Natural Rights and the New Republicanism*, Princeton University Press

II. POLICY AND PROJECT DOCUMENTS

United States Agencies

Bayley (2001)	David H. Bayley, 'Democratizing the Police Abroad: What to Do and How to Do It', Department of Justice, National Institute of Justice (June 2001)
Blair and Hansen (1994)	Harry Blair and Garry Hansen, 'Weighing in on the Scales of Justice: Strategic Approaches for Donor-Supported Rule of Law Programs', USAID (1994)
Bonicelli (2007)	Remarks by Paul J. Bonicelli, USAID Assistant Administrator for Latin America and the Caribbean, 'Assessing the State of Democracy in the Hemisphere', Council of the Americas (November 8, 2007)
CBJ FY2009	Congressional Budget Justification, Foreign Assistance, Fiscal Year 2009, Department of State (undated [2008])
Cranston (1992)	Senator Alan Cranston, testimony before Congress (March 5, 1992) in NSIAD, Foreign Aid: Police Training and Assistance; Report to Congressional Requesters (1992)

DIILS (2004)	Defense Institute for International Legal Studies, Human Rights and Terrorism (undated, 2004)
DIILS (2008)	Defense Institute for International Legal Studies, *Rule of Law and Disciplined Military Operations Course*, offered at various US Military Schools (undated, 2008)
DOC (2008)	US Dept. of Commerce, A Basic Guide to World Bank Business Opportunities: A Primer for US Companies (2008)
DOD (2006a)	Department of Defense Budget for Fiscal Year 2007, Financial Summary Tables (February 2006)
DOD (2006b)	Department of Defense FY 2006 Supplemental request for Operation Iraqi Freedom and Operation Enduring Freedom (February 2006)
DOJ (2006)	Department of Justice, Stewards of the American Dream: FY 2007–FY 2012 Strategic Plan (undated [2006])
DOJ (2008)	Department of Justice, Factsheet: Department of Justice Efforts in Iraq (February 2008)
DOS (2005)	United States Department of State and the Broadcasting Board of Governors, Office of Inspector General, Report of Inspection, Inspection of Rule-of-Law Programs, Embassy Baghdad, Report Number ISP-IQO-06-01 (October 2005)
DOS (2005)	'Rule of Law Is Key to Advancing Democracy, Rice Says', US Dept. of State, Office of the Spokesman (November 9, 2005)
DOS (2007)	Department of State, Supporting Human Rights and Democracy, The U.S. Record 2006 (undated, 2007)
DOS FY2008	U.S. Department of State, FY 2008 Performance Summary (February 2007)
El Salvador DSP (1993)	Republic of El Salvador, Democratic Strengthening Program, Ministry of Planning and Coordination for Social and Economic Development, PN-ABS-571 (March 1993)
GAO (1992)	General Accountability Office, NSIAD, Foreign Aid: Police Training and Assistance, Report to Congressional Requesters (March 1992)
GAO (1999a)	General Accountability Office, Foreign Assistance: Status of Rule of Law Program Coordination, Report B-283714, GAO/NSIAD-00-8R Rule of Law Coordination (October 13, 1999)

252 BIBLIOGRAPHY

GAO (1999b)	General Accountability Office, Foreign Assistance: Rule of Law Funding Worldwide for Fiscal Years 1993–98, Report B-282584, GAO/NSIAD-99-158 Rule of Law Funding (June 1999)
Hyman (2008)	Gerald F. Hyman, 'Assessing Secretary of State Rice's Reform of U.S. Foreign Assistance', Carnegie Endowment for International Peace, Democracy and Rule of Law Program, Carnegie Papers, No. 90 (February 2008)
IFES (2006)	IFES/Keith Henderson, Global Lessons and Best Practices: Fighting Corruption and Promoting the Rule of Law through Transparency, Openness and Judicial Independence, IFES Rule of Law White Paper Series, International Foundation for Electoral Systems (2006)
IFES (2007)	IFES/Ilia Shalhoub, Comparative Report on the State of the Judiciary in Egypt, Jordan, Lebanon and Morocco, International and Arab Center for the Development of Rule of Law and Integrity (May 2007)
INL FY2008	United States Department of State, Bureau for International Narcotics and Law Enforcement Affairs, Fiscal Year 2008 Budget Program and Budget Guide (2007)
MCC FY2007	Millennium Challenge Corporation, Fiscal Year 2007 Guidance for Compact-Eligible Countries (2006)
MCC FY2008	Millennium Challenge Corporation, Guide to the MCC Indicators and the Selection Process Fiscal Year 2008 (2007)
MSI (2002)	Management Systems International, 'Achievements in Building and Maintaining the Rule of Law: MSI's Studies in LAC, E&E, AFR, and ANE', USAID Occasional Papers Series (November 2002)
NSS (2002)	National Security Strategy of the United States of America 2002, White House (2002)
NSS (2006)	National Security Strategy of the United States of America 2006, White House (March 2006)
OIG (2005)	U.S. Department of State and the Broadcasting Board of Governors, OIG, Inspection of Rule-of-Law Programs, Embassy Baghdad, Report Number ISP-IQO-06-01 (October 2005)
USAID (1991)	USAID, Policy, Democracy and Governance (November 1991)

USAID (1998)	USAID, Center for Democracy and Governance, Alternative Dispute Resolution Practitioners' Guide (March 1998)
USAID (1999a)	USAID, A Handbook on Fighting Corruption (1999)
USAID (1999b)	USAID, The Role of Media in Democracy: A Strategic Approach (1999)
USAID (1999c)	USAID, Political Party Development Assistance (1999)
USAID (2000)	USAID, Handbook on Legislative Strengthening (2000)
USAID (2001)	USAID, A Global Guide to Judicial Independence (2001)
USAID (2002a)	USAID, Foreign Aid in the National Interest: Promoting Freedom, Security and Opportunity (2002)
USAID (2002b)	USAID, Guidance for Promoting Judicial Independence and Impartiality (2002)
USAID (2002c)	USAID, Understanding Representation: Implications for Legislative Strengthening (2002)
USAID (2003)	USAID, Money in Politics Handbook: A Guide to Increasing Transparency in Emerging Democracies (2003)
USAID (2004a)	USAID, White Paper: U.S. Foreign Aid: Meeting the Challenges of the Twenty-first Century, Bureau for Policy and Program Coordination, USAID (January 2004)
USAID (2004b)	USAID, USAID Promotes the Rule of Law in Latin American and Caribbean Democracies (undated, 2004)
USAID (2005a)	USAID, At Freedom's Frontiers: A Democracy and Governance Strategic Framework (2005)
USAID (2005b)	USAID, Fragile States Strategy (January 2005)
USAID (2006a)	USAID, Strategic Framework for Africa (24 February 2006)
USAID (2006b)	USAID/Economic Growth, Agriculture and Trade Operational Plan FY 2006 (June 13, 2006)
USAID (2006c)	USAID, Policy Framework for Bilateral Foreign Aid: Implementing Transformational Diplomacy Through Development (2006)
USAID (2008)	USAID, Economic Growth Strategy: Securing the Future, Prepublication edition (April 2008)
USAID/Bulgaria (2007)	USAID/Bulgaria, Assessment Report, Seventeen Years of Partnership in Transition (July 2007)

254 BIBLIOGRAPHY

USAID/Russia (2001)	USAID/Russia, Strategic Objective Close-Out Report. 'Strengthened Rule of Law and Respect for Human Rights' (2001)
USAID/Timor (2007)	USAID, Rule of Law in Timor Leste (June 2007)
USAID Afghanistan (2005)	USAID, Afghanistan Rule of Law Project: Field Study of Informal and Customary Justice in Afghanistan and Recommendations on Improving Access to Justice and Relations Between Formal Courts and Informal Bodies, prepared by Management Systems International (April 30, 2005)
USAID Africa (2007)	USAID Anti-Trafficking in Persons Programs in Africa: A Review, Chemonics International Inc. (April 2007)
USAID Albania (2007)	USAID, Rule of Law Program – Legal Systems that Better Support Democratic Processes and Market Reforms Final Report, by Casals & Associates, Inc. (September 2007)
USAID AOJ (1985)	USAID Project Paper: Regional Administration of Justice, Project No. 596-0133, AID/LAC/P219, USAID (1985)
USAID ATR (2006)	USAID, Assistance For Trade Reform, Final Report, Submitted By Nathan Associates Inc. Under Contract No. PCE-I-00-98-00016-00 Task Order 827 (October 2006)
USAID Benin (2007)	USAID, Benin Decentralization and Anti-Corruption Support Program – Phase II– Extension Increasing Civil Society Participation in Decentralization and Reinforcing Governance through Anti-Corruption Initiatives in Benin, RTI International, Final Performance Report (August 2007)
USAID BiH (2007)	USAID, Assessment of Bosnia Herzegovina's Administrative, USAID Contract Number DFD-I-00-04-00227-00, Task Order RFP No. 168-07-025, by ARD Inc. (December 7, 2007)
USAID Bulgaria (2005)	USAID, Final Report, Assessment of the Bulgarian Enterprise, Growth and Investment Project (EGIP) (Formerly the Policy Reform and Advocacy Strengthening Project), Funded by USAID/Bulgaria, Conducted by Stephen C. Silcox, Kristin Lobron, Neal Nathanson (February 22, 2005)
USAID Bulgaria (2007)	USAID, Judicial Strengthening Initiative for Bulgaria, USAID Contract No. 183-C-00-04-00105-00, Final Report, the East-West Management Institute, Inc. (November 2007)

BIBLIOGRAPHY 255

USAID Bulgaria (2007)	USAID, Bulgaria Financial Sector Integrity Project, Final Report – October 2004–June 2007, Emerging Markets Group Ltd. (June 2007)
USAID Cambodia (2008)	USAID, Evaluation of the Program on Rights and Justice (PRAJ) Final Report, prepared under the USAID/Cambodia – Checchi and Company Consulting, Inc. Contract GS-10F-0425M, Order No. 442-M-00-07-00009-00. The report was authored by Richard Blue, Team Leader, and Robert Underwood (January 2008)
USAID Cape Verde (2005)	Final Report for Cape Verde WTO Accession Project under The Doha Project for WTO Accession and Participation (Contract PCE-I-00-98-00013-00, Task Order 14), prepared by Booz Allen Hamilton (December 2005)
USAID CEE	USAID/CEE/NIS Commercial Law Reform Assessment Task, Final Report (April 15, 2001)
USAID Central Asia (2007)	Chemonics International Inc., Central Asian Republics Rule of Law, Contract # CCN-0007-C-00-4004-00, Final Report (December 2007)
USAID Colombia (2006a)	USAID, Colombia Administration of Justice Program (2001–2006) (USAID Contract No. 514-C-00-01-00113-00) Final Report submitted by Checchi and Company Consulting, Inc. (September 15, 2006)
USAID Colombia (2006b)	USAID, Final Report on Developing a Management Model for a Judicial Services Center under the New Accusatory Criminal System in Colombia, DPK Consulting (September 2006)
USAID Croatia (2004)	USAID, Final Report: Croatia Commercial Law Reform Project, Contract No. PCE-I-00-98-00013, prepared by Frederick G. Yeager, Booz Allen Hamilton (March 2004)
USAID DCHA (2007)	USAID, DCHA/DG, User's Guide to DG Programming, PN-ADJ-300 (June 2007)
USAID DCHA (2008)	USAID DCHA/DG, User's Guide to DG Programming, PN-ADL-400 (June 2008)
USAID DOS (2007)	USAID and US Department of State, Transformational Diplomacy: Strategic Plan Fiscal Years 2007–2012 (revised May 7, 2007)
USAID DOS (FY2007)	US Department of State and USAID, Joint Highlights of Performance, Budget, and Financial Information Fiscal Year 2007 (undated, 2007)
USAID ECOWAS (2005)	USAID, Growth Through Engineering Enterprise in ECOWAS Countries (ECOGEE), A Component of Building Trade Capacity in

256 BIBLIOGRAPHY

	West Africa, Cooperative Agreement No. 688-A-00-02-00064-00, Final Report, submitted by IBI-International Business Initiatives (September 2005)
USAID Egypt (2008)	USAID, Egypt: Combating Violence against Women and Children, Quarterly Progress Report, First Quarter, Fiscal Year 2008, prepared by Chemonics International in partnership with the National Council for Women and National Council for Childhood and Motherhood with support from Subcontractors BlueLaw International and SPAAC (January 30, 2008)
USAID FY1986	Agency for International Development, Congressional Presentation Fiscal Year 1986, Main Volume (undated 1985)
USAID FY1986(III)	Agency for International Development, Congressional Presentation Fiscal Year 1986, Annex III: Latin America and the Caribbean (Vol. I) (undated, 1985)
USAID FY2006	USAID, USAID FY 2006 Performance and Accountability Report (undated, 2006)
USAID Ghana (2005)	USAID, Ghana: Strategic Objective 1 Close-out Report. Increasing Private Sector Growth, implementing partners (1) Sigma One Corporation (2) AMEX International, Inc. (3) Technoserve, Ghana (4) Care International (5) Conservation International (6) Georgia State University (7) Michigan State University (8) Nexant, LLC (August 2005).
USAID Guinea (2006)	USAID, Guinea Agricultural Market Linkages Activity Final Report for Period June 5, 2005–December 31, 2006, Contract No. PCE-I-00-99-00003-00, Task Order No. 29, prepared for USAID/Guinea, NRM SO Ibrahima Camara (December 31, 2006)
USAID Haiti	USAID, Final Evaluation of the Haiti Transition Initiative, prepared by Joel M. Jutkowitz and Deborah R. King with the professional collaboration of Yves F. Pierre, Management Systems International (October 2006)
USAID Iraq (2007)	USAID, Building on Transition: Iraq Civil Society Program (ICSP) Final Evaluation, Final Report, by Kathleen Webb and Stark Biddle, with sample

design and statistical analysis by Robert Torene and Harvey Herr, of International Business & Technical Consultants, Inc. (May 24, 2007)

USAID Karelia (1998)   The Vermont-Karelia Rule of Law Project, Final Report, January 1, 1997–December 31, 1997 (April 28, 1998)

USAID Kazakhstan (2007)   USAID, Strengthening the Rule of Law in Kazakhstan: Kazakhstan Judicial Assistance Project Phase I, Final Report, prepared by Chemonics International (September 2007)

USAID Kenya (2007)   USAID, E-Legislation Policy Development Initiative for the East African Community – Kenya Cyber Law Model, Deliverable No. 6 – Final Report and Final e-Legislation Policies, Funding provided by the United States Agency for International Development, Purchase Order Number: 2985-101101-S-01, submitted to Academy for Educational Development dot-ORG Program (October 1, 2007)

USAID Kosovo (2007)   USAID, Kosovo Economic Development Initiative Final Project Report (June 2007)

USAID Kosovo (2008)   USAID, Kosovo Civil Society Program, Final Evaluation Report, prepared by Democracy International (March 2008)

USAID Lesotho (2007)   USAID, Lesotho: Training of Paralegals in the Leribe District. Women's Legal Rights Initiative Under the Women in Development IQC, Contract No. GEW-I-00-02-00016-00, prepared by the Federation of Women Lawyers (FIDA-Lesotho) in partnership with Chemonics International Inc. and the Centre for Development and Population Activities (CEDPA) (March 2007)

USAID Liberia (2007)   USAID, Final Evaluation: Building Recovery and Reform through Democratic Governance (BRDG) – Liberia USAID/DCHA/OTI (2006–2007), submitted by Martina Nicolls, Susan Kupperstein Social Impact Inc., HDA-I-00-03-00124-00 Task Order 30 (December 24, 2007)

USAID Liberia (2008)   USAID Office of Transition Initiatives BRDG – Liberia Fifth / Final Quarterly Report August 31, 2007–December 15, 2007, Development Alternatives Inc. (DAI) BRDG-Liberia (January 30, 2008)

BIBLIOGRAPHY

USAID LIME (2005) — USAID, Program for a Legal Infrastructure for a Market Economy in Kyrgyzstan and Tajikistan (Commercial Law Reform), Final Report, prepared by ARD Inc. and Checchi & Co. Consulting (September 2005)

USAID LIME2 (2006) — USAID, Assistance in Establishing the Legal and Institutional Framework Necessary to Support a Market-Based Economy (LIME 2), Kyrgyzstan and Tajikistan, Final Report, prepared by ARD Inc. and Checchi & Co. Consulting (June 2006)

USAID Madagascar (2006) — USAID/Madagascar, Madagascar Strategy Statement (Unrestricted Version), USAID (April 2, 2006)

USAID Malawi (2007) — USAID, SUNY Center for International Development, Legislative Strengthening Program/Malawi Quarterly Progress Report, Vol. 1/3, quarter ended December 31, 2006 (2007)

USAID Mongolia (2008) — USAID/ National Center for State Courts, Mongolia Judicial Reform Program, Annual Report 2007, Cooperative Agreement #492-A-00-01-00001, Heike Gramckow, Deputy Director (February 20, 2008)

USAID Montenegro (2007) — USAID, Justice System Reform Project Montenegro, July 1, 2003–March 31, 2007, submitted by Checchi and Co. (2007)

USAID Nepal (2007) — USAID, Nepal: Strengthened Rule of Law and Respect for Human Rights Project, Final Report, prepared by ARD Inc. (August 10, 2007)

USAID Nigeria (2006) — USAID, Democracy and Governance Assessment of Nigeria, prepared by ARD Inc. (December 2006)

USAID Palestine (2007a) — Fostering Respect for the Rule of Law, Final Report of the West Bank/Gaza Supporting Rule of Law Reform Project, by Chemonics International (September 2007)

USAID Palestine (2007b) — USAID, Teaching Law in Palestinian Law Schools, Curriculum Reform Review (April–December 2005), prepared by Chemonics International, Inc. and MASSAR Associates (September 7, 2007)

USAID Peru (2008) — USAID, Strengthening the Peruvian Decentralization Process, The Peru Pro-Decentralization (PRODES) Program, Final Report, USAID Contract No. 527-C-00-03000-4900, implemented by ARD, Inc. (March 2008)

USAID Philippines (2007)	USAID, Investment Climate Improvement Project (ICIP) Final Report for March 2006–February 2007 by John D. Forbes and Richard Umali, Economic Modernization through Efficient Reforms and Governance Enhancement (EMERGE) (May 2007)
USAID Philippines (2008a)	USAID, Transparent Accountable Governance (TAG) Project, Final Report (September 20, 1999–December 31, 2007) by the Asia Foundation (March 14, 2008)
USAID Philippines (2008b)	The Asia Foundation, Strengthening Human Rights in the Philippines Program (Cooperative Agreement No. 492-A-00-07-00016-00), Quarterly Report from the Asia Foundation to USAID, 1 October– 31 December 2007 (January 31, 2008)
USAID Romania (2007)	USAID, Romania: Promoting the Rule of Law, June 1, 2003–September 30, 2007, Final Report, by the American Bar Association-Central European and Eurasian Law Initiative–Romania (December 2007)
USAID Romania (2008)	USAID/World Learning, Romania Civil Society Strengthening Program, Final Report for Cooperative Agreement No. 186-A-00-05-00103-00, submitted by Preeti Shroff-Mehta, World Learning, to USAID/Romania, Ruxandra Datcu (March 31, 2008)
USAID Rwanda (2006)	USAID, Rwanda Decentralization of Judicial Administration and Financial Management Final FY 2006, Jay Carver, Project Director, National Center for State Courts (NCSC), Funded under Indefinite Quantity Contract III, Task Order No. DFD-I-01-04-00176-00 (2006)
USAID Senegal (2007)	USAID, Corruption Assessment Senegal, prepared by MSI, contracted under USAID Contract No. DFD-I-00-03-00144-00, Task Order 1 (August 31, 2007)
USAID Sri Lanka (2007)	USAID, Sri Lanka Anti-corruption Program, Final Project Completion Report, prepared by ARD, Inc. (December 2007)
USAID Tanzania (2007)	DAI PESA Project (Private Enterprise Support Activities) USAID Contract No. PCE-I-99-00002-00 Task Order 817 Final Report (October 10, 2002–February 28, 2007), prepared by Development Alternatives, Inc. (DAI), submitted to Cognizant

260 BIBLIOGRAPHY

	Technical Officer, USAID Tanzania (February 2007)
USAID Timor (2006)	USAID Land Law Program II – Timor-Leste, Final Report by ARD, Inc. (April 30, 2006)
USAID Trafficking (2008)	USAID, Anti-Trafficking Technical Assistance, Thirteenth Quarterly Progress Report, October 1, 2007–December 31, 2007, prepared by Chemonics International (January 31, 2008)
USAID Uganda (2006)	USAID, Uganda Strengthening the Competitiveness of Private Enterprise (SCOPE), Contract #PCE-1-00-98-00015-00, TO #828, prepared by Chemonics International Inc. with Crimson Capital Corporation Inc., International Law Institute – Uganda, Plexus Consulting Group, L.L.C., and International Business Initiatives, Final Report (September 2006)
USAID Ukraine (2007a)	Final Report Phase I, prepared by Chemonics International in partnership with the National Judicial College, MetaMetrics, Institute for Sustainable Communities, and Blue Law (September 2007)
USAID Ukraine (2007b)	USAID, Combating Corruption and Strengthening Rule of Law in Ukraine, Evaluation of the Unified Registry of Court Decisions and Development of an Automated Random Case Assignment Module, by J. Michael Greenwood (November 2007)
USAID Ukraine (2007c)	USAID, Combating Corruption and Strengthening Rule of Law in Ukraine, Assessment of Judicial Selection and Disciplinary Processes, by Laurence Beck (October 2007)
USAID Zambia (2007)	USAID/Zambia, Millennium Challenge Corporation, Report: Zambia Threshold Project (anti-corruption), prepared by Chemonics International Inc., USAID Contract No. AFP-I-06-04-00002-00 (July 2007)
USIP (1999)	Heinrich Klebes, The Quest for Democratic Security: The Role of the Council of Europe and U.S. Foreign Policy, USIP (1999)
USIP (2003a)	United States Institute for Peace, Establishing the Rule of Law in Iraq, USIP Special Report No. 104 (April 2003)
USIP (2003b)	Thomas Barfield, 'Afghan Customary Law and Its Relationship to Formal Judicial Institutions', United States Institute for Peace (2003)

USIP (2003c)	United States Institute for Peace, 'Establishing the Rule of Law in Afghanistan', USIP Special Report 117 (March 2003)
USIP (2007)	Thomas Barfield, Neamat Nojumi, and J. Alexander Thier, The Clash of Two Goods: State and Non-State Dispute Resolution in Afghanistan, United States Institute of Peace (2007).

The World Bank Group and International Monetary Fund

BEEPS (2005)	Business Environment and Enterprise Performance Survey, Screener Questionnaire (2005)
Doing Business 2004	World Bank and International Finance Corporation, Doing Business 2004 – Understanding Regulations (2003)
Doing Business 2005	World Bank and International Finance Corporation, Doing Business 2005 – Removing Obstacles to Growth (2004)
Doing Business 2006	World Bank and International Finance Corporation, Doing Business 2006 – Creating Jobs (2005)
Doing Business 2007	World Bank and International Finance Corporation, Doing Business 2007: How to Reform (2006)
Doing Business 2008	World Bank and International Finance Corporation, Doing Business 2008: Five years of reforms (2007)
Doing Business 2009	World Bank and International Finance Corporation, Doing Business 2009: Five Years of Reforms, Overview (2008)
Governance Matters III	Daniel Kaufmann, Aart Kraay and Massimo Mastruzzi, 'Governance Matters III: Governance Indicators for 1996–2002', World Bank Policy Research Report Series 3106 (2003)
Governance Matters IV	Daniel Kaufmann, Aart Kraay and Massimo Mastruzzi, Governance Matters IV: Governance Indicators for 1996–2004, The World Bank (2005)
Governance Matters VI	Daniel Kaufmann, Aart Kraay and Massimo Mastruzzi, 'Governance Matters VI. Aggregate and Individual Governance Indicators 1996–2006', WPS 4280 (2007)
IMF (2001)	IMF, Review of the Fund's Experience in Governance Issues, Prepared by the Policy

262 BIBLIOGRAPHY

	Development and Review Department (March 28, 2001)
IMF (2003a)	IMF, The Primacy of Institutions (and what this does and does not mean), by Dani Rodrik and Arvind Subramanian in *Finance & Development* 31 (June 2003)
IMF (2003b)	Effects of Financial Globalization on Developing Countries: Some Empirical Evidence, by Eswar Prasad, Kenneth Rogoff, Shang-Jin Wei and M. Ayhan Kose (March 17, 2003)
IMF (2004)	Amar Gande and David Parsley, 'Sovereign Credit Ratings and International Portfolio Flows', IMF (2004)
IMF (2005a)	IMF, Aid, Governance, and the Political Economy: Growth and Institutions by Simon Johnson and Arvind Subramanian. Prepared for the Seminar on Foreign Aid and Macroeconomic Management, Chissano Conference Center, Maputo, March 14–15, 2005 (February 10, 2005)
IMF (2005b)	IMF, 2005 Review of the Poverty Reduction Strategy Approach – Balancing Accountabilities and Scaling Up Results – Synthesis (September 19, 2005)
IMF (2006)	IMF Working Paper WP/06/189, Research Department, Financial Globalization: A Reappraisal, prepared by M. Ayhan Kose, Eswar Prasad, Kenneth Rogoff and Shang-Jin Wei (August 2006)
IMF (2007a)	IMF, Proposals to Modify the PRGF-HIPC Trust Instrument – Further Considerations, Prepared by the Policy Development and Review, African, Finance and Legal Departments (December 19, 2007)
IMF (2007b)	IMF Working Paper WP/07/55, Can the Natural Resource Curse Be Turned Into a Blessing? The Role of Trade Policies and Institutions, prepared by Rabah Arezki and Frederick van der Ploeg (March 2007)
IMF (2007c)	IMF Working Paper WP/07/292, Policy Development and Review Department, Border and Behind-the-Border Trade Barriers and Country Exports, prepared by Azim Sadikov, authorized for distribution by Thomas Dorsey (December 2007)

IMF (2007d)	IMF, Reaping the Benefits of Financial Globalization, prepared by the Research Department, approved by Simon Johnson (June 2007)
IMF (2007e)	IMF Working Paper WP/07/203, African Department, Financial Deepening in Sub-Saharan Africa: Empirical Evidence on the Role of Creditor Rights Protection and Information Sharing, prepared by Calvin McDonald and Liliana Schumacher (August 2007)
IMF (2007f)	IMF Working Paper WP/07/52, Research Department, The Prospects for Sustained Growth in Africa: Benchmarking the Constraints, prepared by Simon Johnson, Jonathan D. Ostry and Arvind Subramanian (March 2007)
IMF (2007g)	IMF Working Paper WP/07/277, Empirical Evidence on the New International Aid Architecture, prepared by Stijn Claessens, Danny Cassimon and Bjorn Van Campenhout (December 2007)
IMF (2007h)	IMF, The Role of the Fund in the Poverty Reduction Strategy (PRS) Process and Its Collaboration with Donors, prepared by the Policy Development and Review Department, approved by Mark Allen (September 21, 2007)
IMF (2007i)	IMF Working Paper WP/07/43, Colonial Origins, Institutions and Economic Performance in the Caribbean: Guyana and Barbados, by Michael DaCosta (February 2007)
IMF (2008)	IMF Working Paper WP/08/26, IMF Institute, Foreign Direct Investment and Structural Reforms: Evidence from Eastern Europe and Latin America, prepared by Nauro F. Campos and Yuko Kinoshita, authorized for distribution by Enrica Detragiache (January 2008)
IMF Albania (2006)	IMF, Albania: Poverty Reduction Strategy Paper – Annual Progress Report 2005, IMF Country Report No. 06/23 (2006)
IMF Cameroon (2008)	IMF Country Report No. 08/2, Cameroon: Poverty Reduction Strategy Paper – Progress Report – Joint Staff Advisory Note (January 2008)
IMF DRC (2007a)	IMF Country Report No. 07/206, Republic of Congo: Selected Issues (June 2007)

264 BIBLIOGRAPHY

IMF DRC (2007b)	IMF Country Report No. 07/331, Democratic Republic of the Congo: Poverty Reduction Strategy Paper – Joint Staff Advisory Note (September 2007)
IMF Gambia (2006)	IMF Country Report No. 06/396, The Gambia: Poverty Reduction Strategy Paper – Second Annual Progress Report (November 2006)
IMF IDA (2006)	IMF & IDA, Heavily Indebted Poor Countries (HIPC) Initiative – Statistical Update, prepared by the Staffs of the IMF and the World Bank, approved by Mark Allen and Danny Leipziger (March 21, 2006)
IMF IDA (2007)	IMF & IDA, Heavily Indebted Poor Countries (HIPC) Initiative and Multilateral Debt Relief Initiative (MDRI) – Status of Implementation, prepared by the Staffs of IDA and IMF, approved by Danny Leipziger and Mark Allen (August 28, 2007)
IMF Uzbekistan (2008)	International Monetary Fund, Republic of Uzbekistan: Poverty Reduction Strategy Paper, IMF Country Report No. 08/34 (January 2008)
Reyes (1995)	Luis Manriquez Reyes, 'Modernization of Judicial Systems in Developing Countries: The Case of Chile', in World Bank (1995d)
Shihata (1988)	Ibrahim Shihata, 'The World Bank and Human Rights' [1988] in Shihata (1991a)
Shihata (1990)	Ibrahim Shihata, 'The World Bank and "Governance" Issues in Its Borrowing Members' [1990] in Shihata (1991a)
Shihata (1991a)	Ibrahim Shihata, *The World Bank in a Changing World: Selected Essays*, Franziska Tschofen and Antonio Parra (eds.), Martinus Nijhoff (1991)
Shihata (1991b)	Ibrahim Shihata, 'The World Bank and Private Sector Development – A Legal Perspective', in Shihata (1991a)
Shihata (1991c)	Ibrahim Shihata, 'Promotion of Foreign Direct Investment – A General Account with Particular Reference to the Role of the World Bank Group', in Shihata (1991a)
Shihata (1991d)	Ibrahim Shihata, 'The World Bank Facing the 21st Century – Developments in the 1980s and Prospects for the 1990s', in Shihata (1991)
WB Albania (2006)	Implementation Completion Report (IDA-33270) on a Credit in the Amount of SDR 6.6 Million

BIBLIOGRAPHY 265

	(US$ 9.0 Million Equivalent) to Albania for a Legal and Judicial Reform Project (June 12, 2006)
WB Argentina (2005)	Project Appraisal Document on a Proposed Loan in the Amount of US$ 40 Million to the Argentine Republic for a Sub-National Governments Public Sector Modernization Project (November 17, 2005)
WB Armenia (2004)	Project Appraisal Document on a Proposed Credit in the Amount of SDR 6.80 Million (US$10.15 Million Equivalent) to the Republic of Armenia for a Public Sector Modernization Project, Report No. 27563-AM (April 8, 2004)
WB Armenia (2007a)	World Bank Report No: 38361-AM, Project Appraisal Document on a Proposed Credit in the Amount of SDR 15.2 million (US$ 22.5 Million Equivalent) for a Second Judicial Reform Project, Republic of Armenia (February 9, 2007)
WB Armenia (2007b)	Implementation Completion and Results Report (IDA-34170) on a Credit Amount of SDR 8.6 Million (US$ 11.4 Million Equivalent) to Republic of Armenia for a Judicial Reform Project, Report No. ICR0000493 (June 28, 2007)
WB Azerbaijan (2006)	Project Appraisal Document on a Proposed Credit in the Amount of SDR 14.8 Million (US$ 21.6 Million Equivalent) to the Republic of Azerbaijan for a Judicial Modernization Project (June 5, 2006)
WB Bissau (2002)	Project Appraisal Document on a Proposed Credit in the Amount of SDR 21.0 Million (US$ 26.0 Million Equivalent) to the Republic of Guinea-Bissau for a Private Sector Rehabilitation and Development Project (February 28, 2002)
WB Colombia (2001)	Project Appraisal Document on a Proposed Learning and Innovation Loan in the amount of US$ 5 Million to the Republic of Colombia for a Judicial Conflict Resolution Improvement Project, Report No. 23184-CO (November 8, 2001)
WB Croatia (2007)	Implementation Completion and Results Report on a Loan in the Amount of US$7.3 Million to Croatia for a Technical Assistance for Institutional and Regulatory Reform for Private Sector Development Project (January 31, 2007)
WB DRC (2007)	World Bank, DRC: Emergency Demobilization & Reintegration – Additional Financing, Project

	Information Document, Concept Stage, Report No. AB 3448 (Prepared: November 9, 2007)
WB DRC (2008)	World Bank, DRC Private Sector Development and Competitiveness – Additional Financing, Project Information Document, Appraisal Stage, Report No. AB3042 (Board Approval: April 22, 2008)
WB Ethiopia (2004)	Legal Vice Presidency, The World Bank, Ethiopia: Legal and Judicial Sector Assessment (2004)
WB Gambia (2001)	Project Appraisal Document on a Proposed Credit in the Amount of SDR 12 Million (US$ 15 Million Equivalent) to the Republic of the Gambia for a Capacity Building for Economic Management Project, Report No. 22516 GM (July 6, 2001)
WB Georgia (1999)	Project Appraisal Document on a Proposed Credit in the Amount of SDR 9.9 Million (US$ 13.4 Million Equivalent) to Georgia for a Judicial Reform Project, Report No. 19346-GE (June 7, 1999)
WB Georgia (2007)	Implementation Completion and Results Report (IDA-32630) on a Credit in the Amount of US$ 13.33 Million (SDR 9.87 Million Credit) to Georgia for Judicial Reform Project, Report No. ICR000026 (May 17, 2007)
WB Ghana (2003)	Project Appraisal Document on a Proposed Credit in the Amount of SDR 15.1 Million (US$ 20.5 Million Equivalent) to the Republic of Ghana for a Land Administration Project (July 8, 2003)
WB Honduras (2005)	Project Appraisal Document on a Proposed Credit in the Amount of SDR 10.0 Million (US$ 15 Million Equivalent) to the Republic of Honduras for a Judicial Branch Modernization Project, Report No. 32128-HN (June 6, 2005)
WB IDA (2006)	International Development Association, IDA's Performance-Based Allocation System: A Review of the Governance Factor, International Development Association Resource Mobilization (FRM) 37911 Public Disclosure (October 2006)
WB IFC (2006)	Lukasz Rozdeiczer and Alejandro Alvarez de la Campa, *Alternative Dispute Resolution Manual: Implementing Commercial Mediation*, International Finance Corporation (2006)

WB Indonesia (2003)	Project Appraisal Document on a Proposed Loan in the Amount of US$ 17.1 million to the Republic of Indonesia for a Private Provision of Infrastructure Technical Assistance Loan (Report No. 25820 (April 25,2003)
WB Ivoire (2007)	Implementation Completion Report on a Credit in the Amount of SDR 8.9 Million (US$ 12.9 Million) to the Republic of Cote d'Ivoire for a Private Sector Capacity Building Project (June 17, 2005)
WB Kosovo (2004)	Implementation Completion Report (TF-27806) on a Grant in the Amount Of US$ 3.0 Million to Kosovo, Serbia and Montenegro for a Private Sector Development Technical Assistance Grant (November 10, 2004)
WB LVP (2004)	Legal Vice Presidency, The World Bank, Initiatives in Legal and Judicial Reform (2004)
WB Malawi (2007)	Project Appraisal Document on a Proposed Grant in the Amount of SDR 10 Million (US$ 15 Million Equivalent) to the Republic of Malawi for a Business Environment Strengthening Technical Assistance Project (BESTAP), Report No. 39633-MW (April 27, 2007)
WB Morocco (2004)	Implementation Completion Report (SCL-45630) on a Loan in the Amount of US$ 5.3 Million to the Kingdom of Morocco for a Legal and Judicial Development Project (December 30, 2004)
WB Pakistan (2006)	Project Appraisal Document on a Proposed Credit in the Amount of SDR 30.35 Million (US$ 45.65 Million Equivalent) to the Islamic Republic of Pakistan for a Punjab Land Records Management and Information Systems, Report No. 36450-PK (December 21, 2006)
WB Peru (2004)	Project Appraisal Document on Proposed Loan in the Amount of US$ 12 Million to the Republic of Peru for a Justice Services Improvement Project (February 9, 2004)
WB Philippines (2003)	Project Appraisal Document on a Proposed Loan in the Amount of US$ 21.9 Million to the Republic of the Philippines for a Judicial Reform Support Project, Report No. 25504 (July 8, 2003)
WB Romania (2005a)	Implementation Completion Report (PPFB-P3610 SCL-44910) on a Loan in the Amount of US$ 25 Million to Romania for a Private Sector Institution Building Project (PIBL) (April 25, 2005)

268   BIBLIOGRAPHY

WB Romania (2005b)	Project Appraisal Document on a Proposed Loan in the Amount of Euro 110.0 Million (US$ 130 Million Equivalent) to Romania for a Judicial Reform Project (November 22, 2005)
WB Russia (2006)	Implementation Completion Report (CPL-40350 TF-29492) on a Loan in the Amount of US$ 58 Million to the Russian Federation for a Legal Reform Project, Report No. 36549 (June 28, 2006)
WB Russia (2007)	Project Appraisal Document on a Proposed Loan in the Amount of US$ 50 Million to the Russian Federation for a Judicial Reform Support Project (January 19, 2007)
WB Salvador (2002)	Project Appraisal Document on a Proposed Loan in the Amount of US$ 18.2 Million to the Republic of El Salvador for a Judicial Modernization Project (July 5, 2002)
WB Venezuela (1997)	Project Appraisal Document on a Proposed Learning and Innovation Loan in the Amount of US$ 4.7 Million to the Republic of Venezuela for a Supreme Court Modernization Project (December 9, 1997)
WB Venezuela (2003)	Implementation Completion Report on a Loan in the Amount of US$ 30 Million to the Bolivarian Republic of Venezuela for a Judicial Infrastructure Development Project (June 28, 2003)
WB West Bank (2004)	Implementation Completion Report (TF-26063 TF-23757) on a Credit in the Amount of US$ 2.49 Million to the West Bank and Gaza for a Legal Development Project, Report No. 29066 (June 9, 2004)
WB Yemen (2003)	Implementation Completion Report (IDA-32740) on a Credit in the Amount of SDR 1.8 Million Equivalent to the Republic of Yemen for a Legal and Judicial Development Project, Report No. 27561 (December 30, 2003)
WB Yemen (2008)	World Bank Independent Evaluation Group, Project Performance Assessment Report, Republic of Yemen, Institutional Development for Public Administration Project (Credit No. 2015-YEM), Legal and Judicial Development Project (Credit No. 3274-YEM), Public Sector Management Adjustment Credit (Credit No. 3178-YEM), Country Evaluation and Regional Relations (October 16, 2008)

WB Zambia (2008)	IDA, Country Assistance Strategy for the Republic of Zambia, World Bank Report No: 43352-ZM, Country Management Unit: AFCS2 (April 8, 2008)
WBES (2004)	Geeta Batra, Daniel Kaufmann, Andrew H. W. Stone, The Investment Climate Around the World: Voices of the Firms from the World, Business Environment Survey (2004)
WDR 1979	World Bank, World Development Report 1979: Structural Change and Development Policy (1978)
WDR 1985	World Bank, World Development Report 1985: International Capital and Economic Development (1984)
WDR 1987	World Bank, World Development Report 1987: Industrialization and Foreign Trade (1986)
WDR 1988	World Bank, World Development Report 1988: Public Finance in Development (1987)
WDR 1989	World Bank, World Development Report 1989: Financial Systems and Development (1988)
WDR 1991	World Bank, World Development Report 1991: The Challenge of Development (1990)
WDR 1995	World Bank, World Development Report 1995: Workers in an Integrating World (1994)
WDR 1996	World Bank, World Development Report 1996: From Plan to Market (1995)
WDR 1997	World Bank, World Development Report 1997: The State in a Changing World (1996)
WDR 2002	World Bank, World Development Report 2002: Building Institutions for Markets (2001)
WDR 2005	World Bank, World Development Report 2005: A Better Investment Climate for Everyone (2004)
WDR 2006	World Bank, World Development Report 2006: Equity and Development, Vol. 1 (2005)
World Bank (1989a)	Brian Van Arkadie, 'The Role of Institutions in Development', in Proceedings of the World Bank Annual Conference on Development Economics (1989)
World Bank (1989b)	World Bank, Sub-Saharan Africa: From Crisis to Sustainable Growth. A Long-Term Perspective Study (1989)
World Bank (1989c)	World Bank, 'Developing the Private Sector: A Challenge for the World Bank Group' (1989)
World Bank (1991a)	Deborah Brautigam, 'Governance and Economy: A Review', Policy Research Working Papers 815, World Bank (December 1991)

World Bank (1991b)	Beatrice Buyck, 'The Bank's Use of Technical Assistance for Institutional Development', The World Bank WPS 578 (January 1991)
World Bank (1991c)	World Bank, 'Private Sector Development: Strengthening the Bank Group Effort', Paper R91-79 (April 1991)
World Bank (1991d)	World Bank, 'Managing Development: The Governance Dimension', A Discussion Paper, World Bank (August 29, 1991)
World Bank (1992)	World Bank, 'Governance and Development' (1992)
World Bank (1994)	Shahid Amjad Chaudhry, Gary James Reid and Waleed Haider Malik (eds.), 'Civil Service Reform in Latin America and the Caribbean Proceedings of a Conference', World Bank Technical Paper No. 259 (October 1994)
World Bank (1995a)	Cheryl W. Gray and Kathryn Hendley, 'Developing Commercial Law in Transition Economies: Examples from Hungary and Russia', The World Bank (1995)
World Bank (1995b)	Jonathan Isbam, Daniel Kaufmann and Lant Pritchett, 'Governance and Returns on Investment: An Empirical Investigation', Policy Research Working Paper 1550 (November 1995)
World Bank (1995c)	Robert Klitgaard, 'Institutional Adjustment and Adjusting to Institutions', World Bank Discussion Papers 303 (1995)
World Bank (1995d)	Malcom Rowat, Waleed H. Malik and Maria Dakolias (eds.), 'Judicial Reform in Latin America and the Caribbean: Proceedings of a World Bank Conference', World Bank Technical Paper No. 280 (1995)
World Bank (1996)	Mamadou Dia, 'Africa's Management in the 1990s and Beyond: Reconciling Indigenous and Transplanted Institutions', World Bank (1996)
World Bank (1998a)	World Bank, 'Africa Can Compete! A Framework For World Bank Group Support for Private Sector Development in Sub-Saharan Africa' (August 1998)
World Bank (1998b)	Craig Burnside and David Dollar, 'Aid, the Incentive Regime and Poverty Reduction', World Bank Policy Research Working Paper 1937 (June 1998)
World Bank (1999a)	World Bank, The Law and Economics of Judicial Systems, PREM Notes No. 26 (July 1999)

World Bank (1999b)	Maria Dakolias and Javier Said, 'Judicial Reform: A Process of Change Through Pilot Courts', World Bank, Legal and Judicial Reform Unit (May 1999)
World Bank (1999c)	Deepa Narayan, *Can Anyone Hear Us? Voices From 47 Countries, Voices of the Poor Volume 1*, World Bank (1999)
World Bank (1999d)	Edgardo Buscaglia and Maria Dakolias, 'An Analysis of the Causes of Corruption in the Judiciary', The World Bank, Legal and Judicial Reform Unit (August 1999)
World Bank (2000a)	Mark Dietrich, 'Legal and Judicial Reform in Central Europe and the Former Soviet Union, Voices from Five Countries', The World Bank (August 2000)
World Bank (2000b)	W. Paatii Ofosu-Amaah, 'Reforming Business-Related Laws to Promote Private Sector Development: The World Bank Experience in Africa' (2000)
World Bank (2000c)	Deepa Narayan, Robert Chambers, Meera K. Shah and Patti Petesch, *Voices of the Poor: Crying Out for Change*, Oxford University Press (2000)
World Bank (2000d)	World Bank, 'Reforming Public Institutions and Strengthening Governance: A World Bank Strategy', The World Bank, Public Sector Group Poverty Reduction and Economic Management (PREM) Network (November 2000)
World Bank (2000e)	Linn Hammergren, 'Judicial Independence and Judicial Accountability: Shifting Balance in Reform Goals', The World Bank (October 2000)
World Bank (2000f)	Stiin Claessens, Simeon Djankov and Tatiana Nenova, 'Corporate Risk Around the World', Policy Research Working Paper 2271, World Bank (2000)
World Bank (2001)	World Development Report 2002, Building Institutions for Markets, Overview (2001)
World Bank (2002a)	Navin Girishankar, Linn Hammergren, Malcolm Holmes, Stephen Knack, Brian Levy, Jennie Litvack, Nicholas Manning, Richard Messick, Jeffrey Rinne and Helen Sutch, 'Governance' in World Bank, Poverty Reduction Strategy Sourcebook (2002)
World Bank (2002b)	Deepa Narayan and Patti Petesch (eds.), 'Voices of the Poor: From Many Lands', World Bank (2002)

272 BIBLIOGRAPHY

World Bank (2003a)	Simeon Djankov, Edward L. Glaesar, Rafael La Porta, Florencio Lopez-de-Silanes and Andrei Shleifer, 'The New Comparative Economics', Institute of Economic Research Harvard University Discussion Paper No. 2002; The World Bank Policy Research Working Paper No. 3054 (2003)
World Bank (2003b)	World Bank, Building Capacity in Post-Conflict Countries, Social Development Notes, No. 14 (December 2003)
World Bank (2003c)	World Bank Group, Making Government an Effective Partner: Civil Service Reform in Sub-Saharan Africa, Findings, Africa Region, No. 4 (October 1993)
World Bank (2003d)	Branko Milanovic, 'Is Inequality in Africa Really Different?' World Bank Development Research Group, WPS3169 (2003)
World Bank (2004)	World Bank, 2004 Annual Review of Development Effectiveness: The Bank's Contribution to Poverty Reduction (2004)
World Bank (2005a)	Richard E. Messick, 'What Governments Can Do to Facilitate the Enforcement of Contracts', Public Sector Group, World Bank (2005)
World Bank (2005b)	Russell Muir and Xiaofang Shen, 'Land Markets: Promoting the Private Sector by Improving Access to Land', Public Policy for the Private Sector (World Bank Group), Note No. 317 (2005)
World Bank (2005c)	World Bank, Alternative Dispute Resolution – When It Works, When It Doesn't, PREM Notes No. 99 (2005)
World Bank (2005d)	Leila Chirayath, Caroline Sage and Michael Woolcock, 'Customary Law and Policy Reform: Engaging with the Plurality of Justice Systems', Prepared as a background paper for the World Development Report 2006: Equity and Development (undated 2005)
World Bank (2005e)	Robert Danino, 'Reforming Legal and Judicial Systems', in Ruth Kagia (ed.), *Balancing the Development Agenda: The Transformation of the World Bank under James D. Wolfensohn, 1995–2005*, World Bank (2005)
World Bank (2005f)	Klaus Decker, Caroline Sage and Milena Stefanova, 'Law or Justice: Building Equitable Legal Institutions', prepared as a background

	paper for the World Development Report 2006: Equity and Development (undated, 2005)
World Bank (2005g)	John M. Ackerman, 'Social Accountability in the Public Sector: A Conceptual Discussion', Social Development Papers No. 82, World Bank (2005)
World Bank (2005h)	World Bank, Perspectives on Development (2005)
World Bank (2005i)	Simeon Djankov, Darshini Manraj, Caralee McLiesh, Rita Ramalho, 'Doing Business Indicators. Why Aggregate and How to Do It', Washington, DC: World Bank Group (December 2005)
World Bank (2005j)	James Anderson, David Bernstein and Cheryl Gray, 'Judicial Systems in Transition Economies: Assessing the Past, Looking to the Future', World Bank (2005)
World Bank (2005k)	The World Bank, Perspectives on Development (2005)
World Bank (2006a)	Mehnaz Safavian, Heywood Fleisig and Jevgenijs Steinbuks, 'Unlocking Dead Capital: How Reforming Collateral Laws Improves Access to Finance', Viewpoint (World Bank Group), Note No. 307 (March 2006)
World Bank (2006b)	Mary McNeil and Takawira Mumvuma, 'Demanding Good Governance: A Stocktaking of Social Accountability Initiatives by Civil Society in Anglophone Africa', World Bank Community Empowerment and Social Inclusion Learning Program (2006)
World Bank (2006c)	Sunita Kikeri, Thomas Kenyon and Vincent Palmadem, 'Reforming the Investment Climate: Lessons for Practitioners', World Bank Policy Research Working Paper 3986 (August 2006)
World Bank (2006e)	Kirsti Samuels, 'Rule of Law Reform in Post-Conflict Countries Operational Initiatives and Lessons Learnt', World Bank Conflict Prevention and Reconstruction Paper No. 37 (October 2006)
World Bank (2006f)	World Bank, The World Bank Annual Report 2006 (2006)
World Bank (2006g)	Simeon Djankov, Caralee McLiesh and Rita Ramalho, 'Regulation and Growth', World Bank (March 17, 2006)
World Bank (2006h)	The World Bank Group, 2006 Questionnaire on Labor and Social Security Laws, Doing Business

	Project, International Finance Corporation (undated, 2006)
World Bank (2007a)	Joseph J. Norton, 'Taking Stock of the "First Generation" of Financial Sector Legal Reform', Law and Development Working Papers Series No. 4, World Bank Legal Vice Presidency (undated, 2007)
World Bank (2007b)	James H. Anderson and Cheryl W. Gray, 'Transforming Judicial Systems in Europe and Central Asia', World Bank (2007)
World Bank (2007c)	Douglass C. North, John Joseph Wallis, Steven B. Webb, Barry R. Weingast, 'Limited Access Orders in the Developing World: A New Approach to the Problems of Development', The World Bank Independent Evaluation Group, Policy Research Working Paper 4359 (September 2007)
World Bank (2007d)	Dory Reiling, Linn Hammergren, Adrian Di Giovanni, 'Justice Sector Assessments: A Handbook', World Bank (undated [2007])
World Bank (2007e)	World Bank, Guyana Investment Climate Assessment, Volume I: Main Findings and Policy Recommendations (June 21, 2007)
World Bank (2007f)	Ksenia Yudaevam, Editorial, *Beyond Transition*, World Bank (April-June 2007)
World Bank (2007g)	Daniel Kaufman and Aart Kraay, 'Governance Indicators: Where are we, where should we be going?' Policy Research Working Paper WPS 4370, World Bank (2007)
World Bank (2007h)	World Bank, The World Bank Annual Report 2007 (2007)
World Bank (2007i)	World Bank, Strengthening World Bank Group Engagement on Governance and Anticorruption (March 21, 2007)
World Bank (2007j)	World Bank, Implementation Plan for Strengthening World Bank Group Engagement on Governance and Anti-corruption (September 28, 2007)
World Bank (2008a)	Sunita Kikeri and Verena Phipps, 'Privatization Trends: A Record Year in 2006', Public Policy for the Private Sector (World Bank Group), Note No. 317 (January 2008)
World Bank (2008b)	World Bank, Public Sector Reform: What Works and Why? (2008)
World Bank (2008c)	Sunita Kikeri and Verena Phipps, 'Privatization Trends: A Record Year for Initial Public Offerings

in 2007', Public Policy for the Private Sector (World Bank Group), Note No. 321 (October 2008)

United Nations

A/49/512	A/49/512, Strengthening the Rule of Law, Report of the Secretary-General (14 October 14 1994)
A/50/653	A/50/653, Strengthening the Rule of Law, Report of the Secretary-General (20 October 1995)
A/51/555	A/51/555, Strengthening the rule of law, Report of the Secretary-General (25 October 1996)
A/51/950	A/51/950, Renewing the United Nations, A Programme for Reform, Report of the Secretary-General (14 July 1997)
A/55/177	A/55/177, Strengthening the Rule of Law, Report of the Secretary-General (20 July 2000)
A/55/305–S/2000/809	A/55/305–S/2000/809, Comprehensive Review of the Whole Question of Peacekeeping Operations in All Their Aspects (21 August 2000) ['Brahimi Report']
A/57/275	A/57/275, Report of the Secretary-General, Strengthening the Rule of Law (5 August 2002)
A/57/387	A/57/387, Strengthening of the United Nations: An Agenda for Further Change, Report of the Secretary-General (9 September 2002)
A/57/711	A/57/711, Implementation of the Recommendations of the Special Committee on Peacekeeping Operations, Report of the Secretary-General (16 January 2003)
A/58/382	A/58/382, Review of Technical Cooperation in the United Nations, Report of the Secretary-General (19 September 2003)
A/59/19/Rev.1	A/59/19/Rev.1, Report of the Special Committee on Peacekeeping Operations and its Working Group (2005)
A/59/2005	A/59/2005, In Larger Freedom: Towards Development, Security and Human Rights for All (21 March 2005)
A/59/37	A/59/37, Report of the Ad Hoc Committee established by General Assembly Resolution 51/210 of 17 December 1996 (2004)
A/59/894	A/59/894, Letter dated 3 August 2005 from the Chairman of the Sixth Committee addressed to the President of the General Assembly (12 August 2005), Appendix II, Draft comprehensive

276   BIBLIOGRAPHY

	convention against international terrorism, Consolidated text prepared by the coordinator for discussion (2005)
A/60/10	A/60/10, Report of the International Law Commission, Fifty Seventh Session (2005)
A/60/692	A/60/692, Investing in the United Nations: for a Stronger Organization Worldwide, Report of the Secretary-General (7 March 2006)
A/61/636–S/2006/980	A/61/636–S/2006/980, Report of the Secretary-General, Uniting Our Strengths: Enhancing United Nations Support for the Rule of Law (14 December 2006)
A/62/121	A/62/121, The Rule of Law at the National and International Levels: Comments and Information Received from Governments (11 July 2007)
A/62/121/Add.1	A/62/121/Add.1, The Rule of Law at the National and International Levels: Comments and Information Received from Governments [Switzerland] (6 September 2007)
A/62/261	A/62/261, The Rule of Law at the National and International Levels, Interim Report of the Secretary-General (15 August 2007)
A/62/454	A/62/454, The Rule of Law at the National and International Levels, Report of the Sixth Committee (20 November 2007)
A/63/37	A/63/37, Report of the Ad Hoc Committee Established by General Assembly Resolution 51/210 of 17 December 1996 (25 and 26 February and 6 March 2008)
A/CONF.157/23	A/CONF.157/23, Vienna Declaration and Program of Action (12 July 1993)
A/HRC/10/3	A/HRC/10/3, Report of the Special Rapporteur on the Promotion and Protection of Human Rights and Fundamental Freedoms while Countering Terrorism, Martin Scheinin (4 February 2009)
A/RES/50/179	A/RES/50/179, Resolution Adopted by the General Assembly [on the Report of the Third Committee (A/50/635/Add.2)] Strengthening of the Rule of Law (28 February 1996)
A/RES/51/96	A/RES/51/96, Resolution Adopted by the General Assembly [on the Report of the Third Committee (A/51/619/Add.2)] Strengthening of the Rule of Law (3 March 1997)
A/RES/56/161	A/RES/56/161, Resolution adopted by the General Assembly [on the Report of the Third

	Committee (A/56/583/Add.2)], Human Rights in the Administration of Justice (20 February 2002)
A/RES/60/1	A/RES/60/1, 2005 World Summit Outcome (24 October 2005)
A/RES/62/70	A/RES/62/70, The Rule of Law at the National and International Levels (January 8, 2008)
Carlson (2006)	Scott Carlson, 'Legal and Judicial Rule of Law Work in Multi-Dimensional Peacekeeping Operations: Lessons-Learned Study', Peacekeeping Best Practices (March 2006)
CCPR/C/21/Rev.1/Add.11	CCPR/C/21/Rev.1/Add.11, Human Rights Committee, General Comment No. 29 on States of Emergency (2001)
DP/2001/4	DP/2001/4, Executive Board of the United Nations Development Programme and of the United Nations Population Fund, Role of UNDP in Crisis and Post-Conflict Situations (27 November 2000)
DPA (2006a)	UN Department of Political Affairs, UN Peacemaker, Operational Guidance Note, Addressing the Rule of Law and the Administration of Justice In Peace Processes and Agreements (undated, 2006)
DPA (2006b)	UN Department of Political Affairs, UN Peacemaker, Operational Guidance Note, Transforming Conflict and Promoting Good Governance Through Peace Processes (undated, 2006)
DPA (2007)	UN Department of Political Affairs, UN Peacemaker, Operational Guidance Note, Disarmament, Demobilization and Reintegration (DDR) (undated, 2007)
DPKO (2006)	DPKO, United Nations Primer for Justice Components in Multidimensional Peace Operations: Strengthening the Rule of Law (December 2006)
DPKO (2008)	DPKO, United Nations Peacekeeping Operations: Principles and Guidelines (the 'Capstone Principles') (2008)
DPKO Surge 2006	DPKO, 'Surge 2006', prepared by DPKO/External Relations, Media Affairs Office, 1 November 2006
E/CN.4/2006/120	E/CN.4/2006/120, Situation of detainees at Guantánamo Bay. Report of the Chairperson of the Working Group on Arbitrary Detention, Ms. Leila Zerrougui; the Special Rapporteur on

278 BIBLIOGRAPHY

	the independence of judges and lawyers, Mr Leandro Despouy; the Special Rapporteur on torture and other cruel, inhuman or degrading treatment or punishment, Mr Manfred Nowak; the Special Rapporteur on freedom of religion or belief, Ms. Asma Jahangir; and the Special Rapporteur on the right of everyone to the enjoyment of the highest attainable standard of physical and mental health, Mr Paul Hunt (15 February 2006)
ECPS (2002)	Final Report of the Executive Committee on Peace and Security Task Force for Development of Comprehensive Rule of Law Strategies for Peace Operations of 15 August 2002, approved by the Executive Committee on 30 September 2002
EOSG (2006)	Executive Office of the Secretary-General, Inventory: United Nations Capacity in Peacebuilding (2006)
Flinterman and Zwamborn (2003)	Cees Flinterman and Marcel Zwamborn, 'From Development of Human Rights to Managing Human Rights Development: Global Review of the OHCHR Technical Cooperation Programme. Revised Draft Synthesis Report', Netherlands Institute of Human Rights (SIM) in partnership with MEDE European Consultancy (September 2003)
MONUC (2008)	William Elachi Alwiga/MONUC, 'Congolese Military Justice Officials Trained in Sex Crime Investigation' (February 8, 2008)
More Secure World (2004)	'A More Secure World: Our Shared Responsibility', Report of the High-level Panel on Threats, Challenges and Change, United Nations (2004)
OHCHR (2006a)	OHCHR, Rule-of-Law Tools for Post-Conflict States: Mapping the Justice Sector (2006)
OHCHR (2006b)	OHCHR, Rule-of-Law Tools for Post-Conflict States: Monitoring Legal Systems (2006)
OHCHR (2006c)	OHCHR, Rule-of-Law Tools for Post-Conflict States: Prosecution Initiatives (2006)
OHCHR (2006d)	OHCHR, Rule-of-Law Tools for Post-Conflict States: Vetting: An Operational Framework (2006)
OHCHR (2006e)	OHCHR, Rule-of-Law Tools for Post-Conflict States: Truth Commissions (2006)
OHCHR (2007)	OHCHR, Making Peace Our Own: Victims' Perceptions of Accountability, Reconciliation and

BIBLIOGRAPHY 279

	Transitional Justice in Northern Uganda, United Nations (2007)
OHCHR/IBA (2003)	Office of the High Commissioner for Human Rights in Cooperation with the International Bar Association, Human Rights in the Administration of Justice: A Manual for Judges, Prosecutors and Lawyers, Professional Training Series No. 9 (2003)
S/2004/616	S/2004/616, The Rule of Law and Transitional Justice in Conflict and Post-Conflict Societies (23 August 2004)
S/2006/367	S/2006/367, Letter dated 7 June 2006 from the Permanent Representative of Denmark to the United Nations addressed to the Secretary-General (7 June 2006)
S/PRST/2004/34	S/PRST/2004/34, Statement by the President of the Security Council (6 October 2004)
S/PRST/2006/28	S/PRST/2006/28, Statement by the President of the Security Council (22 June 2006)
S/PV.4833	S/PV.4833, Security Council 4833rd Meeting, Justice and the Rule of Law: the United Nations Role (24 September 2003)
S/PV.4835	S/PV.4835, Security Council 4835th Meeting. Justice and the Rule of Law: the United Nations Role (30 September 2003)
S/RES/1327 (2000)	S/RES/1327 (2000), Resolution 1327 (2000) Adopted by the Security Council at its 4220th meeting, on 13 November 2000 (13 November 2000)
S/RES/1706 (2006)	S/RES/1706 (2006), Resolution 1706 (2006) Adopted by the Security Council at its 5519th meeting (31 August 2006)
S-G Decision 2006/47	Decision of the Secretary-General, 7 November 2006, Policy Committee Meeting, Decision No. 2006/47 (24 November 2006)
UNDP (1997)	UNDP, Corruption and Good Governance: Discussion Paper 3, Management, Development and Governance Division Bureau for Policy and Programme Support, UNDP (July 1997)
UNDP (2002)	Nicole Ball, Enhancing Security Sector Governance: A Conceptual Framework for UNDP (October 2002)
UNDP (2003)	UNDP, Security Sector Reform and Transitional Justice: A Crisis Post-Conflict Programmatic Approach (March 2003)

UNDP (2004) UNDP, Governance Indicators: A User's Guide, UNDP in collaboration with Eurostat (2004)
UNDP (2005) UNDP, Afghanistan Human Development Report, Bridging Modernity and Tradition: Rule of Law and the Search for Justice (2005)
UNDP (2007) UNDP, Strengthening Rule of Law Within an Early Recovery Framework: The UNDP Programme in Darfur (March 2007)
UNDP (2008) UNDP, Strengthening the Rule of Law in Conflict/Post-Conflict Situations A Global Programme for Justice and Security 2008–2011, UNDP BCPR (2008)
UN-EU (2006) United Nations, The Partnership between the UN and the EU: The United Nations and the European Commission Working Together in Development and Humanitarian Cooperation (2006)
UNHCR (2002) EC/52/SC/INF.2, UNHCR Update on Coordination Issues, 21 *Refugee Survey Quarterly* 217 (2002)
UNMIL (2007a) UNMIL *Focus* 10, Vol. 3 No. 2 (December 2006-February 2007)
UNMIL (2007b) UNMIL *Focus* 12, Vol. 3 No. 4 (June-August 2007)
UNMIL (2008) UNMIL *Focus* 15, Vol. 4 No. 3 (March–May 2008)
UNODC (2000) UNODC, Report of the First Meeting of the Judicial Group on Strengthening Judicial Integrity, Global Programme Against Corruption (April 2000)
UNODC (2005) UNODC, Crime and Development in Africa: Why Fighting Crime Can Assist Development in Africa: Rule of Law Protection of the Most Vulnerable (2005)
UNODC (2006a) UNODC, The Independence, Impartiality and Integrity of the Judiciary, Criminal Justice Assessment Toolkit (2006)
UNODC (2006b) UNODC, Preventing Terrorist Acts: A Criminal Justice Strategy Integrating Rule of Law Standards in Implementation of United Nations Anti-Terrorism Instruments, Technical Assistance Working Paper, Terrorism Prevention Branch (2006)
UNODC (2007) UNODC, Judicial Ethics Training Manual for the Nigerian Judiciary (undated, 2007)
UNODC (2008) 'Rule of law : A "missing" Millennium Development Goal', speech by Antonio Maria Costa, head of UNODC, at the 17th session

of the United Nations Commission on Crime Prevention and Criminal Justice in Vienna (15 April 2008)

Other sources

ABA (2006)	American Bar Association, Task Force on Presidential Signing Statements and the Separation or Powers Doctrine, Report (July 2006).
ABA (2008)	ABA, The World Justice Project ('media resource kit' for the World Justice Forum 2008)
ABA Mission	American Bar Association, Mission and Association Goals (www.abanet.org)
ADB (2003a)	Asian Development Bank, Performance-Based Allocation at ADB: Strengthening the Policy and its Implementation, Asian Development Fund, ADF IX Donors' Meeting, Tokyo, 9–11 December 2003 (November 2003)
ADB (2003b)	Asian Development Bank, Use of ADF IX Resources, Asian Development Fund, ADF IX Donors' Meeting, Tokyo, 9–11 December 2003 (November 2003)
ADB (2004)	Asian Development Bank, ADF IX Donors' Report: Development Effectiveness for Poverty Reduction (June 2004)
COE (2005)	RES/LISB/PL/RAP (2005) 1, Council of Europe Co-operation Programme to Strengthen the Rule of Law for 2005, Seventh Plenary Meeting of the Lisbon Network (European Network for the exchange of information between persons and entities responsible for the training of judges and public prosecutors) (November 2005)
COE (2006)	Council of Europe, 'Building Europe together on the Rule of Law'. Leaflet on the activities of the Directorate General I – Legal Affairs (March 2006)
COE (2007a)	Council of Europe, 'How to Measure the Rule of Law: A Comparison of Three Studies' by Dr Pim Albers, Special Advisor of the CEPEJ [European Commission for the Efficiency of Justice] (undated, 2007)
COE (2007b)	Opinion No. 408/2006, European Commission For Democracy Through Law (Venice Commission), Opinion on the Law on

282 BIBLIOGRAPHY

	Disciplinary Responsibility and Disciplinary Prosecution of Judges of Common Courts of Georgia, adopted by the Venice Commission at its 70th Plenary Session (Venice, 16–17 March 2007)
DFID (2002a)	Department for International Development, Understanding and Supporting Security Sector Reform (undated, 2002)
DFID (2002b)	Department for International Development, Safety Security and Accessible Justice: Putting Policy into Practice (July 2002)
DFID (2003)	DFID, Promoting Institutional and Organisational Development (March 2003)
DFID (2005a)	Claire Vallings and Magüi Moreno-Torres, 'Drivers of Fragility: What Makes States Fragile?' Department for International Development PRDE Working Paper No. 7 (April 2005)
DFID (2005b)	Michael Anderson, Andrew Branchflower, Magüi Moreno-Torres, Marie Besançon, DFID PRDE Working Paper No. 6, Measuring Capacity and Willingness for Poverty Reduction in Fragile States (January 2005)
DFID (2005c)	Christopher Stone, Joel Miller, Monica Thornton, and Jennifer Trone, 'Supporting Security, Justice, and Development: Lessons for a New Era', Vera Institute of Justice (for DFID and FCO) (2005)
DFID (2007a)	DFID, Governance, Development and Democratic Politics: DFID's Work in Building More Effective States (2007)
DFID (2007b)	DFID Briefing, Civil Society and Good Governance (September 2007)
DFID (2007c)	DFID, The UK and the World Bank 2006/2007 (2007)
DFID White Paper (1997)	DFID, Eliminating World Poverty: A Challenge for the 21st Century. White Paper on International Development (1997)
DFID White Paper (2000)	DFID, Eliminating World Poverty: Making Globalisation Work for the Poor. White Paper on International Development (2000)
DFID White Paper (2006)	DFID, Eliminating World Poverty: Making Governance Work for the Poor. White Paper on International Development (2006)
Dietrich (2002)	Mark Dietrich, 'Three Foundations of the Rule of Law: Education, Advocacy and Judicial Reform', in EBRD (2002)

EBRD (2002)	European Bank for Reconstruction and Development, Law in Transition: Ten Years of Legal Transition (2002)
EBRD (2005)	Elisabetta Falcetti, Tatiana Lysenko and Peter Sanfey, 'Reforms and Growth in Transition: Re-examining the Evidence', EBRD Working Paper no. 90 (March 2005)
EC (1990)	European Commission, The European Community and its Eastern Neighbours, Periodical 8/1990 (1990)
Empowerment Commission (2008a)	Commission on Legal Empowerment of the Poor, Making the Law Work for Everyone, Vol. 1, Report of the Commission on Legal Empowerment of the Poor (2008)
Empowerment Commission (2008b)	Commission on Legal Empowerment of the Poor, Making the Law Work for Everyone, Vol. II, Working Group Reports (2008)
EU (2003)	European Commission, A Secure Europe in a Better World, European Security Strategy (12 December 2003)
EU (2004a)	European Union, EU Rule of Law Mission to Georgia, Facts on EUJUST Themis (undated, 2004)
EU (2004b)	SEC(2004) 1041, Implementation of the Commission Communication on the EU's Role in Promoting Human Rights and Democratisation in Third Countries (2004)
EU (2004c)	European Commission, Handbook on Promoting Good Governance in EC Development and Co-operation (undated, 2004)
EU (2005)	European Union Factsheet. EU Rule-of-Law Mission for Iraq, EULEX (February 2005)
EU (2006a)	EUPOL-KINSHASA The first European Police Mission in Africa (Press document) (October 2006)
EU (2006b)	DG RELEX/B/1 JVK 70618, European Instrument for Democracy and Human Rights (EIDHR) Strategy Paper 2007 – 2010
EU (2007a)	European Commission, Furthering Human Rights and Democracy Across the Globe (2007)
EU (2007b)	Fadil Miftari and Jelena Markovic, Rule of Law a Basis to Attract Investments [*M Magazine* interview with Casper Klynge, head of planning of the EU rule of law mission (EULEX) in post-status Kosovo, from EUPT website] (2007)

EU (2007c)	European Commission, The EU in the World: The Foreign Policy of the European Union (2007)
EU (2007d)	European Union Planning Team for Kosovo, Training Needs for Personnel in the Future ESDP Mission in Kosovo – Draft Training Concept as of 30 August 2007 (30 August 2007)
Howard and Bruce (2002)	Jessica Howard & Bruce Oswald, 'The Rule of Law on Peace Operations: A "Challenges of Peace Operations" Project Conference', Asia-Pacific Centre for Military Law (2002)
HRW (2001)	Human Rights Watch, World Report 2001 (2001)
IBA (2007)	Program of the 2nd Annual IBA Bar Leader's Conference, 16–17 May 2007, Zagreb, Croatia (2007)
IDEA (2008)	Luc Huyse and Mark Salter (eds), 'Traditional Justice and Reconciliation after Violent Conflict: Learning from African Experiences', International Institute for Democracy and Electoral Assistance [IDEA] (2008)
IDRC (2008)	IDRC, IDRC on Private Sector Development (undated brochure, 2008)
JRRI (2007)	William G. O'Neill, 'JRR Options Paper', Justice Rapid Response Institute (draft; February 22, 2007)
Lintjer (2003)	Joint Statement of the African and Asian Development Banks Regarding Regional Development Bank Implementation of the Monterrey Consensus Plenary Session of the High Level Dialog on Financing for Development, by Mr John Lintjer, Vice President, Asian Development Bank UN Headquarters, New York, (October 2003)
OECD (1998)	OECD, Harmful Tax Competition: An Emerging Global Issue, OECD (1998)
OECD (2006)	OECD, DAC Guidelines and Reference Series, A DAC Reference Document, Promoting Private Investment for Development, The Role of ODA (2006)
OECD (2007)	OECD, Enhancing the Delivery of Justice and Security Governance, Peace and Security (2007)
Poku (2005)	Presentation of Ambassador Fritz Poku, Ghana's Envoy to the United States, on the Occasion of the International Rule of Law Symposium in Washington DC, hosted by the American Bar Association (November 2005)

RAND Europe (2005)	Greg Hannah, Kevin O'Brien, and Andrew Rathmell, 'Intelligence and Security Legislation for Security Sector Reform', Technical Report, RAND Europe (2005)
SDC (1998)	Swiss Agency for Development Cooperation/ Federal Department of Foreign Affairs, The Rule of Law-Concept: Significance in Development Cooperation (1998)
SDC (2004)	SDC, Independent Evaluation of SDC's Human Rights and Rule of Law Guidance Documents: Influence, Effectiveness and Relevance within SDC (March 2004)
Standard and Poor's (2005)	Standard and Poor's, 'Sovereign Ratings in Latin America', New York (September 2005)
Wiarda (1997)	Howard J. Wiarda, 'Modernizing the State in Latin America', Economic Reform Today, Center for International Private Enterprise, Number One (1997)

III. NEWSPAPER ARTICLES AND PRESS RELEASES

'A Victory for the Rule of Law', *New York Times*, editorial (June 30, 2006)

'Cubans in Miami Await News on Castro', AP Press (August 1, 2006)

'Iraq: UN Envoy Warns that Violence Threatens Government Authority to Enforce Rule of Law', UN News Centre (July 19, 2006)

'The Law Poor', *The Economist* (June 5, 2008)

'The Rule of Law: Limits of Congressional Rights; Recognizing the Power of the Courts, Finally', *New York Times*, editorial (July 12, 2006)

American Bar Association, 'Proposals to Strengthen the Rule of Law Incubated at World Justice Forum; Funding for Projects Announced' (July 7, 2008)

Bream, Rebecca, 'Stability tempts mining companies back to Congo', *Financial Times* (February 21, 2007)

Cole, David, 'Why the Court Said No', *New York Review of Books*, Vol. 53 No. 13 (August 10, 2006)

Danner, Mark, 'US Torture: Voices from the Black Sites', *New York Review of Books*, Vol. 56, No. 6 (April 9, 2009)

Dombey, Daniel, 'World Bank Chief Calls For Rethink Over Failed States', *Financial Times* (September 12, 2008)

Dworkin, Ronald, 'What the Court Said', *New York Review of Books* Vol. 51, No. 13 (August 12, 2004)

Feldman, Noah, 'Who Can Check the President?', *New York Times Magazine* (January 8, 2006), 52

Hoffman, Stanley, 'The Foreign Policy the US Needs', *New York Review of Books*, Vol. 53, No. 13 (August 10, 2006)

Kahn, Joseph, 'Scuffles in China as Trial of Peasants' Rights Advocate Is Postponed', *New York Times* (July 21, 2006)
Lacey, Mark, 'Hargeysa Journal; The Signs Say Somaliland, but the World Says Somalia', *New York Times* (June 5, 2006)
Siniora, Hanna, 'This Week in Palestine', *Jerusalem Times* (February 12, 2006)
White House, Office of the Press Secretary, '2007 U.S.–EU Summit Promoting Peace, Human Rights and Democracy Worldwide' (April 2007)
White, Josh and Carol D. Leonnig, 'U.S. Cites Exception in Torture Ban McCain Law May Not Apply to Cuba Prison', *Washington Post* (March 3, 2006), A04
Wintour, Patrick and Alan Travis, 'The Longest Day', *The Guardian* (March 12, 2005)
World Food Programme, 'Number of World's Hungry Tops a Billion' (June 19, 2009), online at www.wfp.org/stories/number-world-hungry-tops-billion
Zernike, Kate, 'Iraqi Leader Embraces Terror Fight in Speech to Congress', *New York Times* (July 27, 2006)

Index

accountability
  governance and, 190
  judicial system, 73, 201, 204, 205
  public opinion and, 201
  rhetoric, 175, 187
  rule of law and, 145, 147
  United Nations and, 167
  USAID and, 129, 200
administrative state
  Dicey's opposition to, 58, 59–62
  meaning of administrative law, 66
Afghanistan, 150, 153, 179
Agamben, Giorgio
  Homo Sacer, 100
  law colonising life itself, 106
  law of sovereignty, 98–106
  state of exception, 99–101
Albania, 184, 201
Allott, Anthony, 222
alternative dispute resolution, 202–203
Althusser, Louis, 119
American Bar Association, 127, 231
ancient Greece, 89, 97
Aquinas, Thomas, 96
Arendt, Hannah
  on Aristotle, 91, 92
  on Greek *polis*, 49
  on Plato, 92, 94
  public-private divide, 45, 55
  rise of the social, 45
  separation of powers, 106
Aristotle
  aristocracy, 37
  democracy, 38, 90, 91–92, 103
  kyrios, 98, 190
  nomarchy, 89–95
  political tradition, 41, 96–98
  Politics, 89, 90
  rule of law as *habitus*, 29
  slavery, 90

  sovereignty of law, 89–95
  terminology, 90–92
Armenia
  Constitution, 184
  foreign investor discrimination, 197
  World Bank, 181, 196–197, 199, 201, 206
Asquith, H. H., 59
Australia, British penal code, 118
Azerbaijan, World Bank and, 180, 201

Bangladesh, 177
Barker, Ernest, 93
Belgium, 172
Benjamin, Walter, 102
Berlin, General Act of (1885), 111
Berlin Conference (1884-5), 111
bias
  institutional bias, 57
  Lochner v. *New York*, 67–75
  realist critique of formation, 66–75
    blindness to bias, 73–75
    choice of evidence, 72–73
    choice of policy, 70–72
    choice of rights, 69–70
Bingham, Tom, 4
Bismarck, Otto von, 59
Blackstone, William, 31, 33, 41
Bodin, Jean, 37, 41, 96, 106
Bolivia, USAID in, 203
Bracton, Henry de, 96
Brahimi Report (2000), 156–157, 158
Brussels, General Act of (1890), 112
Brussels Conference (1890), 111, 112
Bulgaria, 184
Burke, Edmund, 31, 33, 41, 52

Calhoun, Craig, 50
Cape Verde, 184
Capstone Principles (DPKO), 161–162, 164

288 INDEX

Carothers, Thomas, 220
Chalmers, D.F., 118
Chamberlain, Joseph, 112
Chanock, Martin, 222
chiefs, colonial law and, 114, 115
China, WTO membership, 215
civil society
    global civil society, 231
    meaning, 49
    morality play actors, 175
    poor and, 207
    public and private spheres, 194–195
    public education role, 204–207
    transnationalism, 195
civilisation, 223
Coase, Ronald, 87
coffee-shops, 48
Cohen, Morris, 82
Coke, Edward, 14, 33, 41, 59, 97
Cold War, 43
Colombia, 207, 216
colonialism
    amnesia about, 13
    chiefs, 114, 115
    civilisation and, 223
    criminal justice, 117–118
    customary law and, 113, 117, 170
    development and, 112
    humanitarianism and, 112, 114
    international law and, 111–112
    land rights, 116–117
    legacy, 170, 171–172
    legal dualism, 114–115
    legal intervention, 109–121, 222
    legalism and, 119–121
    modernisation and, 179–180, 183
    native courts, 114, 115
    natural order, 164
    precursors, 17–18, 109–121
    rule of law promotion and, 223
    social chaos and reform, 211
    state-building in Africa, 113–119
    sub-Saharan Africa, 110
    World Bank and, 133–134
command economies, 177
common law systems, 62
communism, 179–180, 183
community justice centres, 203
concept of rule of law
    See also specific theorists
    amnesia and, 13–14
    archetypes of, 56
    Aristotelian tradition, 96–98
    between state and society, 44–55
    democracy and, 42–43
    equality, 50
    discipline and, 168–171
    family resemblances, 43–44

    generality, see universalism
    historical and cultural contingency, 43,
        56, 77, 163, 187
    immanence, 29–44
    indicators, 20–21
    latent theory, 11
    legalism, 44
    legitimacy, 42–43, 44, 224
    liberty, 43
    modern society and, 41–44
    non-discrimination, see equality
    non-instrumentalism, 43, 44, 223
    organic concept, 43
    overview, 3–5
    paradoxes, 12–13
    parameters, 29
    political and economic motives, 13
    public and private distinction, 44–55
    rationality, 50
    social glue, 29–30, 39
    stakes of, 5
    tolerance among strangers, 43
    transformation, 223–225
    transparency, 51
    universalism, 56, 220–221
    welfarism and, 9, 76–77, 84–88
        compatibility, 83–84
        incompatibility, 77–83
Congo, Democratic Republic of
    colonialism, 111
    MONUC, 161, 168
    World Bank and, 165
Cook, Walter Wheeler, 71
corruption
    Corruption Perceptions Index, 192
    elites, 186, 208
    governance and, 7, 190
    morality play, 175
    privatisations and, 193–194
    public and private spheres, 191–192
    regressive tax on the poor, 208
    UN Convention against, 192
    World Bank and, 208
    World Justice Forum and, 1
counter-terrorism
    international convention negotiations,
        102
    rule of law, 89
    United States, 150, 165
criminal justice
    attraction, 166–173
    colonialism, 117–118
    deactivating function, 166–167
    justice for victims, 167, 170
    naturalised, 168
    personnel, 168–169
    rule of law promotion, 162–166
        legitimacy, 170–172

INDEX 289

Critical Legal Studies, 78, 80–83
customary law
 colonialism and, 113, 117, 170
 human rights and, 170
 modernisation, 179
Cyprus, British penal code, 118

Darfur (Sudan), 170
Delavignette, Robert, 114
democracy
 Aristotle, 38, 90, 91–92, 103
 democratic policing, 169
 rule of law and, 42–43
Denmark, 160
deregulation, 9
derogation, 99
detention without trial, 75
development
 colonialism and, 112
 rule of law and, 138–147
 rule of law, assistance for, 9–11
 World Bank, 134, 138–147
Dicey, A. V.
 accountability and public opinion, 201
 administrative state and, 58, 59–62
  judicial protection, 67
 autonomy, 63, 221
 concept of rule of law, 14, 30–35
  coherence, 90
  democracy and, 42
  Englishness, 43, 221
  legitimacy, 42–43
 on Constitutions, 31, 38
 expansive legalism and, 107
 focus on, 30
 habit of self-government, 30–35
 Hayek and, 78
 legal certainty, 75
 parliamentary sovereignty, 34
 positivism, 34
 public opinion, 53
 safeguards, 52
 social fabric, 210
 Weber and, 66
disarmament, demobilisation and reintegration (DDR), 160, 165
discipline, 168–171
Dominican Republic, 200
donors, 2, 6
Doss, Alan, 171

economy
 development. *See* development
 economic governance, 57, 161
 Hayek and, 79–80
 irrelevance to rule of law, 13
 Lochner v. *New York*, 71

 modernisation, 177
 planning, 177
 rule of law promotion and, 138–147
 World Bank and, 138–147
Egypt, 177, 183
El Salvador, USAID programme, 125
Elias, A. O., 170
emergencies, 99–101
empowerment, legal, 211–213
Empowerment Commission, 1, 211–213
Enlightenment, 45, 52, 180, 232
Ethiopia, World Bank, 180
European Union, 146, 172
exceptionalism, 99–101
extraordinary rendition, 165

Ferguson, Adam, 49
Fiji, 118
financial services, 129
formalism. *See* legal formalism
Foucault, Michel, 104–105, 106, 107, 168
France
 administrative law, 33, 60
 colonialism, 114, 119
 Constitution, 31
 Dicey and, 31, 33, 60
 Revolution, 101
 rule of law promotion, 172
 state of exception, 100, 101
free trade
 colonialism and, 111
 global integration, 214–217
 US foreign assistance and, 125
 World Bank and, 208
Fuller, Lon, 4
funders, 2, 6

Gambia, 118, 177
gender, 189, 211
Georgia, 184, 187, 198, 199, 201
Germany, 59, 78, 101
Geuss, Raymond, 45
Ghana
 colonial land rights, 116
 colonial penal code, 118
 land law, 178
Ghéhenno, Jean-Marie, 157
Giddens, Anthony, 182
global integration, 213–217
Glorious Revolution (1688), 14, 33, 86
Gold Coast. *See* Ghana
governance
 economic governance, 57, 161
 morality play, 175
 public and private spheres, 190–191
 World Bank and, 132, 133–135, 177, 208
Guinea Bissau, 177

habeas corpus, 33, 163
Habermas, Jürgen
  accountability and public opinion, 201
  basic rights, 52
  civil society, 204
  complex social interactions, 43
  concept of rule of law, 14
    legitimacy, 40-41, 42-43
    mutual respect between strangers, 38-41, 44
  democracy and rule of law, 42
  discourse principle, 40
  failure of transnational rule of law, 230
  focus on, 30
  German enlightenment tradition, 41
  on illiteracy, 50
  later works, 230
  modernity, 45, 182
  private autonomy, 40
  public autonomy, 40-41
  public opinion, 52-53
  public sphere, 187
    collapse of public-private divide, 55
    equality, 50
    ideal of, 232
    overview, 228-229
    private sphere and, 44-55, 207
    public of private persons, 46-49, 188
    rationality, 50
    representative publicity, 50
    rise, 231
    transparency, 51
    tripartite distinction, 53-55, 188
  role of state coercion, 42
  social rights, 86
  Structural Transformation of the Public Sphere, 44, 56
  terminology, 49
Hailey, Malcolm, 116, 117, 171
Hale, Robert, 69-70, 80-81, 84
Hall, W. E., 112
Hamilton, Alexander, 100
Hayek, Friedrich
  Constitution of Liberty, 78
  Hale compared with, 80-81
  individual freedom, 61
  market competition, 79-80
  Road to Serfdom, 78
  rule of law, 78-80
    welfare and, 82
    World Bank and, 87, 143
  worldview, 88
Hegel, Georg, 41, 48, 49, 53, 204
Hickman, Tom, 99
Hill, General James, 104

historical contingencies, 43, 56, 77, 163, 187
Hobbes, Thomas, 37, 41, 164
Hohfeld, Wesley, 70
Holmes, Oliver Wendell, 68, 70, 71-72, 73-74, 85
Honduras, 201
Hong Kong, 118
Horwitz, Morton, 82
hubris, 2
human rights
  balancing rights, 69-70, 85
  customary law and, 170
  democratic policing, 169
  promotion, 7
  public and private spheres, 192
  rule of law and, 4
  social and economic rights, 57-58, 83-84, 86
  training, 168
humanitarianism, 112, 114

ignorance, 1, 3-4
IMF, 217
impunity culture of, 166-167
India, 118, 121
indicators of rule of law, 20-21
Indonesia, 151
institutions, 3
instrumentalism
  rule of law as non-instrumental, 43, 44, 223
  World Bank, 145, 148
International Association of the Congo, 111
International Bank for Reconstruction and Development (IBRD), *see* World Bank
International Commission of Jurists, 5, 222
international community, rule of law promotion and, 172-173
international criminal tribunals, 167
International Development Authority (IDA), 131, 190, 191
International Finance Corporation (IFC), 131, 143, 202, 217
International Foundation for Electoral Systems (IFES), 127
international law
  colonialism and, 111-112
  derogations, 99
International Rescue Committee (IRC), 127
Iraq
  Central Criminal Court, 153-154
  legality of 2003 invasion, 155
  Rule of Law Coordinator, 154

US projects in, 150, 151, 154, 166
Italy, 101

James I, 33, 97
Jowett, Benjamin, 90
judiciary
    accountability of, 201
    alternatives of, 202–203
    autonomy, 196–198
    modernisation, 132
    morality play actors, 175
    prestige, 198–201
justice
    punishment of perpetrators, 169–170
    restorative justice, 117
    traditional justice, 179
    victims' desire for, 167

Kant, Immanuel, 40, 41, 47, 48, 182
Kasson, John, 113
Kazakhstan, 176, 181
Kennedy, Duncan, 55
Kenya, 208
Kosovo, 153

labour laws, flexibility, 201
laissez faire, 68, 79
Landis, James, 72
Latin America, US legal interventions, 120, 181
law and order
    attraction, 166–173
    rule of law project literature and, 162
    rule of law promotion, 162–166
        legitimacy, 170–172
    security personnel, 168–169
legal empowerment, 211–213
Legal Empowerment Commission 1, 211–213
legal formalism
    legal realist challenge to, 55, 66–75
legal realism
    challenge to legal formalism, 55, 66–75
    critique of formalism, 66–75
        blindness to bias, 73–75
        choice of evidence, 72–73
        choice of policy, 70–72
        choice of rights, 69–70
    focus on, 58
Leopold, King of the Belgians, 111
Liberia, 161, 163, 169, 171
Lincoln, Abraham, 101
Llewellyn, Karl, 72
Lochner v. New York, 67–75
Locke, John, 48, 52, 164
Lugard, Frederick, 115, 117

McCormick, John, 55
Macedonia, 184
Magna Carta, 14, 33, 86, 163
Malawi, 208
Mamdani, Mahmood, 113, 115
Mandeville, Bernard de, 31, 198
Marbury v. Madison, 14
market. *See* economy
media, 175, 195, 230
Messimy, Adolphe, 119
Mexico, 216
Mill, John Stuart, 48, 52, 53
Millennium Challenge Corporation, 127
modernisation
    chronological, 176–178
    modernity and, 182–183
    motivating theme, 175, 176–187
    reform constituency, 183–187
    technological, 180–182
    topographical, 178–180
    World Bank and, judicial modernisation, 132
Mongolia, 177, 182
Montesquieu, Charles de, 48, 96
MONUC (United Nations Organization Mission in the Democratic Republic of Congo), 161, 168
morality play, 169–170, 175–176

NAFTA (North American Free Trade Agreement), 216
native courts, 114, 115
natural justice, 4
Nepal, 177
Netherlands, 172
New Deal, 58, 67, 72, 76, 78, 101
Nigeria, 117, 118, 186
nomos, 89–95
Nonet, Philippe, 82
North, Douglass, 87
Northern Ireland, democratic policing, 169

Oakeshott, Michael
    concept of rule of law, 14
        legitimacy, 42
        moral association, 35–38
    democracy and rule of law, 37–38, 42
    educated sensibility, 43, 44
    European political tradition, 41
    focus on, 30
    nomocracy, 38
    state coercion, role, 42
    teleocracy, 38
    value-neutral, 38
OECD, 152

OSCE, 152
Ostwald, Martin, 92

Pakistan, 154
Palestinians, 151
paralegals, 211
paternalism, 69, 179
peace and security
   Capstone Principles (DPKO), 161–162, 164
   Counter-terrorism, 89, 165
   disarmament, demobilisation and reintegration (DDR), 151, 160
   discipline, 168–171
   rule of law promotion and, 149–162
      attraction, 166–173
      colonial overtones, 171–172
      United Nations, 155–162
      United States, 149–155
Philippines, 177, 204, 207
Plato
   ideal state, 97
   Laws, 93–94, 95
   parental sovereignty, 98
   philosopher king, 94
   supremacy of law, 37, 92, 93–94
pluralism, 39, 42, 43, 163, 167, 179, 215
police, 169
post-structuralism, 74
Pound, Roscoe, 71, 84
poverty
   civil society and the poor, 207
   global integration and, 213–217
   legal empowerment of the poor, 211–213
   poor as investors in waiting, 207–213
   public services and, 210
   rule of law and, 3–4
   social fabric and, 209
   World Bank and poverty reduction, 143, 207–211
   World Justice Forum and, 1
private sphere. *See* public sphere
privatisation
   corruption and, 193–194
   morality play, 175
   poor constituencies and, 210
   self-abdication, 218
   theoretical framework, 193–194
   US foreign assistance and, 125
   World Bank and, 135–138, 144
project literature
   on international consensus, 172
   law and order and, 162
   modernisation themes, 176–177, 184–187
   rule of law language, 139, 145–147
   source, 19
   terminology, 3
property rights
   colonialism, 116–117
   Empowerment Commission and, 212
   judiciary and, 201
   private autonomy, 48
   USAID and, 129
public interest
   private investors and, 198
public opinion, 52–53, 175, 201
public sphere
   civil society, 204–207
   Habermas. *See* Habermas, Jürgen
   corruption, 191–192
   governance, 190–191
   poor as investors in waiting, 207–213
   private investors and public interest, 198
   public sphere of private investors, 194–195
   roles, 187–195
   retreat of, 229–230
   rise of, 231
   transnationalism, 225–232

Raz, Joseph, 4, 5
Read, James, 117
realism. *See* legal realism
restorative justice, 117
Roberts-Wray, Kenneth, 222
Roman Empire, 91
Romania, 193, 204, 205
Roosevelt, Franklin, 101
rule by law, 162, 172
rule of law
   concept. *See* concept of rule of law
   promotion. *See* rule of law promotion
rule of law promotion
   See also USAID; World Bank; UN; *and country entries*
   attraction, 166–173
   colonial overtones, 171–172
   deactivating function, 166–167
   discipline, foregrounding, 168–171
   as field of practice, 6–9
   global integration, 213–217
   impoverished vision, 163–164
   international consensus, 172–173
   and law and order, 117–118, 162–166
   legitimacy, 170–172
   literature, 7
   main actors, 20
   market promotion, 138–147
   modernisation theme. *See* modernisation

morality tale and spectacle, 169–170, 175–176
national v. international practice, 9–12
naturalising function, 168
overview, 222–223
peace and security. *See* peace and security
public and private lead roles, 187–195
stakeholders, 207
support roles, 195–213
technocratic approach, 8
terminology, 3
theatre, overview, 18–25
theory and practice, overview, 12–25
unreflective approach, 8
US foreign assistance, 125–131
Rumsfeld, Donald, 104
Russia, 176, 184, 201
Rwanda, 156

St Lucia, 118
salons, 48
Schmitt, Carl, 101–102, 103
security forces, 9, 168–169
self-reflexivity, 182
Selznick, Philip, 82
Senegal, 154, 208
Shihata, Ibrahim, 131, 135, 136–138, 143
Shklar, Judith, 43, 225
sickness, 1
slave trade, 112, 116
slavery, 90, 101, 116
Smith, Adam, 31, 49
social fabric
  Dicey, 210
  the poor, 209
  rule of law and, 29–30, 39
Soto, Hernando de, 198, 212
South Africa, 169
sovereignty
  Agamben, 98–106
  definition of sovereign, 101
  rule of law promotion and, 13
  state sovereignty, 172–173
sovereignty of law
  Aristotelian tradition, 96–98
  Aristotle, 89–95
Soviet Union, 78
Sri Lanka, 121
state
  centrality to rule of law, 224
  dysfunctional states, 147
  modernisation, 178
  monopoly on violence, 63, 81, 191
  sovereignty, international rule of law promotion and, 172–173
  state and law perspectives, 59–66

state-building, colonial Africa, 113–119
strong state, 164
technological conception, 224
strategic literature. *See* project literature
Strauss, Leo, 94, 95
structuralism, 74
Sudan, 118, 150, 170
Switzerland, 31

Tajikistan, 184–185, 216
technological concept of state, 224
technological modernisation, 180–182
teleocracy, 224
terrorism. *See* counter-terrorism
theatre of the rule of law, overview, 18–25, 220–223
Timor-Leste, US police training, 153
Tocqueville, Alexis de, 31–32, 48, 53
tolerance, rule of law and, 43
torture, 104
trade liberalisation. *See* free trade
transition countries, 7, 139, 161, 176, 199, 210
transnational
  civil society, 195
  meaning, 10–11
  transnational public sphere, 225–232
Transparency International, 192

Uganda, 116
Ukraine, 184
UNDP, 156–157, 158–159, 162, 170
Unger, Roberto, 41, 82
United Kingdom
  administrative state, 59, 61
  censorship, 47
    chiefs, 115
    criminal codes, 118
    Foreign Jurisdiction Acts, 112
    land rights, 117
    law and development and, 120
    law and justice, 222
  emergencies, 101
  English Constitution, 30, 41
  rule of law promotion, 172
  safeguards, 51
  UN Security Council presidency, 157
United Nations
  Brahimi Report, 156–157, 158
  DPKO
    Capstone Principles, 161–162, 164
    culture of impunity and, 167
    function, 158
    OROLSI, 160
    Primer, 159, 167
  focus on, 20
  Office of Legal Affairs (OLA), 158

United Nations (cont.)
  OHCHR
    internal discipline, 169
    mandate, 155-156
    rule of law promotion, 159
  peacebuilding, 7, 158-159
  Peacebuilding Commission, 158
  peacekeeping operations, 156, 157, 161
  rule of law promotion
    impunity culture and, 167
    international tribunals, 167
    peace and security, 155-162
  UNDP, 156-157, 158-159, 162, 170
  UNODC, 152, 156, 159
United States
  Afghanistan, 150, 153
  Berlin Conference (1884-5), 113
  Brown v. Board of Education, 76, 83, 84
  Constitution, Dicey on, 33
  counterterrorism
    Anti-Terrorism Assistance programme (ATA), 150
    9/11, 89
    techniques, 165
  Defense Institute of International Legal Studies, 154
  due process, substantive due process, 67, 69
  emergencies, 101
  employment regulation
    Lochner v. New York, 67-75
    minimum wage, 75-76
  free trade, 214-215
  freedom of contract, 69-70, 75-76
  ICITAP, 150-151, 152-153
  INL, 150, 152, 153-154
  International Foundation for Electoral Systems (IFES), 127
  International Rescue Committee (IRC), 127
  Interstate Commerce Commission, 67
  Iraq and, 150, 151, 154, 166
  judicial bias, 67-75
  judicial formalism, 58
  judicial politicisation, 71
  Latin America and, 120, 181
  law and development and, 120
  law and economics, 87
  legal realism. *See* legal realism
  Millennium Challenge Account, 127, 151
  National Endowment for Democracy, 127
  National Security Strategies, 151-152, 214
  New Deal, 58, 67, 72, 76, 78, 101
  OPDAT, 150, 152-153
  rule of law promotion
    See also USAID
    channels, 127
    foreign assistance, 125-131
    measuring, 170
    peace and security assistance, 149-155
    security sector reform, 149
  torture, definition, 104
  Vietnam and, 215
  Warren court, 75
  welfarism and rule of law, 76-77
  West Coast Hotel v. Parrish, 76, 83, 84, 85
United States Institute for Peace (USIP), 127
universalism, 220-221
UNMIL, 161, 169
USAID
  administration of justice programmes, 125-126
  ADR and, 202
  bilateral investment treaties, 214-215
  Bolivia, 203
  civil society and, 204, 205
  databases, 181
  Dominican Republic, 200
  Eastern European judiciary and, 198
  Egypt, 183
  focus on, 20
  free trade and, 215
  gender and, 189
  Kazakhstan, 181
  modernisation, 176-177
    political will, 185
  Mongolia, 182
  Nigeria, 186
  peace and security, 151
  reform constituencies and, 183-184
  Romania, 204, 205
  rule of law promotion, 6, 125-131
  Tajikistan, 184-185, 216
  total budget, 126
  World Bank and, 138
  worldview, 128-131
  WTO and, 129, 185, 215
Uzbekistan, 144

Vietnam, 215
violence
  rule of law and, 3-4
  state monopoly, 63, 81, 191
  state violence and rule of law discourse, 9
  World Justice Forum and, 1

Warner, Michael, 54
Weber, Max
  autonomy, 63
  bureaucracy, 64-66, 87-88, 171, 195

compulsory political association, 62–66
Dicey and, 66
Economy and Society, 55, 62
freedom of contract, 63, 64
German enlightenment tradition, 41
Habermas and, 39, 55
ideal types, 46
kadi justice, 65
modern western law, 62–63, 107, 178, 221
public and private sphere boundaries, 98
Rechtsstaat, 62, 65
rise of capitalism, 62
state monopoly on violence, 63, 191
Weinstein, David, 184
welfare state
 centrality, 57
 laissez faire v. social welfare, 68
 Lochner v New York, 67–75
 political battles, 13
 poor constituencies and, 210
 rhetorical hostility to, 58–59
 rule of law and, 9, 76–77, 84–88
  compatibility, 83–84
  incompatibility, 77–83
Westlake, John, 113, 114
Wolfensohn, James, 141
World Bank
 ADR and, 202
 Africa Study, 133–135
 Albania, 201
 Armenia, 181, 196–197, 199, 201, 206
 Azerbaijan, 180, 201
 civil society and, 204
 Colombia, 207
 concept of rule of law, 216
 contracts, 141
 corruption and, 208
 development concept, 134
 disarmament, demobilisation and reintegration (DDR), 165
 economic governance, 161
 Ethiopia, 180
 focus on, 20
 free trade and, 214–215, 216–217
 Georgia, 187, 198, 199, 201
 governance and, 132, 133–135, 177, 208
 Hayek and, 86–87, 143
 Honduras, 201
 modernisation theme, 132, 176
 Philippines, 204, 207
 post-Cold War, 132–138
 poverty reduction, 143, 207–211
 Poverty Reduction Strategy Papers, 144–145
 private sector development (PSD), 132, 135–138
 privatisation database, 193
 reform process, 184
 Romania, 193
 rule of law promotion, 6, 131
  economy of law, 138–147
  instrumentalism, 145, 148
  legitimacy, 141–142
  post-conflicts, 164
  privileging certain economic structures, 142–146
  project literature, 145–147
 Russia, 201
 shareholders, 145
 Sub-Saharan Africa Study (1989), 133–135
 Yemen, 178, 185
World Development Report (1991), 178
World Development Report (2005), 217
World Justice Forum, 1, 231
WTO, 129, 185, 198, 215, 216

Yemen, 178, 185

Zambia, modernisation, 176
zeitgeist, 1–2
Zoellick, Robert, 139

CAMBRIDGE STUDIES IN INTERNATIONAL AND COMPARATIVE LAW

Books in the series

Theatre of the Rule of Law: Transnational Legal Intervention in Theory and Practice
Stephen Humphreys

Science and Risk Regulation in International Law: The Role of Science, Uncertainty and Values
Jacqueline Peel

Vicarious Liability in Tort: A Comparative Perspective
Paula Giliker

Legitimacy and Legality in International Law: An Interactional Account
Jutta Brunnée and Stephen J. Toope

The Public International Law Theory of Hans Kelsen: Believing in Universal Law
Jochen von Bernstorff

The Concept of Non-International Armed Conflict in International Humanitarian Law
Anthony Cullen

The Challenge of Child Labour in International Law
Franziska Humbert

Shipping Interdiction and the Law of the Sea
Douglas Guilfoyle

International Courts and Environmental Protection
Tim Stephens

Legal Principles in WTO Disputes
Andrew D. Mitchell

War Crimes in Internal Armed Conflicts
Eve La Haye

Humanitarian Occupation
Gregory H. Fox

The International Law of Environmental Impact Assessment: Process, Substance and Integration
Neil Craik

The Law and Practice of International Territorial Administration: Versailles, Iraq and Beyond
Carsten Stahn

Cultural Products and the World Trade Organization
Tania Voon

United Nations Sanctions and the Rule of Law
Jeremy Farrall

National Law in WTO Law: Effectiveness and Good Governance in the World Trading System
Sharif Bhuiyan

The Threat of Force in International Law
Nikolas Stürchler

Indigenous Rights and United Nations Standards
Alexandra Xanthaki

International Refugee Law and Socio-Economic Rights
Michelle Foster

The Protection of Cultural Property in Armed Conflict
Roger O'Keefe

Interpretation and Revision of International Boundary Decisions
Kaiyan Homi Kaikobad

Multinationals and Corporate Social Responsibility: Limitations and Opportunities in International Law
Jennifer A. Zerk

Judiciaries within Europe: A Comparative Review
John Bell

Law in Times of Crisis: Emergency Powers in Theory and Practice
Oren Gross and Fionnuala Ní Aoláin

Vessel-Source Marine Pollution: The Law and Politics of International Regulation
Alan Tan

Enforcing Obligations Erga Omnes *in International Law*
Christian J. Tams

Non-Governmental Organisations in International Law
Anna-Karin Lindblom

Democracy, Minorities and International Law
Steven Wheatley

Prosecuting International Crimes: Selectivity and the International Law Regime
Robert Cryer

Compensation for Personal Injury in English, German and Italian Law: A Comparative Outline
Basil Markesinis, Michael Coester, Guido Alpa, Augustus Ullstein

Dispute Settlement in the UN Convention on the Law of the Sea
Natalie Klein

The International Protection of Internally Displaced Persons
Catherine Phuong

Imperialism, Sovereignty and the Making of International Law
Antony Anghie

Necessity, Proportionality and the Use of Force by States
Judith Gardam

International Legal Argument in the Permanent Court of International Justice: The Rise of the International Judiciary
Ole Spiermann

Great Powers and Outlaw States: Unequal Sovereigns in the International Legal Order
Gerry Simpson

Local Remedies in International Law
C. F. Amerasinghe

Reading Humanitarian Intervention: Human Rights and the Use of Force in International Law
Anne Orford

Conflict of Norms in Public International Law: How WTO Law Relates to Other Rules of Law
Joost Pauwelyn

Transboundary Damage in International Law
Hanqin Xue

European Criminal Procedures
Edited by Mireille Delmas-Marty and John Spencer

The Accountability of Armed Opposition Groups in International Law
Liesbeth Zegveld

Sharing Transboundary Resources: International Law and Optimal Resource Use
Eyal Benvenisti

International Human Rights and Humanitarian Law
René Provost

Remedies Against International Organisations
Karel Wellens

Diversity and Self-Determination in International Law
Karen Knop

The Law of Internal Armed Conflict
Lindsay Moir

International Commercial Arbitration and African States: Practice, Participation and Institutional Development
Amazu A. Asouzu

The Enforceability of Promises in European Contract Law
James Gordley

International Law in Antiquity
David J. Bederman

Money Laundering: A New International Law Enforcement Model
Guy Stessens

Good Faith in European Contract Law
Reinhard Zimmermann and Simon Whittaker

On Civil Procedure
J. A. Jolowicz

Trusts: A Comparative Study
Maurizio Lupoi

The Right to Property in Commonwealth Constitutions
Tom Allen

International Organizations Before National Courts
August Reinisch

The Changing International Law of High Seas Fisheries
Francisco Orrego Vicuña

Trade and the Environment: A Comparative Study of EC and US Law
Damien Geradin

Unjust Enrichment: A Study of Private Law and Public Values
Hanoch Dagan

Religious Liberty and International Law in Europe
Malcolm D. Evans

Ethics and Authority in International Law
Alfred P. Rubin

Sovereignty Over Natural Resources: Balancing Rights and Duties
Nico Schrijver

The Polar Regions and the Development of International Law
Donald R. Rothwell

Fragmentation and the International Relations of Micro-States: Self-determination and Statehood
Jorri Duursma

Principles of the Institutional Law of International Organizations
C. F. Amerasinghe

Printed in Great Britain
by Amazon.co.uk, Ltd.,
Marston Gate.